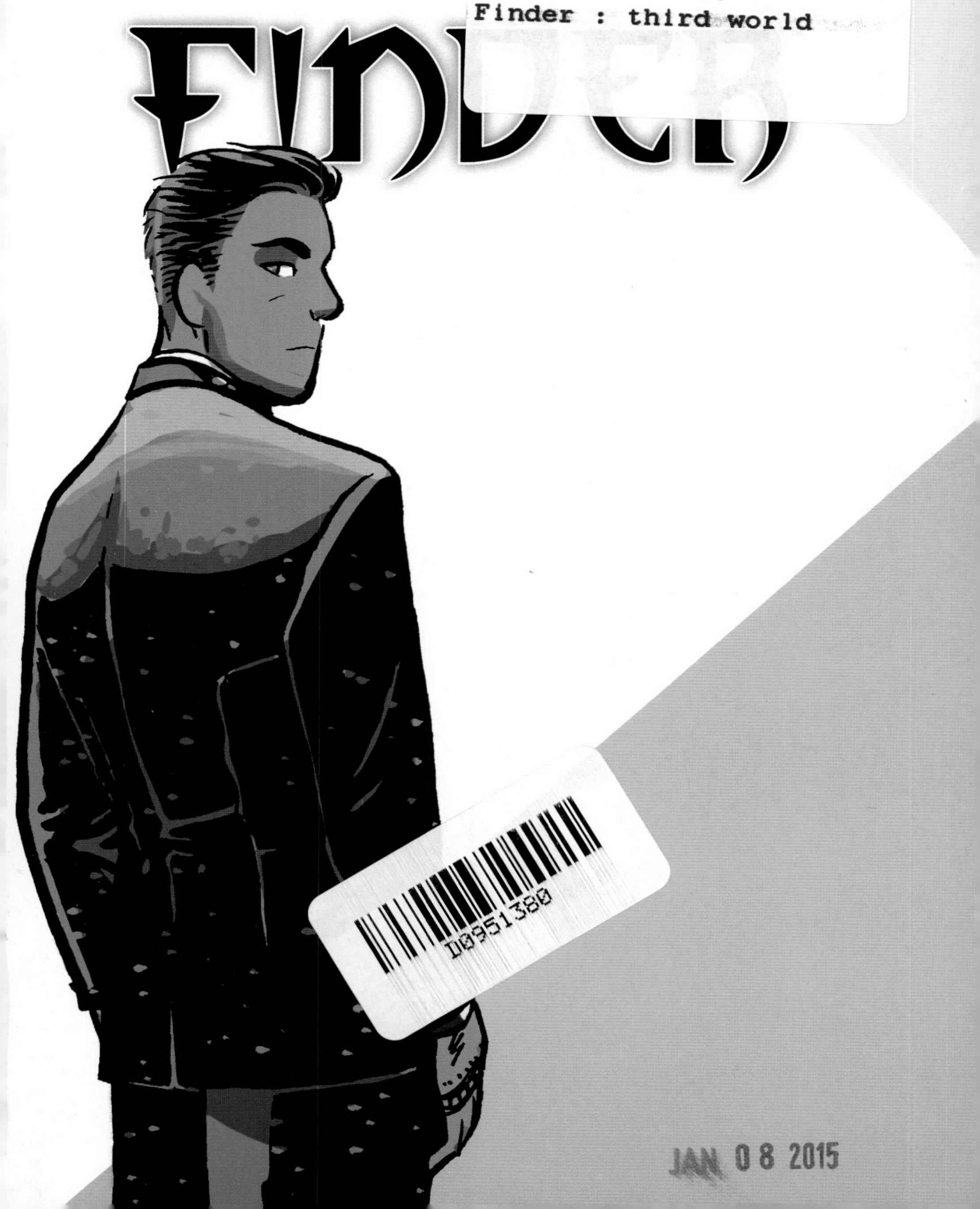
FINDER

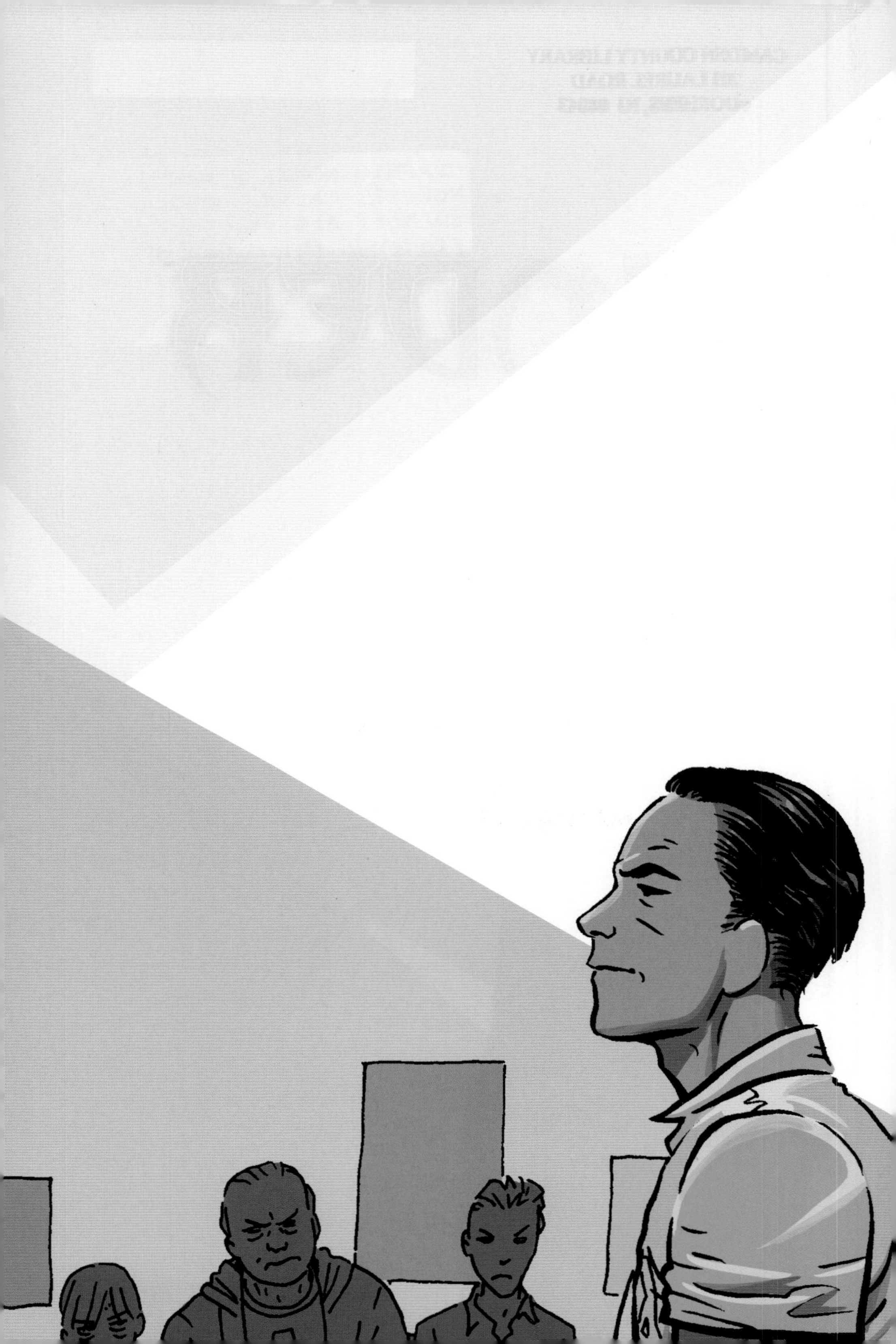

FINDER™

THIRD WORLD

Story, art, and cover by
CARLA SPEED McNEIL

Colors by
JENN MANLEY LEE and BILL MUDRON

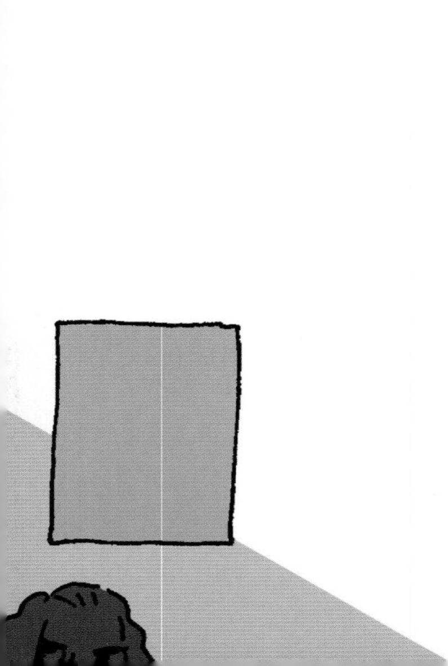

DARK HORSE BOOKS

President and Publisher
Mike Richardson

Editors
Philip R. Simon and **Rachel Edidin**

Assistant Editors
Roxy Polk and **Jemiah Jefferson**

Designer
Sandy Tanaka

Digital Production
Christianne Goudreau

Published by Dark Horse Books
A division of Dark Horse Comics, Inc.
10956 SE Main Street
Milwaukie, OR 97222

DarkHorse.com | LightspeedPress.com

To find a comics shop in your area,
call the Comic Shop Locator Service toll-free at 1-888-266-4226.

First edition: September 2014
ISBN 978-1-61655-467-5

1 3 5 7 9 10 8 6 4 2

Printed in China

NEIL HANKERSON Executive Vice President • **TOM WEDDLE** Chief Financial Officer • **RANDY STRADLEY** Vice President of Publishing • **MICHAEL MARTENS** Vice President of Book Trade Sales • **ANITA NELSON** Vice President of Business Affairs • **SCOTT ALLIE** Editor in Chief • **MATT PARKINSON** Vice President of Marketing • **DAVID SCROGGY** Vice President of Product Development • **DALE LaFOUNTAIN** Vice President of Information Technology • **DARLENE VOGEL** Senior Director of Print, Design, and Production • **KEN LIZZI** General Counsel • **DAVEY ESTRADA** Editorial Director • **CHRIS WARNER** Senior Books Editor • **DIANA SCHUTZ** Executive Editor • **CARY GRAZZINI** Director of Print and Development • **LIA RIBACCHI** Art Director • **CARA NIECE** Director of Scheduling

To David, who is old enough to read the good stuff—
but not yet old enough to read this one.

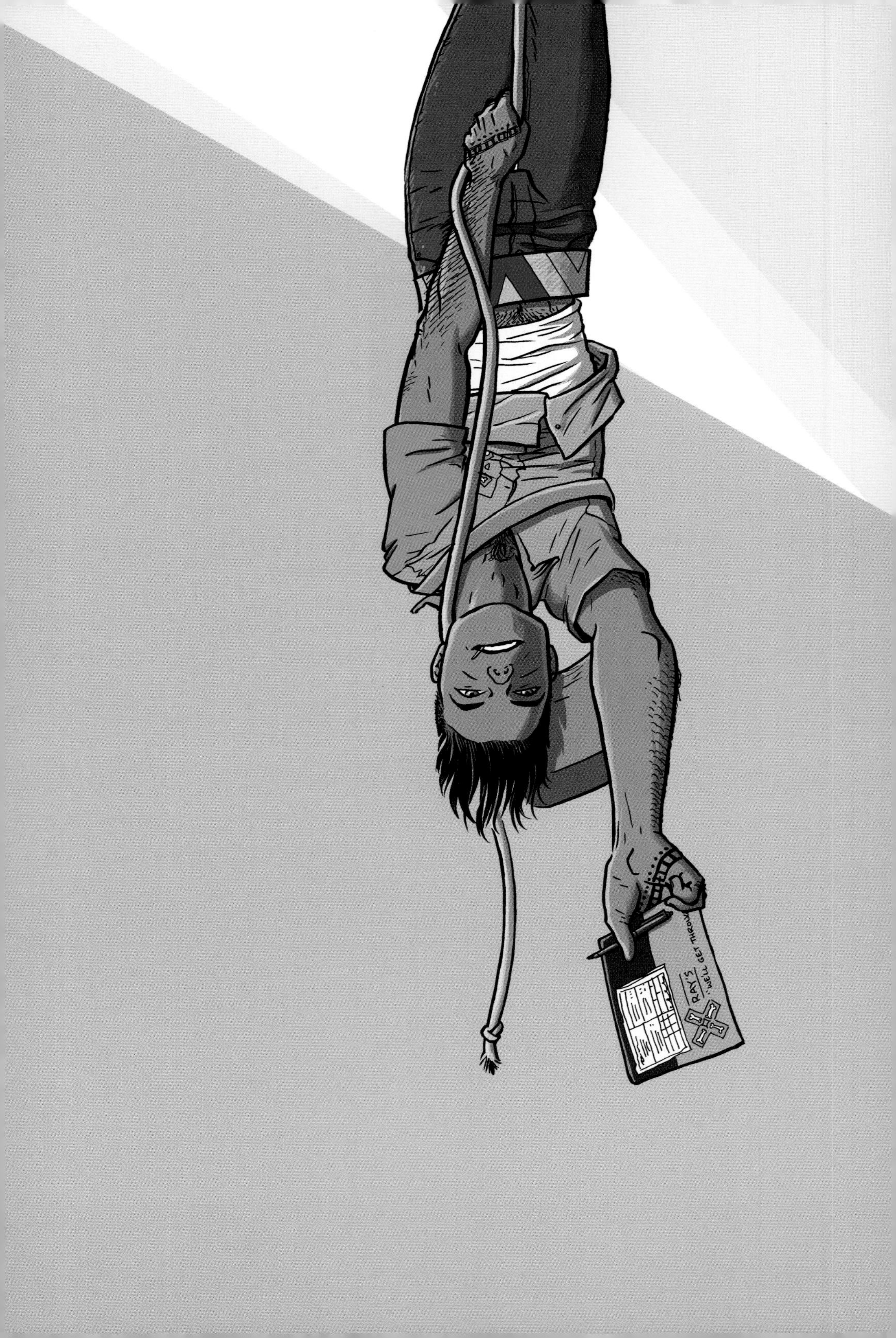
RAY'S
WE'LL GET THROU

PART ONE

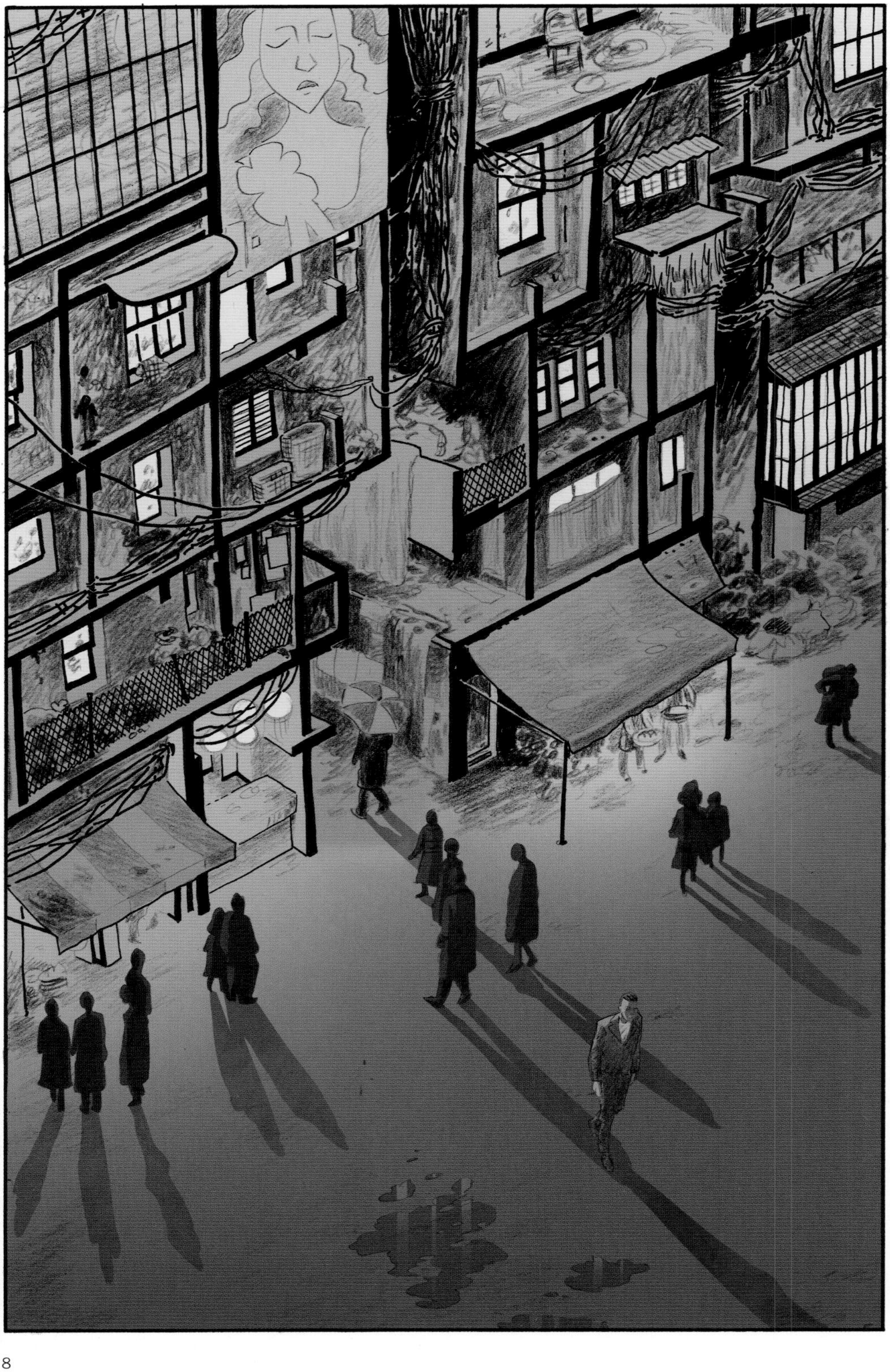

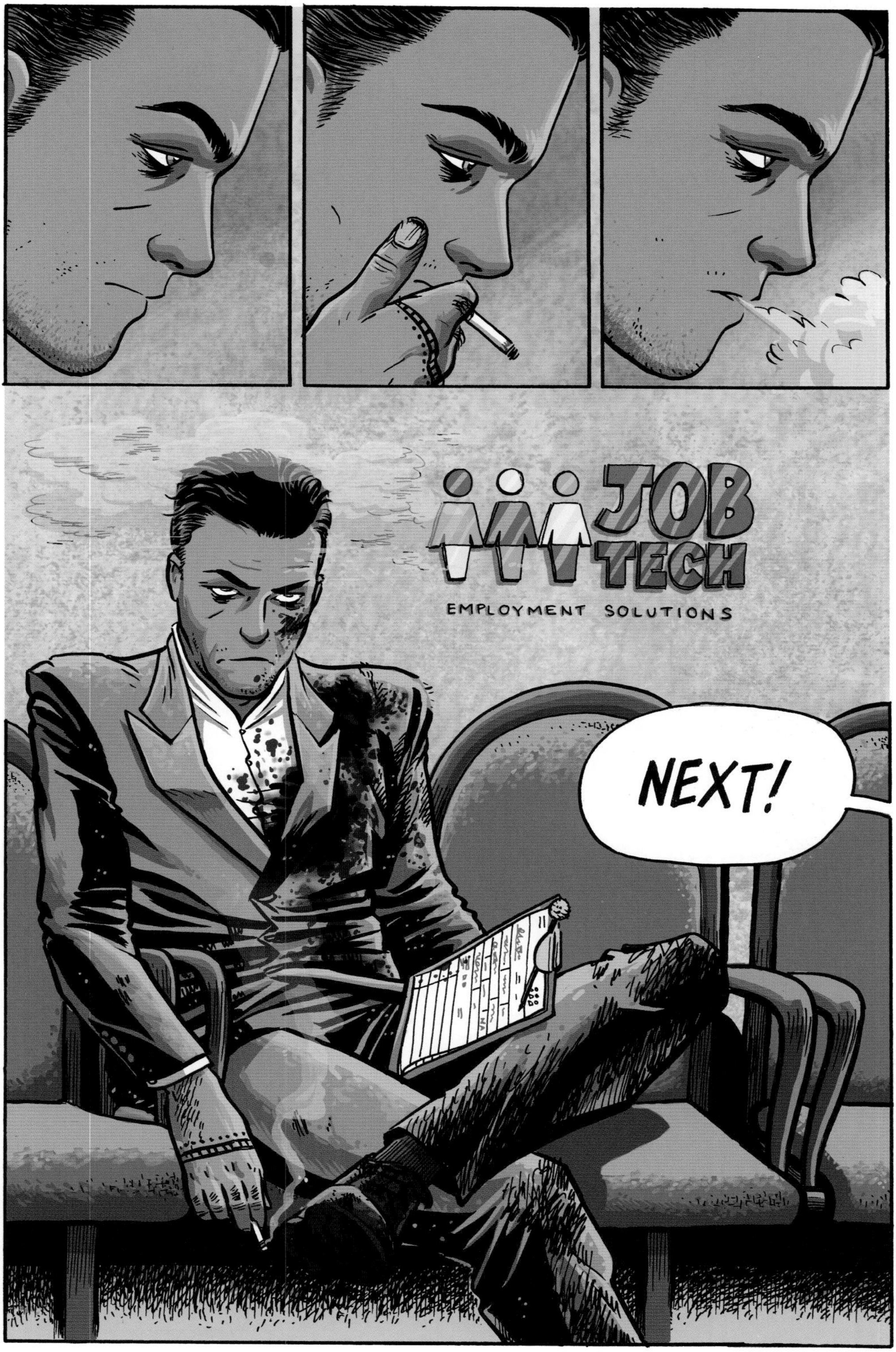
JOB TECH
EMPLOYMENT SOLUTIONS
NEXT!

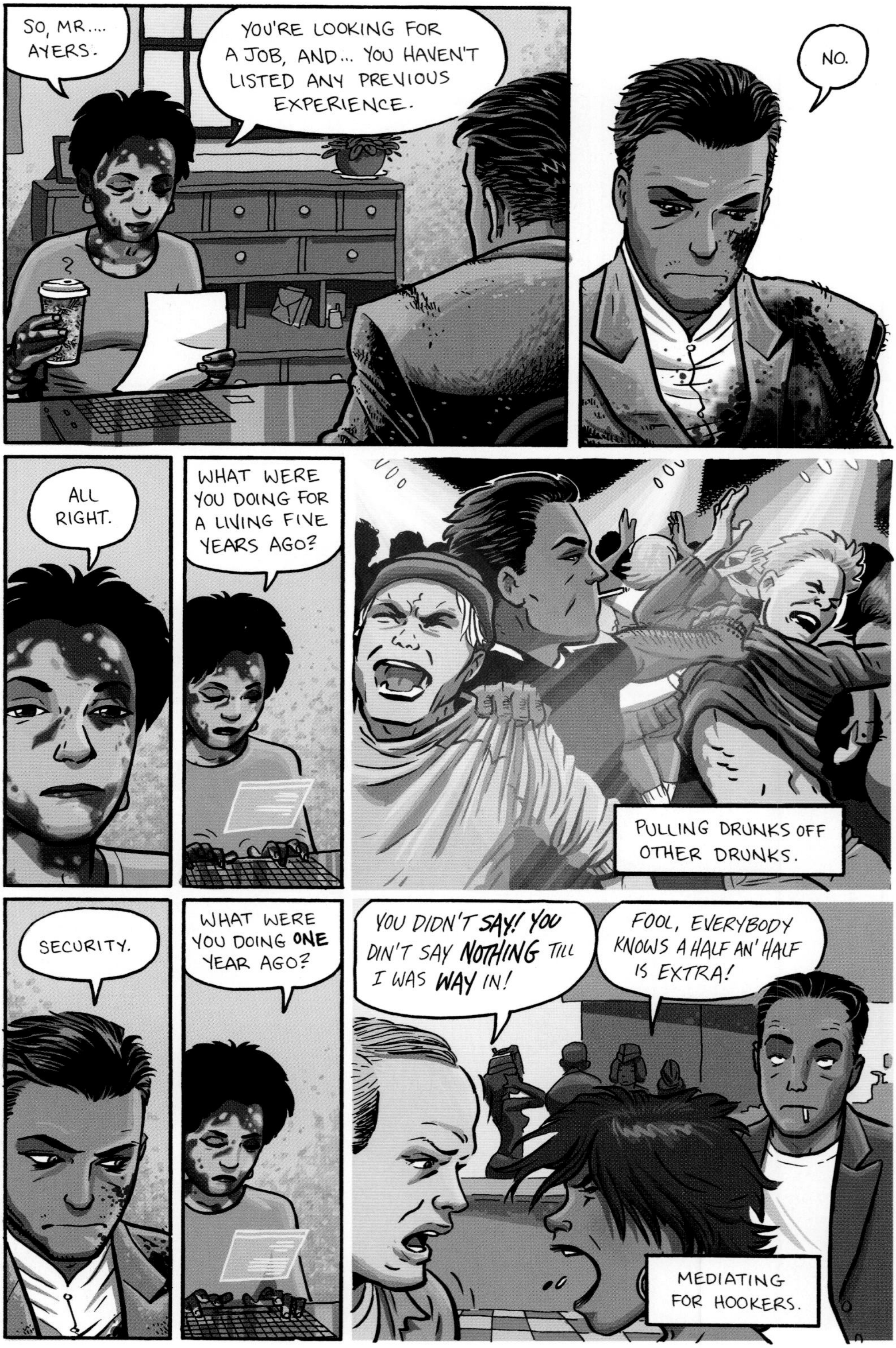
SO, MR.... AYERS.
YOU'RE LOOKING FOR A JOB, AND... YOU HAVEN'T LISTED ANY PREVIOUS EXPERIENCE.
NO.
ALL RIGHT.
WHAT WERE YOU DOING FOR A LIVING FIVE YEARS AGO?
PULLING DRUNKS OFF OTHER DRUNKS.
SECURITY.
WHAT WERE YOU DOING ONE YEAR AGO?
YOU DIDN'T SAY! YOU DIN'T SAY NOTHING TILL I WAS WAY IN!
FOOL, EVERYBODY KNOWS A HALF AN' HALF IS EXTRA!
MEDIATING FOR HOOKERS.

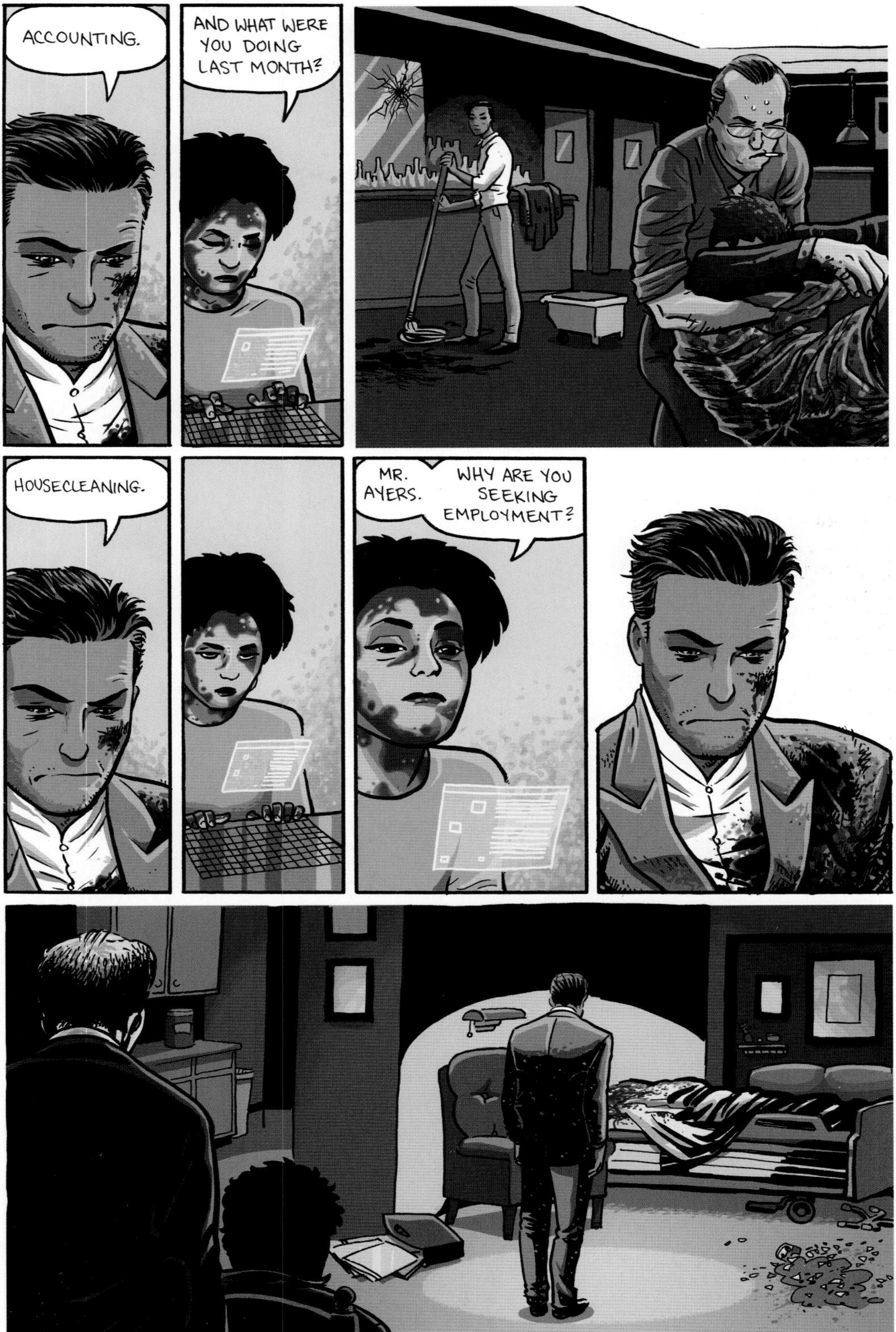
ACCOUNTING.
AND WHAT WERE YOU DOING LAST MONTH?
HOUSECLEANING.
MR. AYERS.
WHY ARE YOU SEEKING EMPLOYMENT?

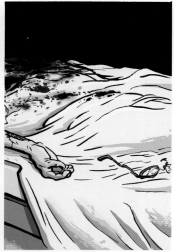

JUST TAKE CARE OF IT.

WE WILL TAKE CARE OF **THIS**.

YOU TAKE CARE OF **THAT**.

MY CURRENT SITUATION LACKS SATISFACTION.

HM.

TAKE THIS TO 662 HUYANERA STREET. PRESENT IT TO TRUDY.

"TELL HER YOU'RE FROM ME."

DESTINATIONS

RATES

X RAY'S

COURIERS: "WE'LL GET THROUGH"

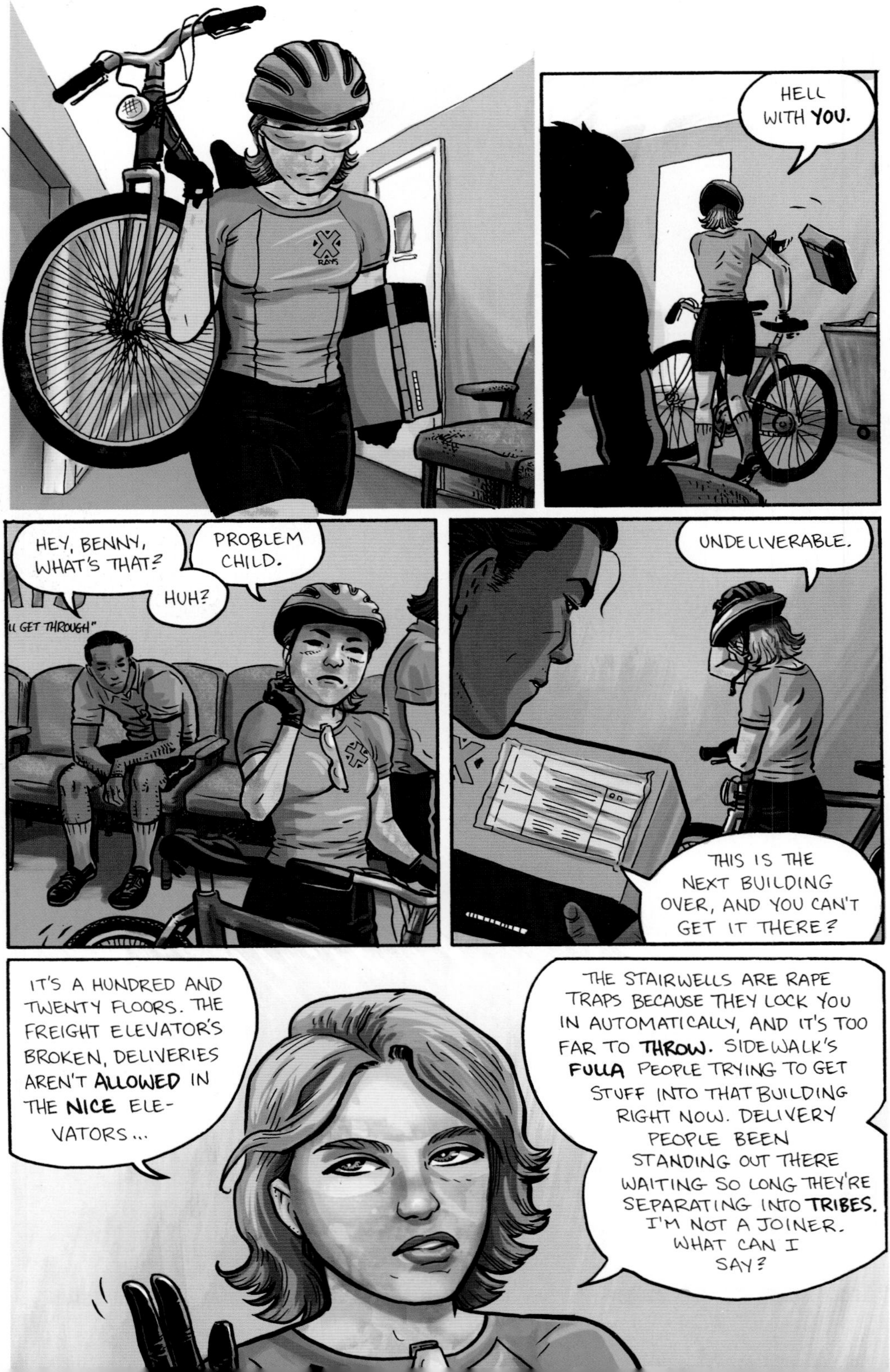
HELL WITH **YOU**.
HEY, BENNY, WHAT'S THAT?
HUH?
PROBLEM CHILD.
UNDELIVERABLE.
THIS IS THE NEXT BUILDING OVER, AND YOU CAN'T GET IT THERE?
IT'S A HUNDRED AND TWENTY FLOORS. THE FREIGHT ELEVATOR'S BROKEN, DELIVERIES AREN'T **ALLOWED** IN THE **NICE** ELE-VATORS...
THE STAIRWELLS ARE RAPE TRAPS BECAUSE THEY LOCK YOU IN AUTOMATICALLY, AND IT'S TOO FAR TO **THROW**. SIDEWALK'S **FULLA** PEOPLE TRYING TO GET STUFF INTO THAT BUILDING RIGHT NOW. DELIVERY PEOPLE BEEN STANDING OUT THERE WAITING SO LONG THEY'RE SEPARATING INTO **TRIBES**. I'M NOT A JOINER. WHAT CAN I SAY?

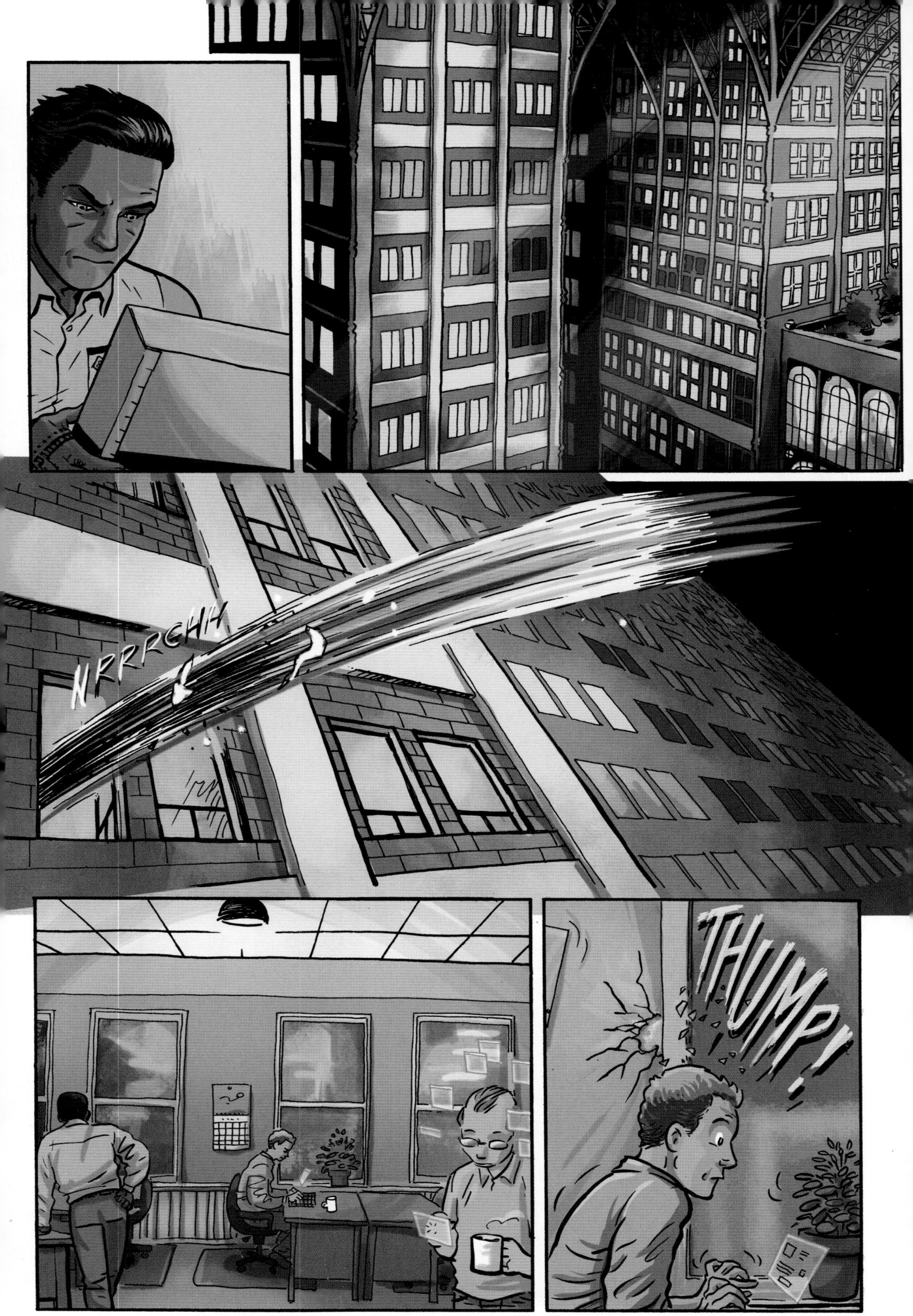
NRRRGHH
THUMP!

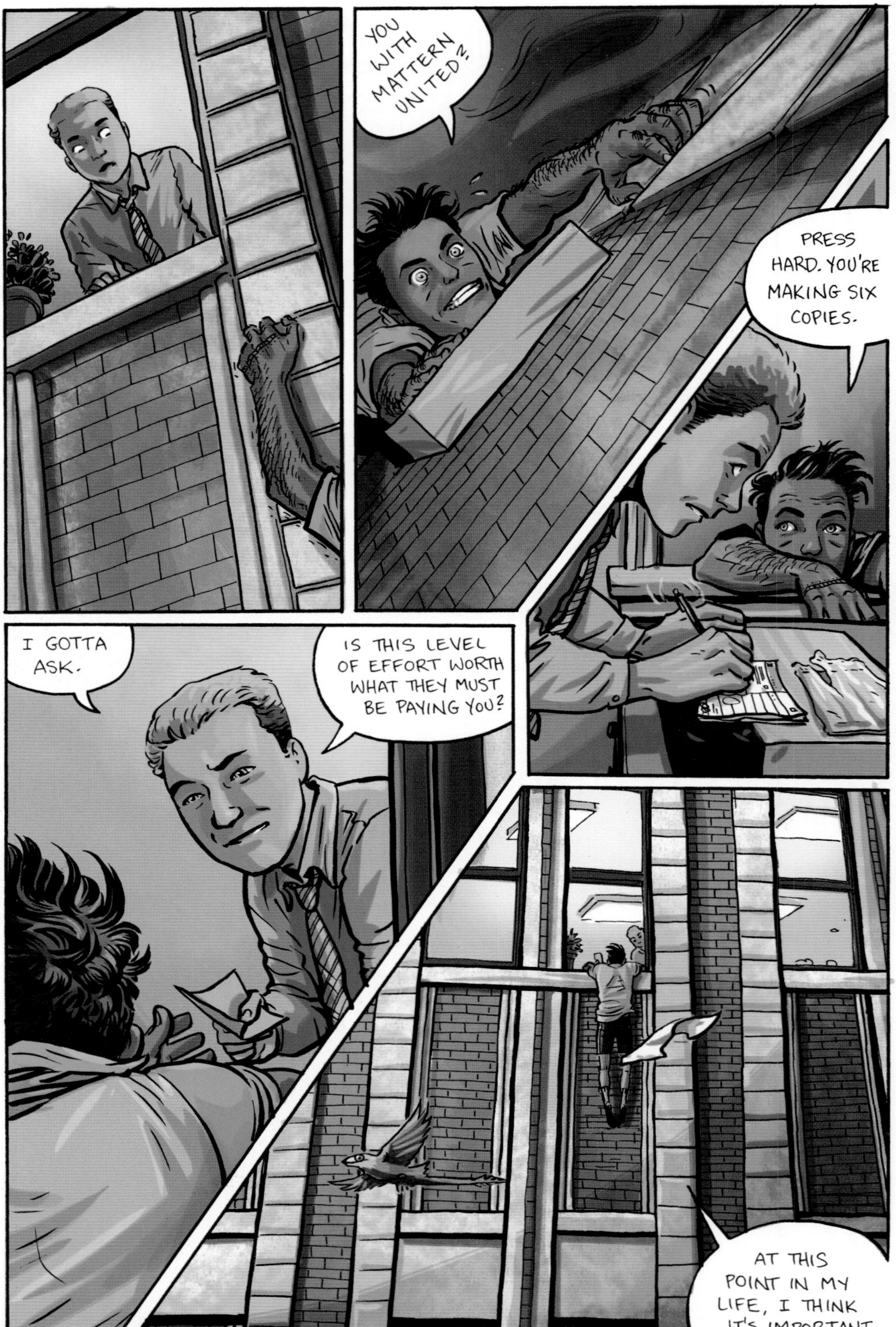
YOU WITH MATTERN UNITED?!
PRESS HARD. YOU'RE MAKING SIX COPIES.
I GOTTA ASK.
IS THIS LEVEL OF EFFORT WORTH WHAT THEY MUST BE PAYING YOU?
AT THIS POINT IN MY LIFE, I THINK IT'S IMPORTANT TO BE HAPPY.

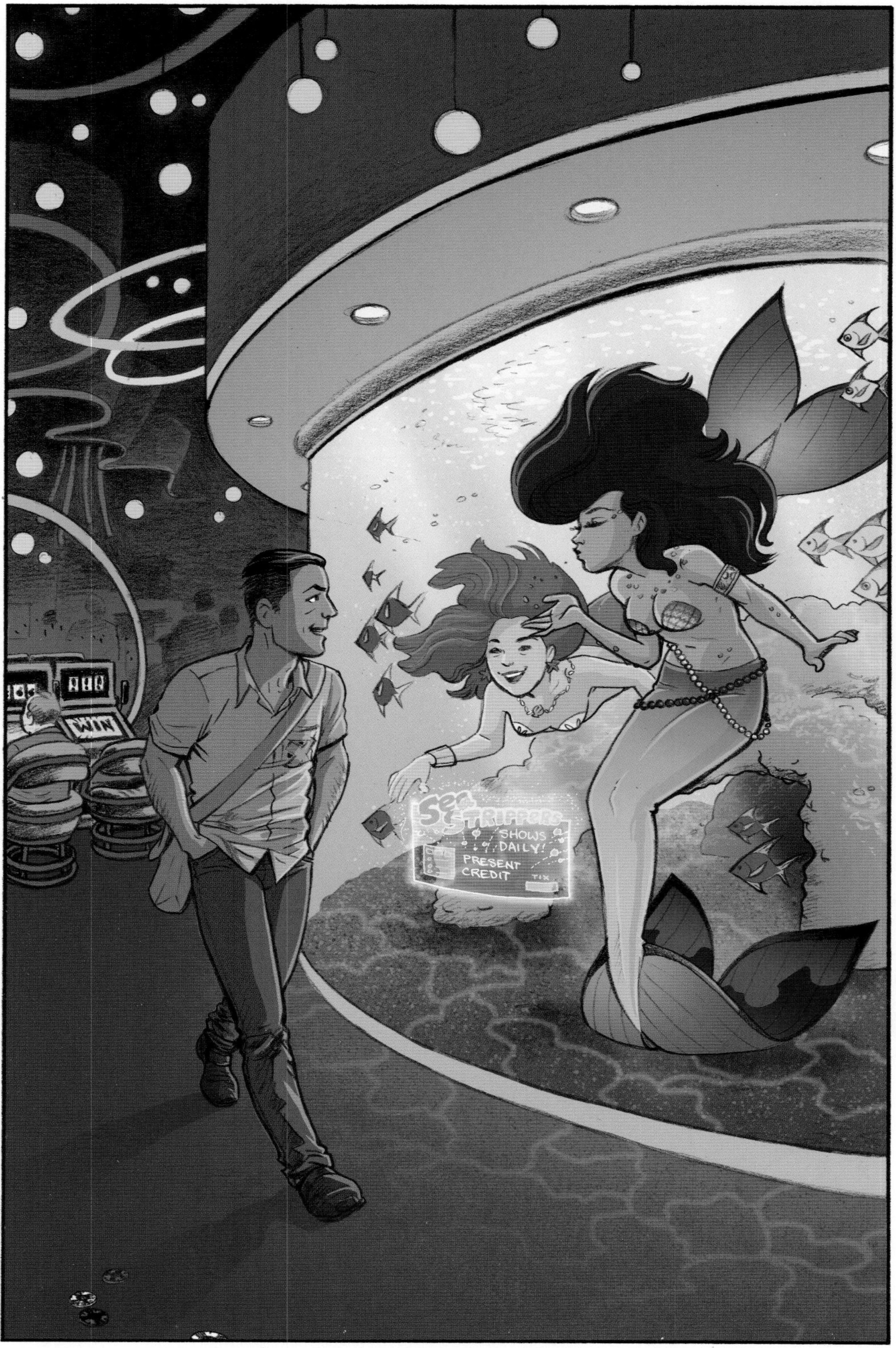
WIN
Sea Strippers
SHOWS DAILY!
PRESENT CREDIT
TIX

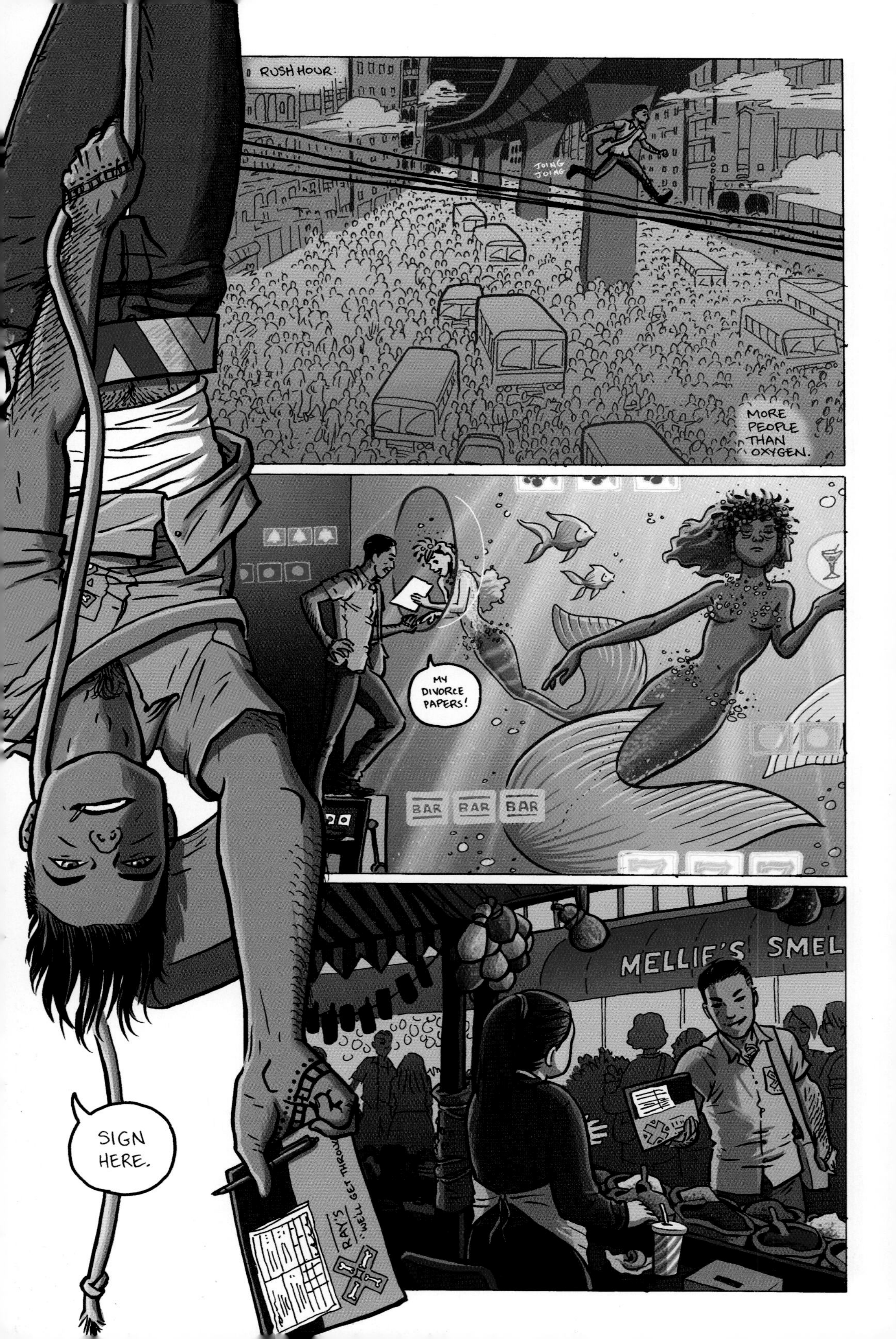
RUSH HOUR:
JOING JOING
MORE PEOPLE THAN OXYGEN.
MY DIVORCE PAPERS!
BAR BAR BAR
MELLIE'S SMEL
RAY'S
SIGN HERE.

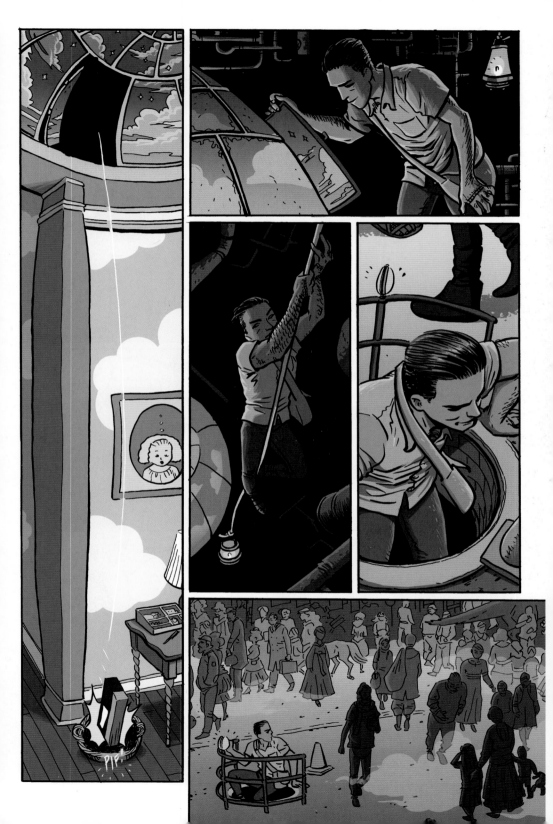

PIP!

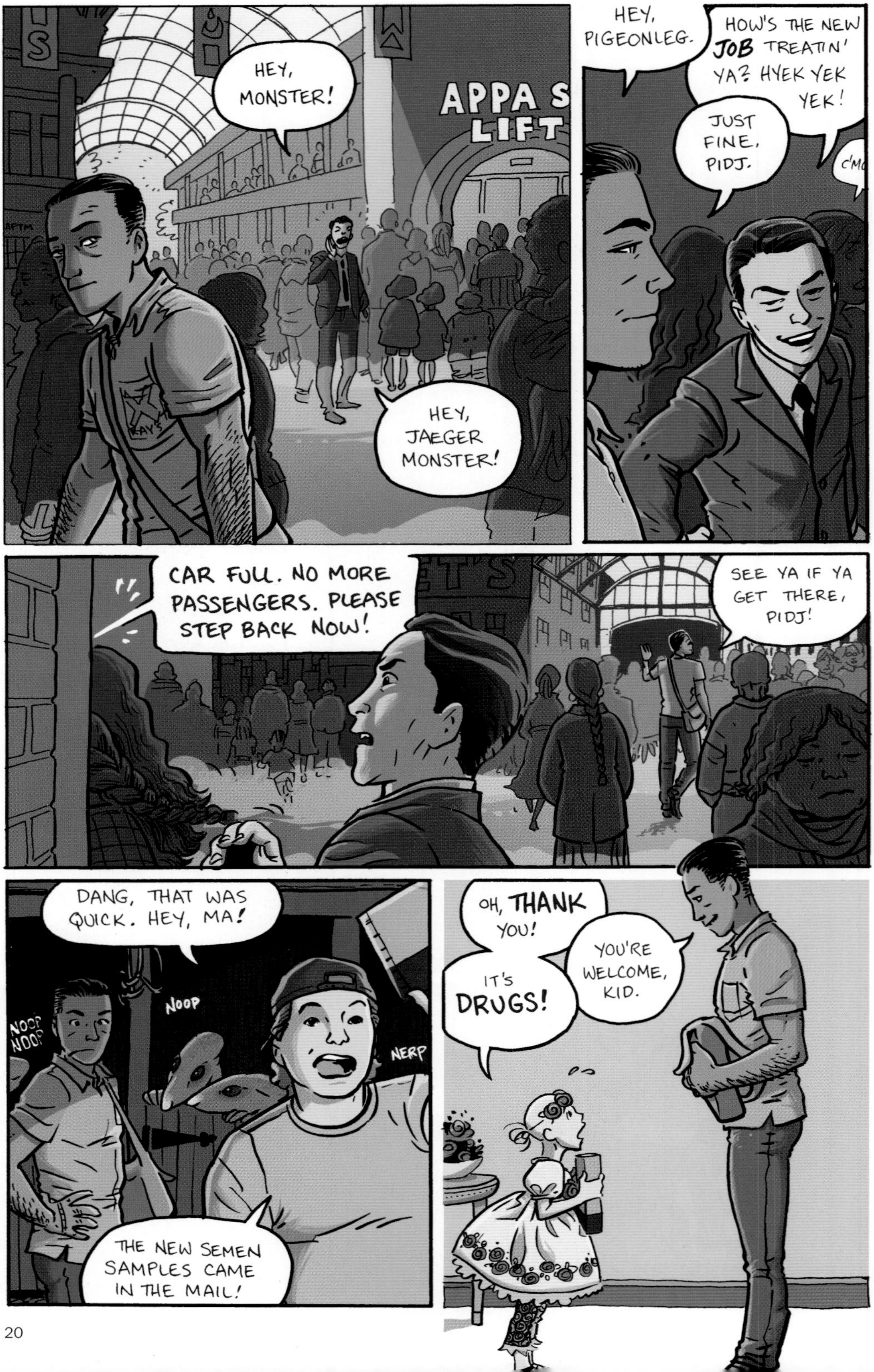
HEY, MONSTER!
APPA S
LIFT
HEY, JAEGER MONSTER!
HEY, PIGEONLEG.
HOW'S THE NEW JOB TREATIN' YA? HYEK YEK YEK!
JUST FINE, PIDJ.
CAR FULL. NO MORE PASSENGERS. PLEASE STEP BACK NOW!
SEE YA IF YA GET THERE, PIDJ!
DANG, THAT WAS QUICK. HEY, MA!
NOOP NOOP
NOOP
NERP
THE NEW SEMEN SAMPLES CAME IN THE MAIL!
OH, THANK YOU!
IT'S DRUGS!
YOU'RE WELCOME, KID.

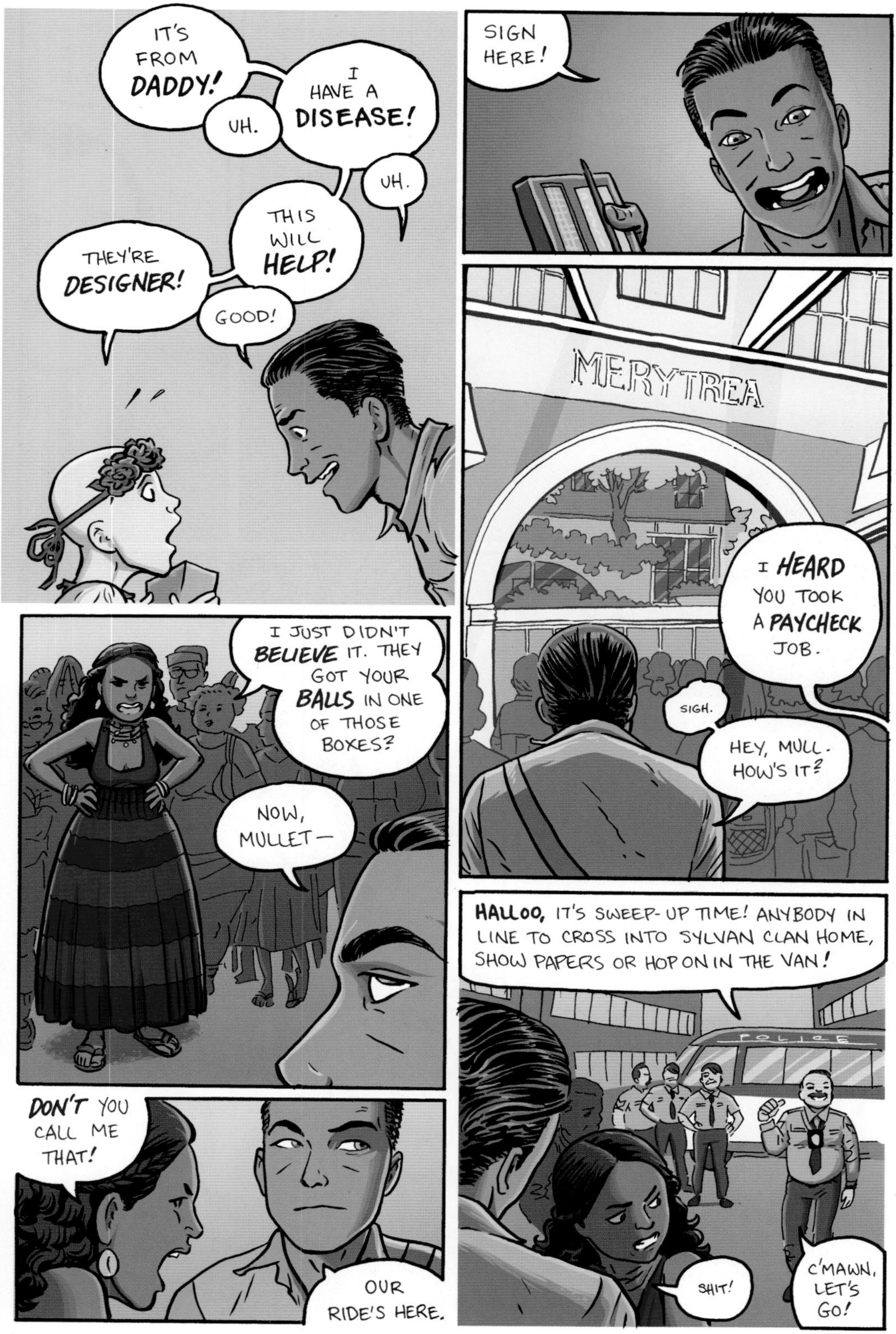
IT'S FROM DADDY!
UH.
I HAVE A DISEASE!
UH.
THEY'RE DESIGNER!
THIS WILL HELP!
GOOD!
SIGN HERE!
I HEARD YOU TOOK A PAYCHECK JOB.
MERYTREA
SIGH.
HEY, MULL. HOW'S IT?
I JUST DIDN'T BELIEVE IT. THEY GOT YOUR BALLS IN ONE OF THOSE BOXES?
NOW, MULLET—
DON'T YOU CALL ME THAT!
OUR RIDE'S HERE.
HALLOO, IT'S SWEEP-UP TIME! ANYBODY IN LINE TO CROSS INTO SYLVAN CLAN HOME, SHOW PAPERS OR HOP ON IN THE VAN!
POLICE
SHIT!
C'MAWN, LET'S GO!

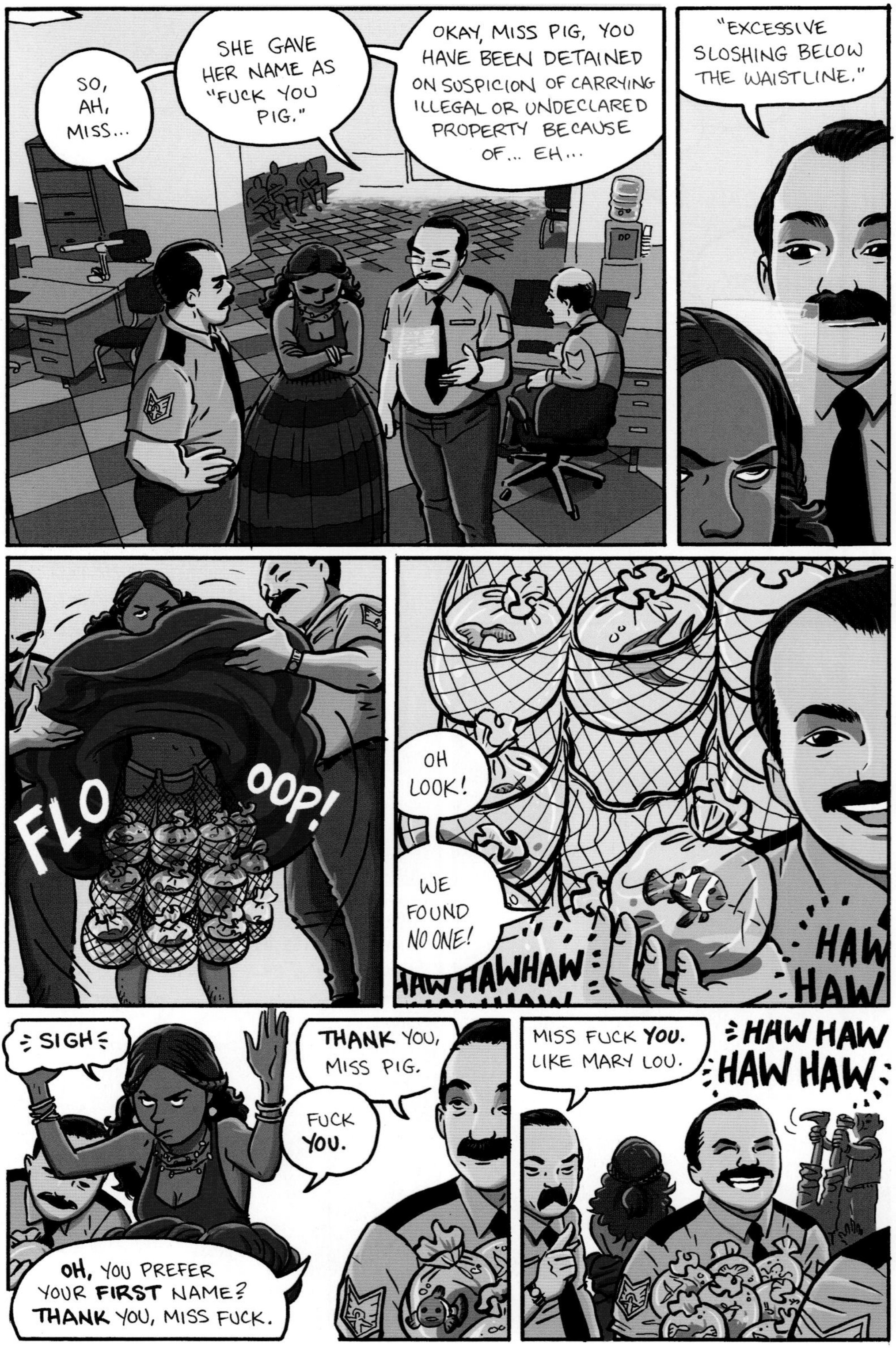
SO, AH, MISS...
SHE GAVE HER NAME AS "FUCK YOU PIG."
OKAY, MISS PIG, YOU HAVE BEEN DETAINED ON SUSPICION OF CARRYING ILLEGAL OR UNDECLARED PROPERTY BECAUSE OF... EH...
"EXCESSIVE SLOSHING BELOW THE WAISTLINE."
FLOOOP!
OH LOOK!
WE FOUND NO ONE!
HAW HAWHAW
HAW HAW
SIGH
OH, YOU PREFER YOUR FIRST NAME? THANK YOU, MISS FUCK.
THANK YOU, MISS PIG.
FUCK YOU.
MISS FUCK YOU. LIKE MARY LOU.
HAW HAW HAW HAW

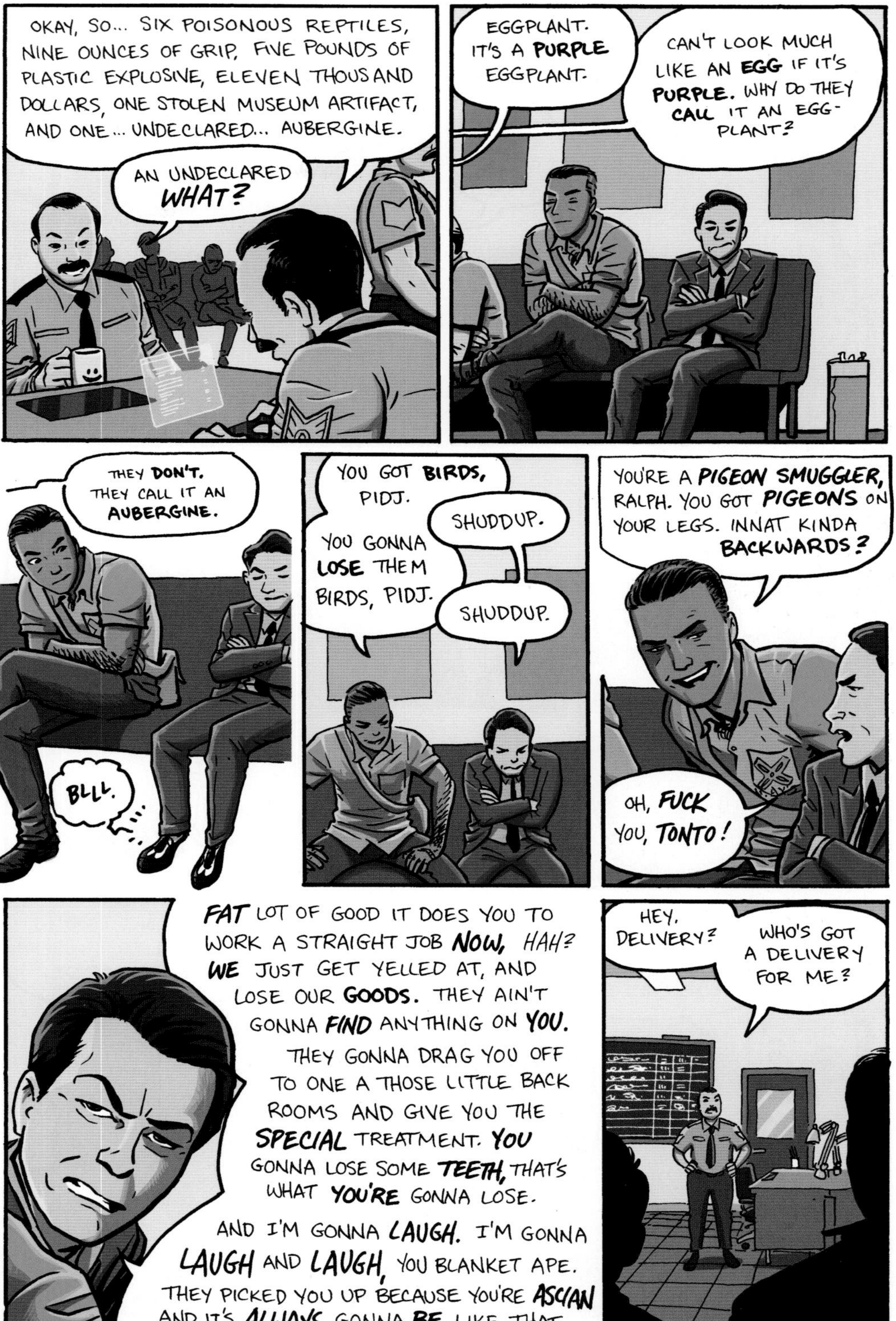
OKAY, SO... SIX POISONOUS REPTILES, NINE OUNCES OF GRIP, FIVE POUNDS OF PLASTIC EXPLOSIVE, ELEVEN THOUSAND DOLLARS, ONE STOLEN MUSEUM ARTIFACT, AND ONE... UNDECLARED... AUBERGINE.
AN UNDECLARED WHAT?
EGGPLANT. IT'S A PURPLE EGGPLANT.
CAN'T LOOK MUCH LIKE AN EGG IF IT'S PURPLE. WHY DO THEY CALL IT AN EGG-PLANT?
THEY DON'T. THEY CALL IT AN AUBERGINE.
BLLL.
YOU GOT BIRDS, PIDJ.
SHUDDUP.
YOU GONNA LOSE THEM BIRDS, PIDJ.
SHUDDUP.
YOU'RE A PIGEON SMUGGLER, RALPH. YOU GOT PIGEONS ON YOUR LEGS. INNAT KINDA BACKWARDS?
OH, FUCK YOU, TONTO!
FAT LOT OF GOOD IT DOES YOU TO WORK A STRAIGHT JOB NOW, HAH? WE JUST GET YELLED AT, AND LOSE OUR GOODS. THEY AIN'T GONNA FIND ANYTHING ON YOU.
THEY GONNA DRAG YOU OFF TO ONE A THOSE LITTLE BACK ROOMS AND GIVE YOU THE SPECIAL TREATMENT. YOU GONNA LOSE SOME TEETH, THAT'S WHAT YOU'RE GONNA LOSE.
AND I'M GONNA LAUGH. I'M GONNA LAUGH AND LAUGH, YOU BLANKET APE. THEY PICKED YOU UP BECAUSE YOU'RE ASCIAN AND IT'S ALWAYS GONNA BE LIKE THAT.
HEY. DELIVERY?
WHO'S GOT A DELIVERY FOR ME?

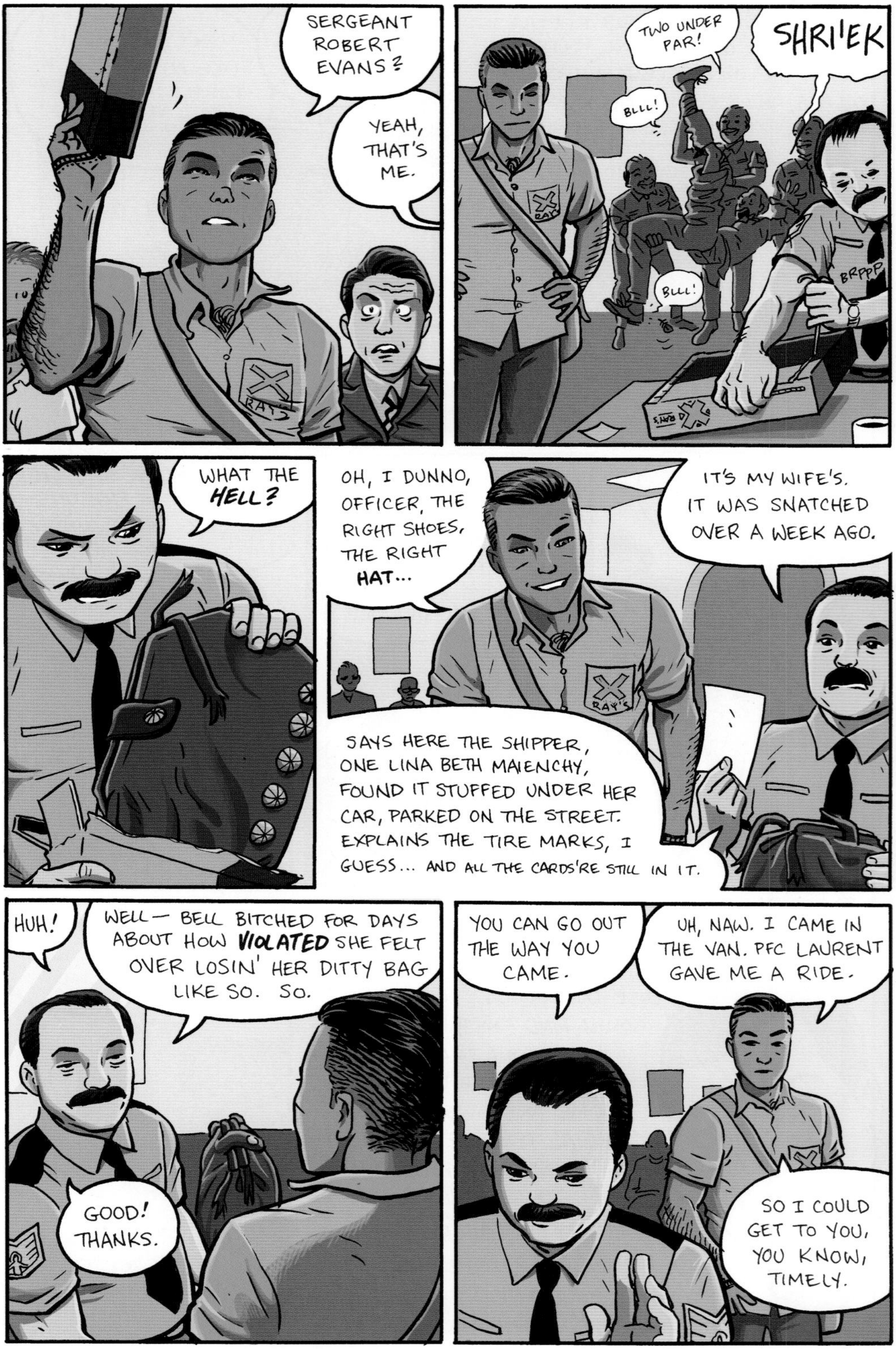
SERGEANT ROBERT EVANS?
YEAH, THAT'S ME.
TWO UNDER PAR!
SHRI'EK
BLLL!
BLLL!
BRPPP
WHAT THE HELL?
OH, I DUNNO, OFFICER, THE RIGHT SHOES, THE RIGHT HAT...
IT'S MY WIFE'S. IT WAS SNATCHED OVER A WEEK AGO.
SAYS HERE THE SHIPPER, ONE LINA BETH MAIENCHY, FOUND IT STUFFED UNDER HER CAR, PARKED ON THE STREET. EXPLAINS THE TIRE MARKS, I GUESS... AND ALL THE CARDS'RE STILL IN IT.
HUH!
WELL— BELL BITCHED FOR DAYS ABOUT HOW VIOLATED SHE FELT OVER LOSIN' HER DITTY BAG LIKE SO. SO.
GOOD! THANKS.
YOU CAN GO OUT THE WAY YOU CAME.
UH, NAW. I CAME IN THE VAN. PFC LAURENT GAVE ME A RIDE.
SO I COULD GET TO YOU, YOU KNOW, TIMELY.

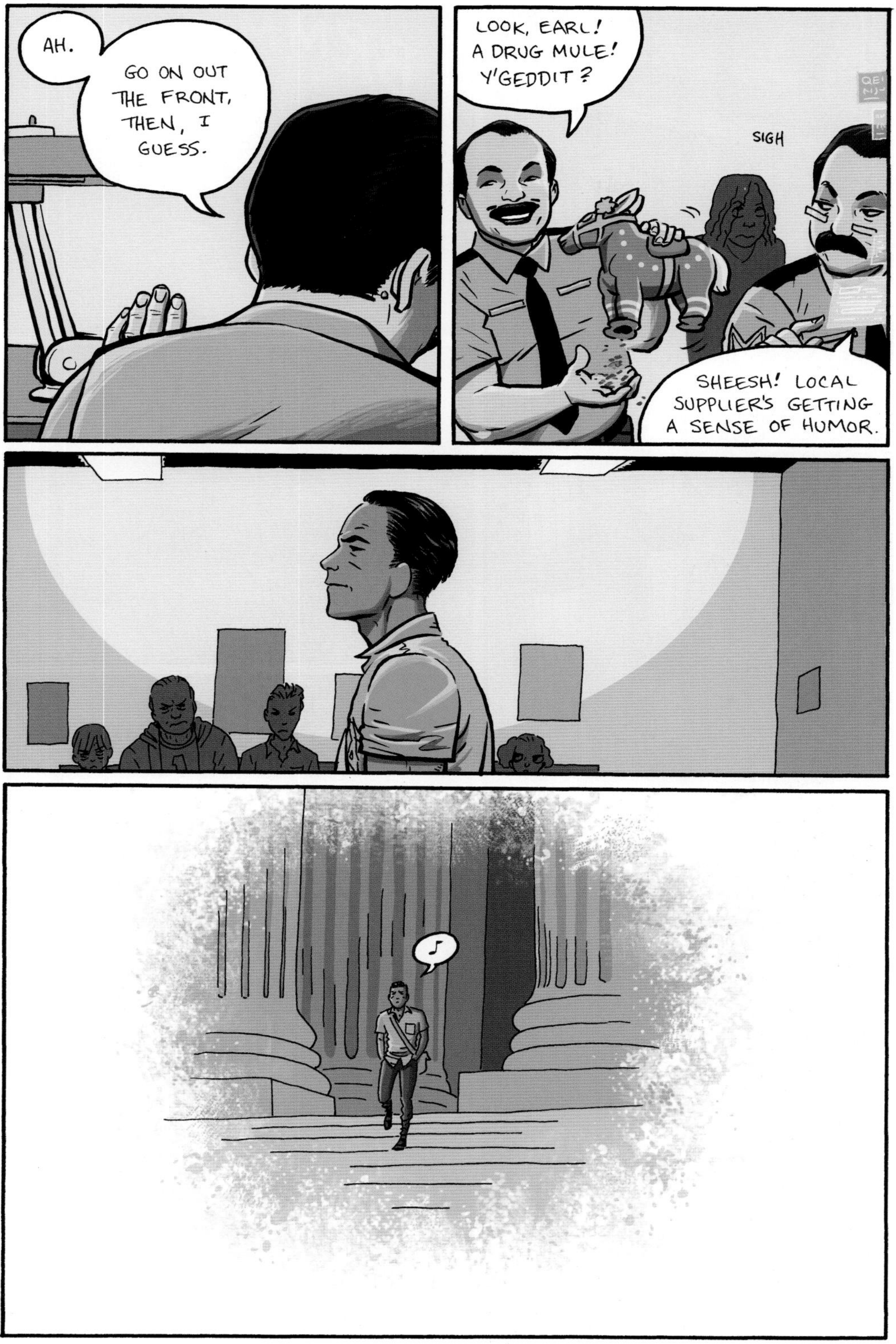
AH.
GO ON OUT THE FRONT, THEN, I GUESS.
LOOK, EARL! A DRUG MULE! Y'GEDDIT?
SIGH
SHEESH! LOCAL SUPPLIER'S GETTING A SENSE OF HUMOR.

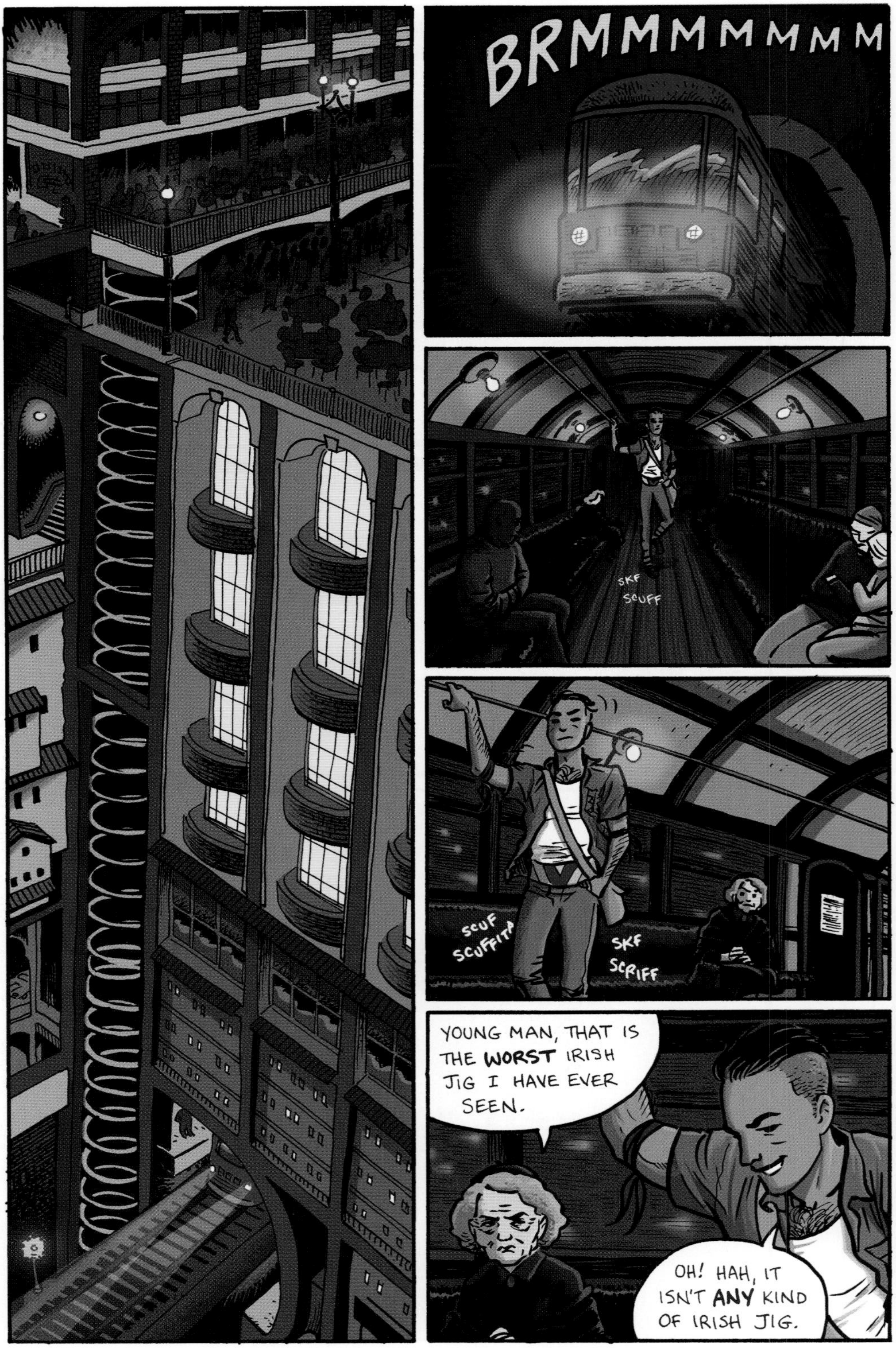
BRMMMMMMMM
SKF
SCUFF
SCUF
SCUFFITA
SKF
SCRIFF
YOUNG MAN, THAT IS THE **WORST** IRISH JIG I HAVE EVER SEEN.
OH! HAH, IT ISN'T **ANY** KIND OF IRISH JIG.

I JUST HAVE ITCHY FEET. I HATE THESE LONG TRAIN RIDES.

NONSENSE. IF YOU'RE GOING TO SCUFF UP YOUR SHOES ANYROAD, YOU OUGHT TO **DO** SOMETHING **WITH** THEM.

HOW'D YOU GET ALL THE WAY OUT HERE ANYWAY? AND HOW'D YOU FIGURE TO GET **BACK**?

SNORT! I FORGOT MY STOP.

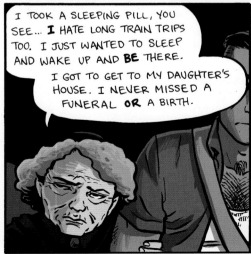

I TOOK A SLEEPING PILL, YOU SEE... **I** HATE LONG TRAIN TRIPS TOO. I JUST WANTED TO SLEEP AND WAKE UP AND **BE** THERE.

I GOT TO GET TO MY DAUGHTER'S HOUSE. I NEVER MISSED A FUNERAL **OR** A BIRTH.

WHICH... NEVER MIND. WE'LL GET YOU THERE, OL' DEAR.

I'M NOT **OLD**. I'M JUST **TIRED**.

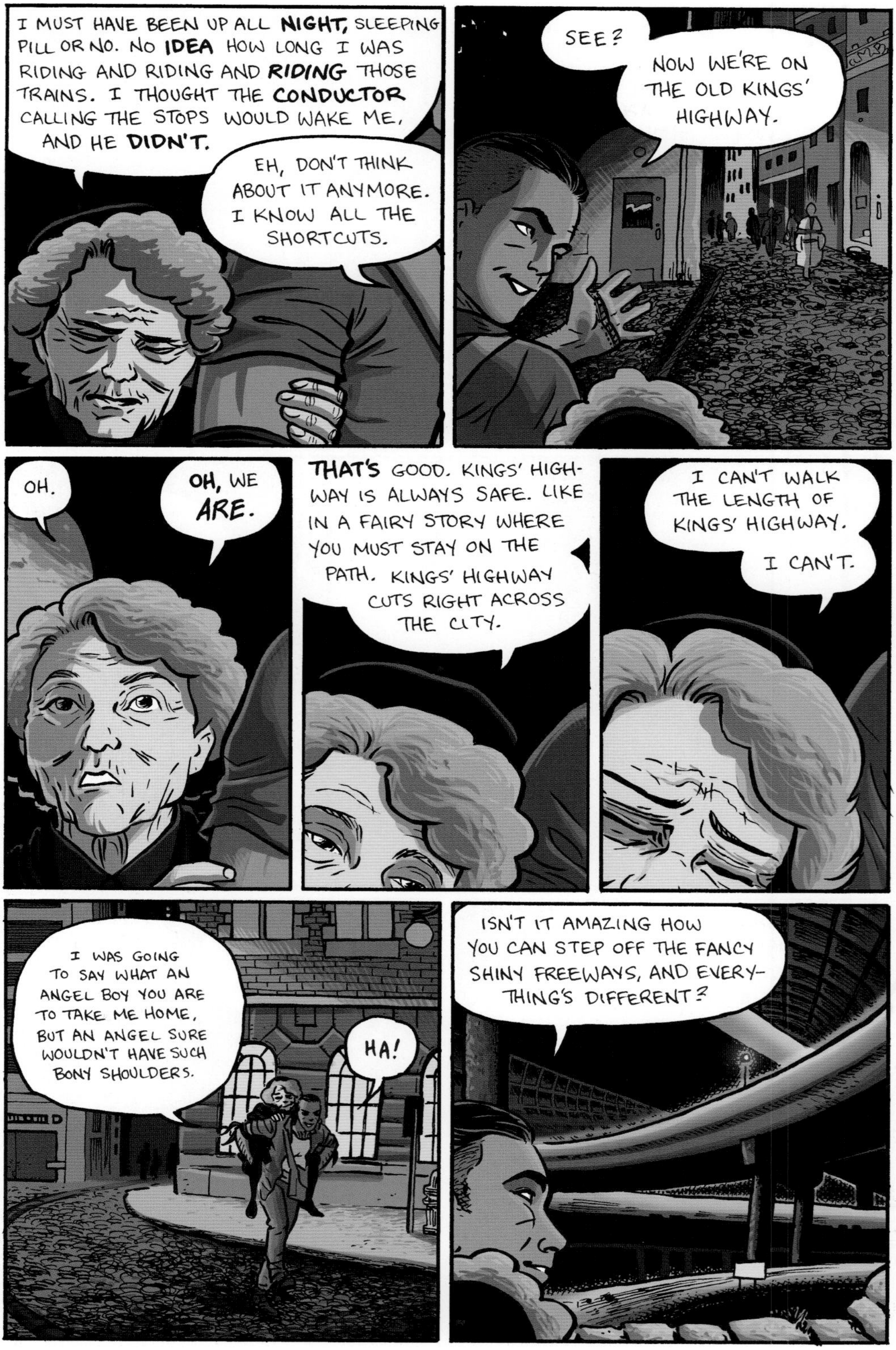
I MUST HAVE BEEN UP ALL NIGHT, SLEEPING PILL OR NO. NO IDEA HOW LONG I WAS RIDING AND RIDING AND RIDING THOSE TRAINS. I THOUGHT THE CONDUCTOR CALLING THE STOPS WOULD WAKE ME, AND HE DIDN'T.
EH, DON'T THINK ABOUT IT ANYMORE. I KNOW ALL THE SHORTCUTS.
SEE?
NOW WE'RE ON THE OLD KINGS' HIGHWAY.
OH.
OH, WE ARE.
THAT'S GOOD. KINGS' HIGHWAY IS ALWAYS SAFE. LIKE IN A FAIRY STORY WHERE YOU MUST STAY ON THE PATH. KINGS' HIGHWAY CUTS RIGHT ACROSS THE CITY.
I CAN'T WALK THE LENGTH OF KINGS' HIGHWAY.
I CAN'T.
I WAS GOING TO SAY WHAT AN ANGEL BOY YOU ARE TO TAKE ME HOME, BUT AN ANGEL SURE WOULDN'T HAVE SUCH BONY SHOULDERS.
HA!
ISN'T IT AMAZING HOW YOU CAN STEP OFF THE FANCY SHINY FREEWAYS, AND EVERYTHING'S DIFFERENT?

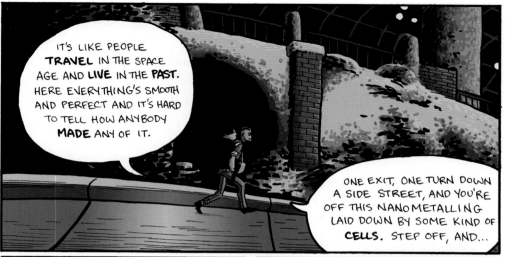

IT'S LIKE PEOPLE **TRAVEL** IN THE SPACE AGE AND **LIVE** IN THE **PAST.** HERE EVERYTHING'S SMOOTH AND PERFECT AND IT'S HARD TO TELL HOW ANYBODY **MADE** ANY OF IT.

ONE EXIT, ONE TURN DOWN A SIDE STREET, AND YOU'RE OFF THIS NANOMETALLING LAID DOWN BY SOME KIND OF **CELLS.** STEP OFF, AND...

BOOM, YOU'RE ON CONCRETE. **CONCRETE,** POURED OUT OF TRUCKS, SMOOTHED OUT BY GUYS WITH RAKES, SCRATCHED AND CRACKED MARKED BY ANIMALS' FOOTPRINTS, LOVERS' NAMES, FOOTRACE ROUTES.

ONE TURN MORE, AND WE'RE ON COBBLE-STONES.

ONE **MORE,** AND LOOK AT *THIS! DIRT!* DIRT ROADS, WAY DOWN HERE AT THE BOTTOM OF *THIS* CITY.

FARMLAND, IF ANYBODY CAN STILL AFFORD SUNLIGHT.

29

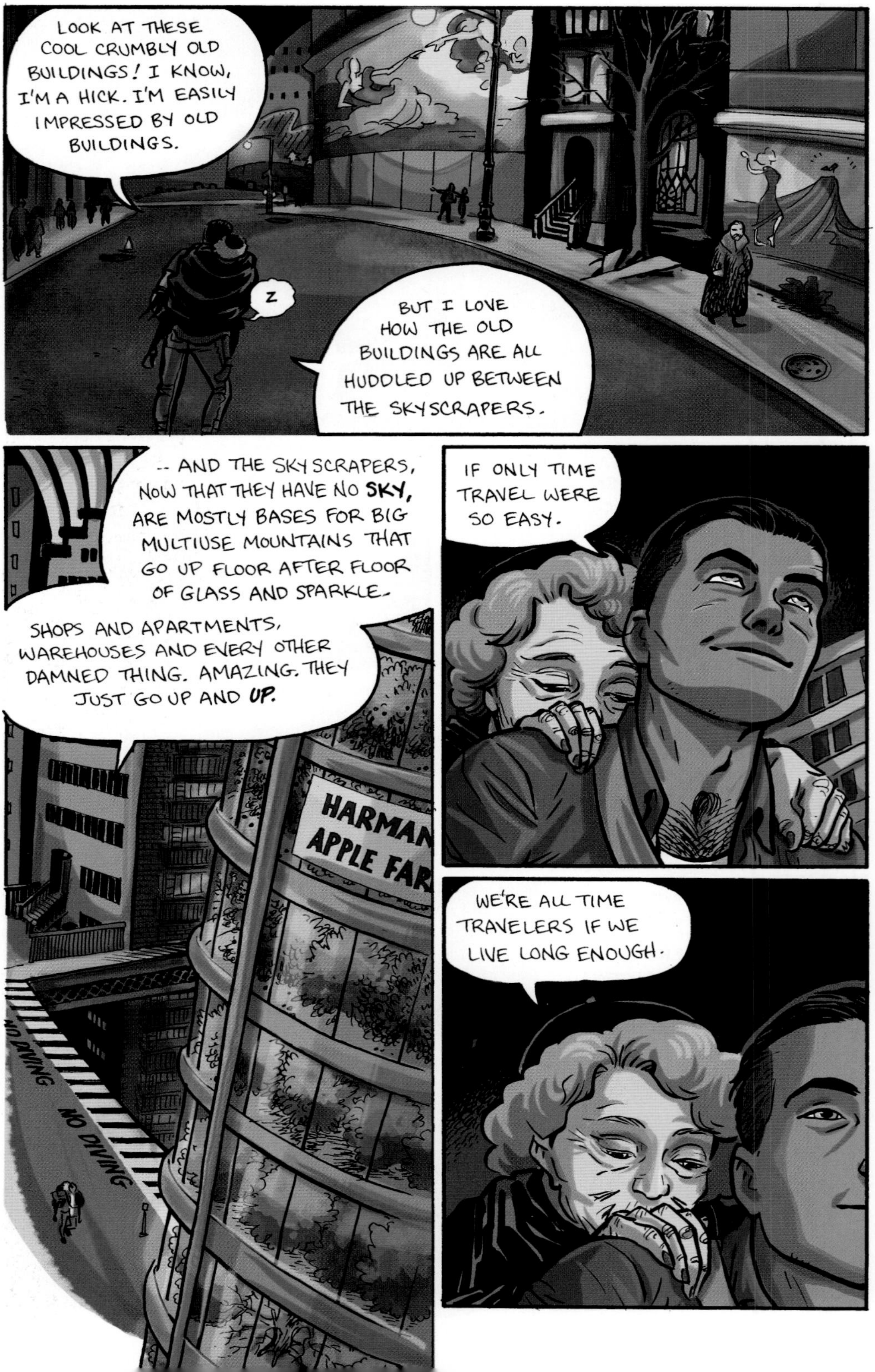
LOOK AT THESE COOL CRUMBLY OLD BUILDINGS! I KNOW, I'M A HICK. I'M EASILY IMPRESSED BY OLD BUILDINGS.
Z
BUT I LOVE HOW THE OLD BUILDINGS ARE ALL HUDDLED UP BETWEEN THE SKYSCRAPERS.
-- AND THE SKYSCRAPERS, NOW THAT THEY HAVE NO SKY, ARE MOSTLY BASES FOR BIG MULTIUSE MOUNTAINS THAT GO UP FLOOR AFTER FLOOR OF GLASS AND SPARKLE.
SHOPS AND APARTMENTS, WAREHOUSES AND EVERY OTHER DAMNED THING. AMAZING. THEY JUST GO UP AND UP.
HARMAN
APPLE FAR
NO DIVING
NO DIVING
NO DIVING
IF ONLY TIME TRAVEL WERE SO EASY.
WE'RE ALL TIME TRAVELERS IF WE LIVE LONG ENOUGH.

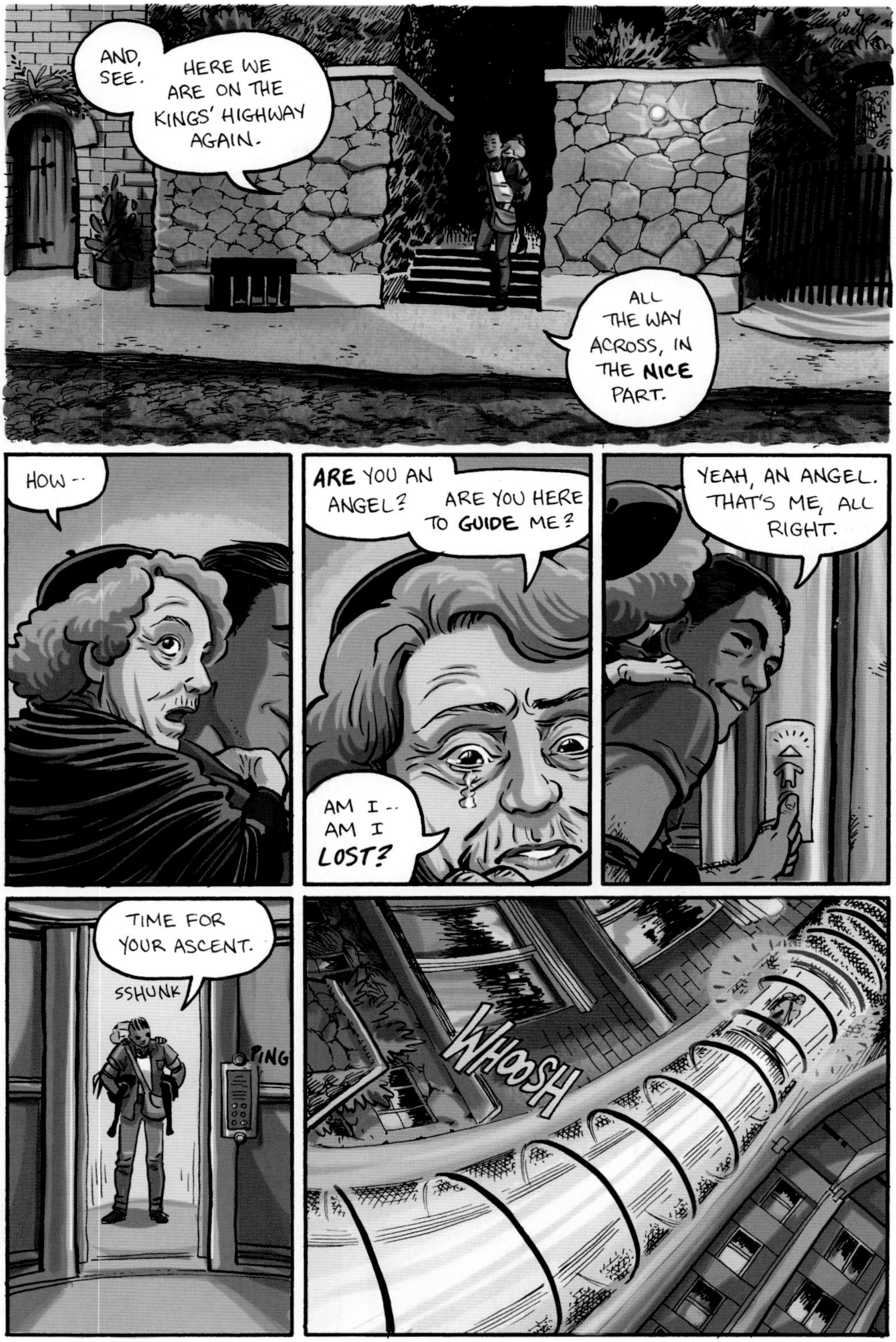
AND, SEE.
HERE WE ARE ON THE KINGS' HIGHWAY AGAIN.
ALL THE WAY ACROSS, IN THE NICE PART.
HOW--
ARE YOU AN ANGEL?
ARE YOU HERE TO GUIDE ME?
AM I-- AM I LOST?
YEAH, AN ANGEL. THAT'S ME, ALL RIGHT.
TIME FOR YOUR ASCENT.
SSHUNK
PING
WHOOSH

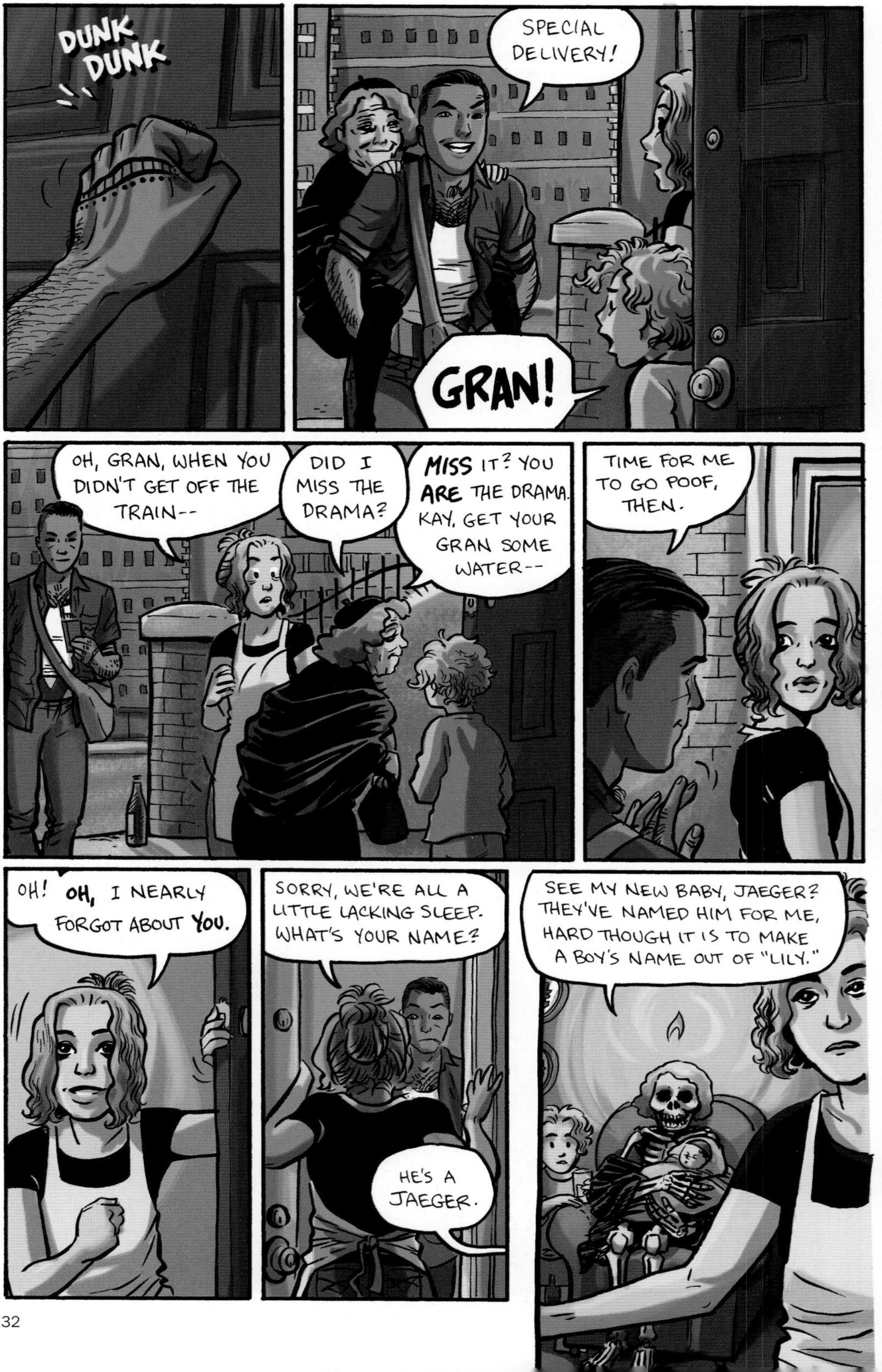
DUNK DUNK
SPECIAL DELIVERY!
GRAN!
OH, GRAN, WHEN YOU DIDN'T GET OFF THE TRAIN--
DID I MISS THE DRAMA?
MISS IT? YOU ARE THE DRAMA. KAY, GET YOUR GRAN SOME WATER--
TIME FOR ME TO GO POOF, THEN.
OH! OH, I NEARLY FORGOT ABOUT YOU.
SORRY, WE'RE ALL A LITTLE LACKING SLEEP. WHAT'S YOUR NAME?
HE'S A JAEGER.
SEE MY NEW BABY, JAEGER? THEY'VE NAMED HIM FOR ME, HARD THOUGH IT IS TO MAKE A BOY'S NAME OUT OF "LILY."

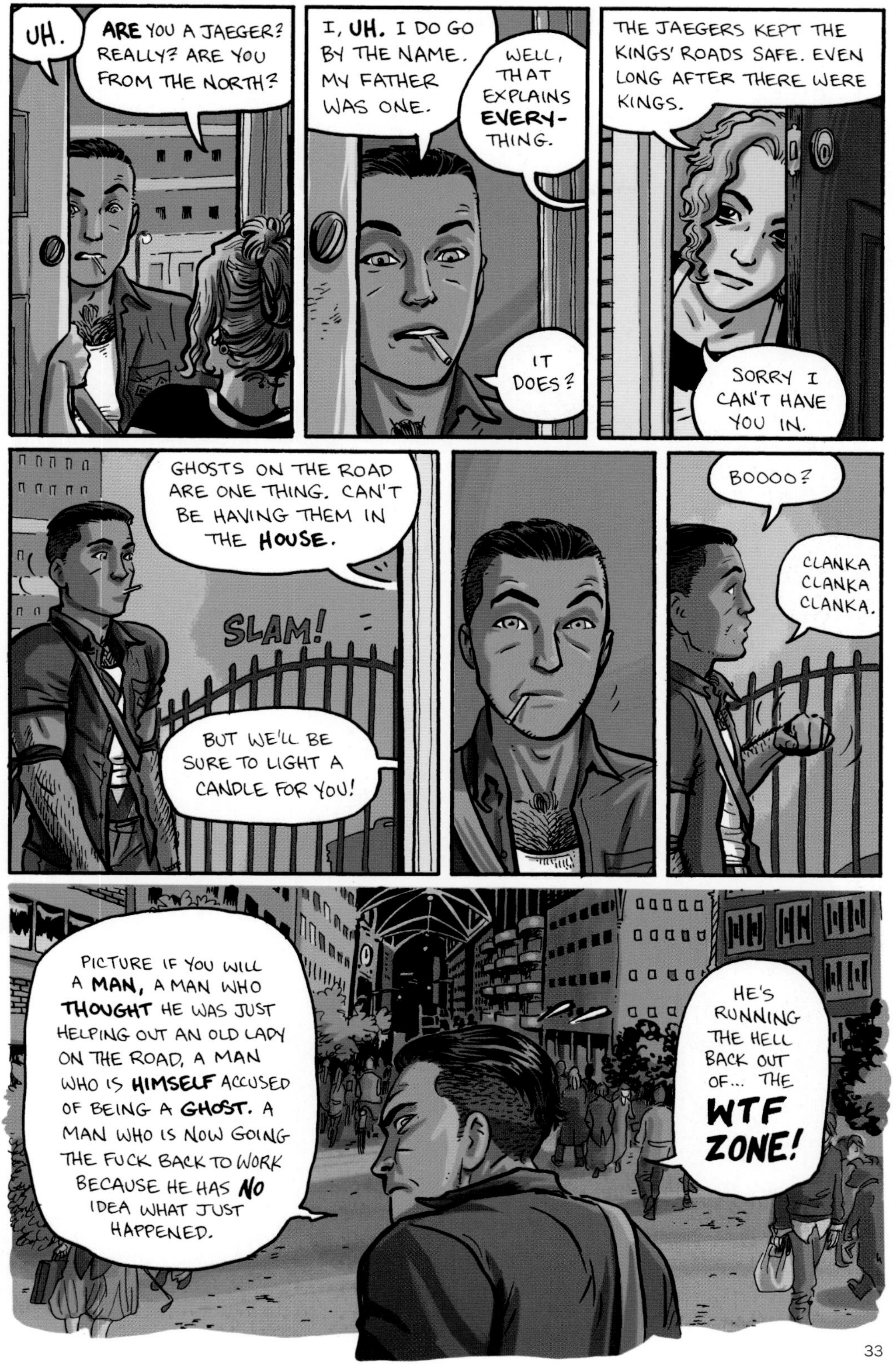
UH.
ARE YOU A JAEGER? REALLY? ARE YOU FROM THE NORTH?
I, UH. I DO GO BY THE NAME. MY FATHER WAS ONE.
WELL, THAT EXPLAINS EVERYTHING.
IT DOES?
THE JAEGERS KEPT THE KINGS' ROADS SAFE. EVEN LONG AFTER THERE WERE KINGS.
SORRY I CAN'T HAVE YOU IN.
GHOSTS ON THE ROAD ARE ONE THING. CAN'T BE HAVING THEM IN THE HOUSE.
SLAM!
BUT WE'LL BE SURE TO LIGHT A CANDLE FOR YOU!
BOOOO?
CLANKA CLANKA CLANKA.
PICTURE IF YOU WILL A MAN, A MAN WHO THOUGHT HE WAS JUST HELPING OUT AN OLD LADY ON THE ROAD, A MAN WHO IS HIMSELF ACCUSED OF BEING A GHOST. A MAN WHO IS NOW GOING THE FUCK BACK TO WORK BECAUSE HE HAS NO IDEA WHAT JUST HAPPENED.
HE'S RUNNING THE HELL BACK OUT OF... THE WTF ZONE!

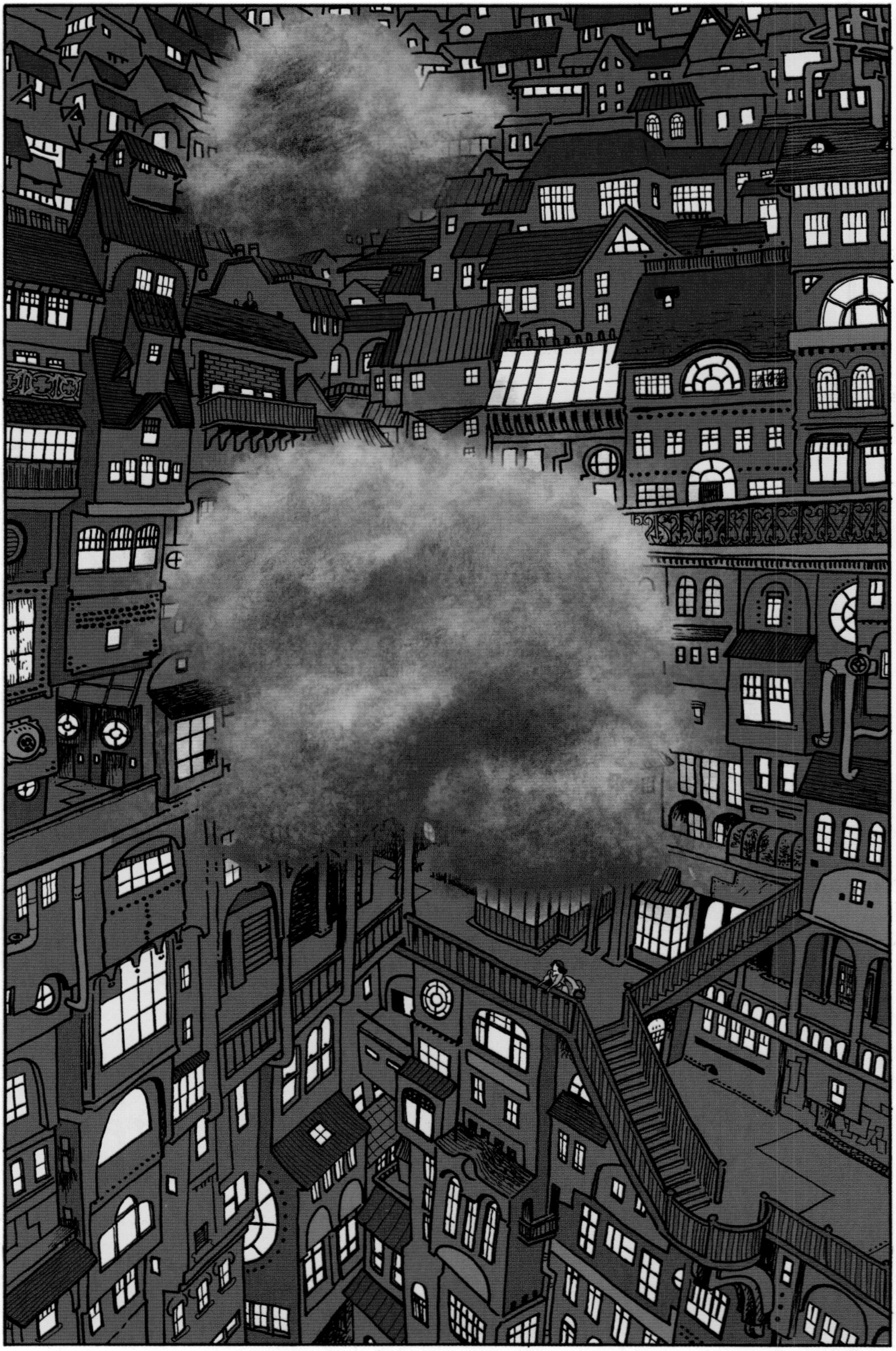

THEY CALL THIS A RUN-AWAY-DAUGHTER JOB. AND IT SEEMS SIMPLE AT FIRST, DOESN'T IT?

YES, IT DOES.

SEEMS LIKE ALL YOU'D HAVE TO DO IS RUN IN LIKE PRINCE RAMBO.

SOCK SOME OL' DOG A GOOD ONE.

ESCORT THE DAMSEL BACK TO THE BOOZUM OF HER FAMILY.

THAT DOES SOUND NICE.

ONE GIRL I KNOW OF STAYED AWAY FOR **TEN YEARS.** AND SHE WORKED SO *HARD* TO CHANGE ALL HER **WAYS** SO HER FOLKS COULDN'T TRACK HER **DOWN,** WHEN SHE *DID* GO BACK SHE WAS SO DIFFERENT THEY DIDN'T RECOGNIZE HER.

"HELEN, PLEASE COME HOME"

LOST SINCE TH
FAMILY WAITS
GIVEN UP HOPE.
"WE KNOW SH
OUT THERE. S
SEE OUR DAI
SAFE. ANYO
REWARD IS
INFORMAT

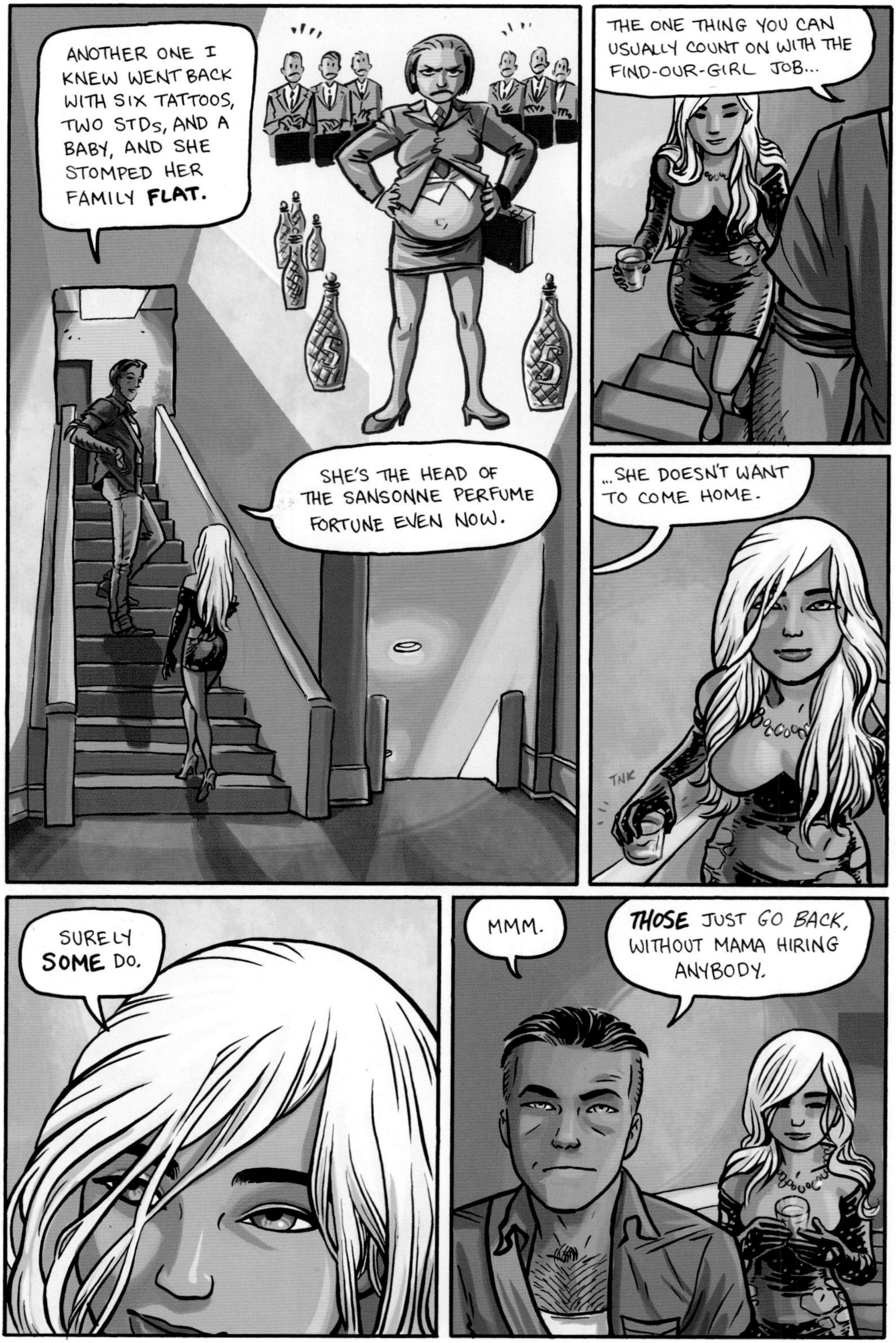
ANOTHER ONE I KNEW WENT BACK WITH SIX TATTOOS, TWO STDs, AND A BABY, AND SHE STOMPED HER FAMILY FLAT.
SHE'S THE HEAD OF THE SANSONNE PERFUME FORTUNE EVEN NOW.
THE ONE THING YOU CAN USUALLY COUNT ON WITH THE FIND-OUR-GIRL JOB...
...SHE DOESN'T WANT TO COME HOME.
TNK
SURELY SOME DO.
MMM.
THOSE JUST GO BACK, WITHOUT MAMA HIRING ANYBODY.

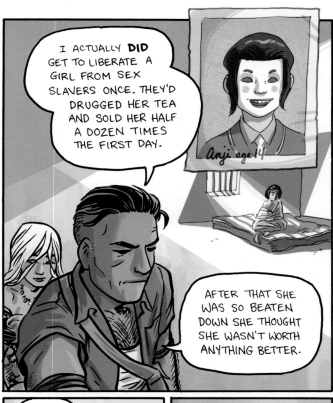

I ACTUALLY **DID** GET TO LIBERATE A GIRL FROM SEX SLAVERS ONCE. THEY'D DRUGGED HER TEA AND SOLD HER HALF A DOZEN TIMES THE FIRST DAY.

Anji age 14

AFTER THAT SHE WAS SO BEATEN DOWN SHE THOUGHT SHE WASN'T WORTH ANYTHING BETTER.

DID **HER** FAMILY WANT HER BACK?

HARD TO SAY, SINCE THEY SOLD HER IN THE FIRST PLACE.

THEY COULDN'T JUST...

SELL HER AGAIN?

WELL, NOT FOR AS **MUCH.**

SO...

DID **YOU** FIND ALL THESE RUNAWAY GIRLS YOURSELF OR ARE YOU THE TYPE WHO TELLS EVERY STORY AS IF IT'S HIS OWN?

HEH!

I DID DO THE ONE ABOUT THE SANSONNE HEIRESS.

AND THE WHOLE POINT OF **YOU** IS, YOU CAN'T GET LOST?

NO.

NOT SO FAR.

NEVER EVER?

EVERYBODY IN THE CITY HAS ACCESS TO MAP SOFTWARE THROUGH OUR SCHOOL IMPLANTS. SO—

NOT **EVERYBODY.**

AND A GOOD THIRD OF THE REALLY GOOD UPS AND DOWNS AND SIDEWAYSES OF THIS CITY AREN'T **ON** THE GENERAL-ACCESS MAPS.

THE RICH FAMILIES CONSIDER ALL KINDS OF STUFF "NEED TO KNOW" ONLY, AND MOST PEOPLE, **THEY** THINK, **DON'T** NEED TO KNOW.

AIN'T THAT RIGHT?

I HAVE A PRETTY GOOD MEMORY—

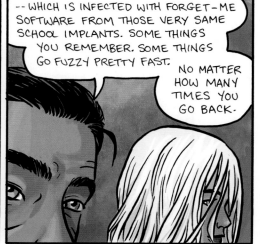

-- WHICH IS INFECTED WITH FORGET-ME SOFTWARE FROM THOSE VERY SAME SCHOOL IMPLANTS. SOME THINGS YOU REMEMBER. SOME THINGS GO FUZZY PRETTY FAST.

NO MATTER HOW MANY TIMES YOU GO BACK.

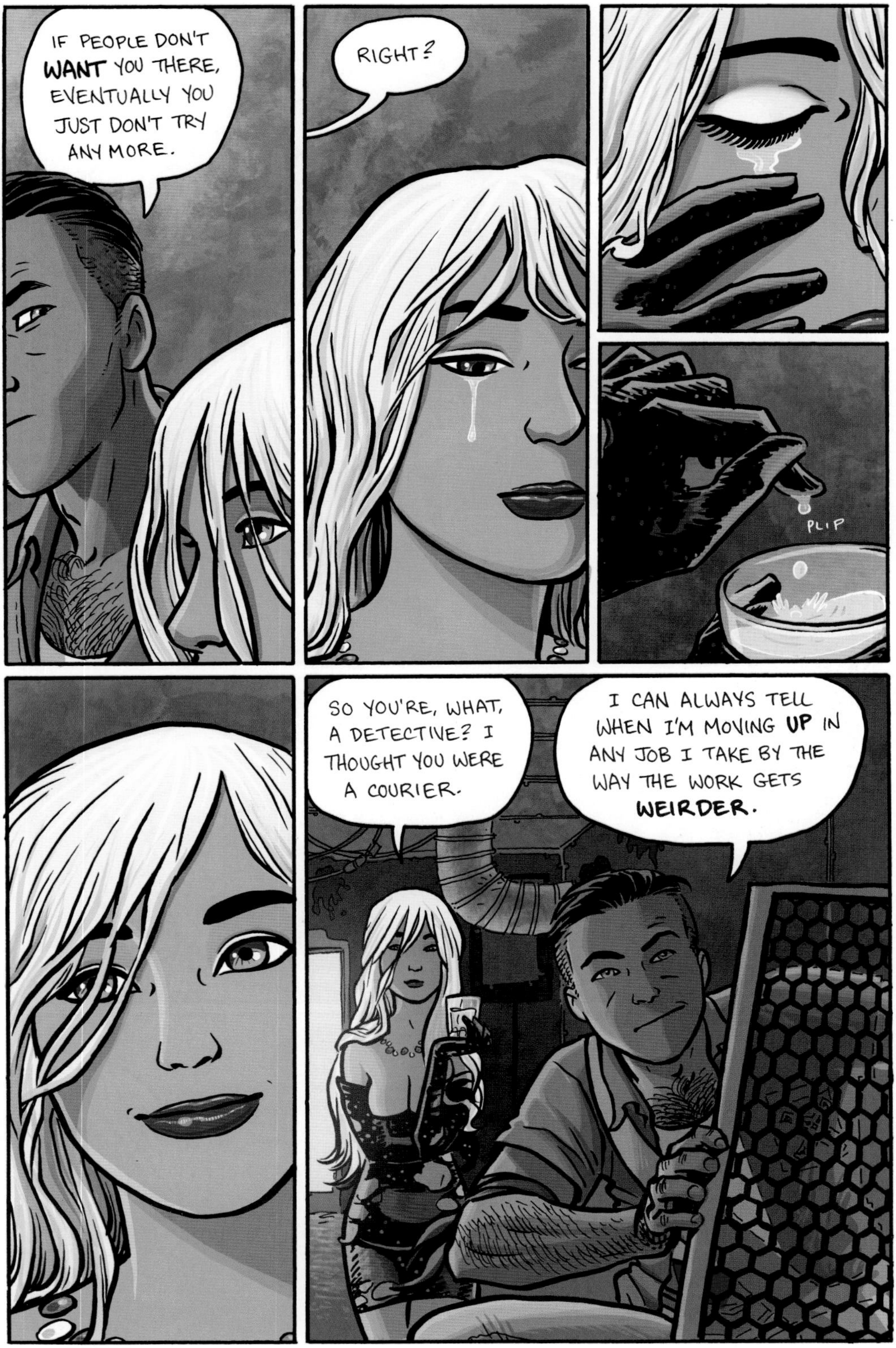
IF PEOPLE DON'T WANT YOU THERE, EVENTUALLY YOU JUST DON'T TRY ANY MORE.
RIGHT?
PLIP
SO YOU'RE, WHAT, A DETECTIVE? I THOUGHT YOU WERE A COURIER.
I CAN ALWAYS TELL WHEN I'M MOVING UP IN ANY JOB I TAKE BY THE WAY THE WORK GETS WEIRDER.

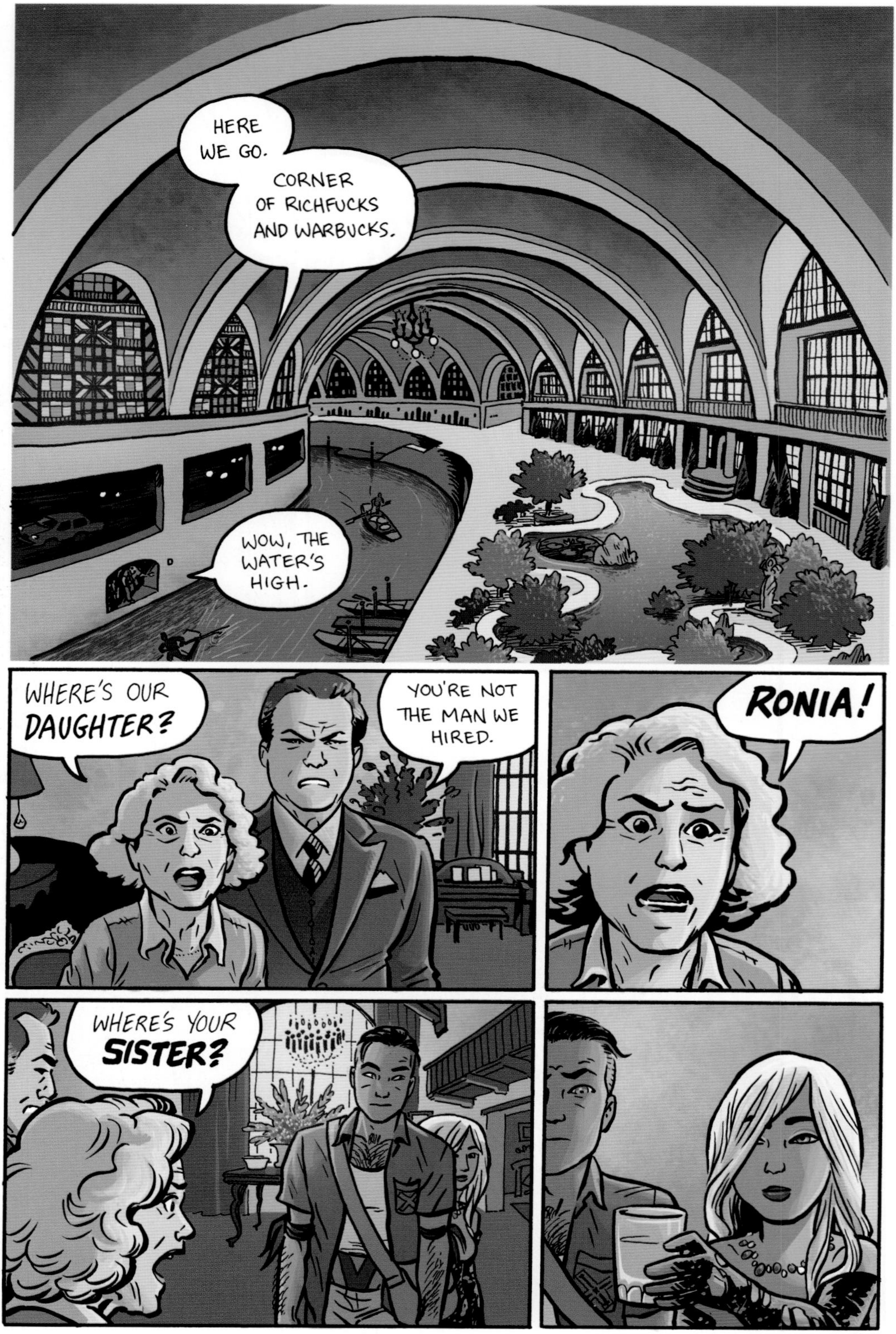
HERE WE GO.
CORNER OF RICHFUCKS AND WARBUCKS.
WOW, THE WATER'S HIGH.
WHERE'S OUR **DAUGHTER?**
YOU'RE NOT THE MAN WE HIRED.
RONIA!
WHERE'S YOUR **SISTER?**

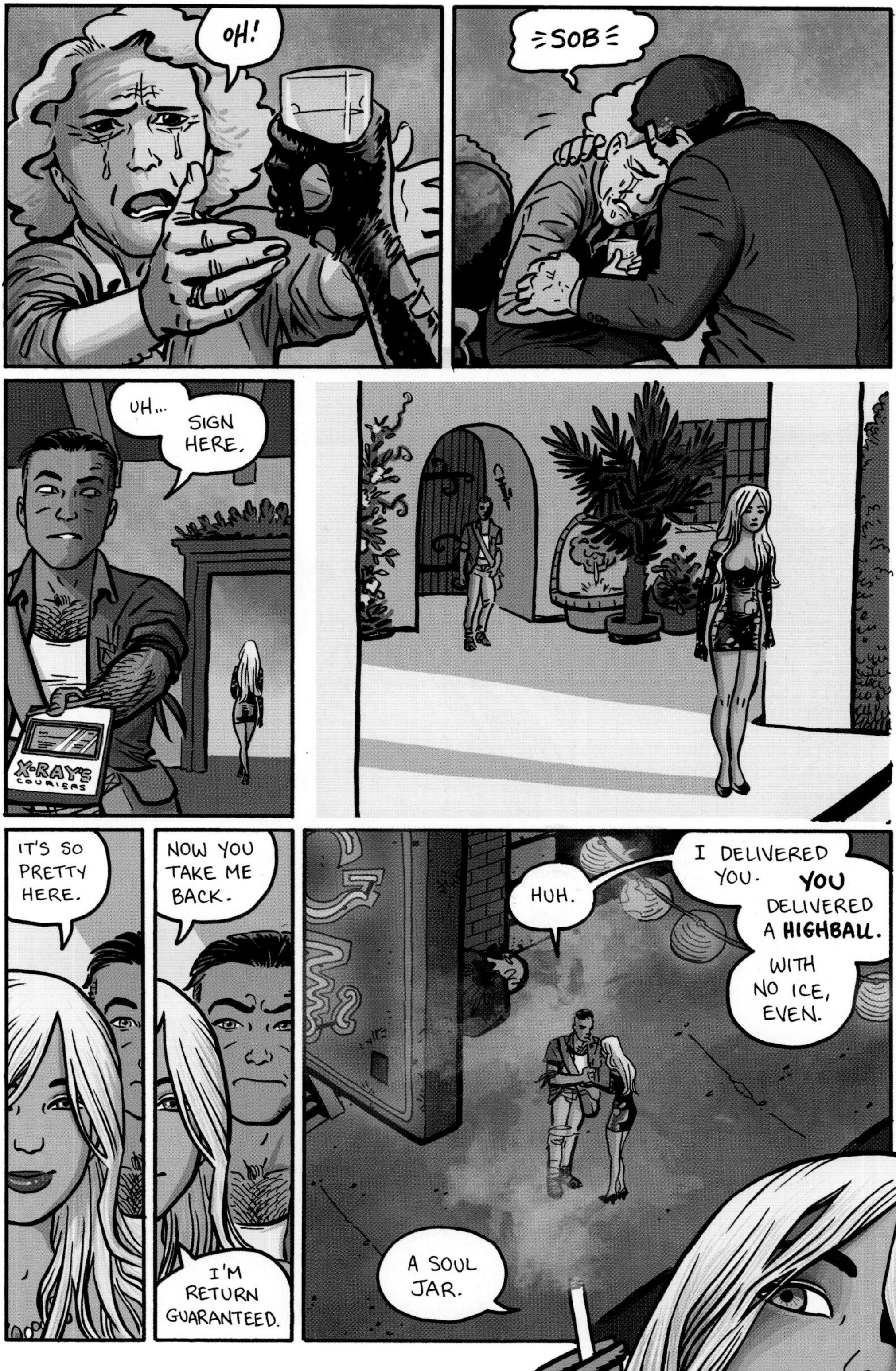
OH!
SOB
UH... SIGN HERE.
X-RAY'S COURIERS
IT'S SO PRETTY HERE.
NOW YOU TAKE ME BACK.
I'M RETURN GUARANTEED.
HUH.
I DELIVERED YOU. YOU DELIVERED A HIGHBALL.
WITH NO ICE, EVEN.
A SOUL JAR.

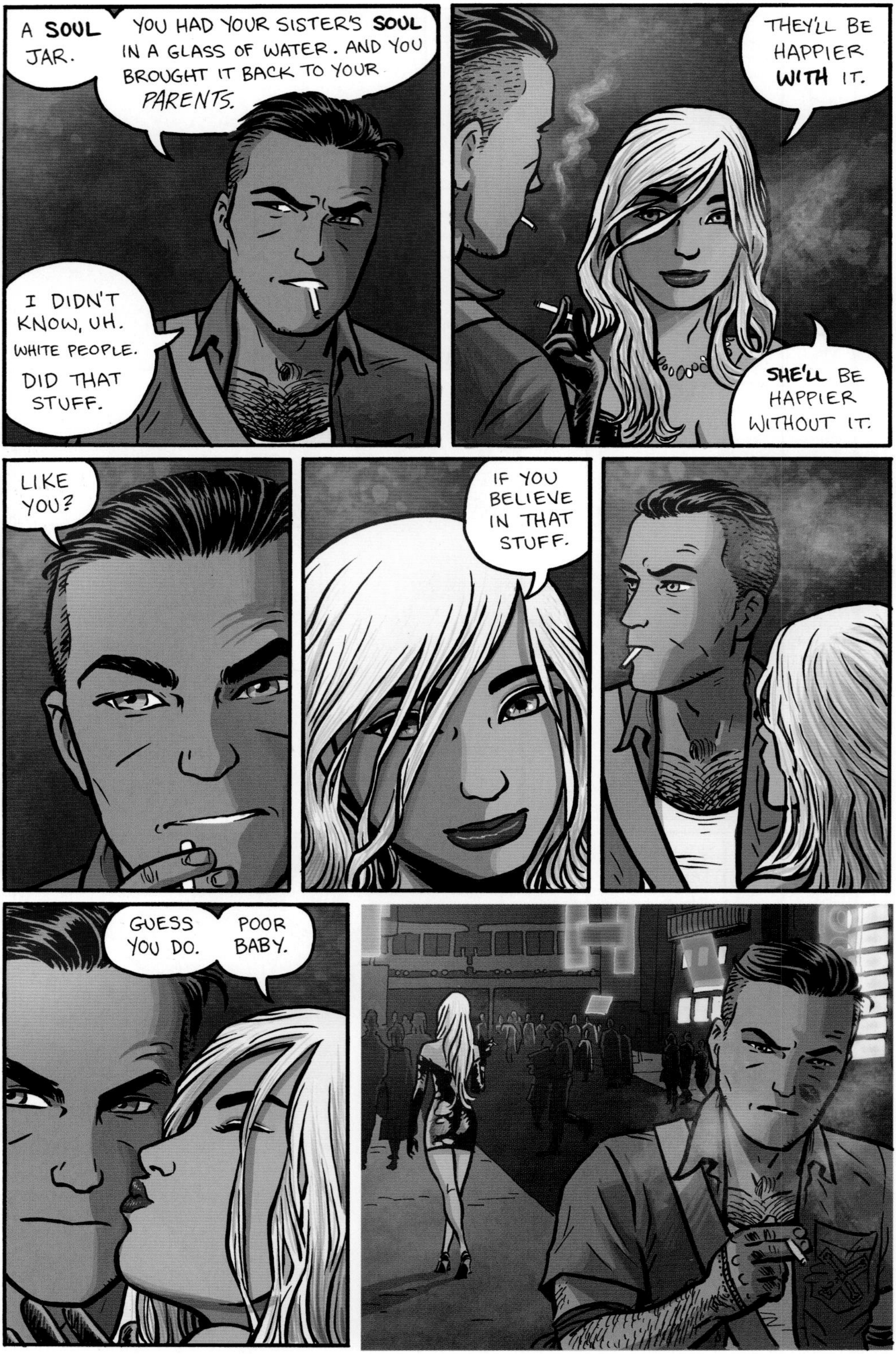
A SOUL JAR.
YOU HAD YOUR SISTER'S SOUL IN A GLASS OF WATER. AND YOU BROUGHT IT BACK TO YOUR PARENTS.
I DIDN'T KNOW, UH. WHITE PEOPLE. DID THAT STUFF.
THEY'LL BE HAPPIER WITH IT.
SHE'LL BE HAPPIER WITHOUT IT.
LIKE YOU?
IF YOU BELIEVE IN THAT STUFF.
GUESS YOU DO.
POOR BABY.

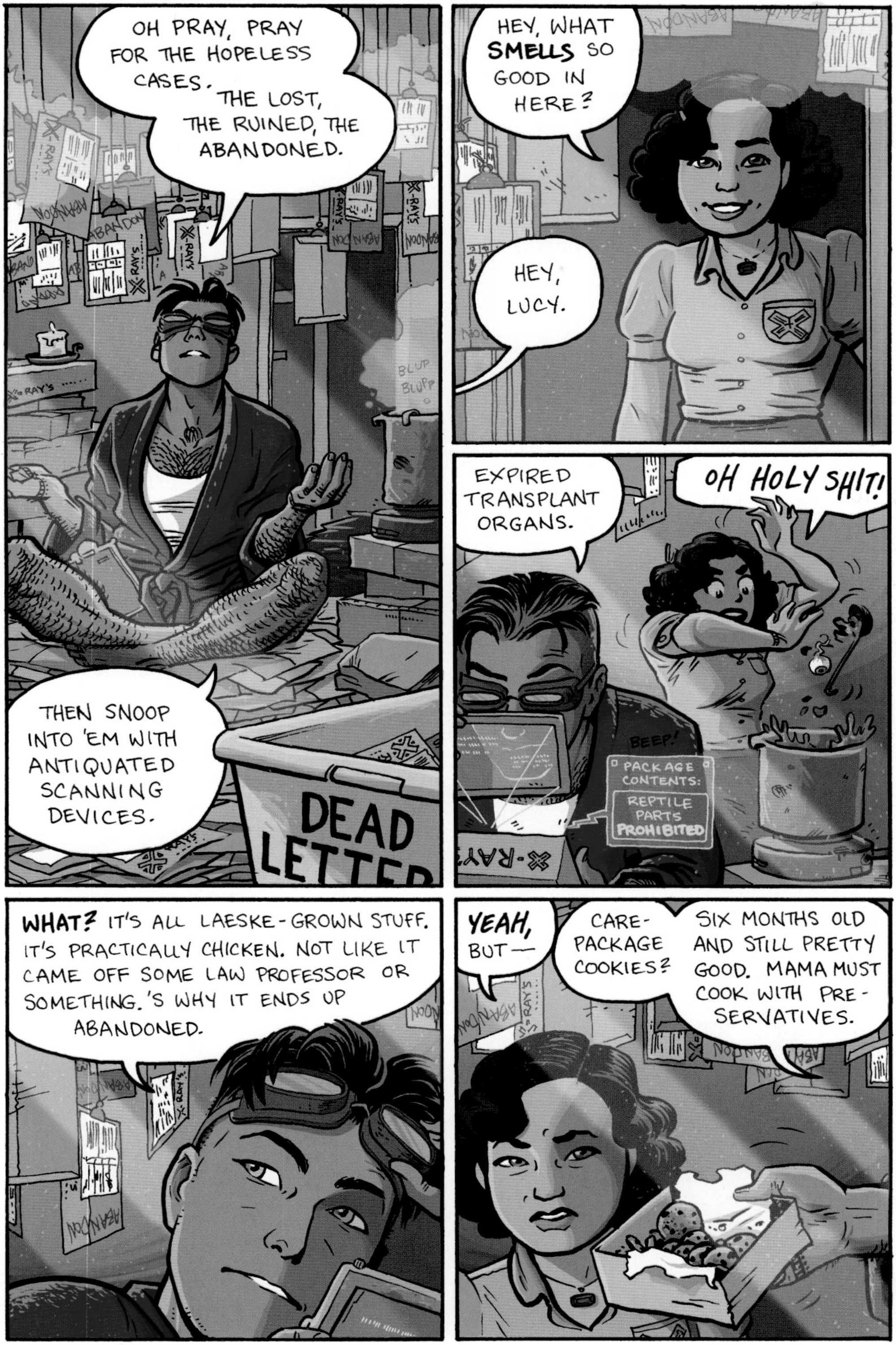
OH PRAY, PRAY FOR THE HOPELESS CASES. THE LOST, THE RUINED, THE ABANDONED.
THEN SNOOP INTO 'EM WITH ANTIQUATED SCANNING DEVICES.
DEAD LETTER
BLUP BLUPP
HEY, WHAT SMELLS SO GOOD IN HERE?
HEY, LUCY.
EXPIRED TRANSPLANT ORGANS.
OH HOLY SHIT!
BEEP!
PACKAGE CONTENTS: REPTILE PARTS PROHIBITED
WHAT? IT'S ALL LAESKE-GROWN STUFF. IT'S PRACTICALLY CHICKEN. NOT LIKE IT CAME OFF SOME LAW PROFESSOR OR SOMETHING. 'S WHY IT ENDS UP ABANDONED.
YEAH, BUT—
CARE-PACKAGE COOKIES?
SIX MONTHS OLD AND STILL PRETTY GOOD. MAMA MUST COOK WITH PRE-SERVATIVES.

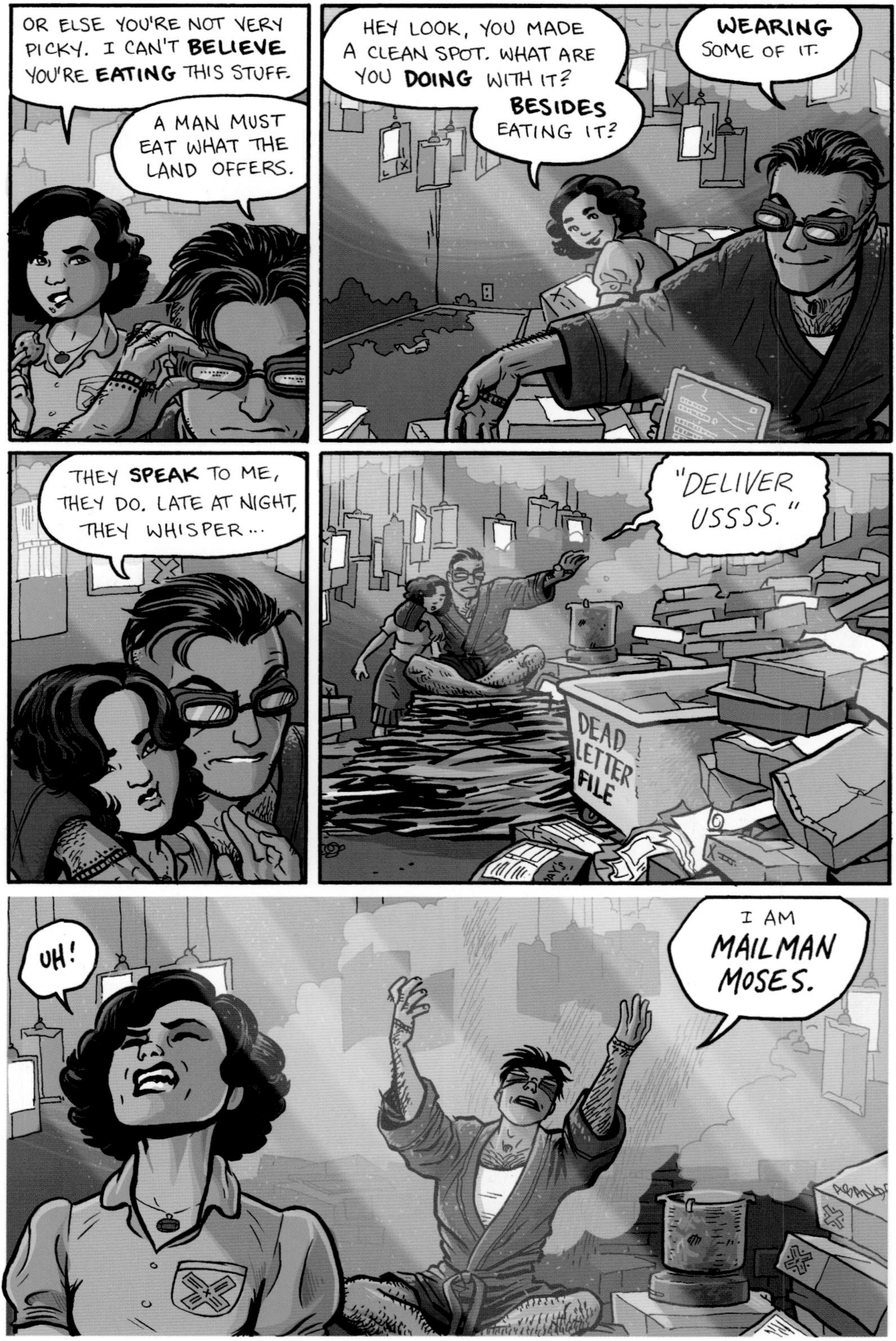

OR ELSE YOU'RE NOT VERY PICKY. I CAN'T BELIEVE YOU'RE EATING THIS STUFF.
A MAN MUST EAT WHAT THE LAND OFFERS.
HEY LOOK, YOU MADE A CLEAN SPOT. WHAT ARE YOU DOING WITH IT?
BESIDES EATING IT?
WEARING SOME OF IT.
THEY SPEAK TO ME, THEY DO. LATE AT NIGHT, THEY WHISPER...
"DELIVER USSSS."
DEAD LETTER FILE
UH!
I AM MAILMAN MOSES.

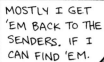

MOSTLY I GET 'EM BACK TO THE SENDERS. IF I CAN FIND 'EM.
BUT THESE ARE ALL MARKED "TREAT AS ABANDONED IF UNDELIVERABLE."
PACKAGE SCAN
PAPER
OBSCENITY
BEEP
PEOPLE ARE STILL PRETTY HAPPY TO GET THEIR STUFF BACK.
OH MY GOD!
I NEVER THOUGHT I'D SEE THIS ART-WORK AGAIN!
IT WAS IN MY CAR I WAS ON MY WAY TO DROP IT OFF AT RAY'S AND THE CAR GOT JACKED!
COPS GOT THE CAR BACK BUT THE BOX WAS GONE!
I SAID, "PIGS! PRIORITIES!" LIKE I CARE ABOUT THE CAR!
WEIRD THIEF, THOUGH, HUH? DROPPED IT OFF AT RAY'S ANY-WAY.
WEIRD OF RAY'S NOT TO DELIVER IT IS WHAT YOU MEAN. WHAT KINDA CHEAP SHIT IS THAT?
IT WASN'T DELIVERED, DUDE, BECAUSE YOU DIDN'T ADDRESS IT.
OH!
CRAP!
ABANDON
DUDE! I'M PARTYIN'!
HAVE A BEER!
MALT LIQU
37 FLAVO

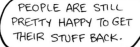

"ERSKINE ROYAL ACADEMY OF PALEONTOLOGY WAS ON MY WAY, SO I DROPPED IN ON A PROFESSOR NAME O' DARNIAN LUDKA.

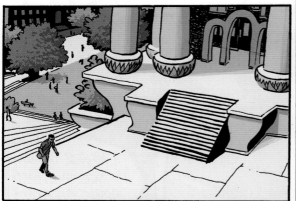

"DR. LUDKA DOES *NOT* **GO** ALONG TO **GET** ALONG."

THIS WAS **NEVER** DELIVERED?

NO.

ARE YOU **SURE?**

YYYES.

NOBODY HAS SEEN THIS?

SHUF

TOK

BRT

PROFESSOR KIMBROUGH! MY **ESTEEMED** COLLEAGUE! **HAHA,** YOU **BASTARD!** YOU'RE **WRONG!** MY RESEARCH **PROVES** IT! **SUCK** IT, YOU SUCKING **SUCK!**

TURN OFF, ROT YOU!

CLICK
CLICK
CLICK
CLICK
CLICK

SHUT **UP**
SHUT **UP**
SHUT **UP**
SHUT **UP!**

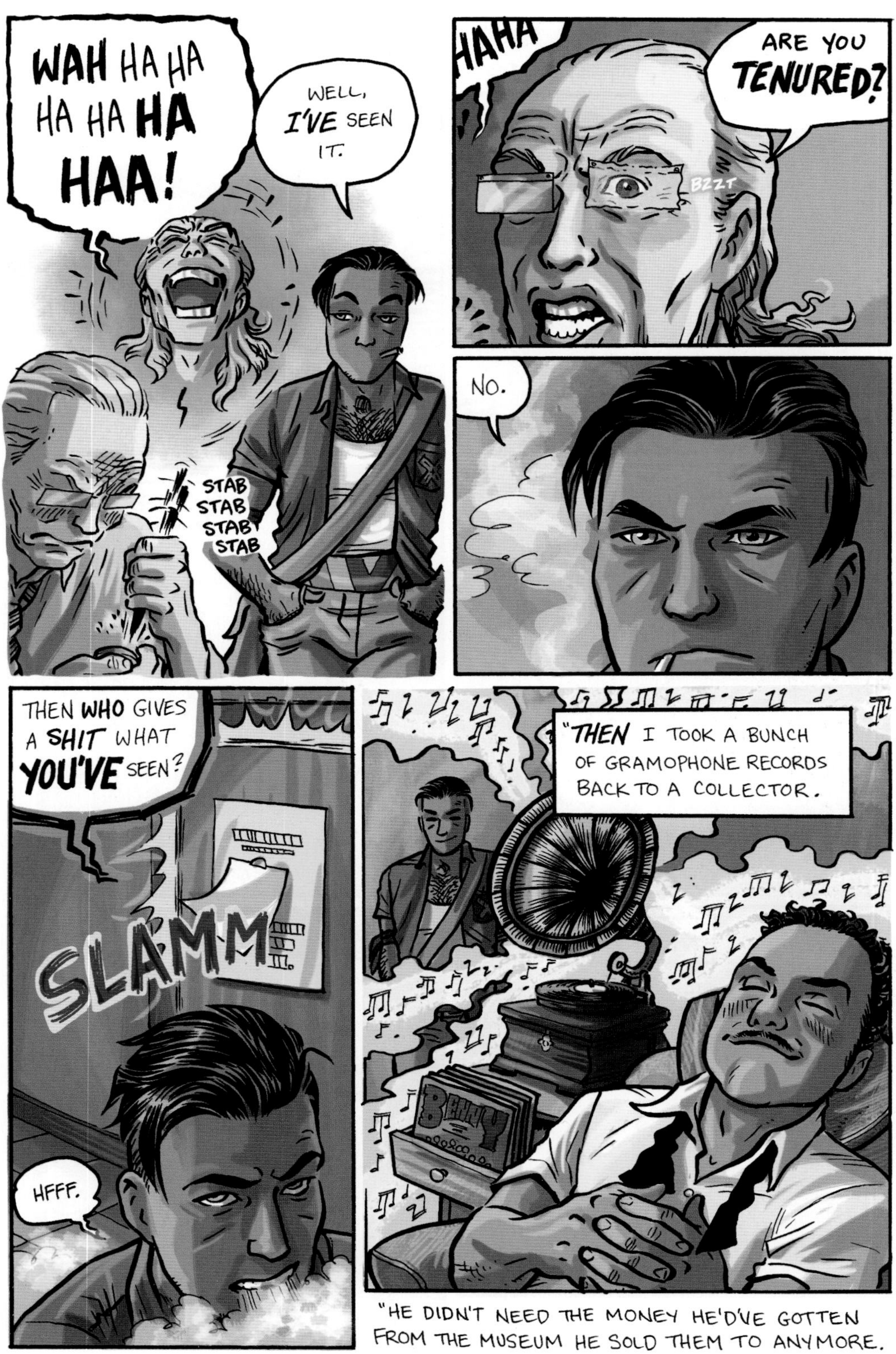
WAH HA HA HA HA HA HA HAA!
WELL, I'VE SEEN IT.
STAB STAB STAB STAB
HAHA
ARE YOU TENURED?
BZZT
NO.
THEN WHO GIVES A SHIT WHAT YOU'VE SEEN?
SLAMM
HFFF.
"THEN I TOOK A BUNCH OF GRAMOPHONE RECORDS BACK TO A COLLECTOR.
"HE DIDN'T NEED THE MONEY HE'D'VE GOTTEN FROM THE MUSEUM HE SOLD THEM TO ANYMORE.

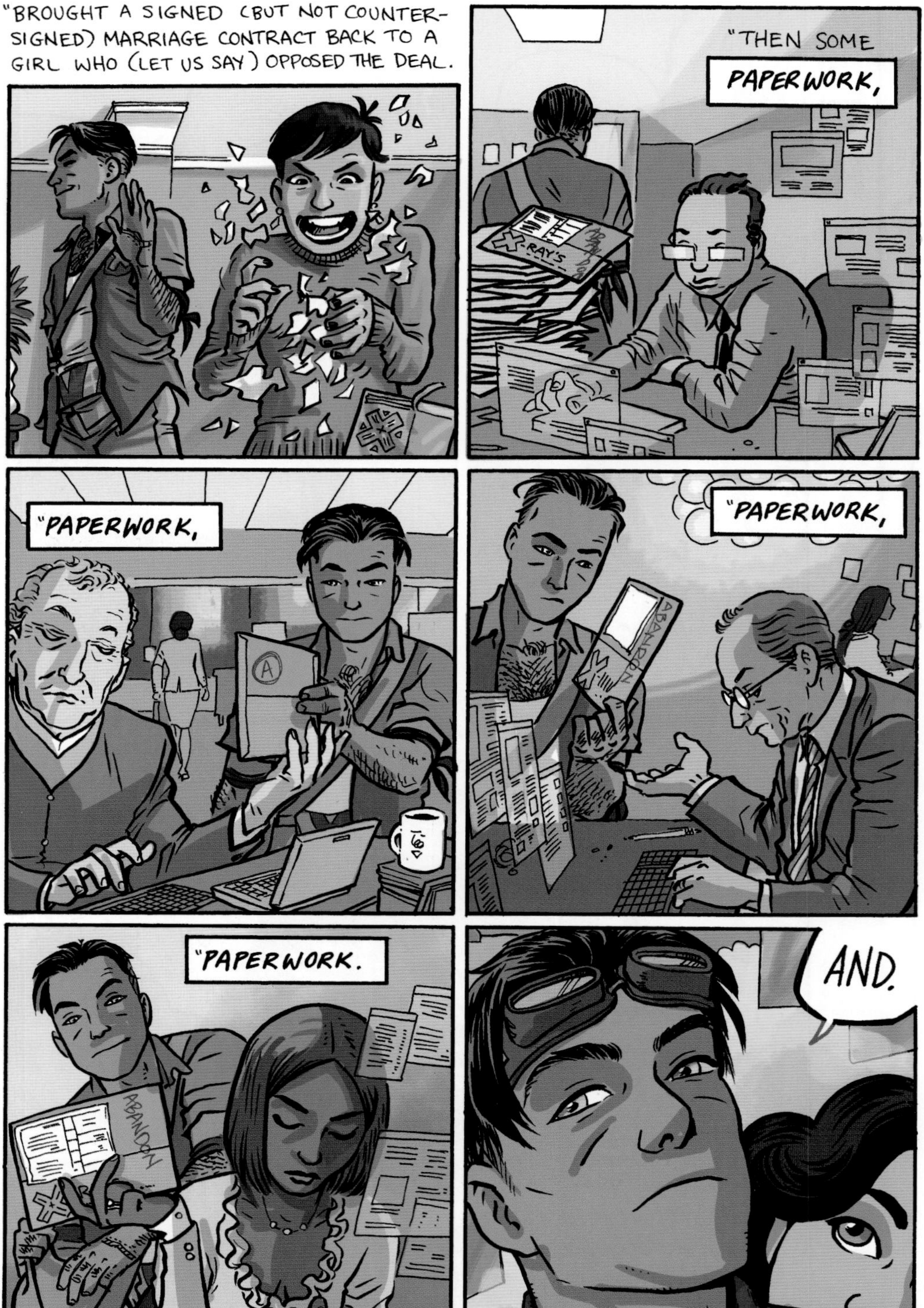
"BROUGHT A SIGNED (BUT NOT COUNTER-SIGNED) MARRIAGE CONTRACT BACK TO A GIRL WHO (LET US SAY) OPPOSED THE DEAL.
"THEN SOME
PAPERWORK,
RAY'S
"PAPERWORK,
"PAPERWORK,
"PAPERWORK.
ABANDON
AND.
"NONE OF WHICH WAS AS URGENT AS THE SENDER ORIGINALLY THOUGHT."

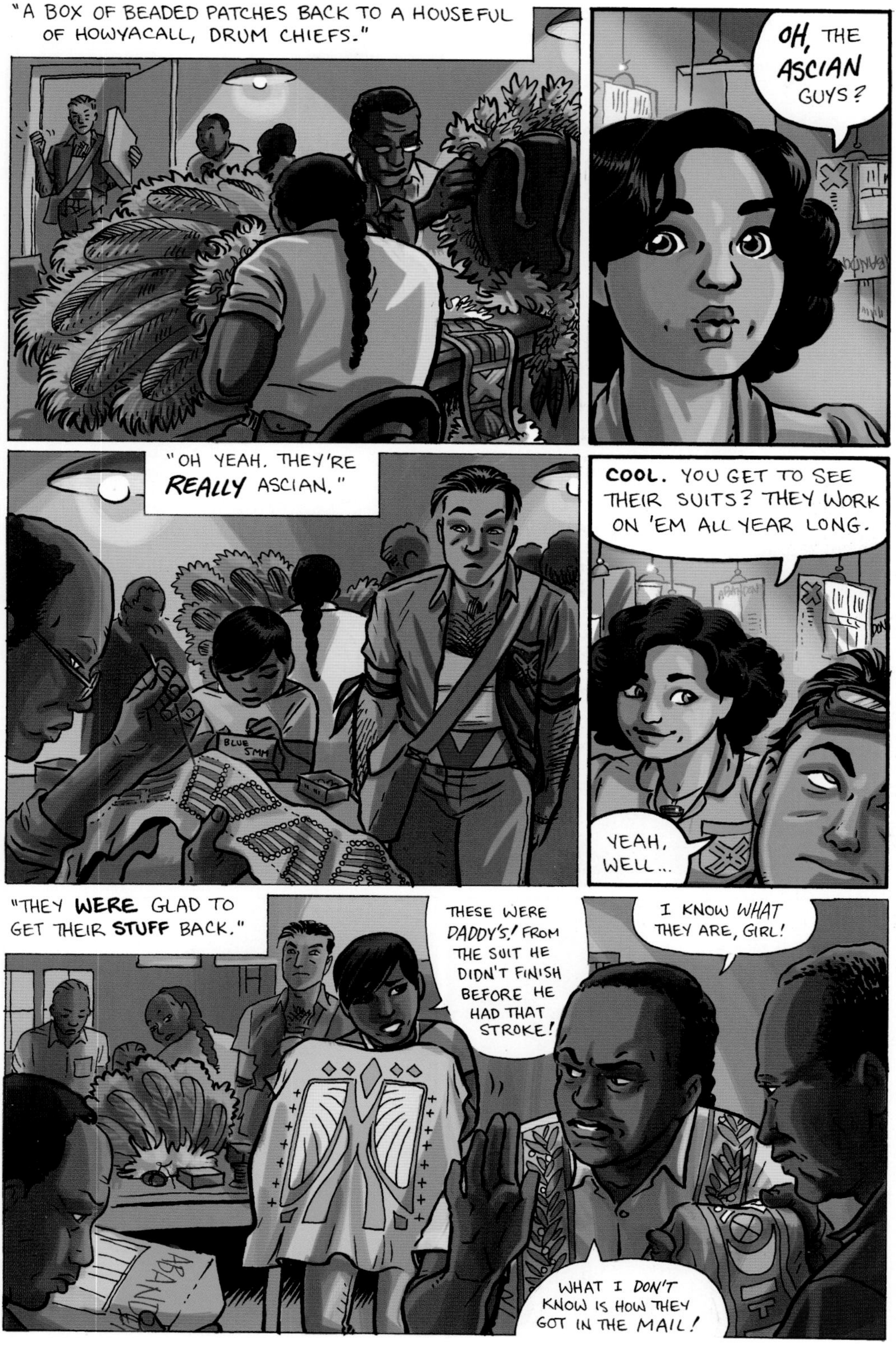
"A BOX OF BEADED PATCHES BACK TO A HOUSEFUL OF HOWYACALL, DRUM CHIEFS."
OH, THE ASCIAN GUYS?
"OH YEAH. THEY'RE REALLY ASCIAN."
COOL. YOU GET TO SEE THEIR SUITS? THEY WORK ON 'EM ALL YEAR LONG.
YEAH, WELL...
"THEY WERE GLAD TO GET THEIR STUFF BACK."
THESE WERE DADDY'S! FROM THE SUIT HE DIDN'T FINISH BEFORE HE HAD THAT STROKE!
I KNOW WHAT THEY ARE, GIRL!
WHAT I DON'T KNOW IS HOW THEY GOT IN THE MAIL!

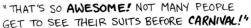
"THAT'S SO **AWESOME!** NOT MANY PEOPLE GET TO SEE THEIR SUITS BEFORE **CARNIVAL!**"

WHAT DO YOU KNOW ABOUT IT, CRIOLLO?

WHO LET YOU UP *IN* HERE IN THE *FIRST* PLACE?

I'M JUST THE MESSENGER...

UH-HUH.

OH, **DON'T** BE LIKE THAT. THE DRUM CHIEFS ARE **PART** OF CARNIVAL. **BEEN** PART OF IT **FOREVER.**

WOULDN'T **BE** CARNIVAL WITHOUT THE CHIEFS.

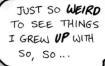
JUST SO **WEIRD** TO SEE THINGS I GREW **UP** WITH SO, SO ...

WHATEVER. LET 'EM EAT THEIR HEARTS OUT.

OR **I** WILL, IF NOBODY **ELSE** WANTS 'EM.

50

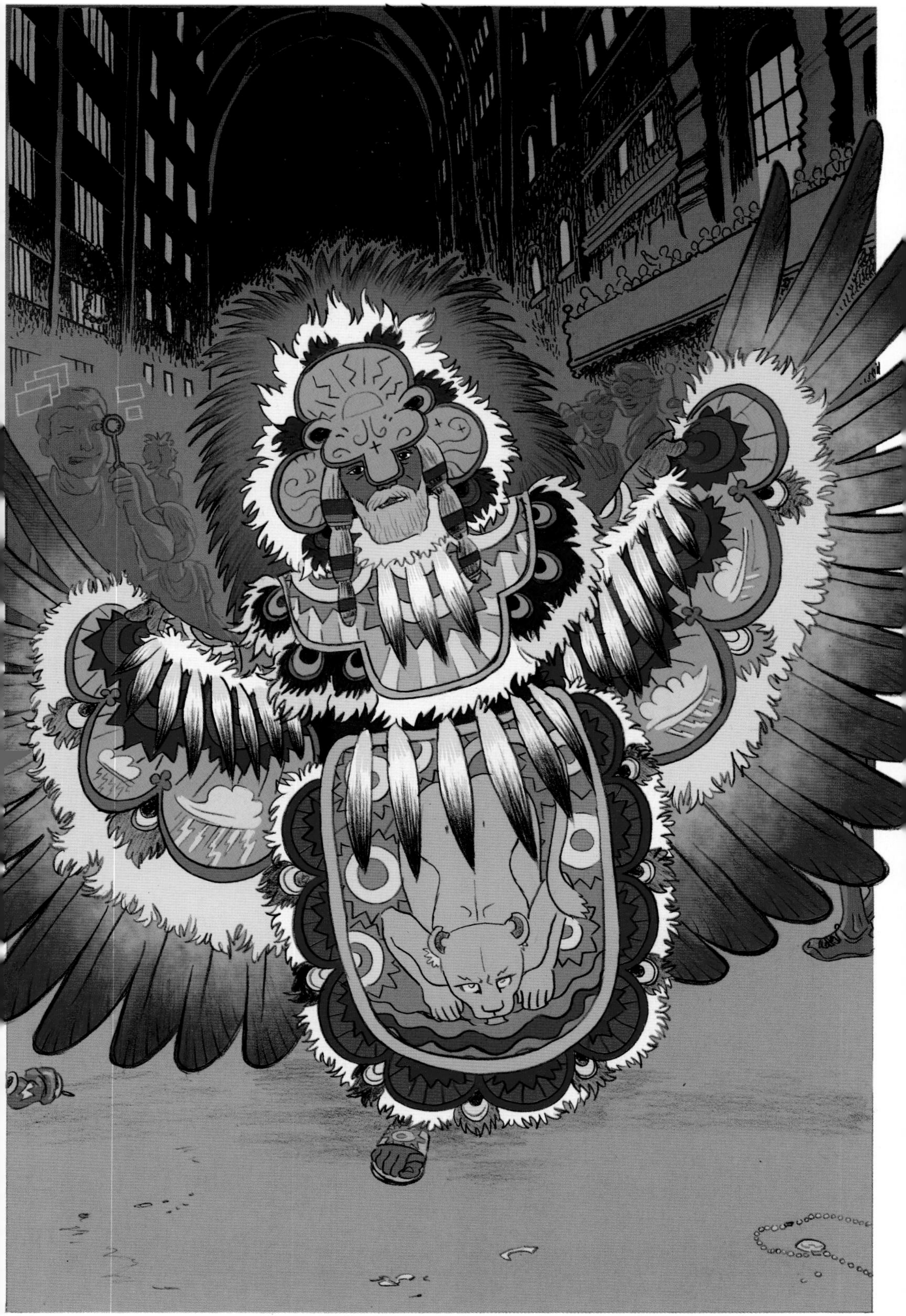

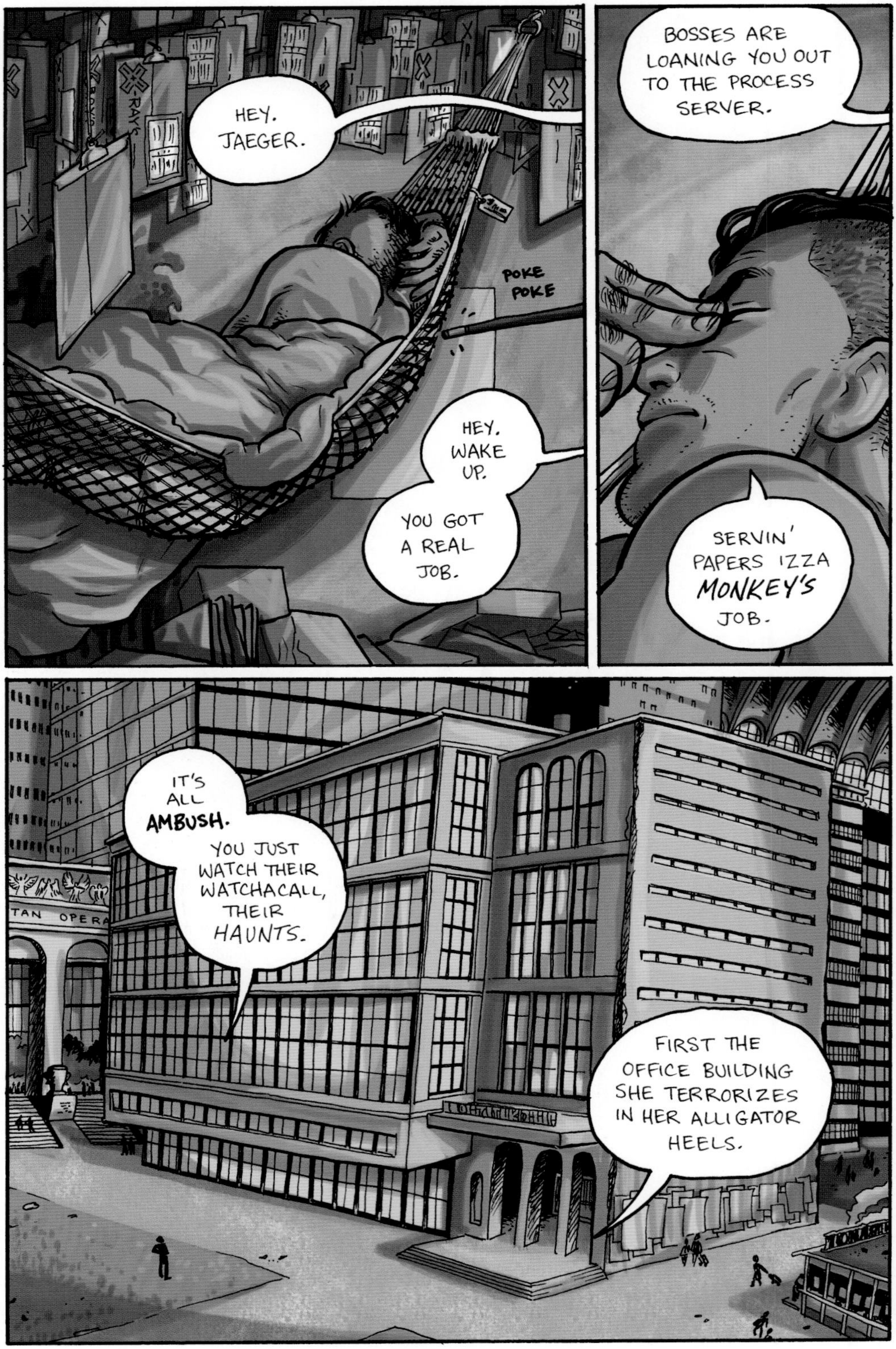
HEY. JAEGER.
POKE POKE
HEY. WAKE UP.
YOU GOT A REAL JOB.
BOSSES ARE LOANING YOU OUT TO THE PROCESS SERVER.
SERVIN' PAPERS IZZA MONKEY'S JOB.
IT'S ALL AMBUSH.
YOU JUST WATCH THEIR WATCHACALL, THEIR HAUNTS.
FIRST THE OFFICE BUILDING SHE TERRORIZES IN HER ALLIGATOR HEELS.
TAN OPERA

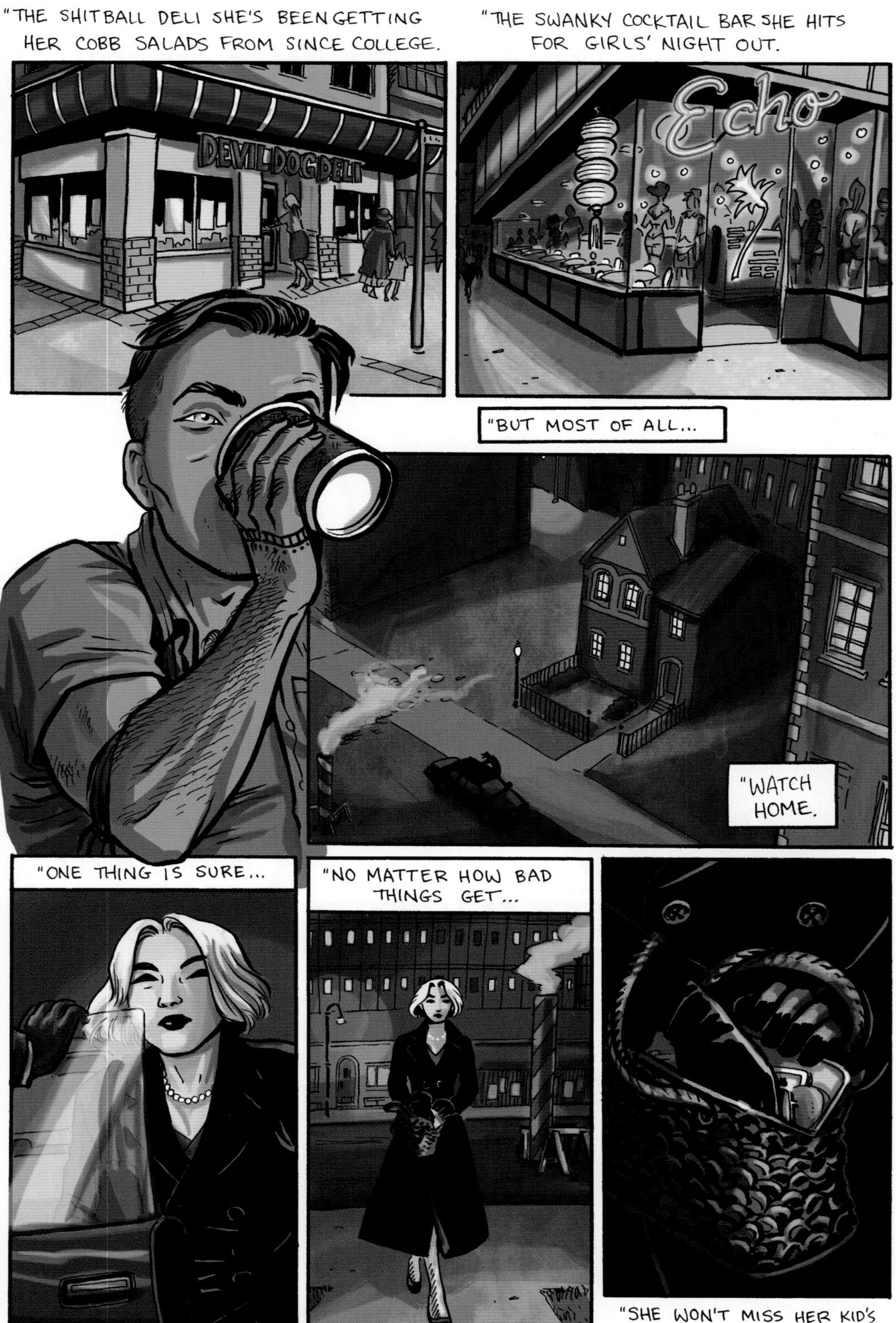
"THE SHITBALL DELI SHE'S BEEN GETTING HER COBB SALADS FROM SINCE COLLEGE.
DEVIL DOG DELI
"THE SWANKY COCKTAIL BAR SHE HITS FOR GIRLS' NIGHT OUT.
Echo
"BUT MOST OF ALL...
"WATCH HOME.
"ONE THING IS SURE...
"NO MATTER HOW BAD THINGS GET...
"SHE WON'T MISS HER KID'S SIXTH BIRTHDAY PARTY."

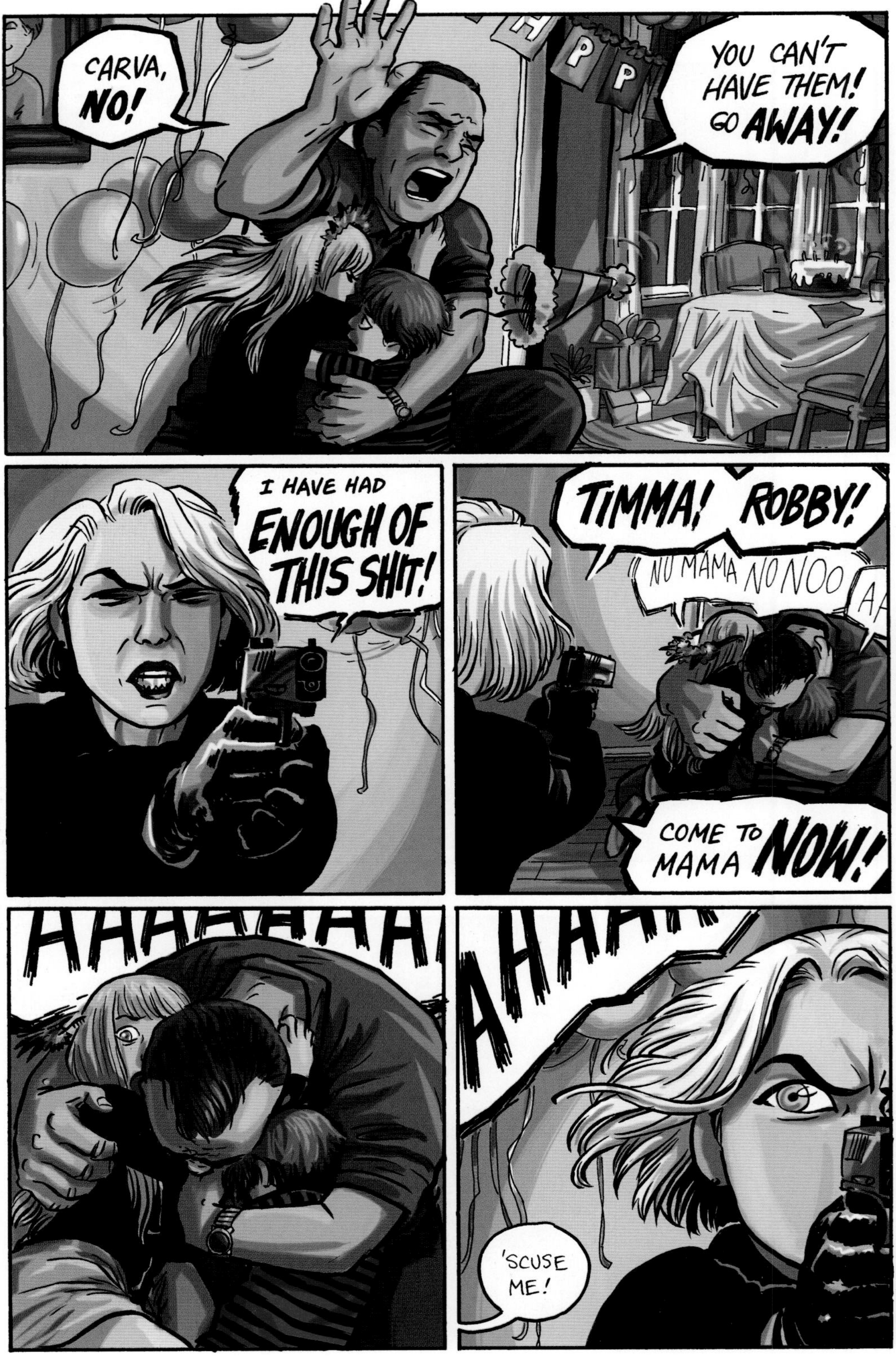

CARVA, NO!
YOU CAN'T HAVE THEM! GO AWAY!
I HAVE HAD ENOUGH OF THIS SHIT!
TIMMA! ROBBY!
NU MAMA NO NOO
COME TO MAMA NOW!
AAAAAAAA
AAAA
'SCUSE ME!

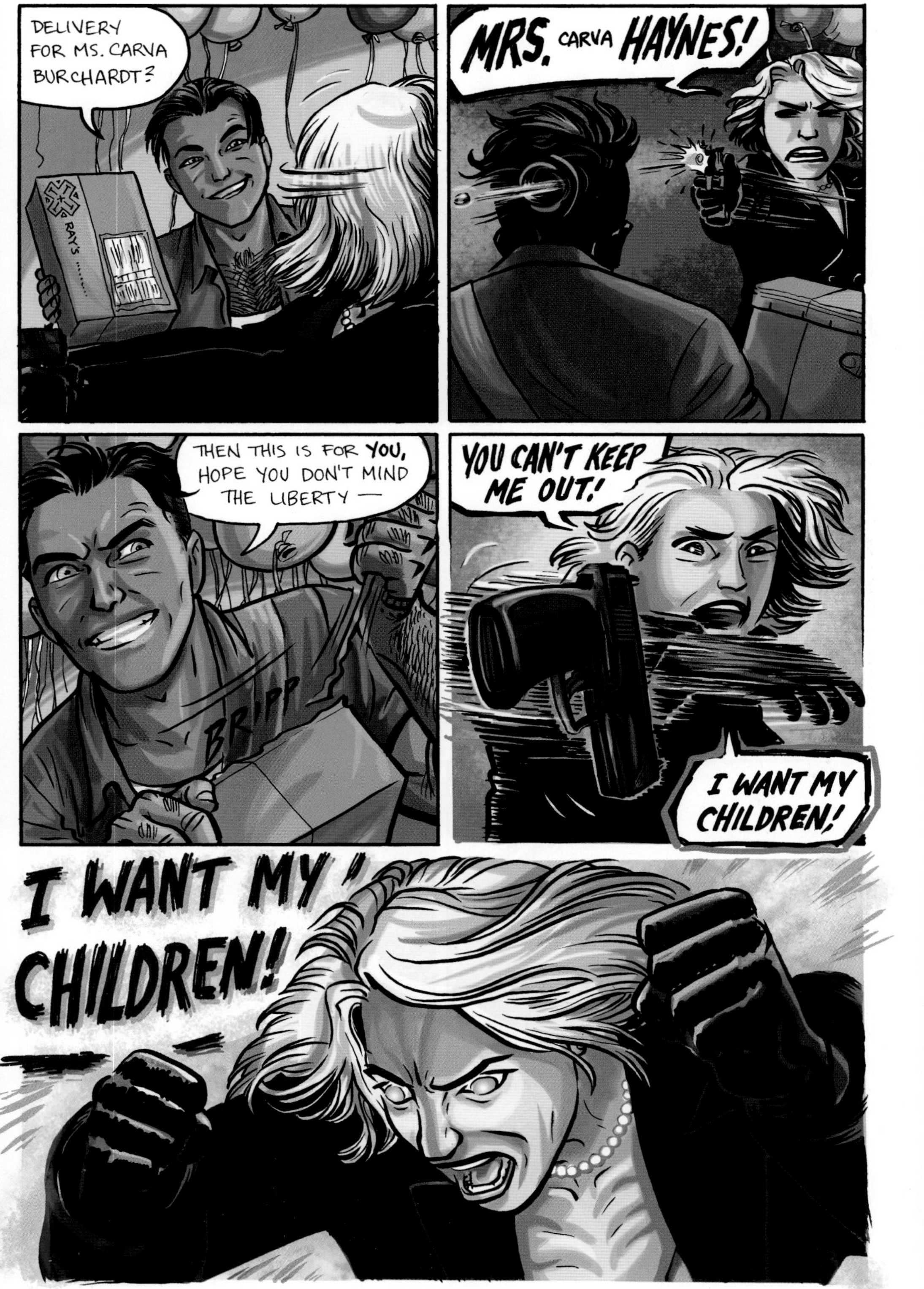

DELIVERY FOR MS. CARVA BURCHARDT?
RAY'S
MRS. CARVA HAYNES!
THEN THIS IS FOR YOU, HOPE YOU DON'T MIND THE LIBERTY —
BRIPP
YOU CAN'T KEEP ME OUT!
I WANT MY CHILDREN!
I WANT MY CHILDREN!

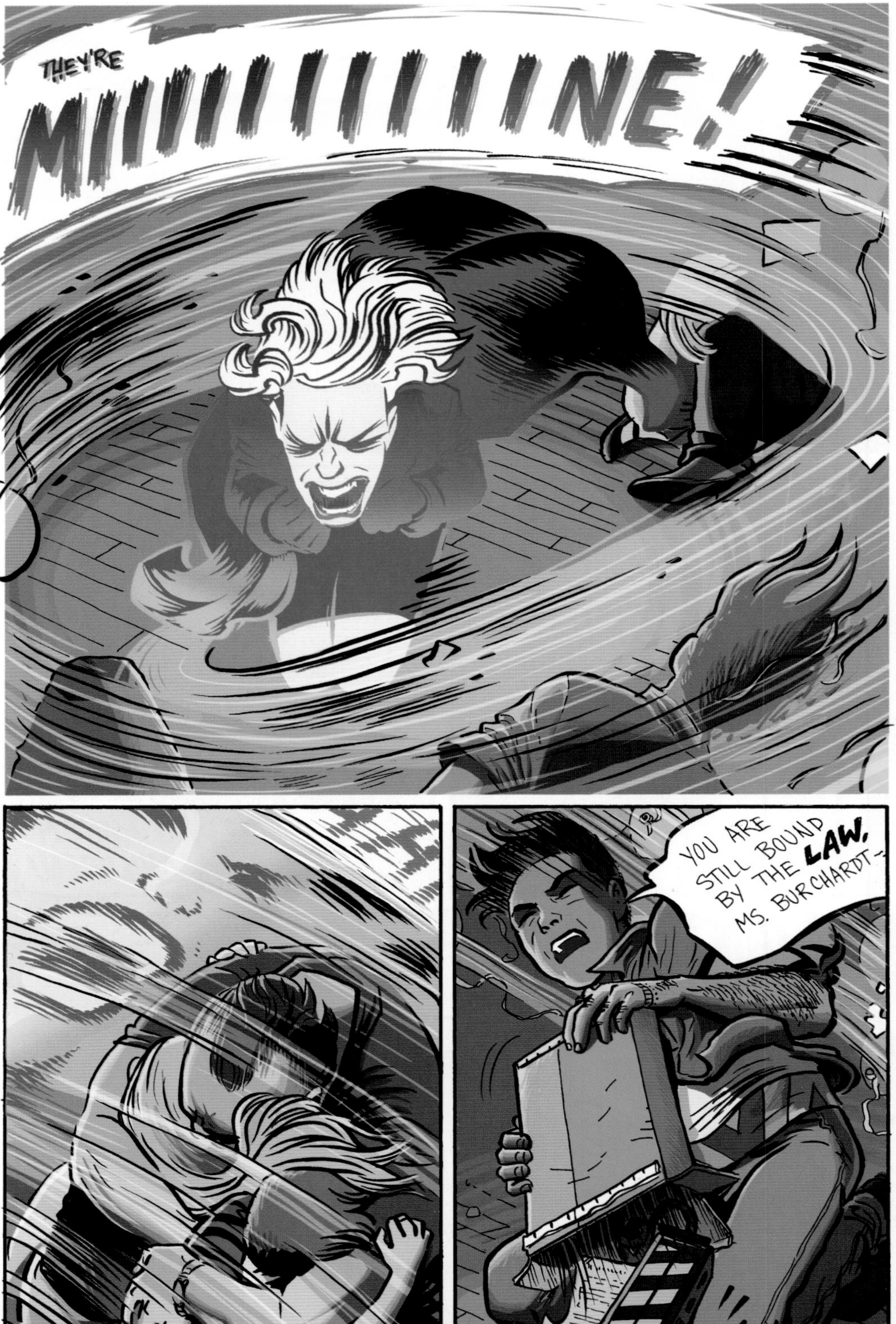
THEY'RE MIIIIIIIIIINE!
YOU ARE STILL BOUND BY THE LAW, MS. BURCHARDT--

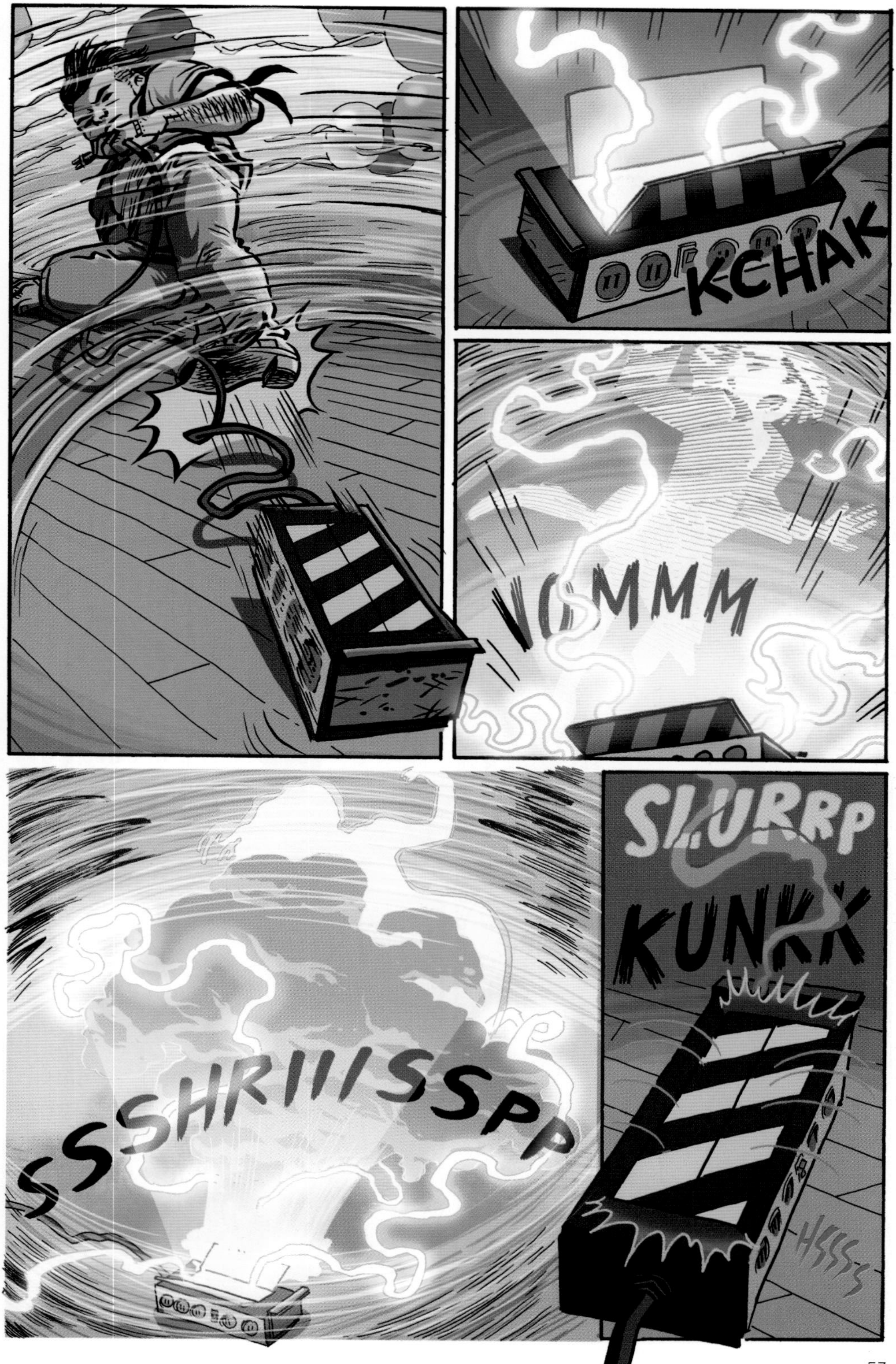
KCHAK
VOMMM
SSSHRIIISSPP
SLURRP
KUNKK
HSSSs

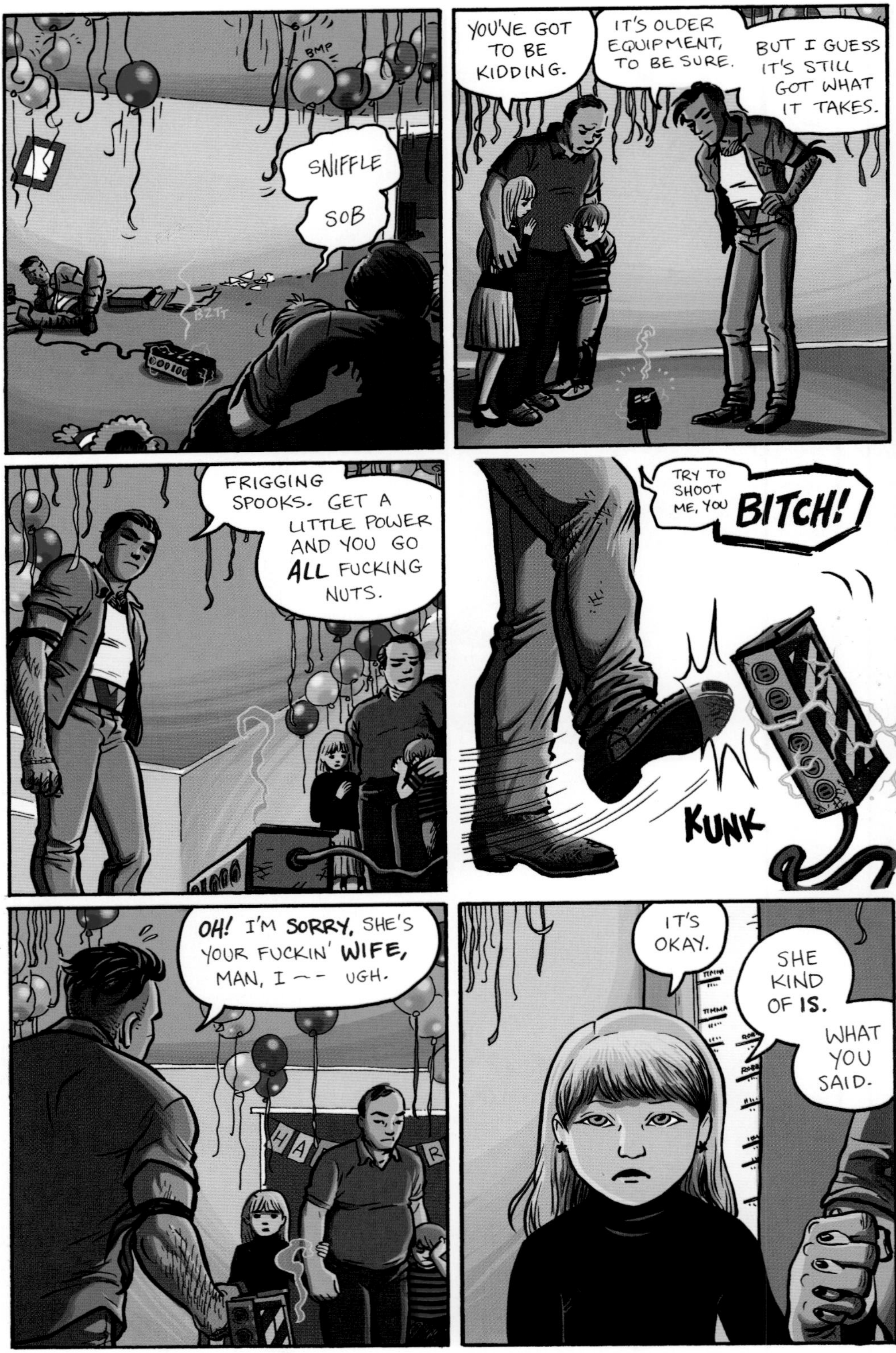
BMP
SNIFFLE
SOB
BZTT
YOU'VE GOT TO BE KIDDING.
IT'S OLDER EQUIPMENT, TO BE SURE.
BUT I GUESS IT'S STILL GOT WHAT IT TAKES.
FRIGGING SPOOKS. GET A LITTLE POWER AND YOU GO ALL FUCKING NUTS.
TRY TO SHOOT ME, YOU BITCH!
KUNK
OH! I'M SORRY, SHE'S YOUR FUCKIN' WIFE, MAN, I -- UGH.
IT'S OKAY.
SHE KIND OF IS.
WHAT YOU SAID.

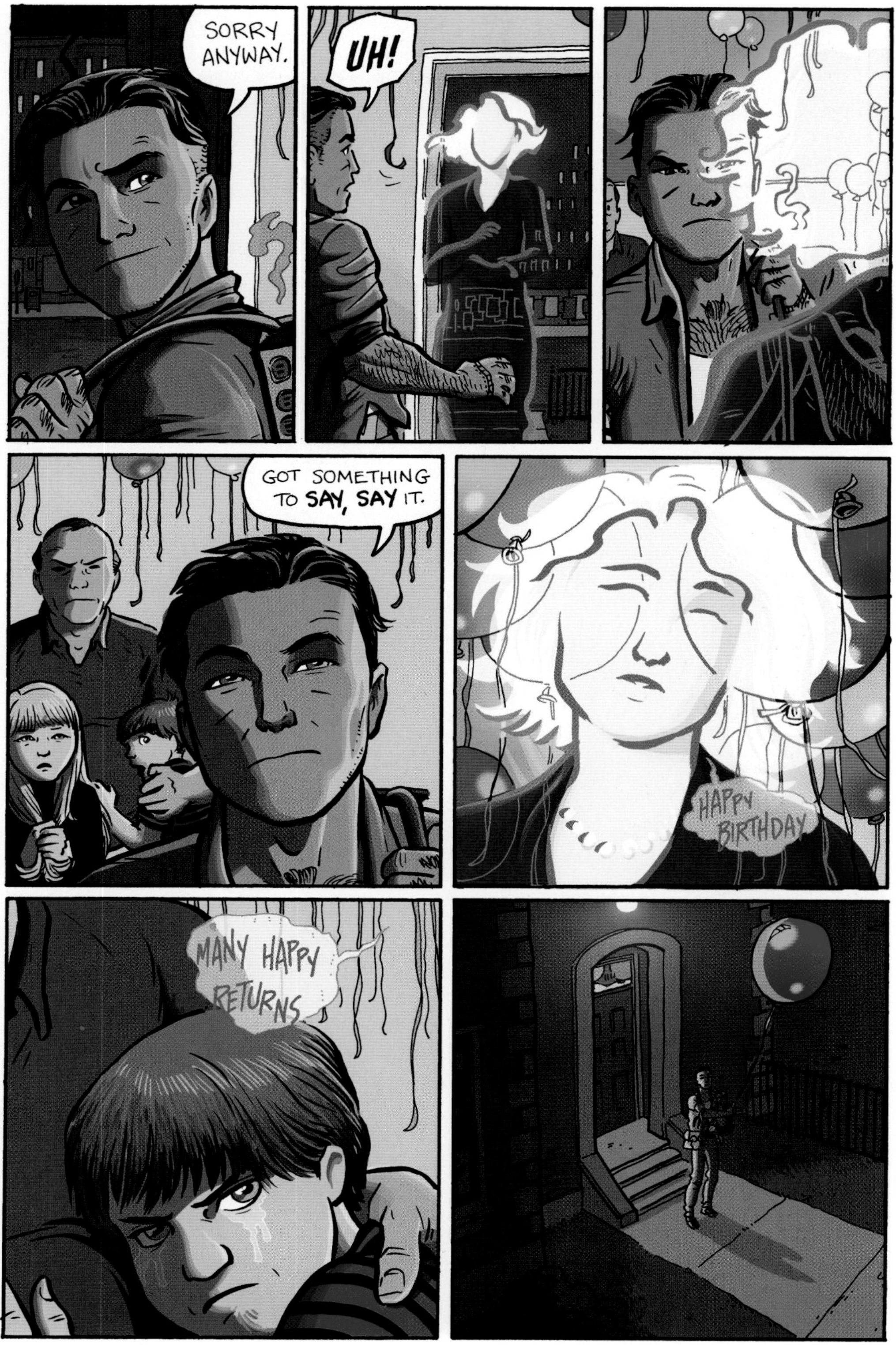
SORRY ANYWAY.
UH!
GOT SOMETHING TO SAY, SAY IT.
HAPPY BIRTHDAY
MANY HAPPY RETURNS

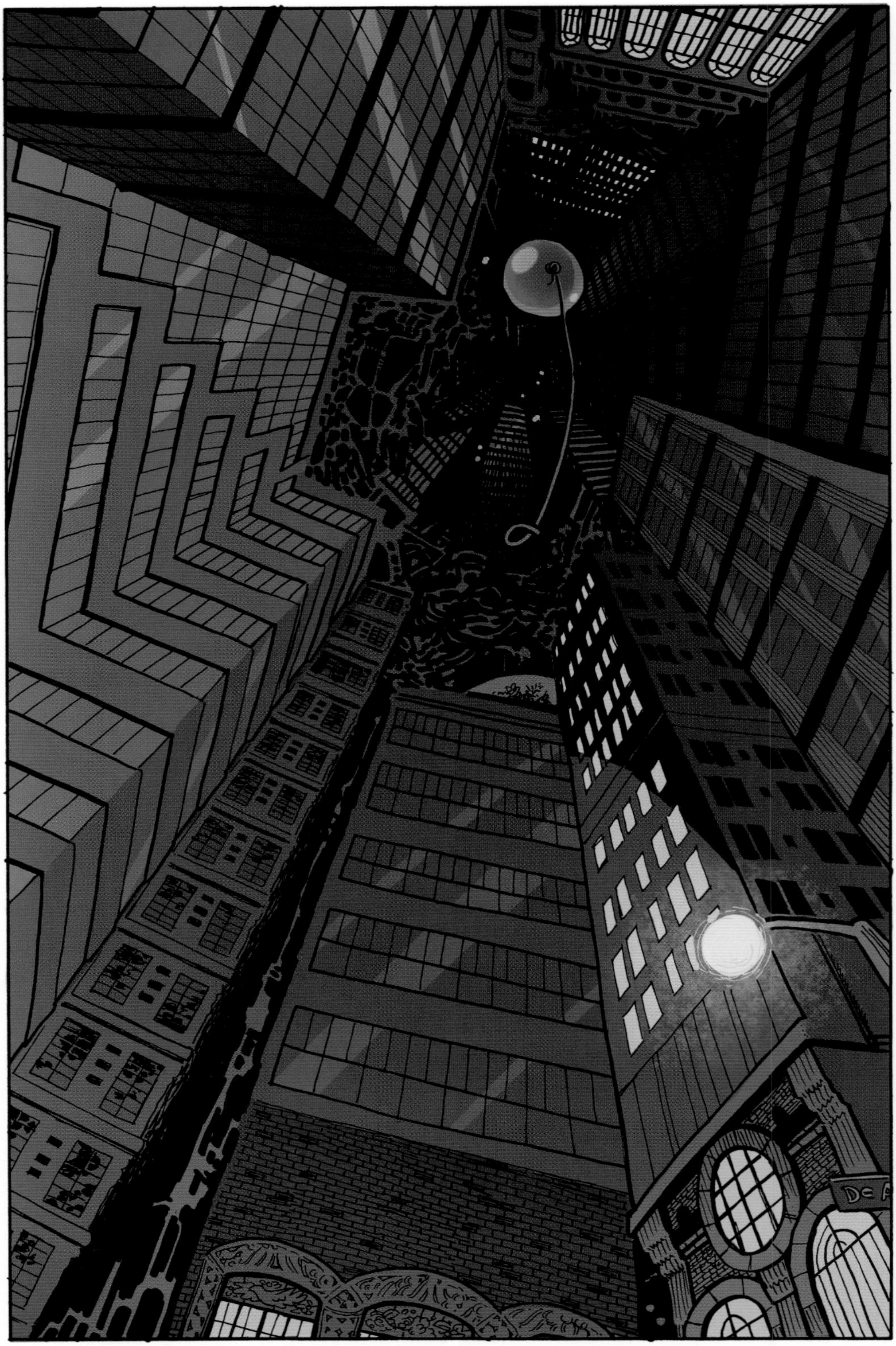

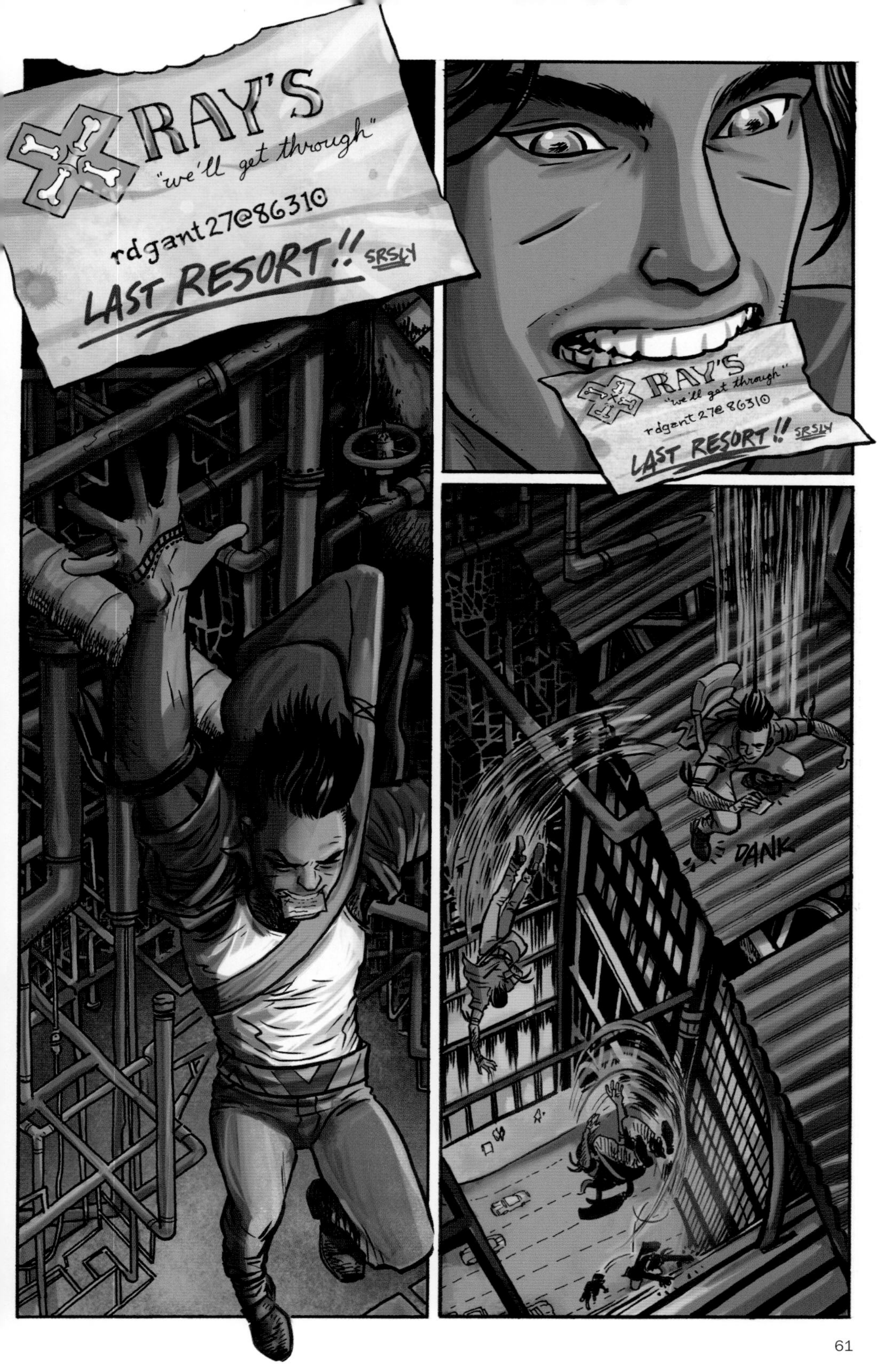
RAY'S
"we'll get through"
rdgant27@86310
LAST RESORT!! SRSLY
RAY'S
"we'll get through"
rdgant27@86310
LAST RESORT!! SRSLY
DANK

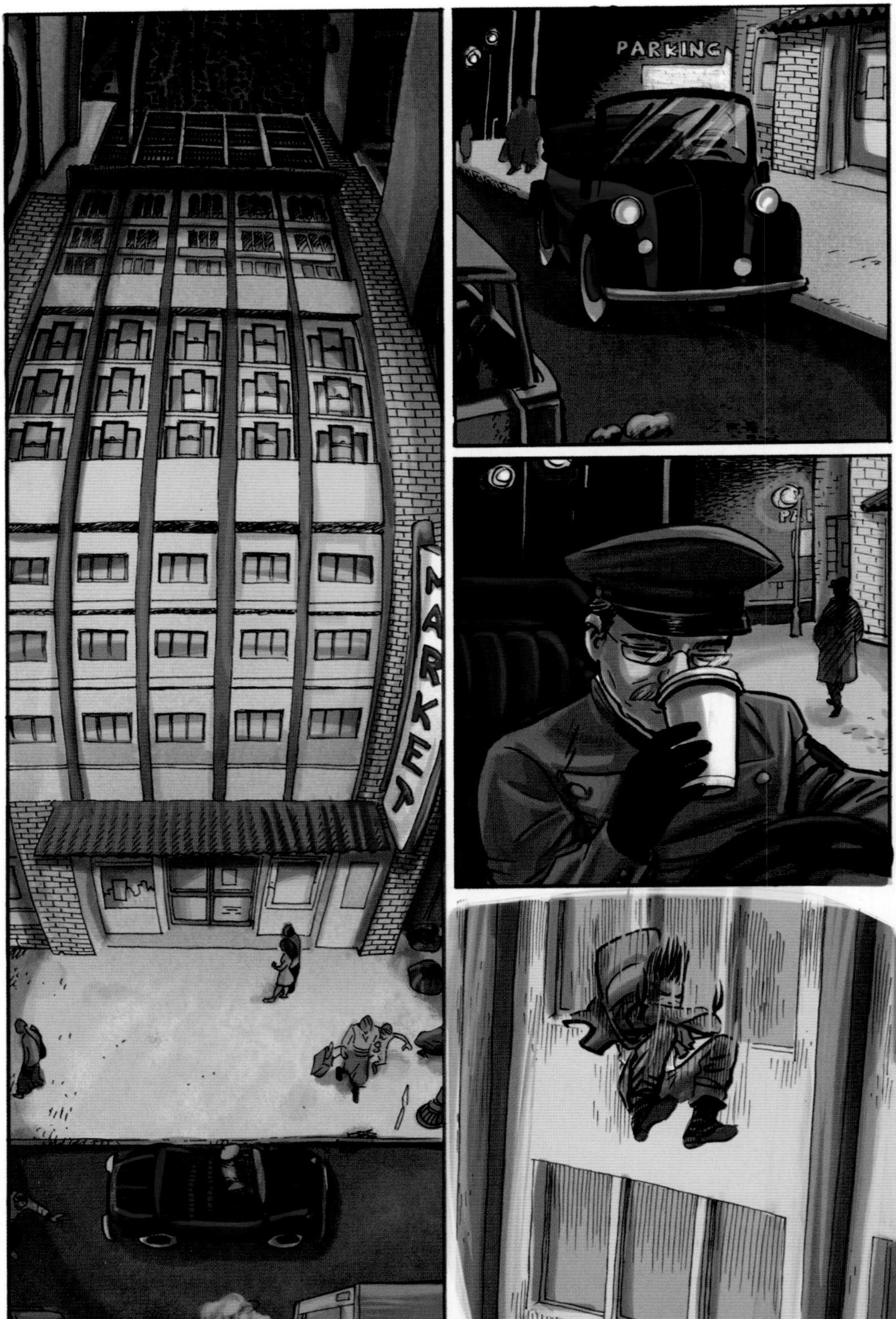
MARKET
PARKING

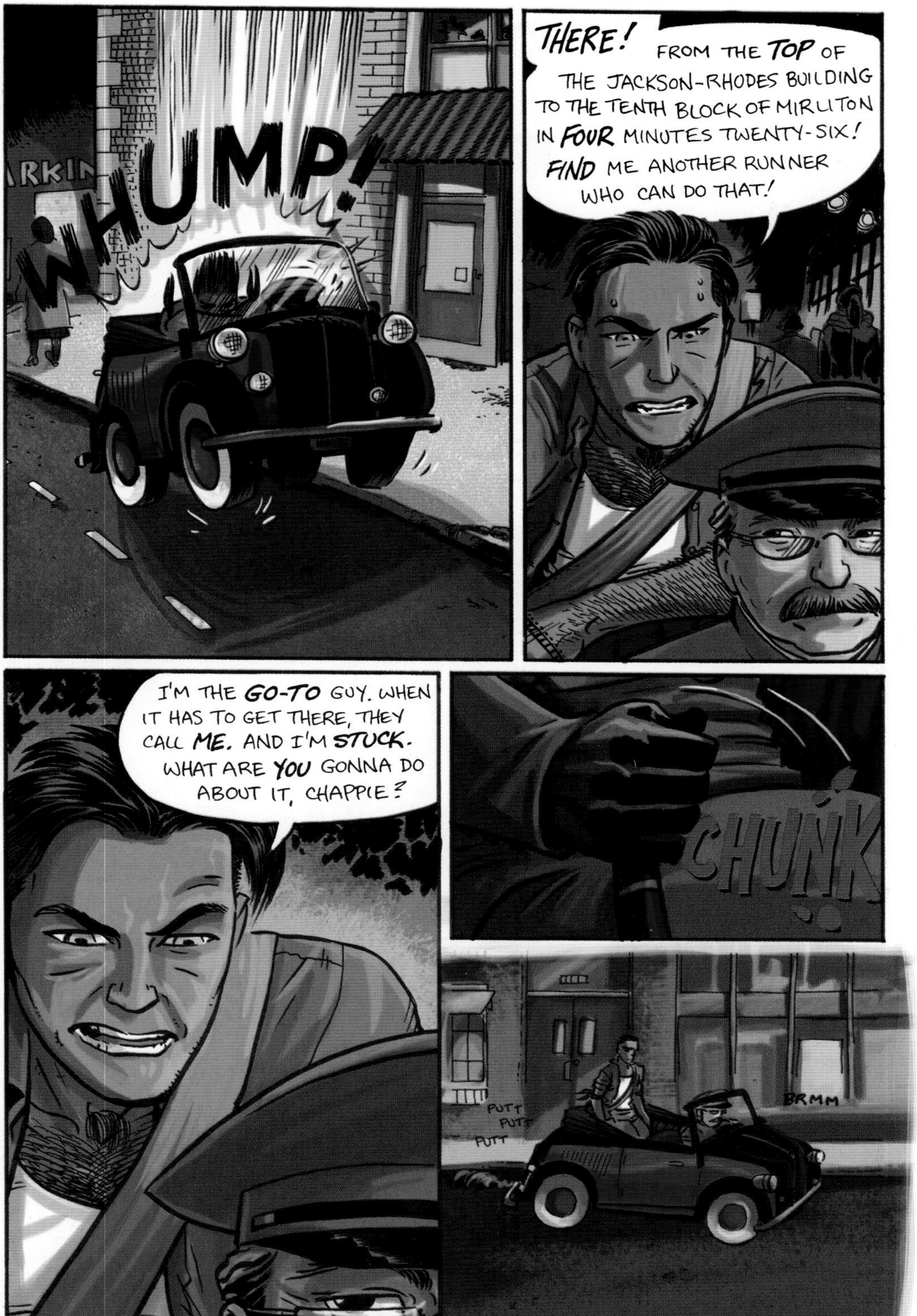
ARKIN
WHUMP!
THERE! FROM THE TOP OF THE JACKSON-RHODES BUILDING TO THE TENTH BLOCK OF MIRLITON IN FOUR MINUTES TWENTY-SIX! FIND ME ANOTHER RUNNER WHO CAN DO THAT!
I'M THE GO-TO GUY. WHEN IT HAS TO GET THERE, THEY CALL ME. AND I'M STUCK. WHAT ARE YOU GONNA DO ABOUT IT, CHAPPIE?
CHUNK
PUTT
PUTT
PUTT
BRMM

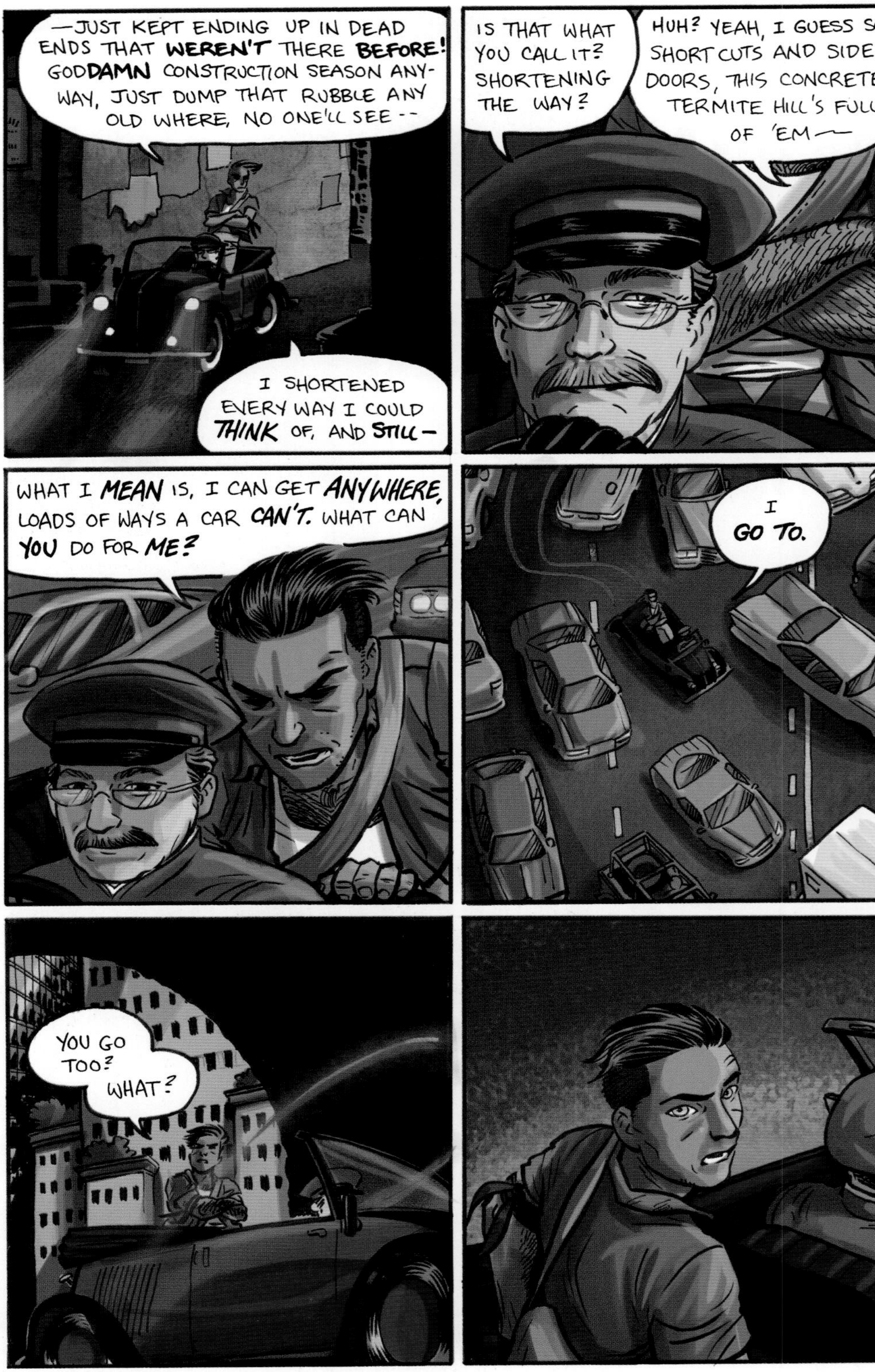
—JUST KEPT ENDING UP IN DEAD ENDS THAT WEREN'T THERE BEFORE! GODDAMN CONSTRUCTION SEASON ANYWAY, JUST DUMP THAT RUBBLE ANY OLD WHERE, NO ONE'LL SEE --
I SHORTENED EVERY WAY I COULD THINK OF, AND STILL—
IS THAT WHAT YOU CALL IT? SHORTENING THE WAY?
HUH? YEAH, I GUESS SO, SHORT CUTS AND SIDE DOORS, THIS CONCRETE TERMITE HILL'S FULL OF 'EM—
WHAT I MEAN IS, I CAN GET ANYWHERE, LOADS OF WAYS A CAR CAN'T. WHAT CAN YOU DO FOR ME?
I GO TO.
YOU GO TOO? WHAT?

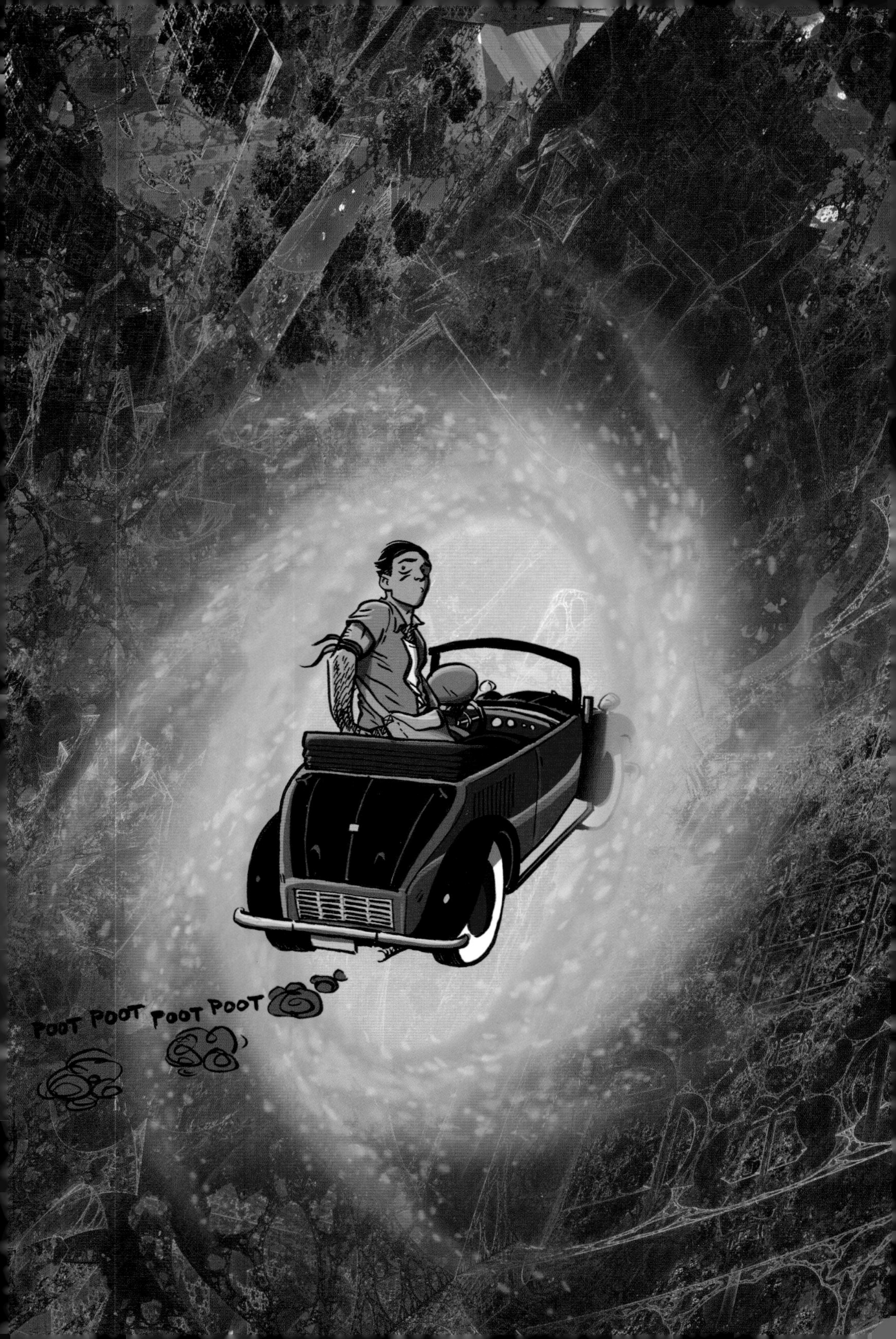
POOT POOT POOT POOT

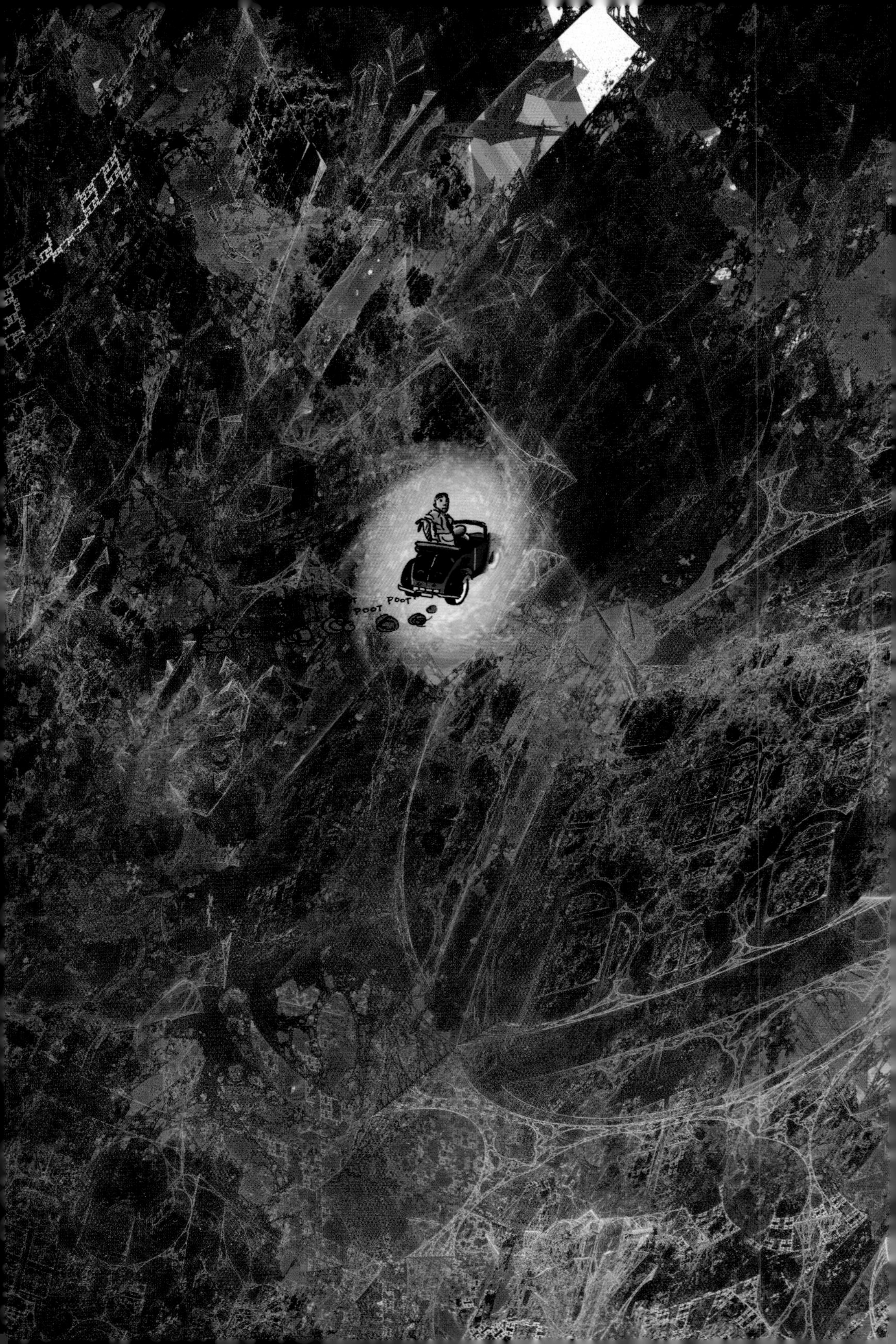
POOT
POOT

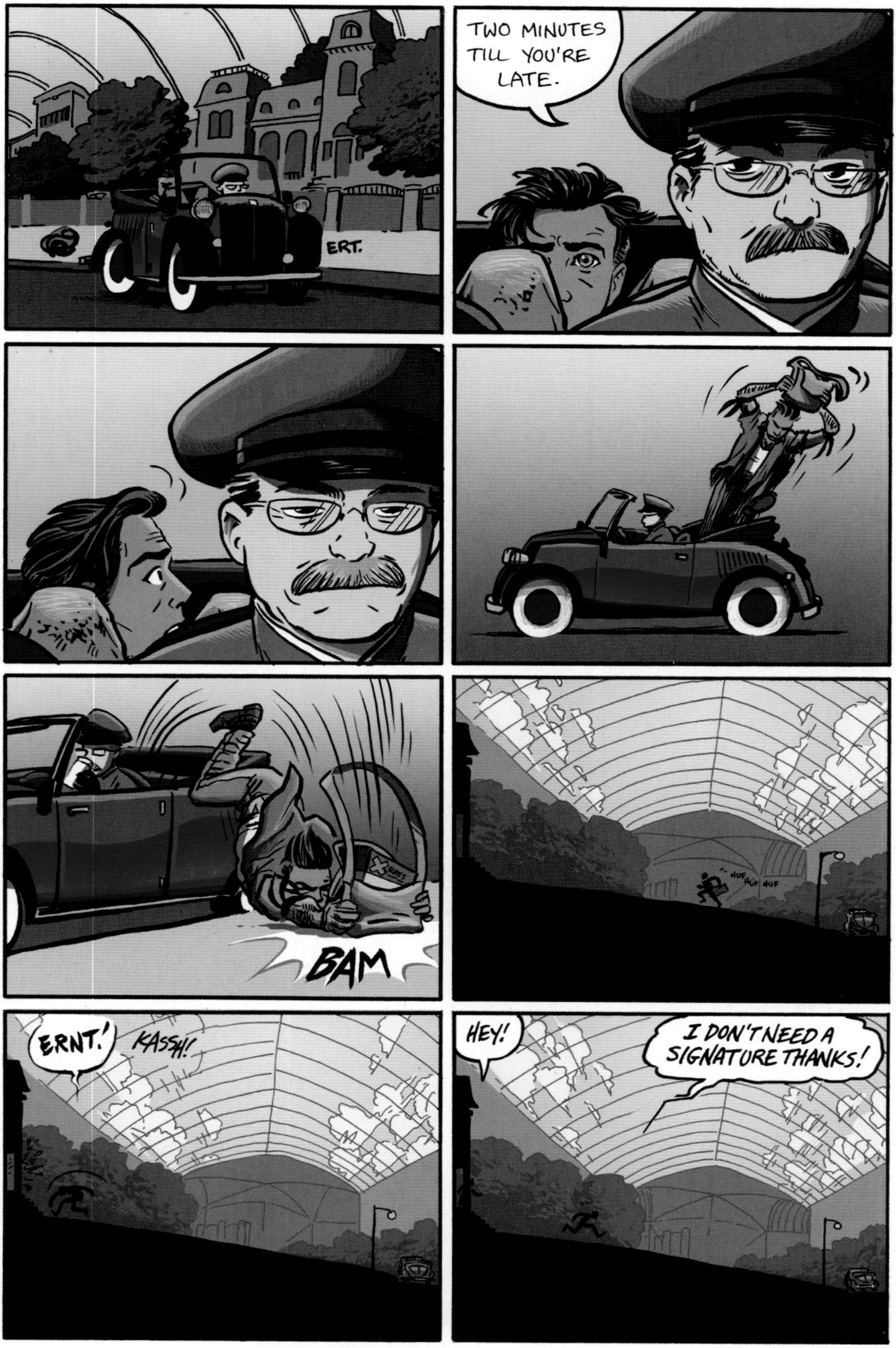
ERT.
TWO MINUTES TILL YOU'RE LATE.
BAM
ERNT!
KASSH!
HEY!
I DON'T NEED A SIGNATURE THANKS!

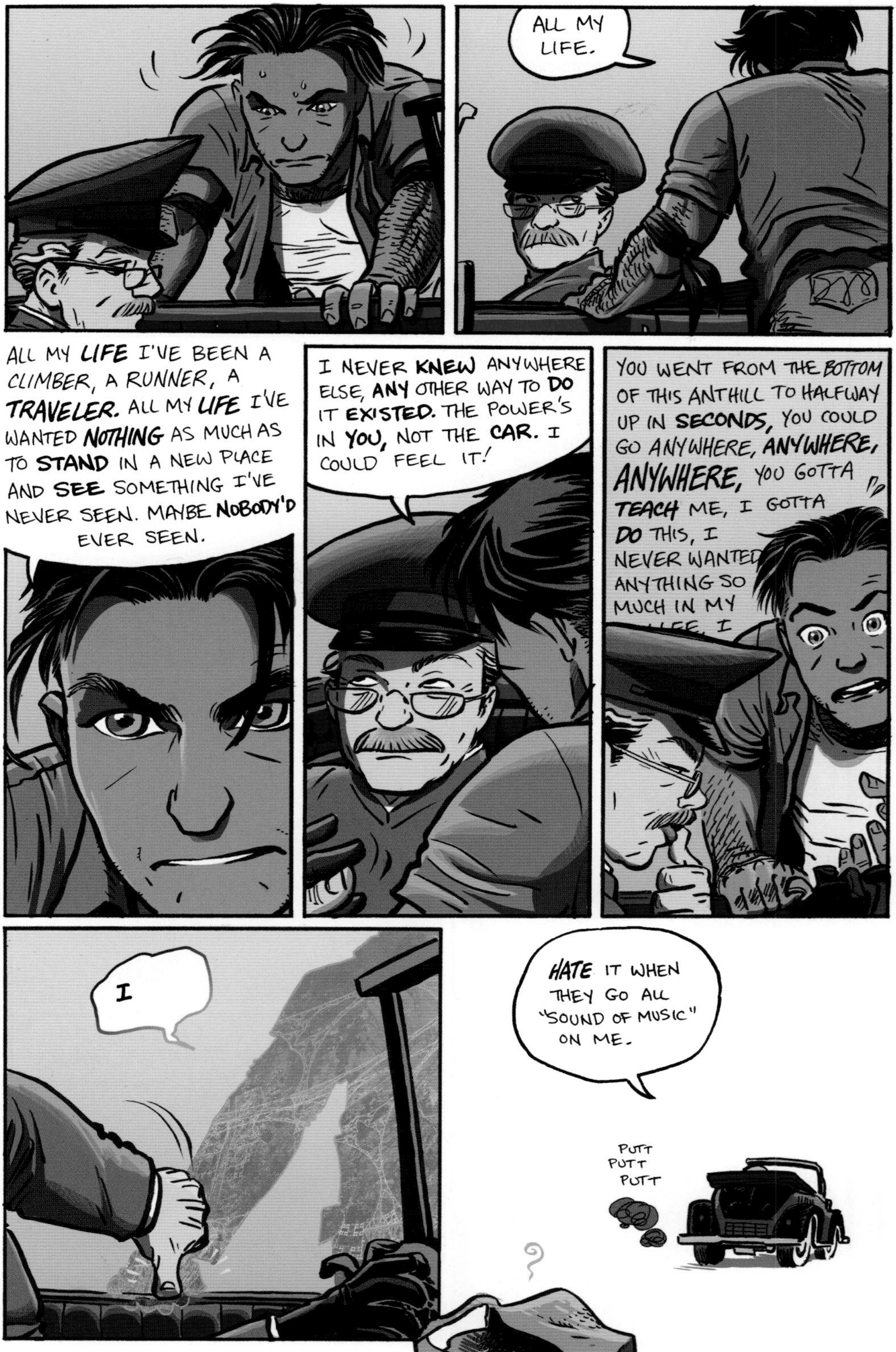
ALL MY LIFE.
ALL MY LIFE I'VE BEEN A CLIMBER, A RUNNER, A TRAVELER. ALL MY LIFE I'VE WANTED NOTHING AS MUCH AS TO STAND IN A NEW PLACE AND SEE SOMETHING I'VE NEVER SEEN. MAYBE NOBODY'D EVER SEEN.
I NEVER KNEW ANYWHERE ELSE, ANY OTHER WAY TO DO IT EXISTED. THE POWER'S IN YOU, NOT THE CAR. I COULD FEEL IT!
YOU WENT FROM THE BOTTOM OF THIS ANTHILL TO HALFWAY UP IN SECONDS, YOU COULD GO ANYWHERE, ANYWHERE, ANYWHERE, YOU GOTTA TEACH ME, I GOTTA DO THIS, I NEVER WANTED ANYTHING SO MUCH IN MY
I
HATE IT WHEN THEY GO ALL "SOUND OF MUSIC" ON ME.
PUTT PUTT PUTT

PART TWO

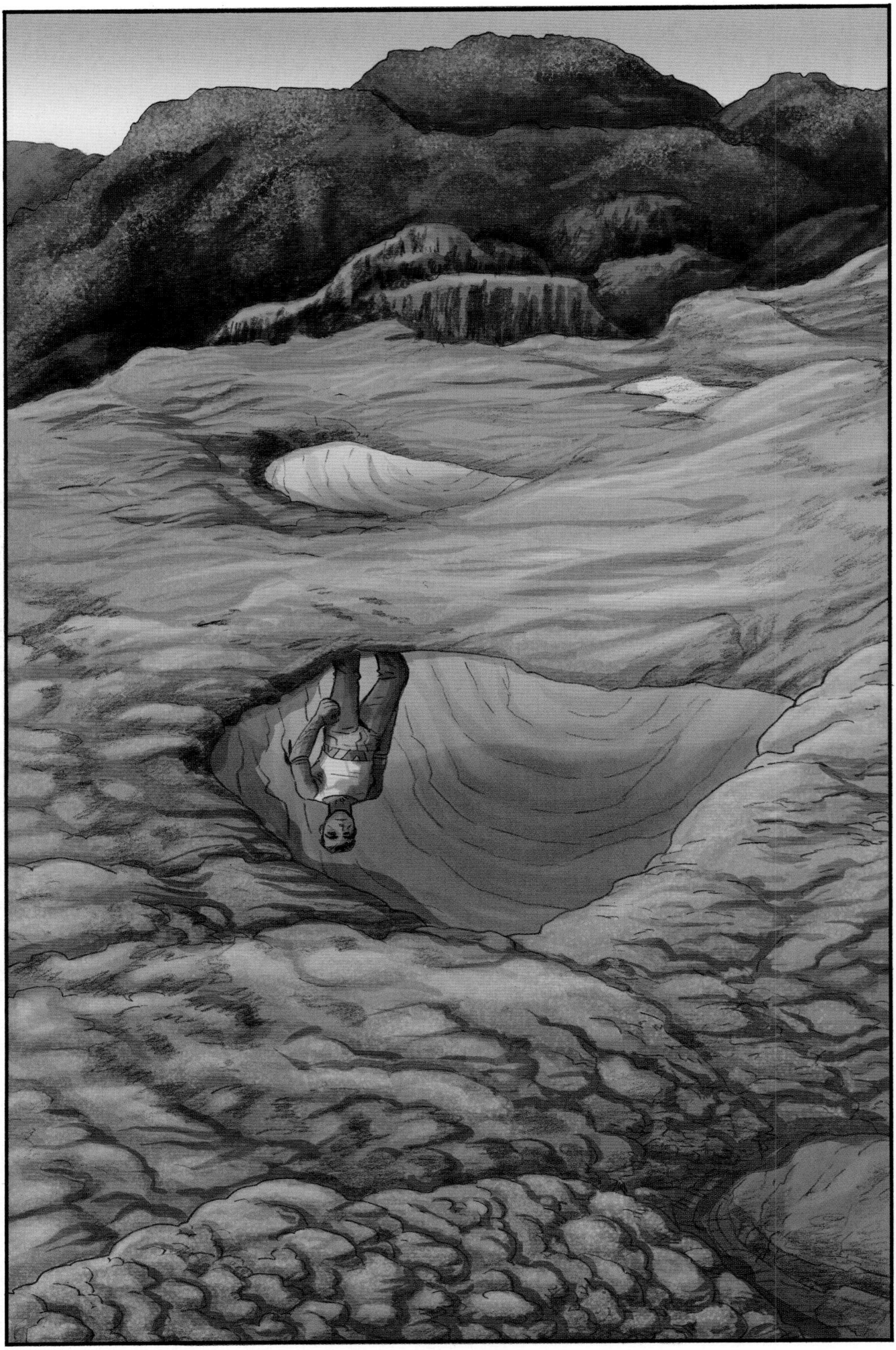

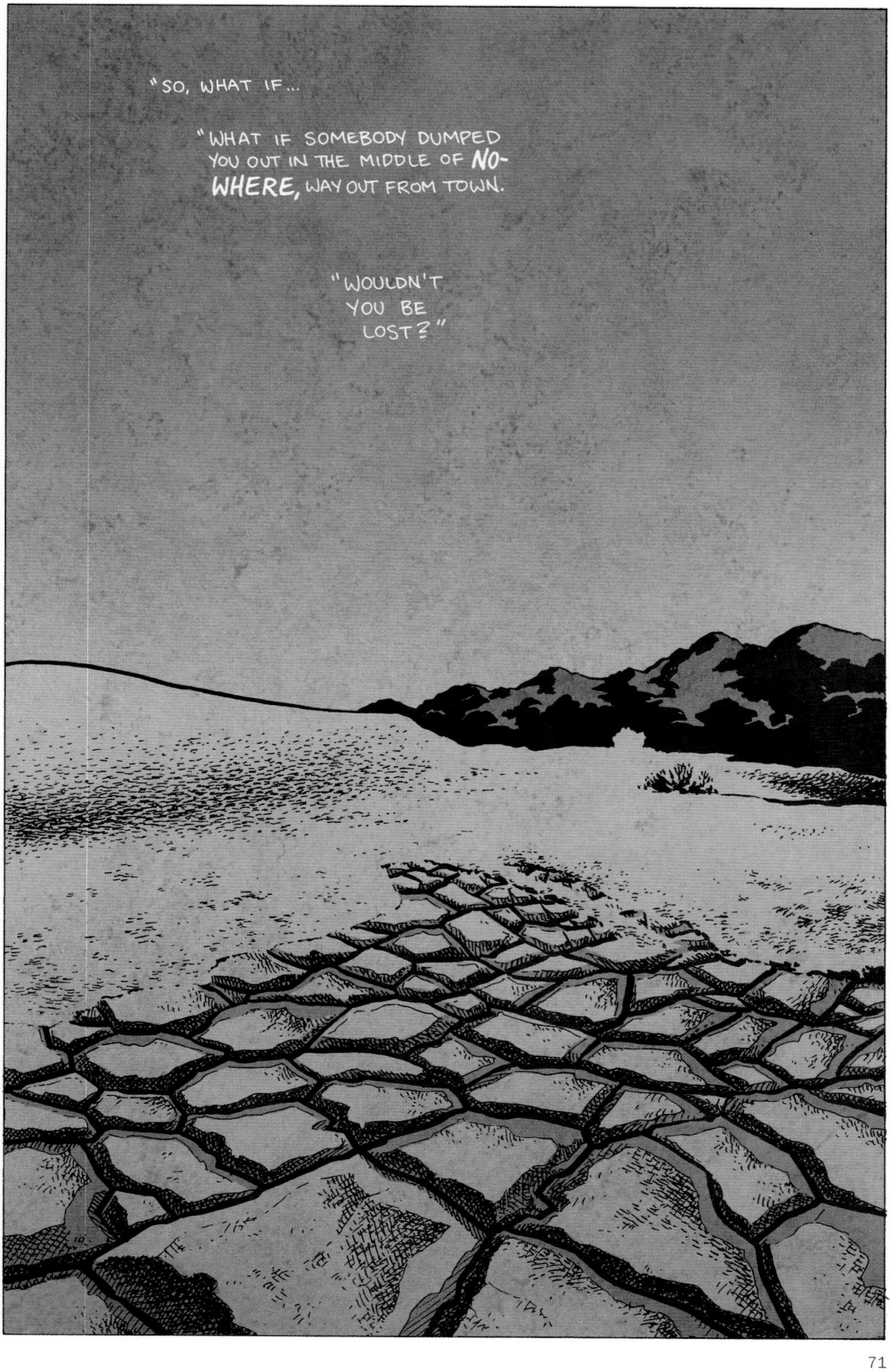
"SO, WHAT IF...
"WHAT IF SOMEBODY DUMPED YOU OUT IN THE MIDDLE OF NO-WHERE, WAY OUT FROM TOWN.
"WOULDN'T YOU BE LOST?"

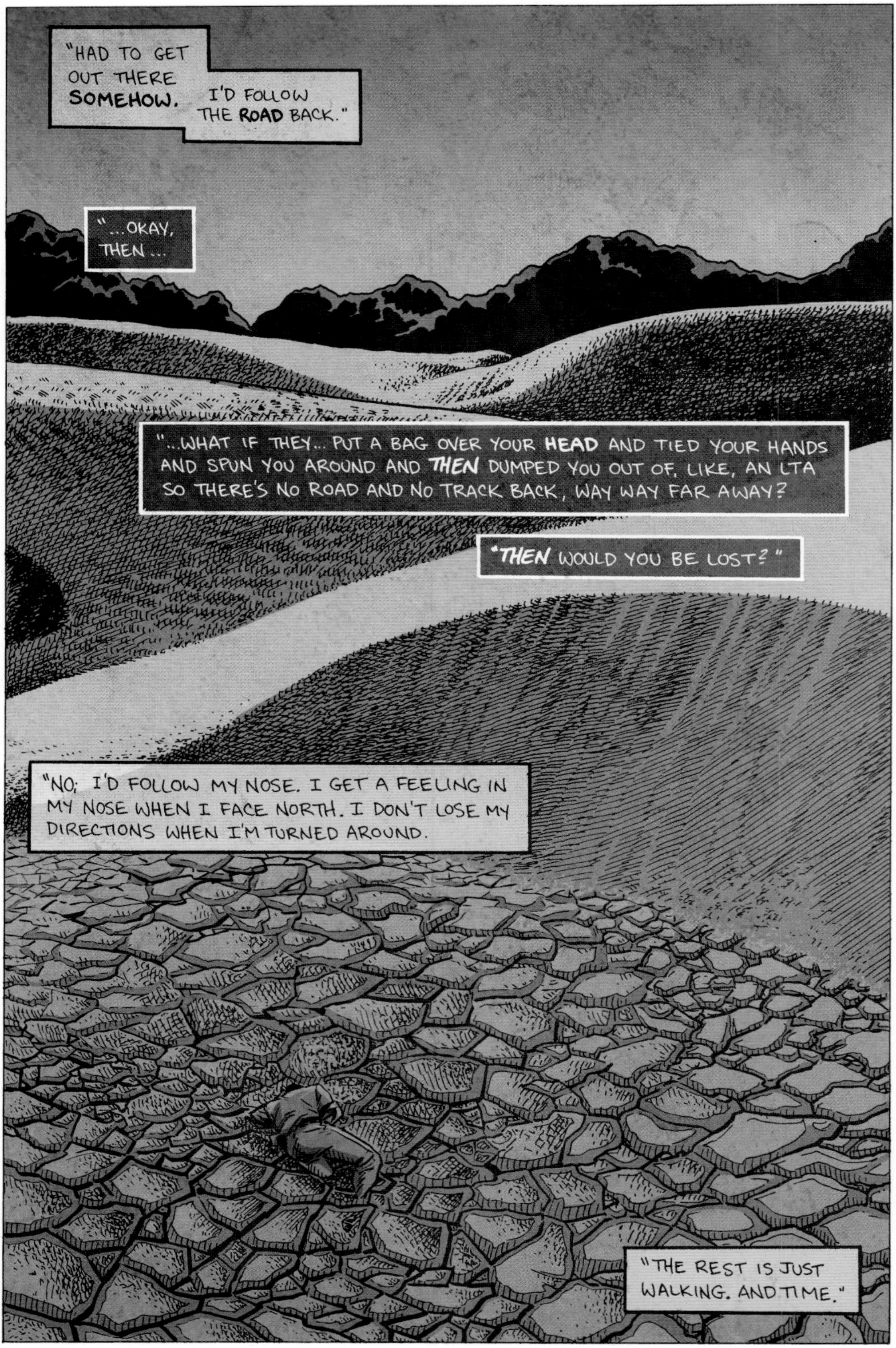
"HAD TO GET OUT THERE SOMEHOW. I'D FOLLOW THE ROAD BACK."
"...OKAY, THEN...
"...WHAT IF THEY... PUT A BAG OVER YOUR HEAD AND TIED YOUR HANDS AND SPUN YOU AROUND AND THEN DUMPED YOU OUT OF, LIKE, AN LTA SO THERE'S NO ROAD AND NO TRACK BACK, WAY WAY FAR AWAY?
"THEN WOULD YOU BE LOST?"
"NO; I'D FOLLOW MY NOSE. I GET A FEELING IN MY NOSE WHEN I FACE NORTH. I DON'T LOSE MY DIRECTIONS WHEN I'M TURNED AROUND.
"THE REST IS JUST WALKING. AND TIME."

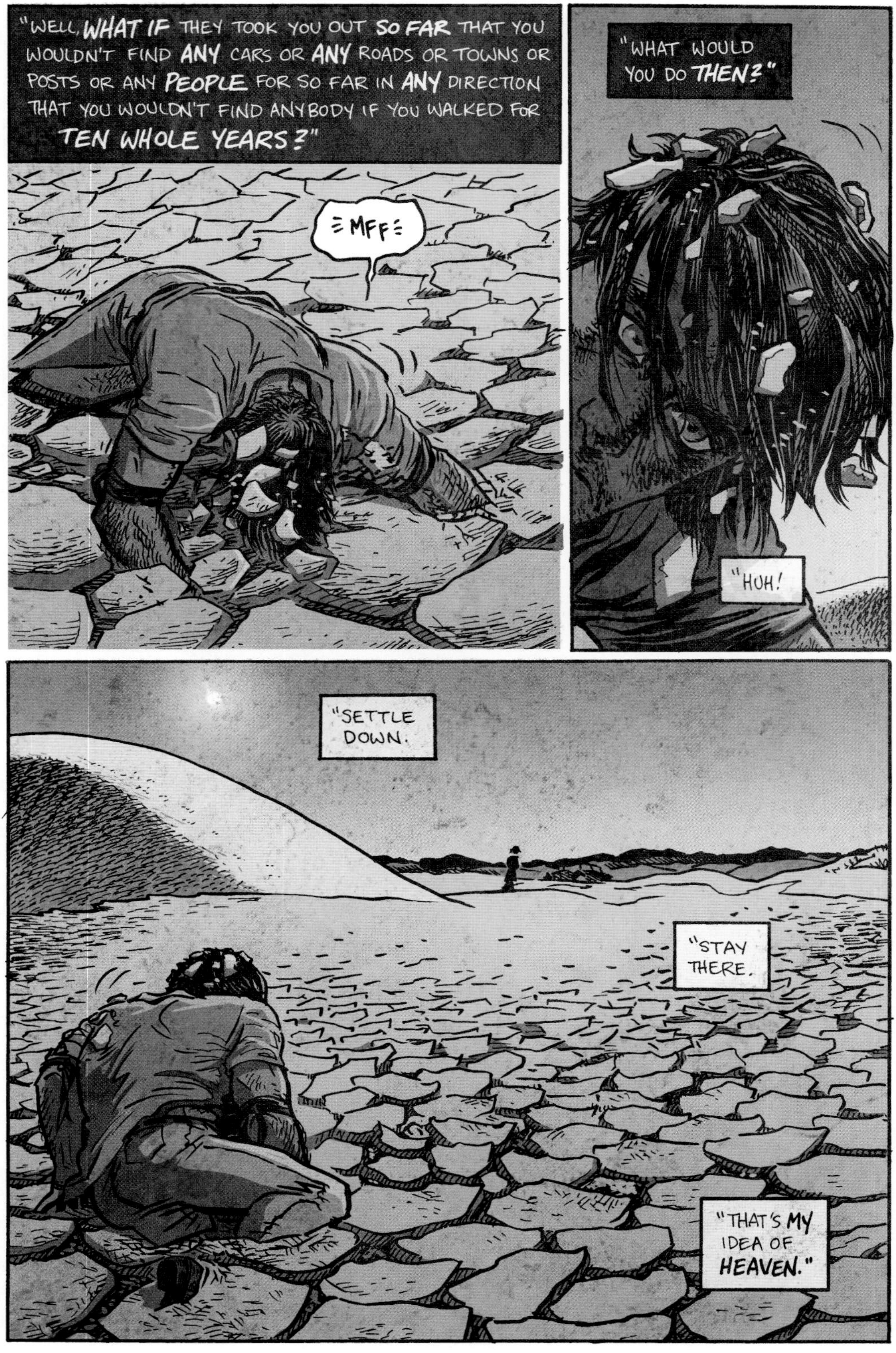
"WELL, WHAT IF THEY TOOK YOU OUT SO FAR THAT YOU WOULDN'T FIND ANY CARS OR ANY ROADS OR TOWNS OR POSTS OR ANY PEOPLE FOR SO FAR IN ANY DIRECTION THAT YOU WOULDN'T FIND ANYBODY IF YOU WALKED FOR TEN WHOLE YEARS?"
MFF
"WHAT WOULD YOU DO THEN?"
"HUH!
"SETTLE DOWN.
"STAY THERE.
"THAT'S MY IDEA OF HEAVEN."

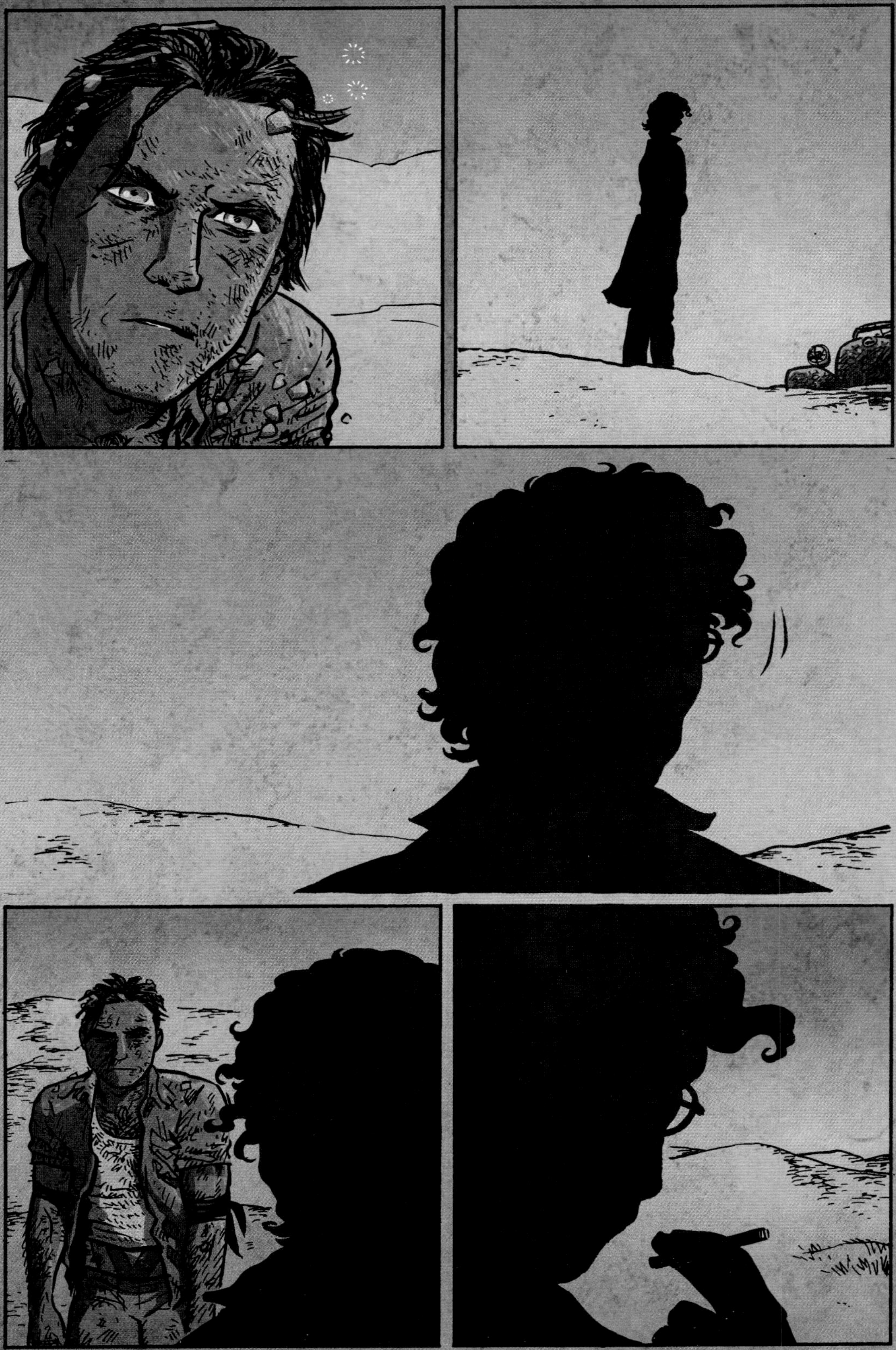

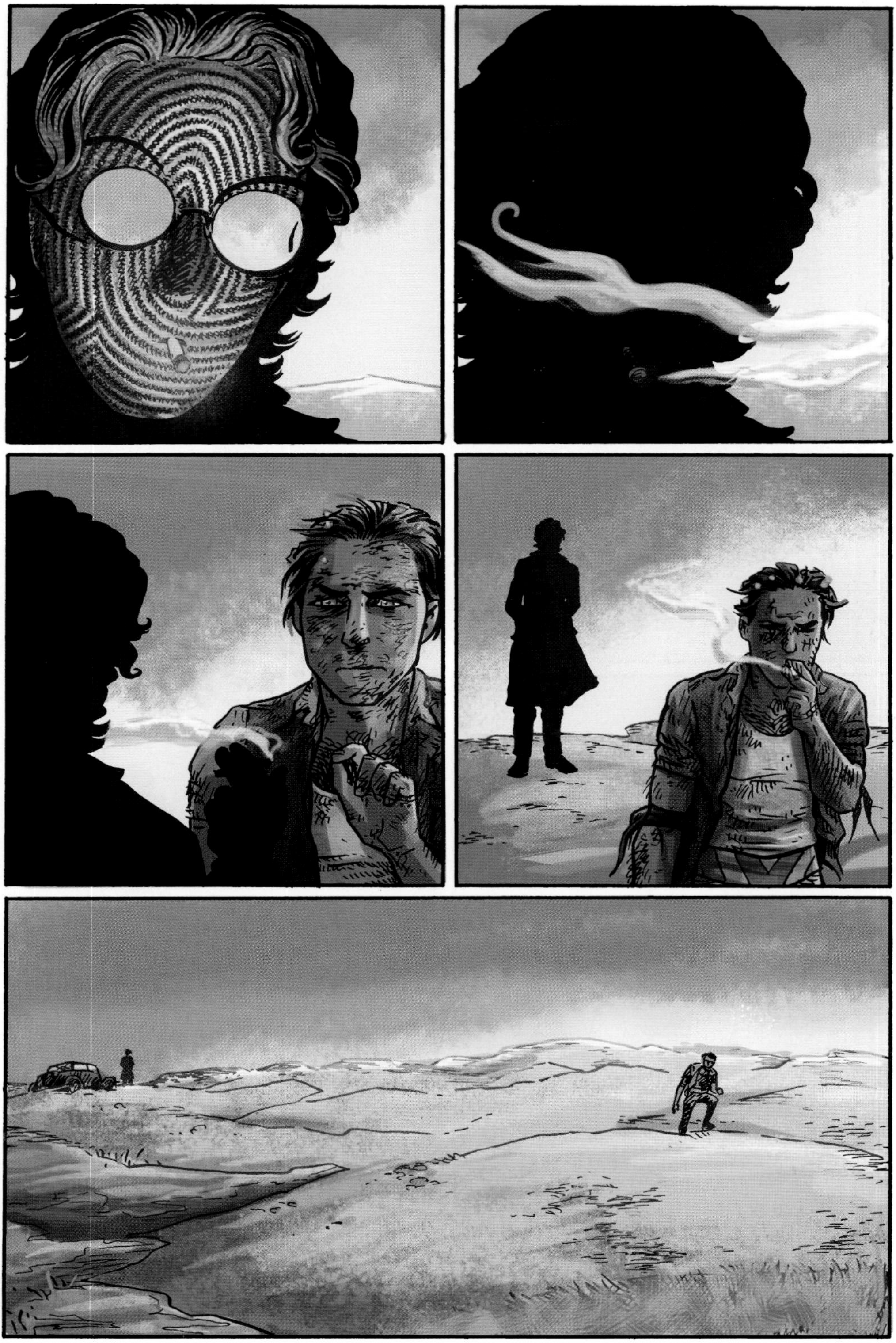

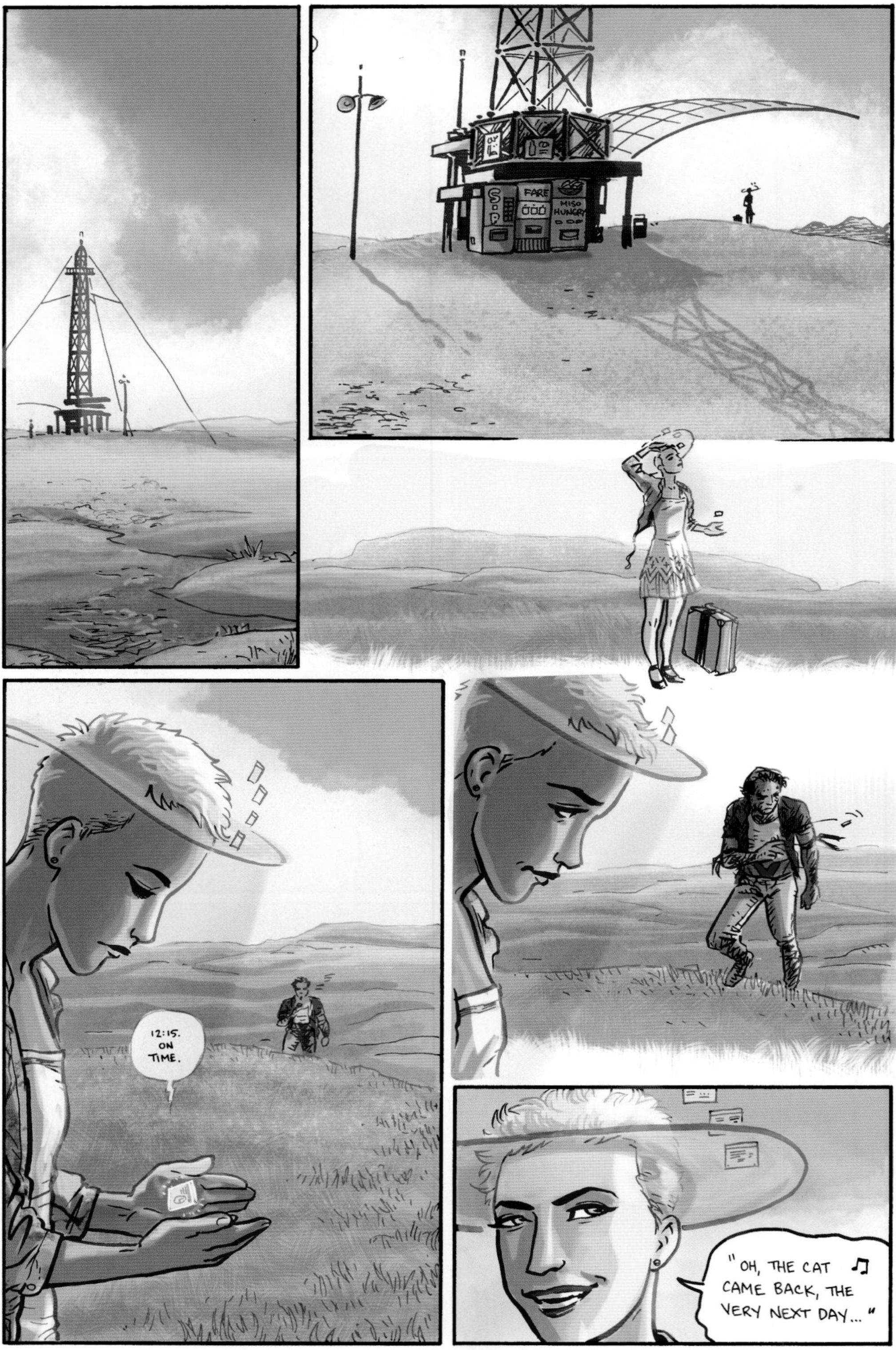
FARE
MISO HUNGRY
12:15. ON TIME.
"OH, THE CAT CAME BACK, THE VERY NEXT DAY..." ♫

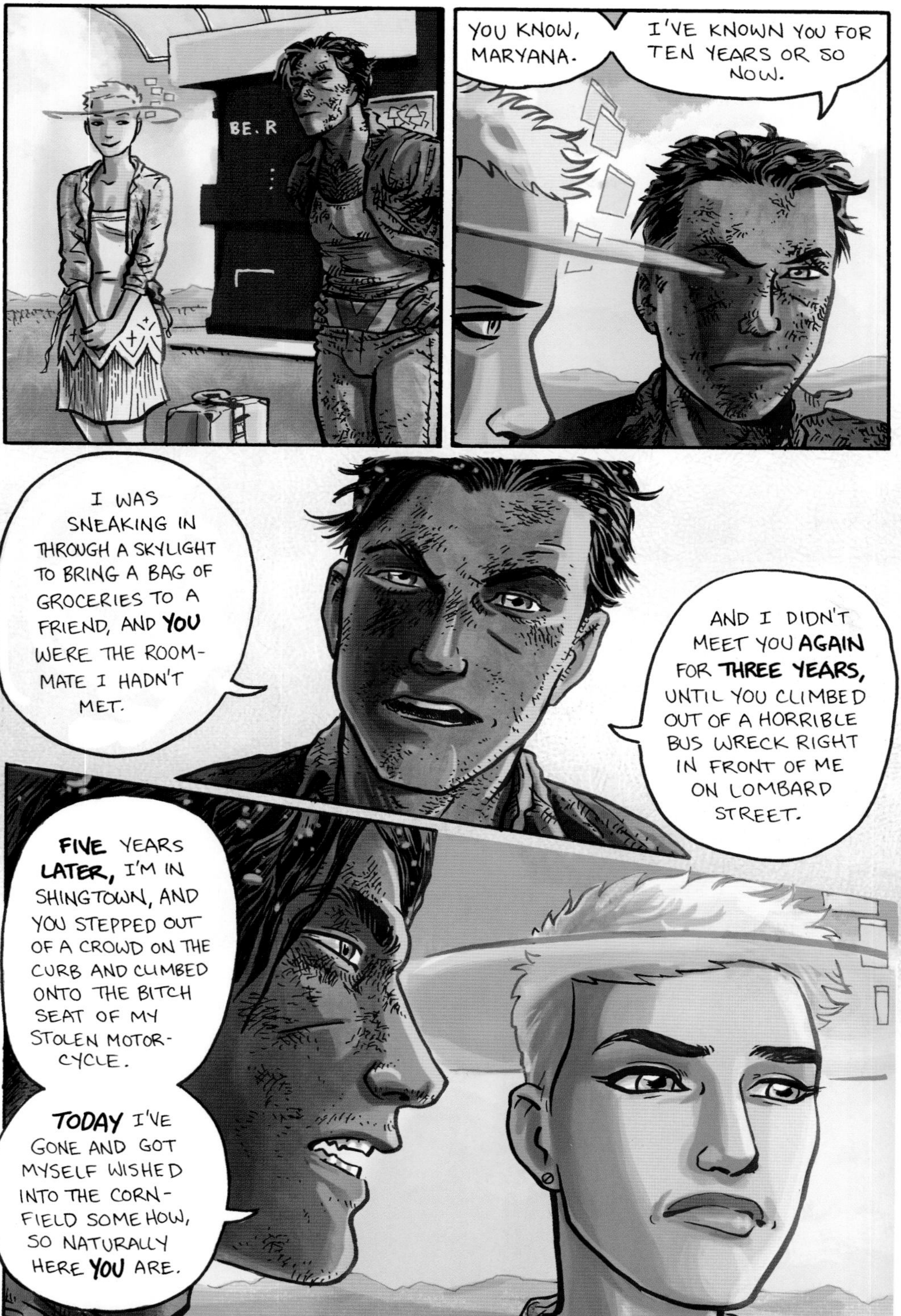
BE. R
YOU KNOW, MARYANA.
I'VE KNOWN YOU FOR TEN YEARS OR SO NOW.
I WAS SNEAKING IN THROUGH A SKYLIGHT TO BRING A BAG OF GROCERIES TO A FRIEND, AND **YOU** WERE THE ROOM-MATE I HADN'T MET.
AND I DIDN'T MEET YOU **AGAIN** FOR **THREE YEARS,** UNTIL YOU CLIMBED OUT OF A HORRIBLE BUS WRECK RIGHT IN FRONT OF ME ON LOMBARD STREET.
FIVE YEARS **LATER,** I'M IN SHINGTOWN, AND YOU STEPPED OUT OF A CROWD ON THE CURB AND CLIMBED ONTO THE BITCH SEAT OF MY STOLEN MOTOR-CYCLE.
TODAY I'VE GONE AND GOT MYSELF WISHED INTO THE CORN-FIELD SOMEHOW, SO NATURALLY HERE **YOU** ARE.

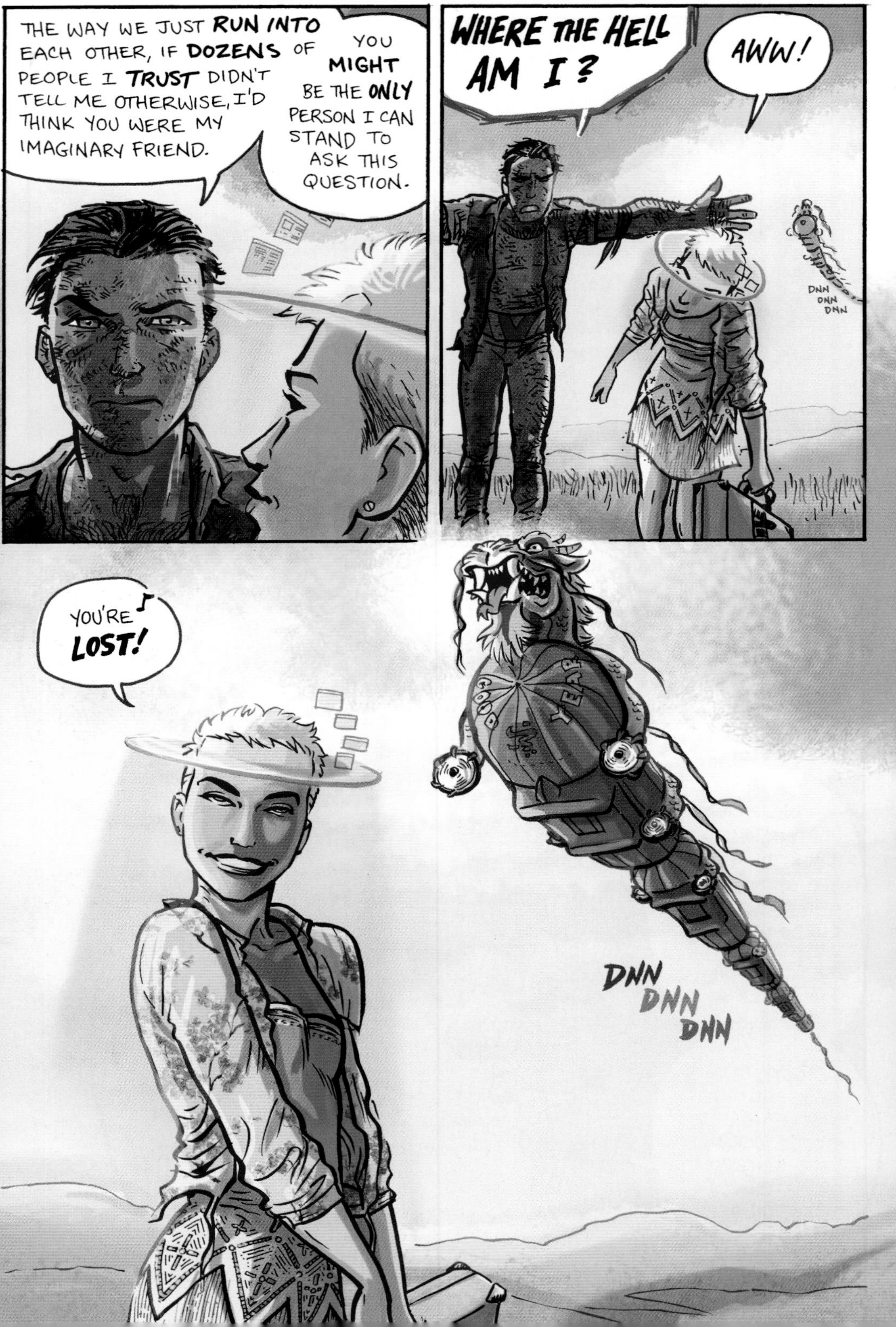
THE WAY WE JUST RUN INTO EACH OTHER, IF DOZENS OF PEOPLE I TRUST DIDN'T TELL ME OTHERWISE, I'D THINK YOU WERE MY IMAGINARY FRIEND.
YOU MIGHT BE THE ONLY PERSON I CAN STAND TO ASK THIS QUESTION.
WHERE THE HELL AM I?
AWW!
DNN DNN DNN
YOU'RE LOST!
GOOD YEAR
DNN DNN DNN

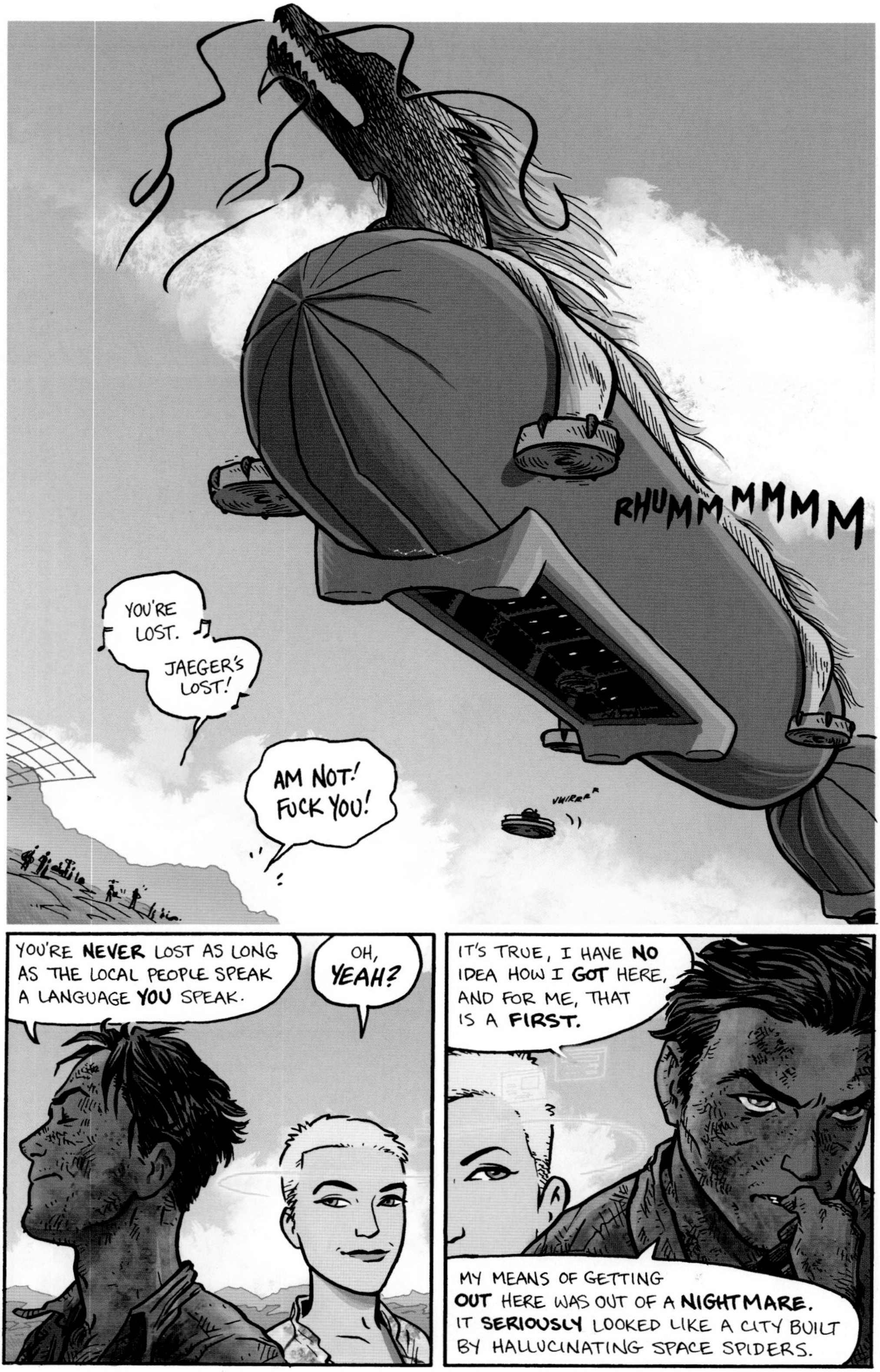
RHUMMMMMM
YOU'RE LOST.
JAEGER'S LOST!
AM NOT! FUCK YOU!
VHIRRR
YOU'RE **NEVER** LOST AS LONG AS THE LOCAL PEOPLE SPEAK A LANGUAGE **YOU** SPEAK.
OH, **YEAH?**
IT'S TRUE, I HAVE **NO** IDEA HOW I **GOT** HERE, AND FOR ME, THAT IS A **FIRST.**
MY MEANS OF GETTING **OUT** HERE WAS OUT OF A **NIGHTMARE.** IT **SERIOUSLY** LOOKED LIKE A CITY BUILT BY HALLUCINATING SPACE SPIDERS.

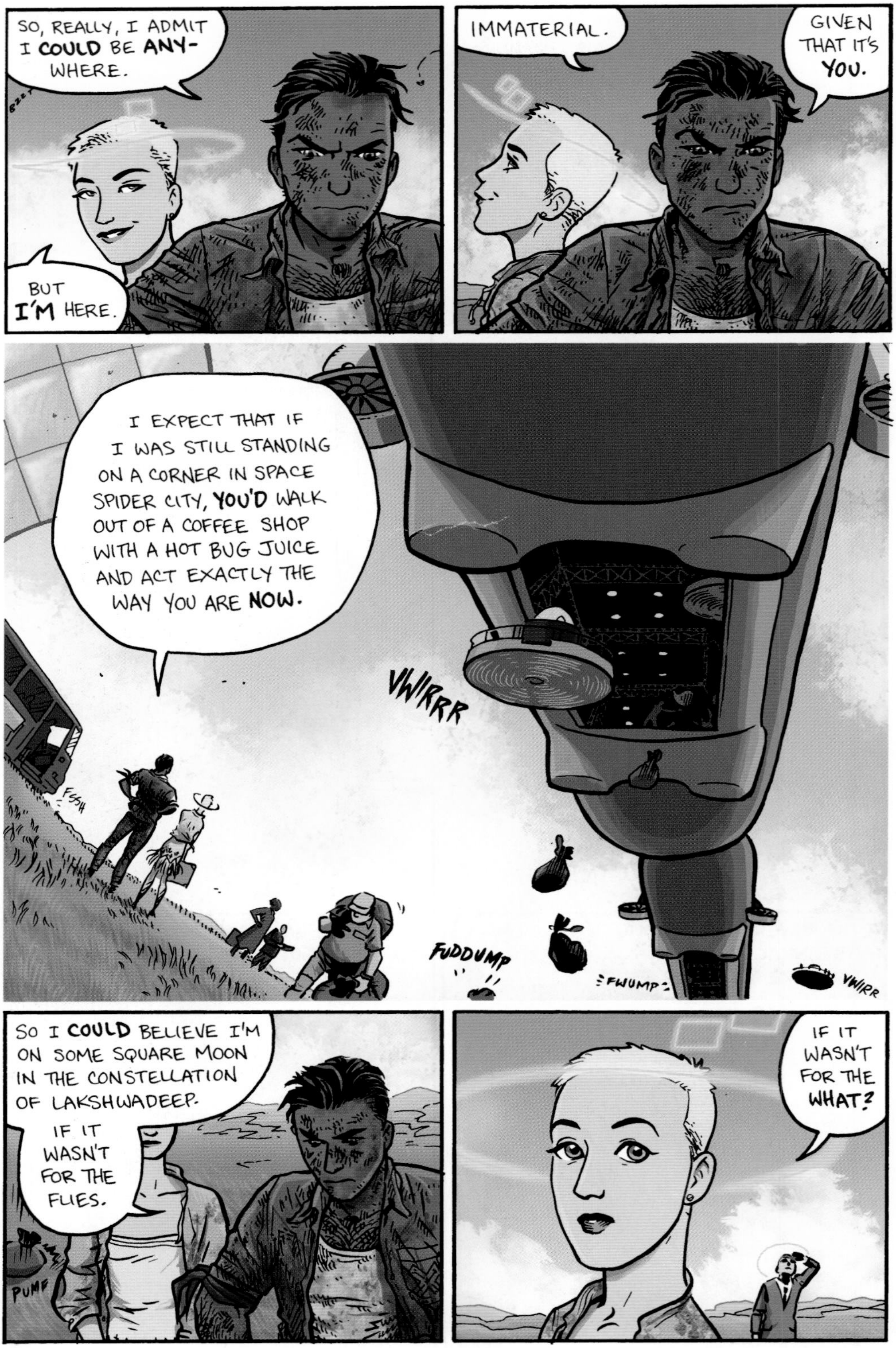
SO, REALLY, I ADMIT I COULD BE ANY-WHERE.
BUT I'M HERE.
IMMATERIAL.
GIVEN THAT IT'S YOU.
I EXPECT THAT IF I WAS STILL STANDING ON A CORNER IN SPACE SPIDER CITY, YOU'D WALK OUT OF A COFFEE SHOP WITH A HOT BUG JUICE AND ACT EXACTLY THE WAY YOU ARE NOW.
VWIRRR
FSSH
FUDDUMP
FWUMP
VWIRR
SO I COULD BELIEVE I'M ON SOME SQUARE MOON IN THE CONSTELLATION OF LAKSHWADEEP.
IF IT WASN'T FOR THE FLIES.
PUMF
IF IT WASN'T FOR THE WHAT?

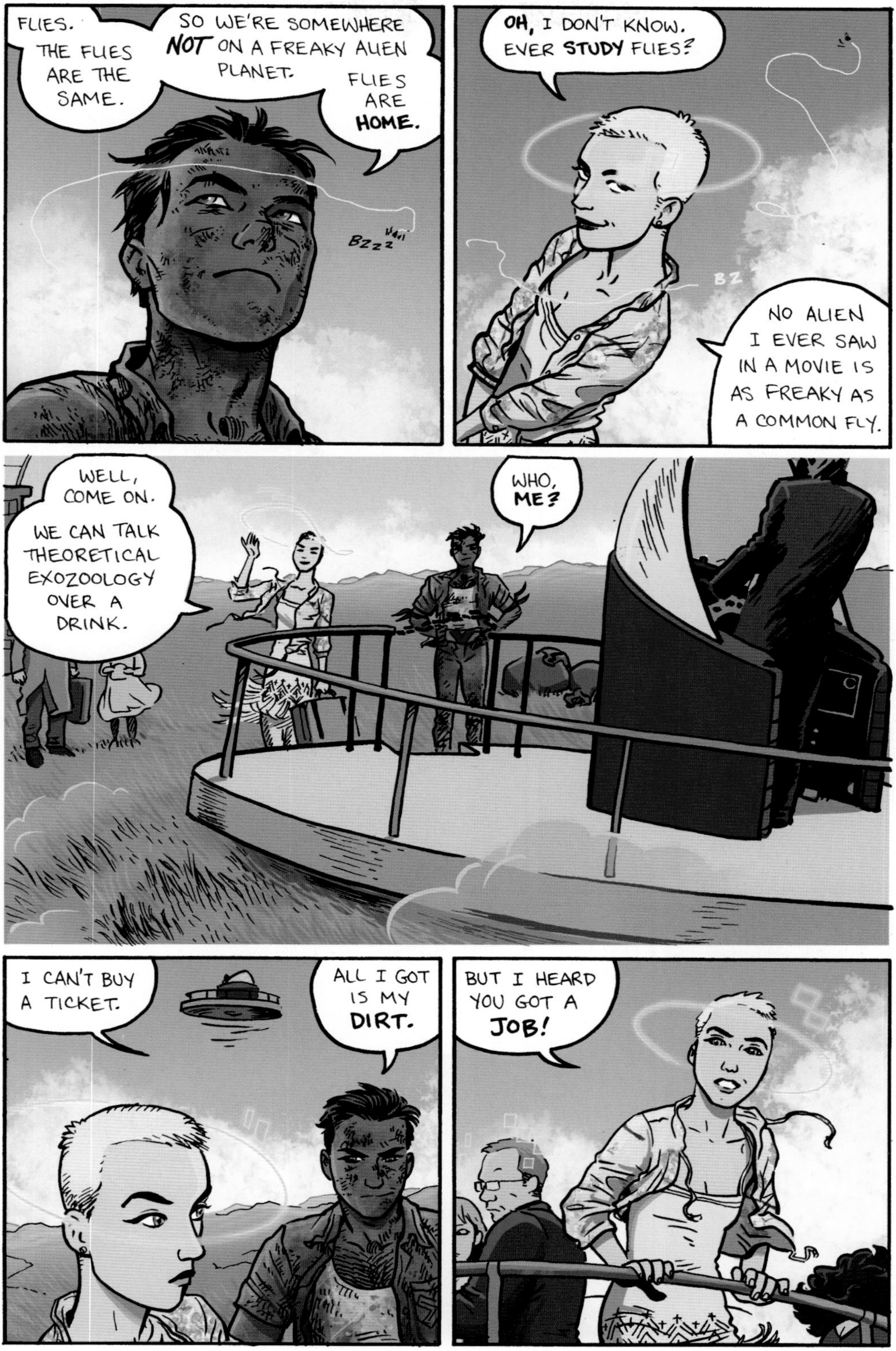

FLIES. THE FLIES ARE THE SAME.
SO WE'RE SOMEWHERE NOT ON A FREAKY ALIEN PLANET.
FLIES ARE HOME.
BZZZ
OH, I DON'T KNOW. EVER STUDY FLIES?
BZ
NO ALIEN I EVER SAW IN A MOVIE IS AS FREAKY AS A COMMON FLY.
WELL, COME ON.
WE CAN TALK THEORETICAL EXOZOOLOGY OVER A DRINK.
WHO, ME?
I CAN'T BUY A TICKET.
ALL I GOT IS MY DIRT.
BUT I HEARD YOU GOT A JOB!

I KNOW IT'S CRAZY, BUT THE LATEST SCIENTIFIC DATA SUGGEST YOU CAN HAVE A JOB AND **STILL** BE **BROKE!**

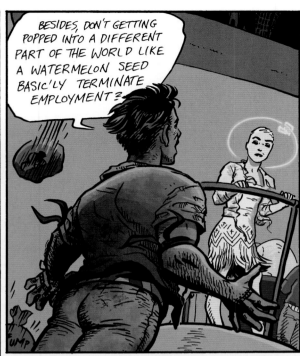

BESIDES, DON'T GETTING POPPED INTO A DIFFERENT PART OF THE WORLD LIKE A WATERMELON SEED BASIC'LY TERMINATE EMPLOYMENT?

WHRUMMMM

SURF...

HEY!

GRAB IT AND COME **ON!**

HUH?

YOU FROM RAY'S COURIERS, RIGHT?

ROY G. TRANSPORT

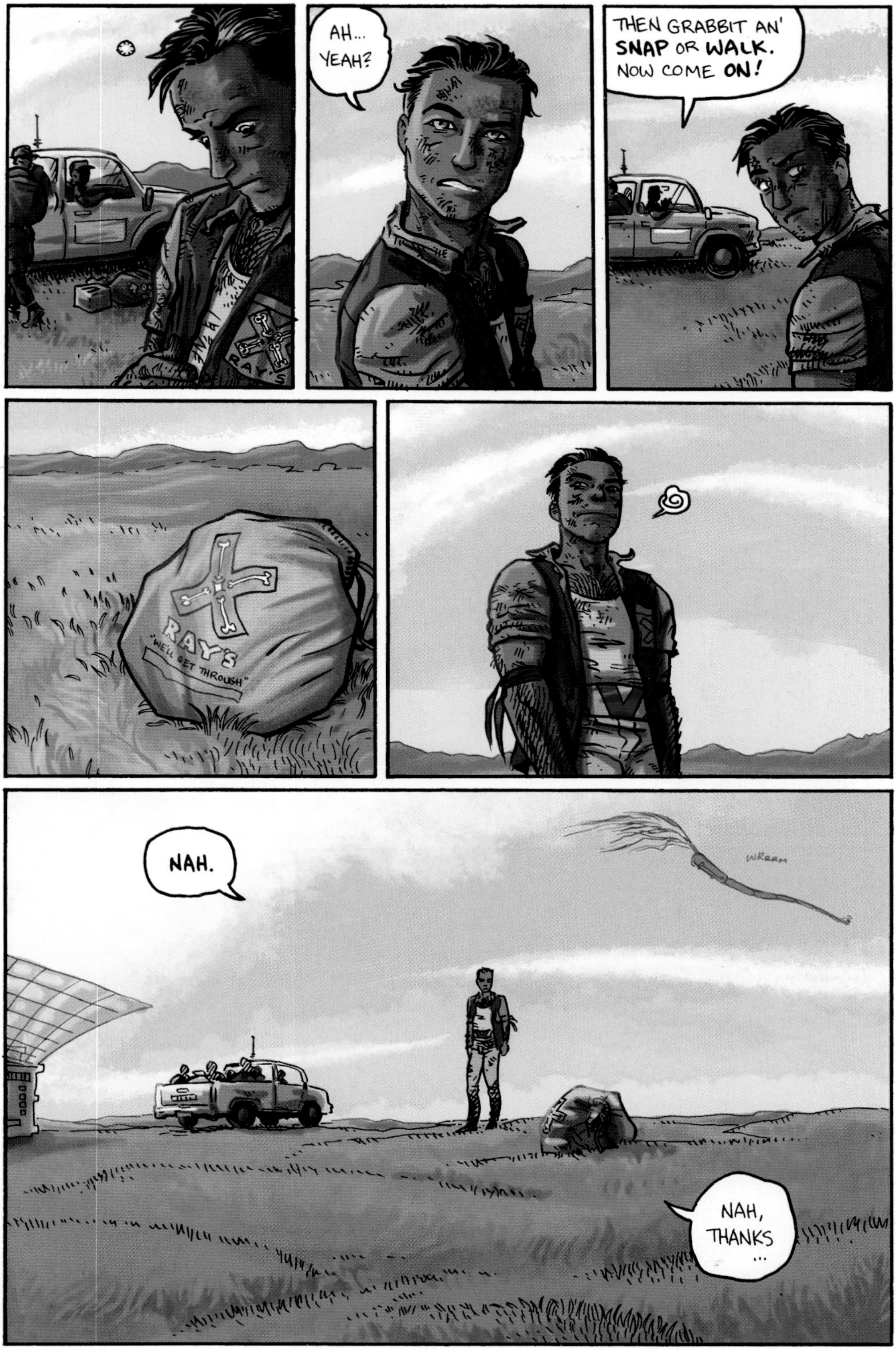

RAY'S
AH... YEAH?
THEN GRABBIT AN' SNAP OR WALK. NOW COME ON!
RAY'S
"WE'LL GET THROUGH"
NAH.
WRRRM
NAH, THANKS ...

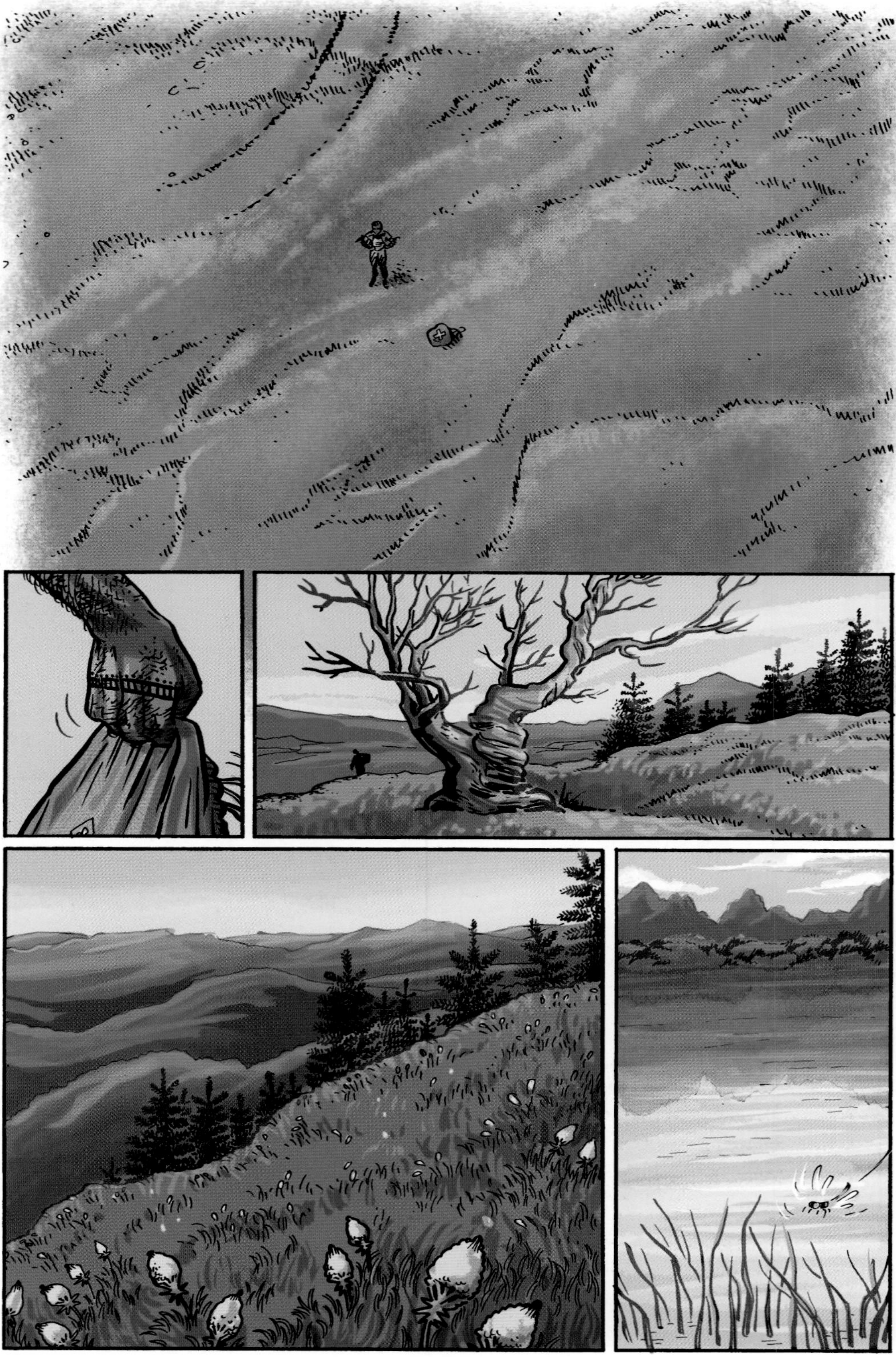

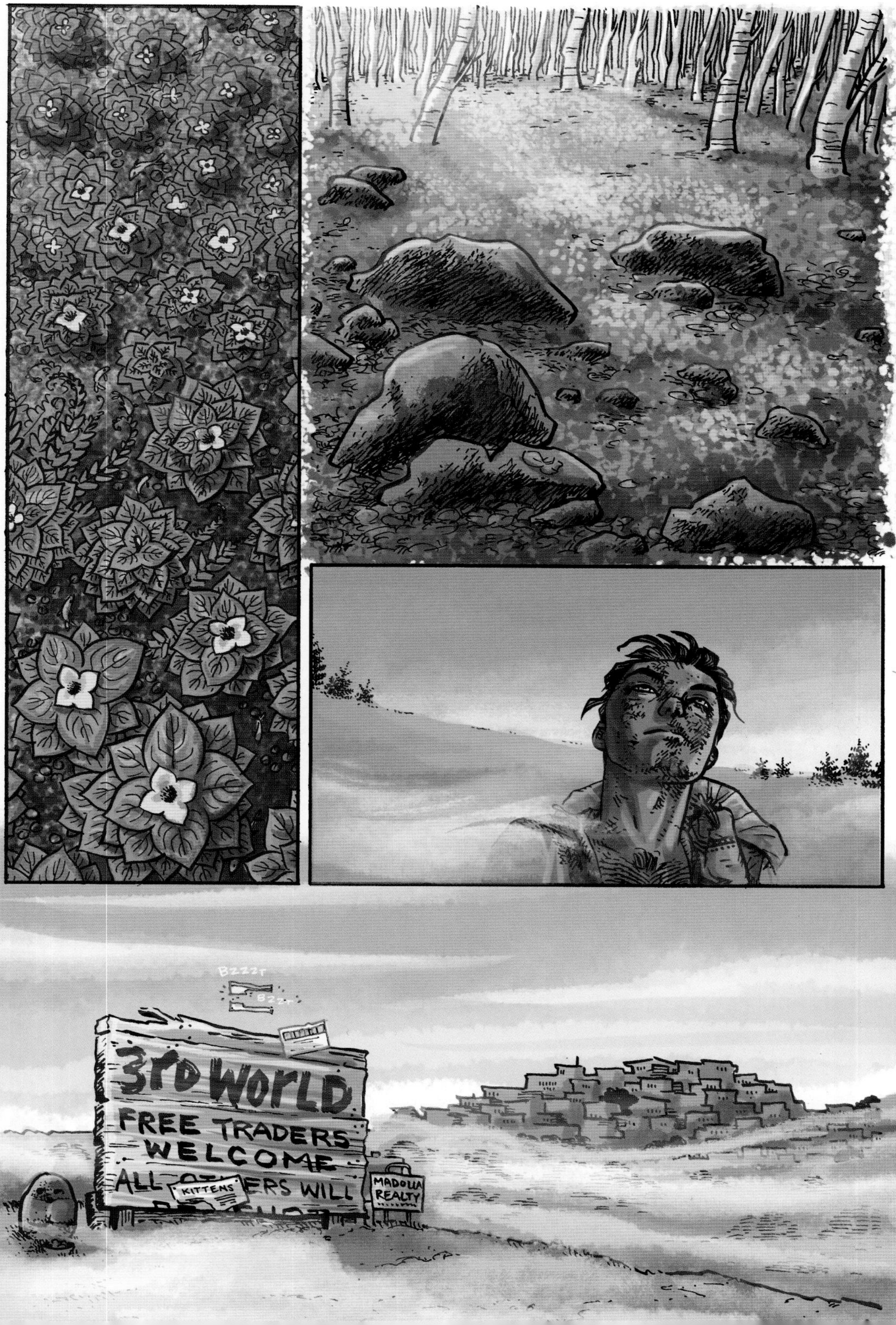
BZZZT
BZZT
3rD WorLD
FREE TRADERS
WELCOME
ALL
KITTENS
ERS WILL
MADOLIA
REALTY

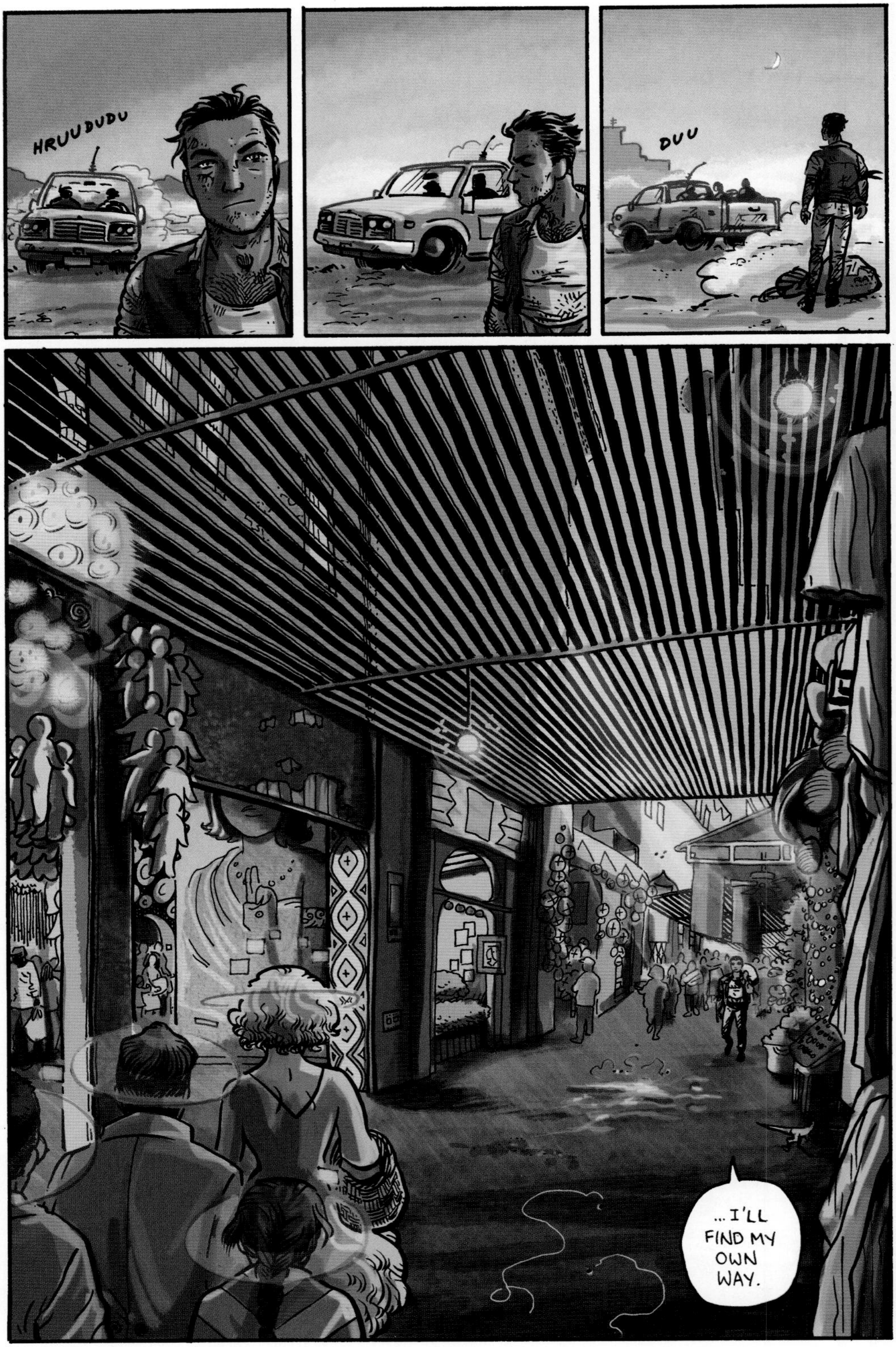
HRUUDUDU
DUU
...I'LL FIND MY OWN WAY.

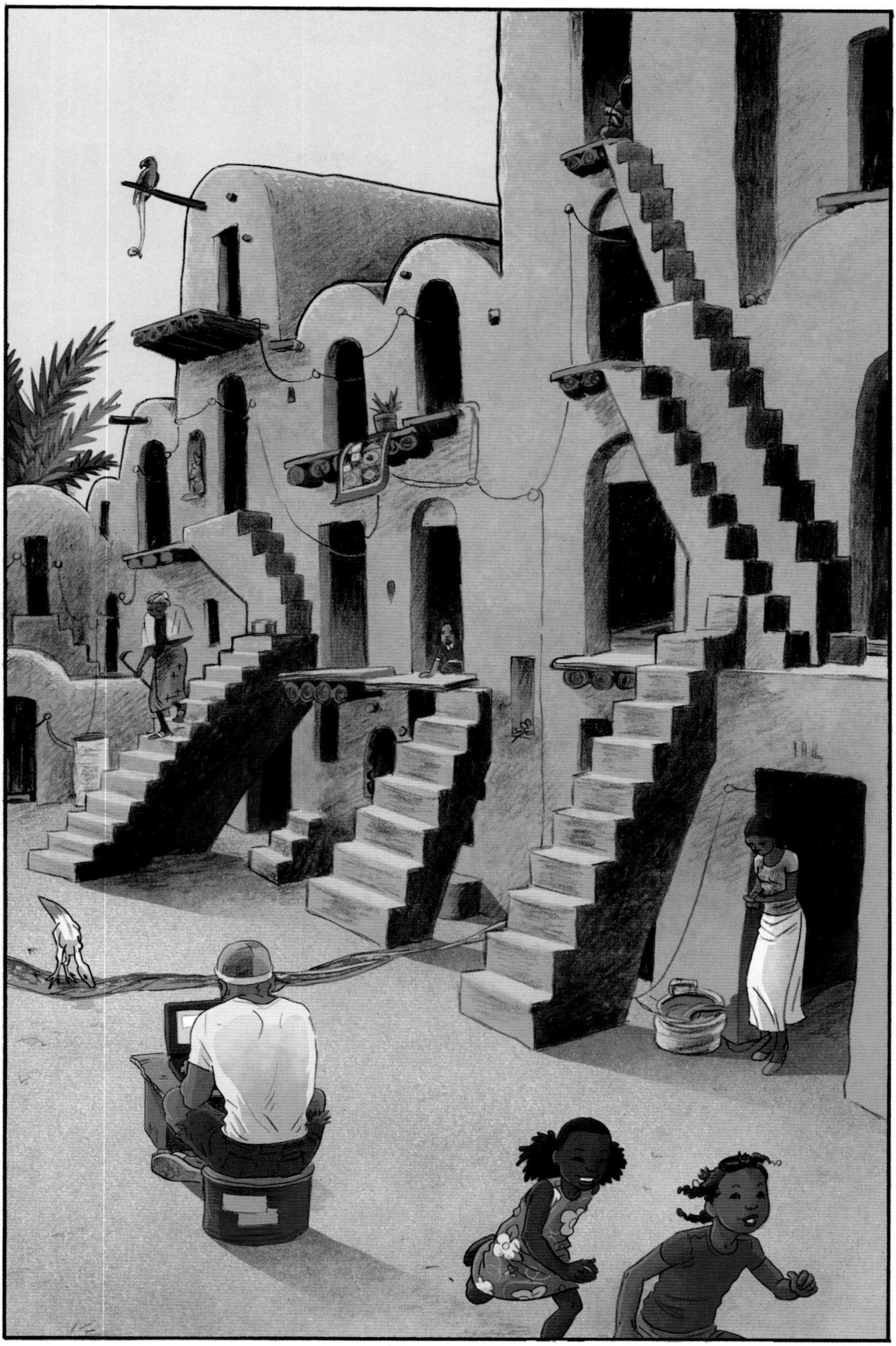

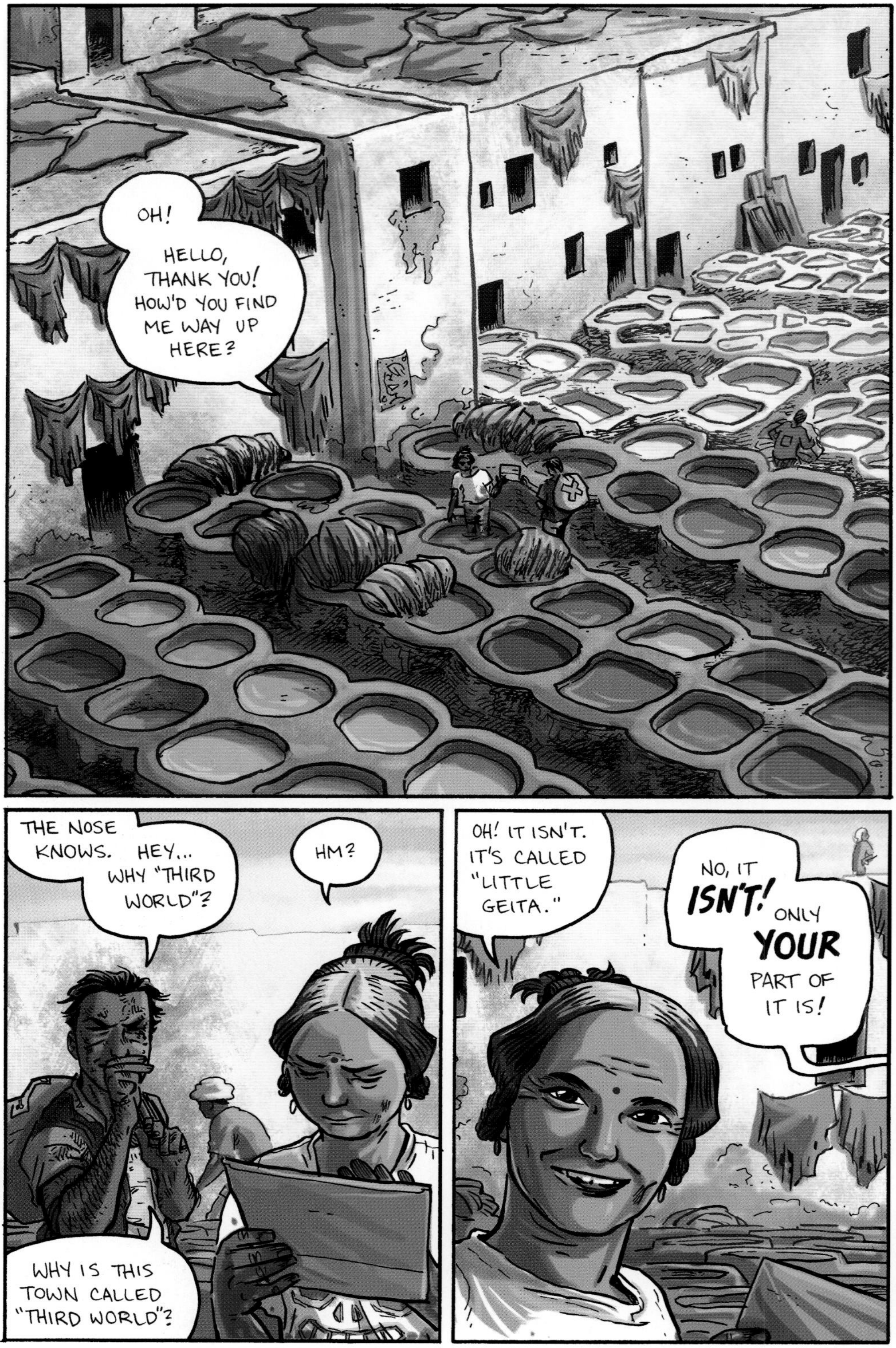
OH!
HELLO, THANK YOU! HOW'D YOU FIND ME WAY UP HERE?
THE NOSE KNOWS. HEY... WHY "THIRD WORLD"?
HM?
WHY IS THIS TOWN CALLED "THIRD WORLD"?
OH! IT ISN'T. IT'S CALLED "LITTLE GEITA."
NO, IT **ISN'T!** ONLY **YOUR** PART OF IT IS!

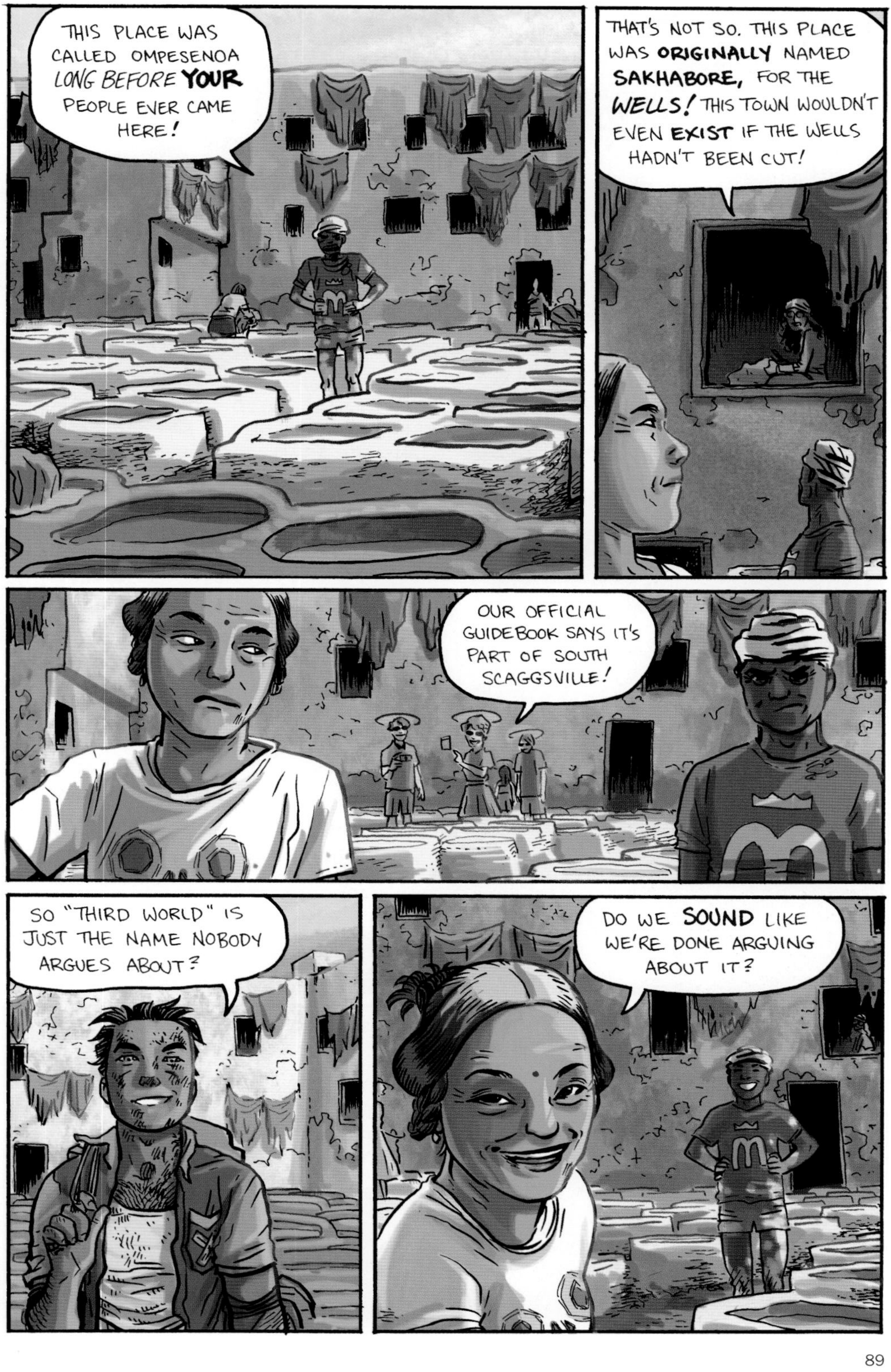
THIS PLACE WAS CALLED OMPESENOA *LONG BEFORE* **YOUR** PEOPLE EVER CAME HERE!
THAT'S NOT SO. THIS PLACE WAS **ORIGINALLY** NAMED **SAKHABORE,** FOR THE **WELLS!** THIS TOWN WOULDN'T EVEN **EXIST** IF THE WELLS HADN'T BEEN CUT!
OUR OFFICIAL GUIDEBOOK SAYS IT'S PART OF SOUTH SCAGGSVILLE!
SO "THIRD WORLD" IS JUST THE NAME NOBODY ARGUES ABOUT?
DO WE **SOUND** LIKE WE'RE DONE ARGUING ABOUT IT?

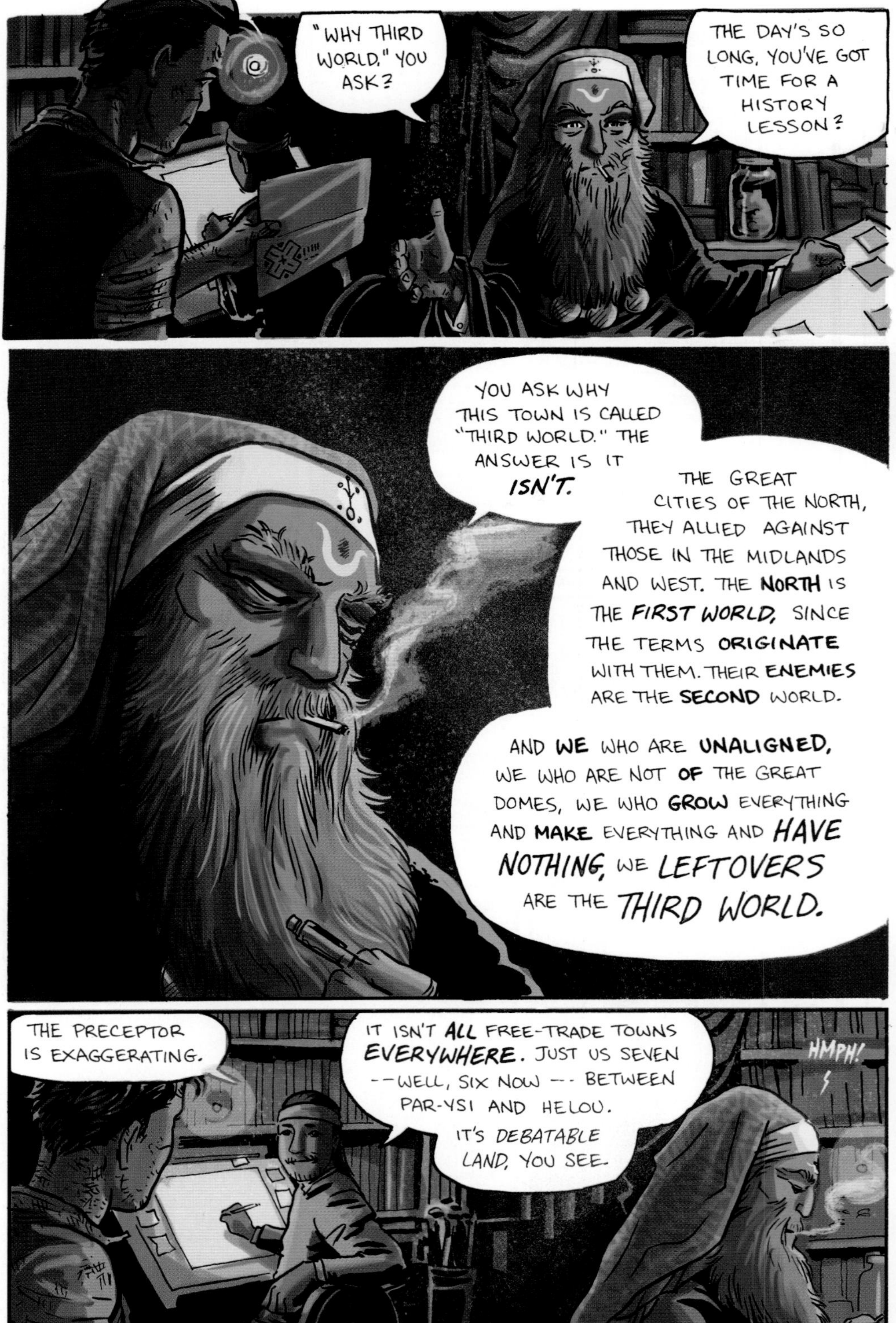
"WHY THIRD WORLD," YOU ASK?
THE DAY'S SO LONG, YOU'VE GOT TIME FOR A HISTORY LESSON?
YOU ASK WHY THIS TOWN IS CALLED "THIRD WORLD." THE ANSWER IS IT ISN'T.
THE GREAT CITIES OF THE NORTH, THEY ALLIED AGAINST THOSE IN THE MIDLANDS AND WEST. THE NORTH IS THE FIRST WORLD, SINCE THE TERMS ORIGINATE WITH THEM. THEIR ENEMIES ARE THE SECOND WORLD.
AND WE WHO ARE UNALIGNED, WE WHO ARE NOT OF THE GREAT DOMES, WE WHO GROW EVERYTHING AND MAKE EVERYTHING AND HAVE NOTHING, WE LEFTOVERS ARE THE THIRD WORLD.
THE PRECEPTOR IS EXAGGERATING.
IT ISN'T ALL FREE-TRADE TOWNS EVERYWHERE. JUST US SEVEN --WELL, SIX NOW -- BETWEEN PAR-YSI AND HELOU.
IT'S DEBATABLE LAND, YOU SEE.
HMPH!

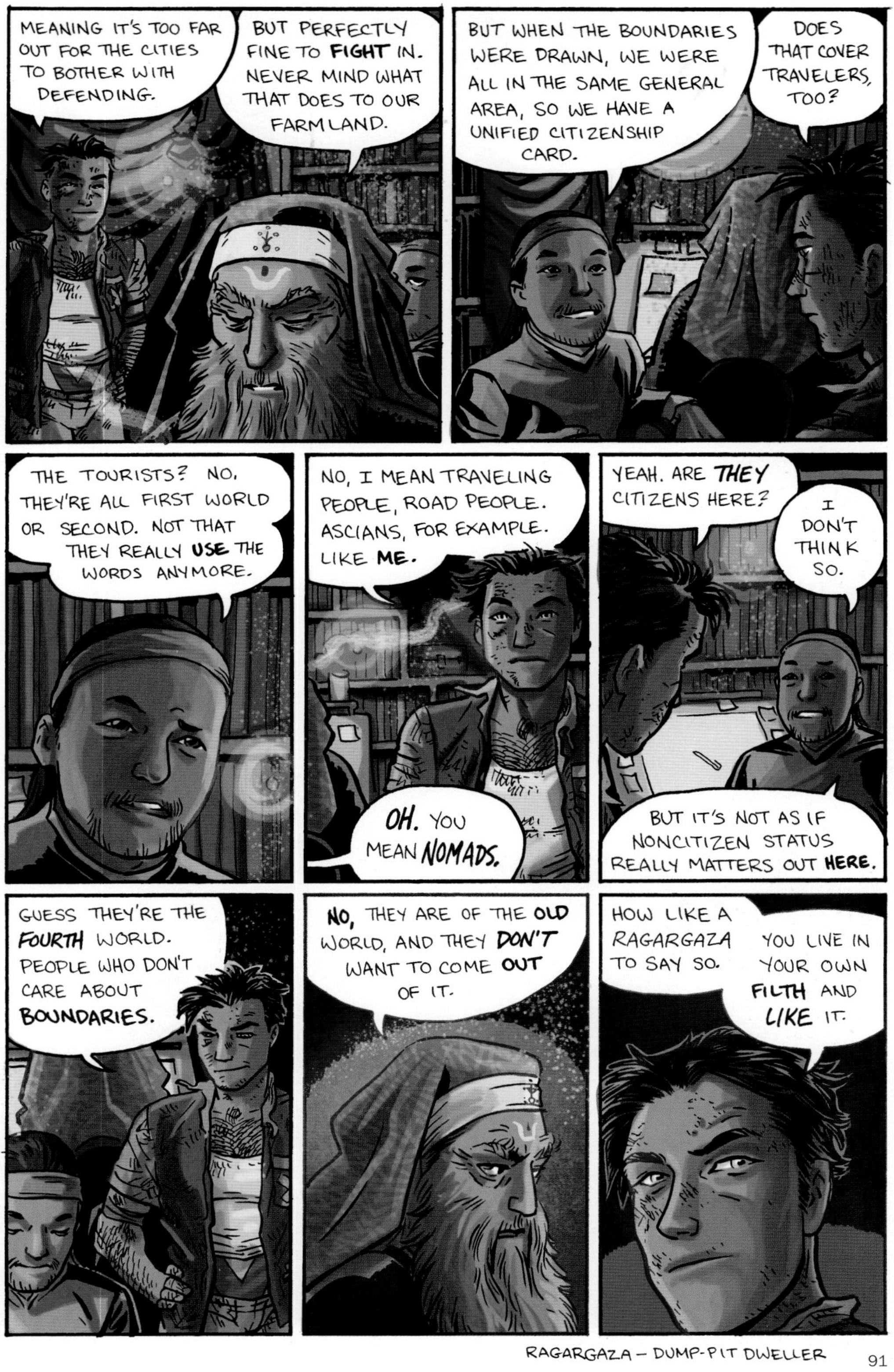
MEANING IT'S TOO FAR OUT FOR THE CITIES TO BOTHER WITH DEFENDING.
BUT PERFECTLY FINE TO **FIGHT** IN. NEVER MIND WHAT THAT DOES TO OUR FARMLAND.
BUT WHEN THE BOUNDARIES WERE DRAWN, WE WERE ALL IN THE SAME GENERAL AREA, SO WE HAVE A UNIFIED CITIZENSHIP CARD.
DOES THAT COVER TRAVELERS, TOO?
THE TOURISTS? NO. THEY'RE ALL FIRST WORLD OR SECOND. NOT THAT THEY REALLY **USE** THE WORDS ANYMORE.
NO, I MEAN TRAVELING PEOPLE, ROAD PEOPLE. ASCIANS, FOR EXAMPLE. LIKE **ME**.
OH. YOU MEAN **NOMADS.**
YEAH. ARE **THEY** CITIZENS HERE?
I DON'T THINK SO.
BUT IT'S NOT AS IF NONCITIZEN STATUS REALLY MATTERS OUT **HERE**.
GUESS THEY'RE THE **FOURTH** WORLD. PEOPLE WHO DON'T CARE ABOUT **BOUNDARIES.**
NO, THEY ARE OF THE **OLD** WORLD, AND THEY **DON'T** WANT TO COME **OUT** OF IT.
HOW LIKE A *RAGARGAZA* TO SAY SO.
YOU LIVE IN YOUR OWN **FILTH** AND **LIKE** IT.

RAGARGAZA — DUMP-PIT DWELLER

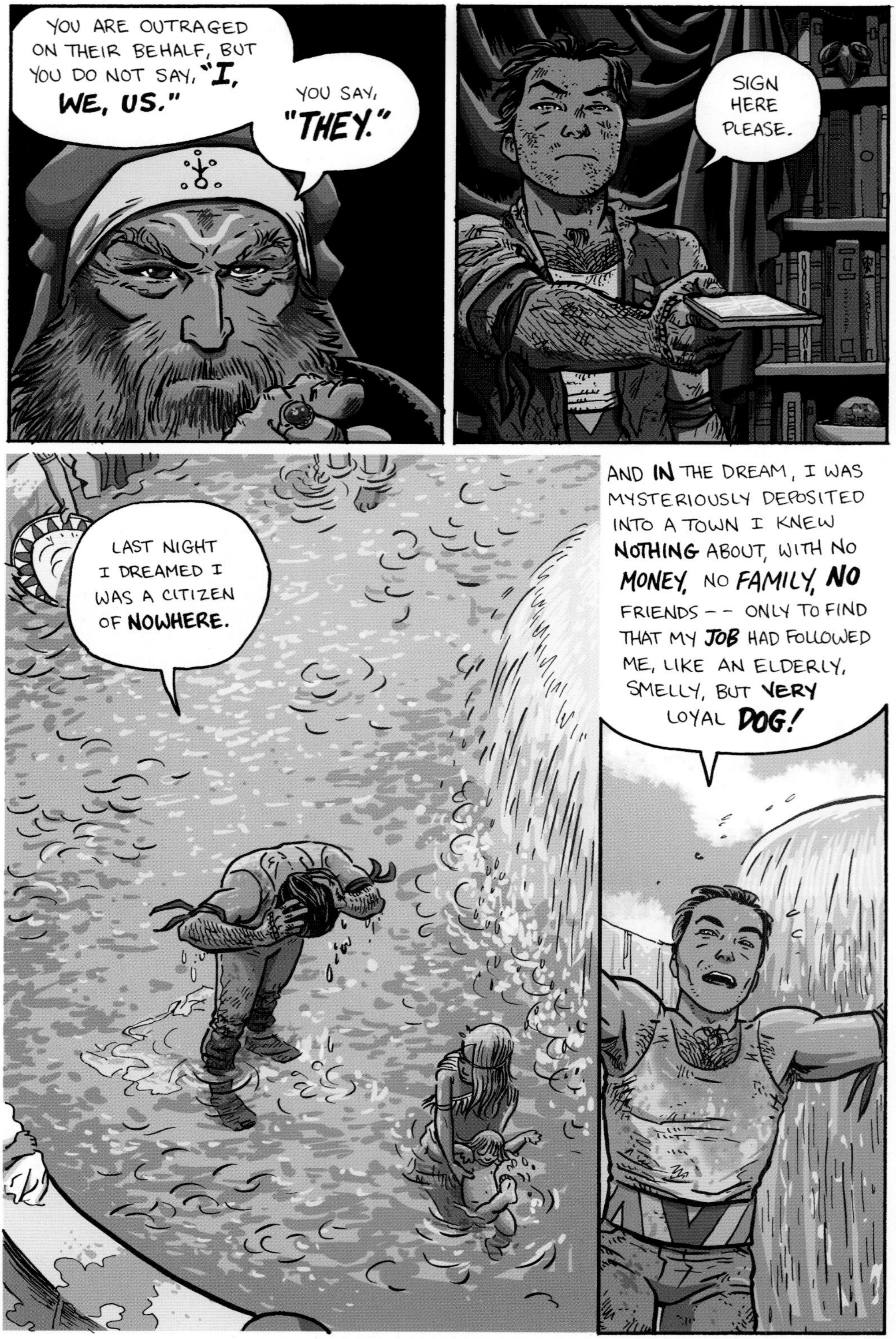
YOU ARE OUTRAGED ON THEIR BEHALF, BUT YOU DO NOT SAY, "I, WE, US."
YOU SAY, "THEY."
SIGN HERE PLEASE.
LAST NIGHT I DREAMED I WAS A CITIZEN OF NOWHERE.
AND IN THE DREAM, I WAS MYSTERIOUSLY DEPOSITED INTO A TOWN I KNEW NOTHING ABOUT, WITH NO MONEY, NO FAMILY, NO FRIENDS -- ONLY TO FIND THAT MY JOB HAD FOLLOWED ME, LIKE AN ELDERLY, SMELLY, BUT VERY LOYAL DOG!

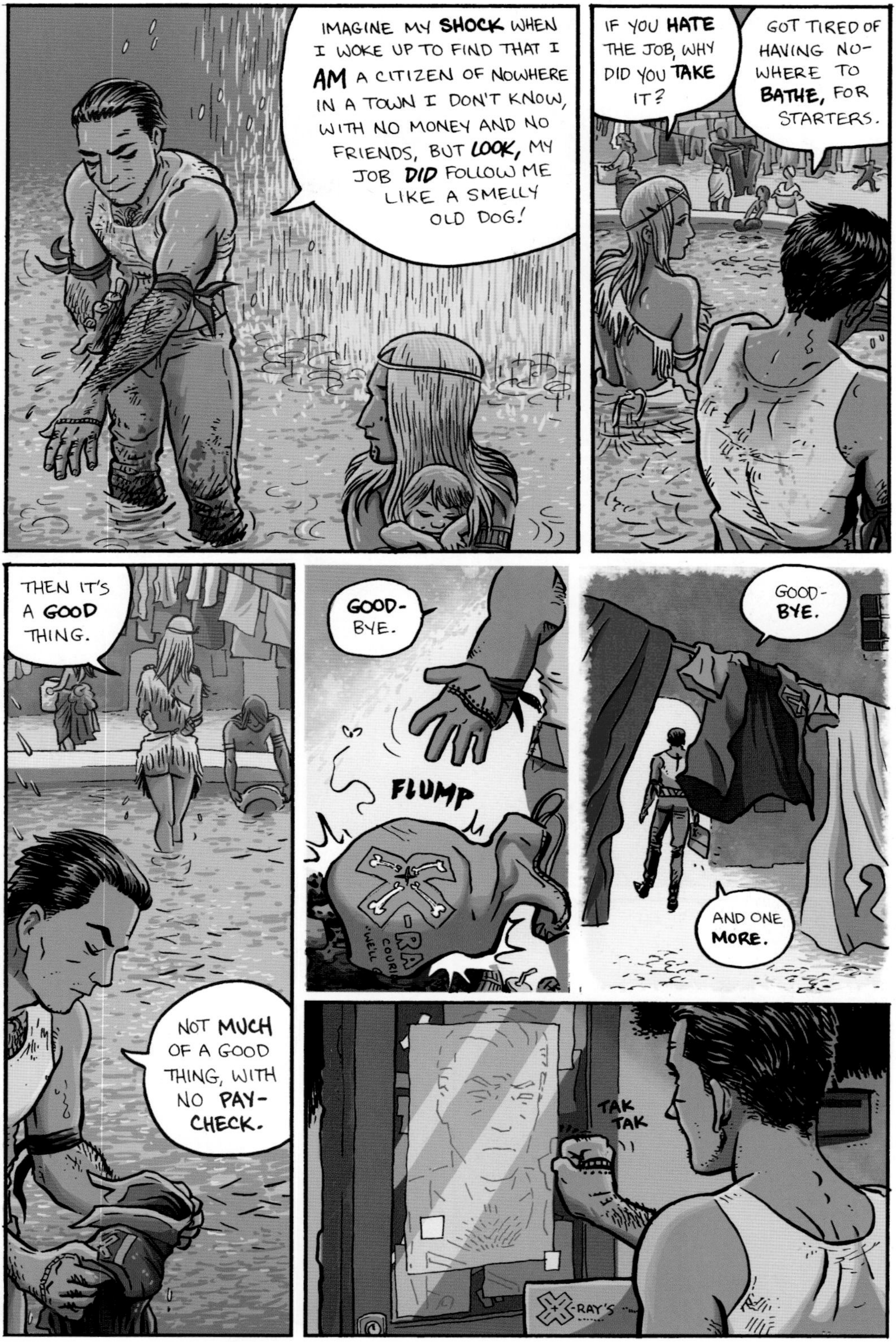
IMAGINE MY SHOCK WHEN I WOKE UP TO FIND THAT I AM A CITIZEN OF NOWHERE IN A TOWN I DON'T KNOW, WITH NO MONEY AND NO FRIENDS, BUT LOOK, MY JOB DID FOLLOW ME LIKE A SMELLY OLD DOG!
IF YOU HATE THE JOB, WHY DID YOU TAKE IT?
GOT TIRED OF HAVING NO-WHERE TO BATHE, FOR STARTERS.
THEN IT'S A GOOD THING.
NOT MUCH OF A GOOD THING, WITH NO PAY-CHECK.
GOOD-BYE.
FLUMP
GOOD-BYE.
AND ONE MORE.
TAK TAK
RAY'S

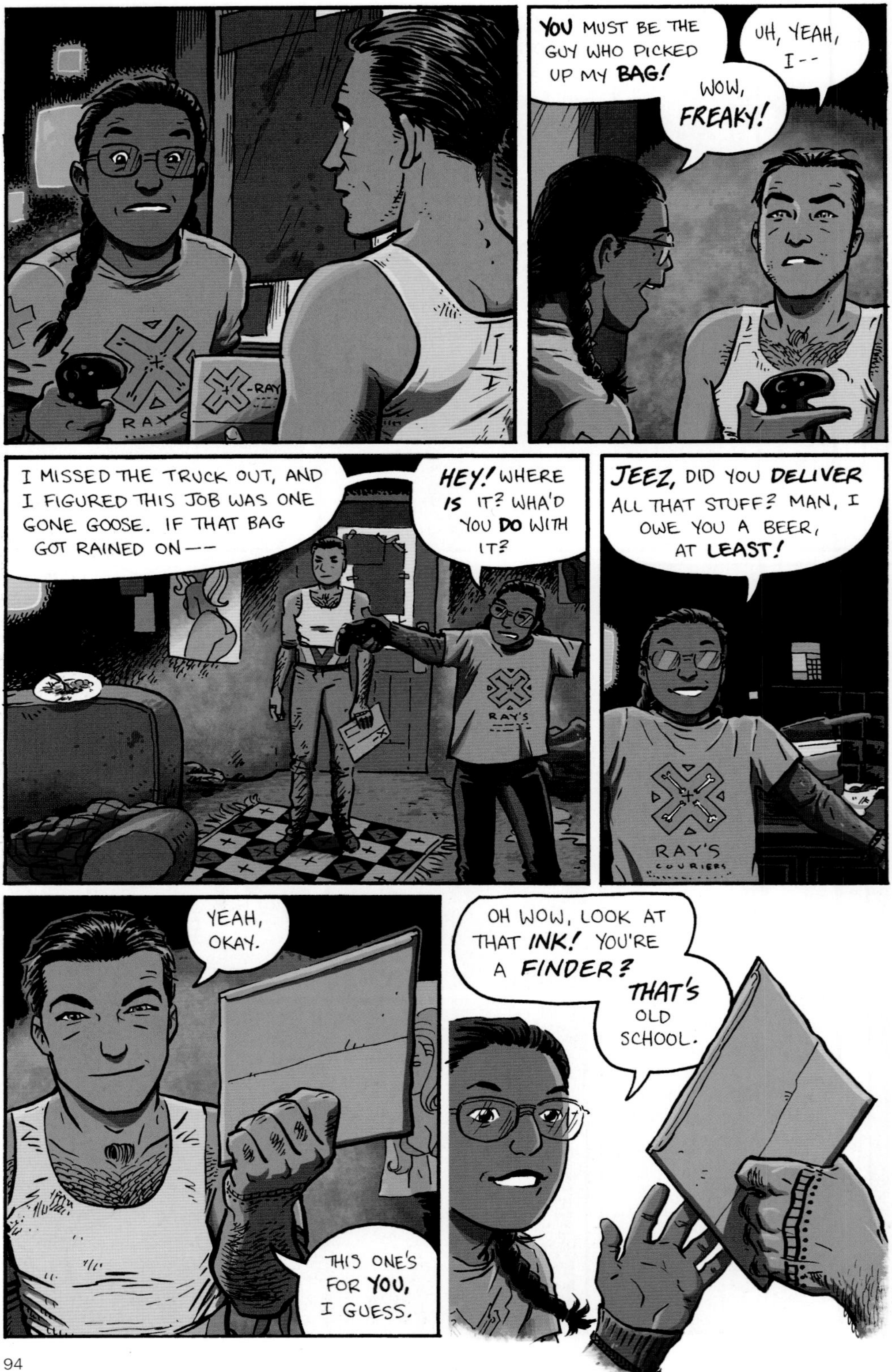
RAY'S
YOU MUST BE THE GUY WHO PICKED UP MY BAG!
UH, YEAH, I--
WOW, FREAKY!
I MISSED THE TRUCK OUT, AND I FIGURED THIS JOB WAS ONE GONE GOOSE. IF THAT BAG GOT RAINED ON--
HEY! WHERE IS IT? WHA'D YOU DO WITH IT?
RAY'S
JEEZ, DID YOU DELIVER ALL THAT STUFF? MAN, I OWE YOU A BEER, AT LEAST!
RAY'S COURIERS
YEAH, OKAY.
THIS ONE'S FOR YOU, I GUESS.
OH WOW, LOOK AT THAT INK! YOU'RE A FINDER? THAT'S OLD SCHOOL.

I'M SALJUDUMI TRIBE. WHO **YOU** FROM?

OH. NORTHERN ANEMOI. ADOPTED.

I **FIGURED**, YOU'RE SUCH A **BEAR**. LONG WAY FROM HOME!

AND YOU'RE **NOT?** WHERE THE HELL **ARE** WE, ANYWAY?

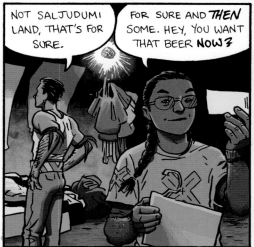

NOT SALJUDUMI LAND, THAT'S FOR SURE.

FOR SURE AND **THEN** SOME. HEY, YOU WANT THAT BEER **NOW?**

'CAUSE I GOT TO GET TO THE BANK WITH **THIS.**

IS THAT A **PAYCHECK?**

FOR **THAT** JOB?

YOU KNOW, THE JOB **I DID?**

OH YOU **BETTER** RUN, YC

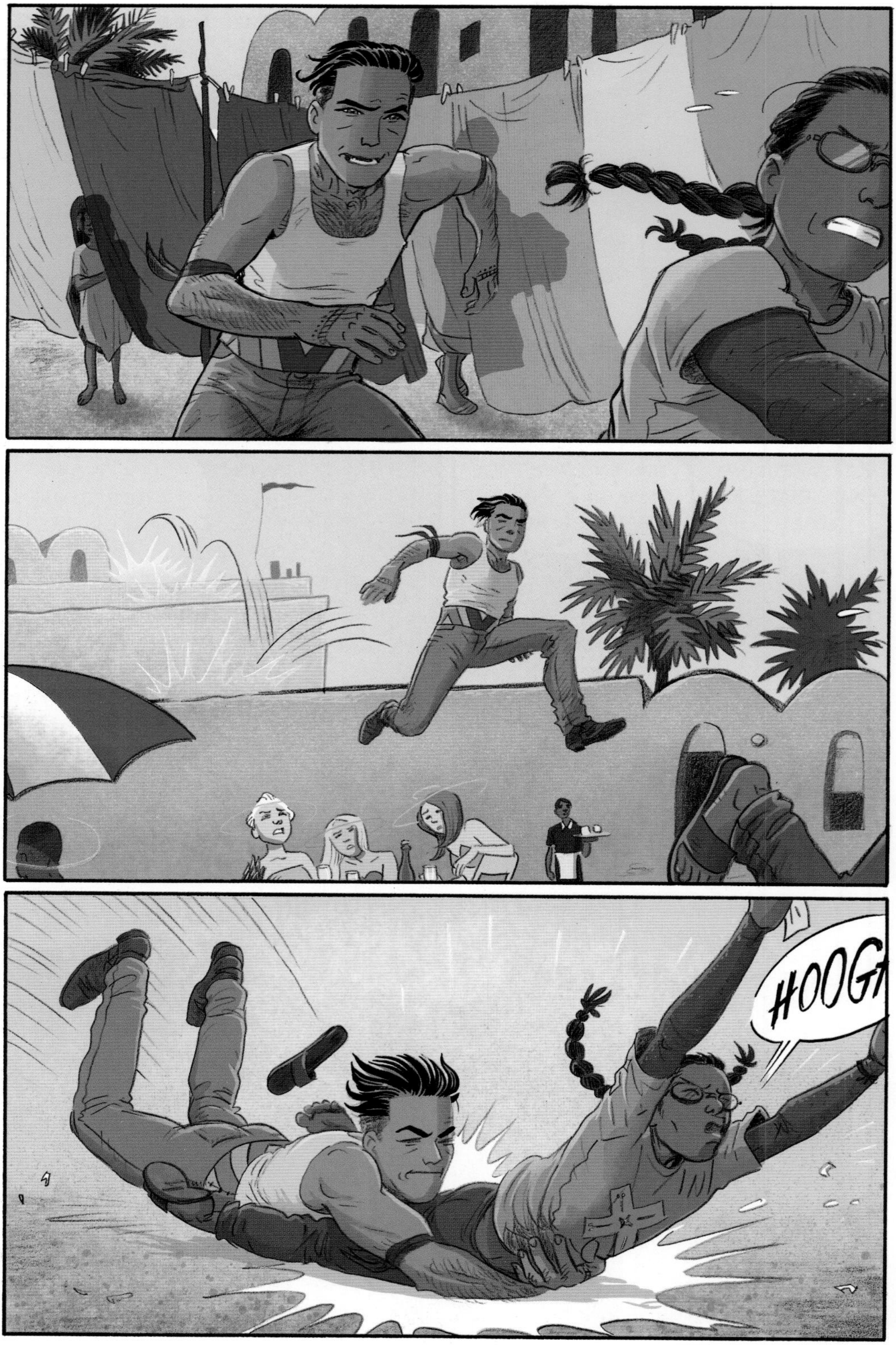
HOOG

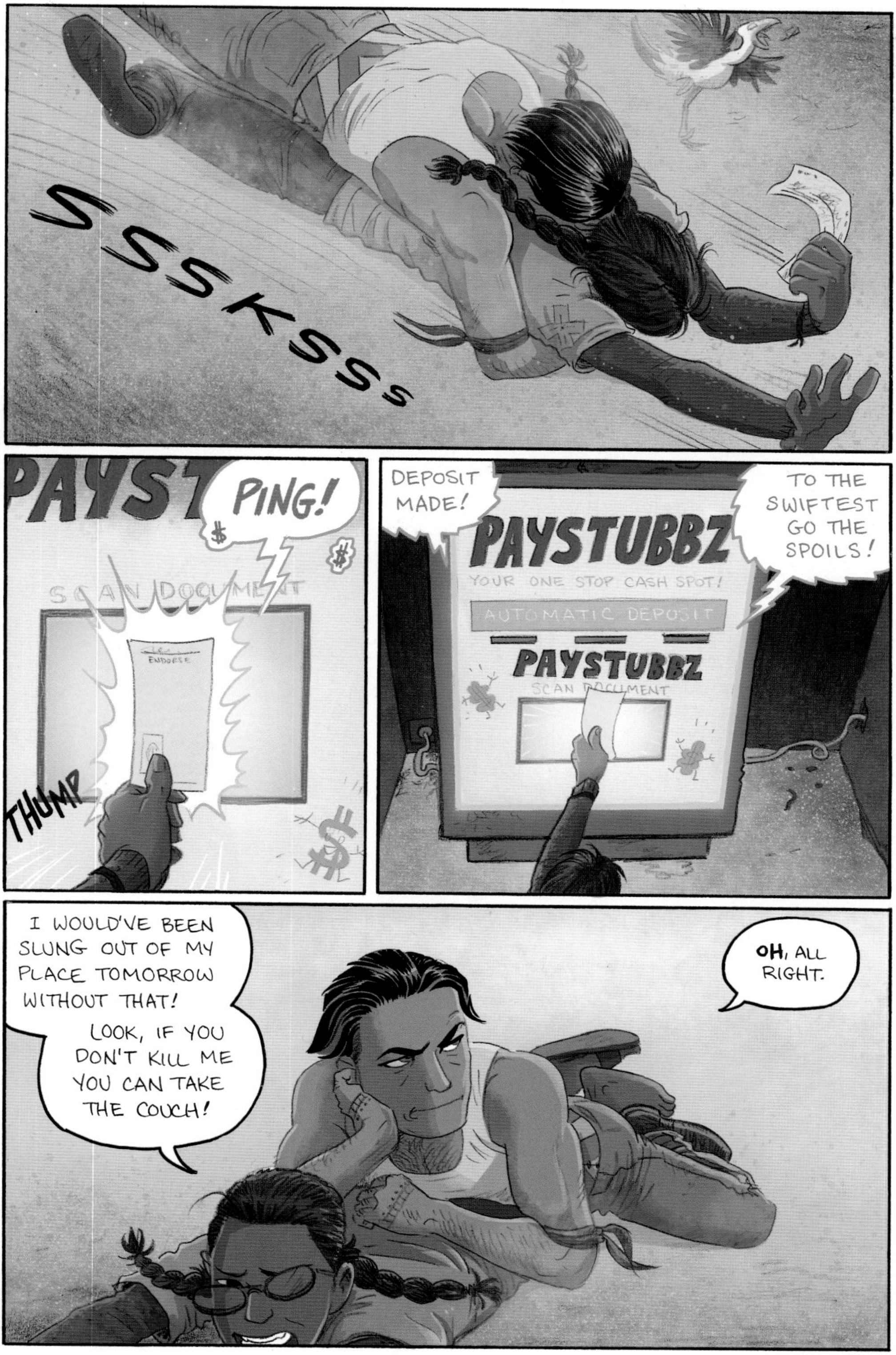
SSSKSSSs
PAYST
PING!
SCAN DOCUMENT
ENDORSE
THUMP
DEPOSIT MADE!
PAYSTUBBZ
YOUR ONE STOP CASH SPOT!
AUTOMATIC DEPOSIT
PAYSTUBBZ
SCAN DOCUMENT
TO THE SWIFTEST GO THE SPOILS!
I WOULD'VE BEEN SLUNG OUT OF MY PLACE TOMORROW WITHOUT THAT!
LOOK, IF YOU DON'T KILL ME YOU CAN TAKE THE COUCH!
OH, ALL RIGHT.

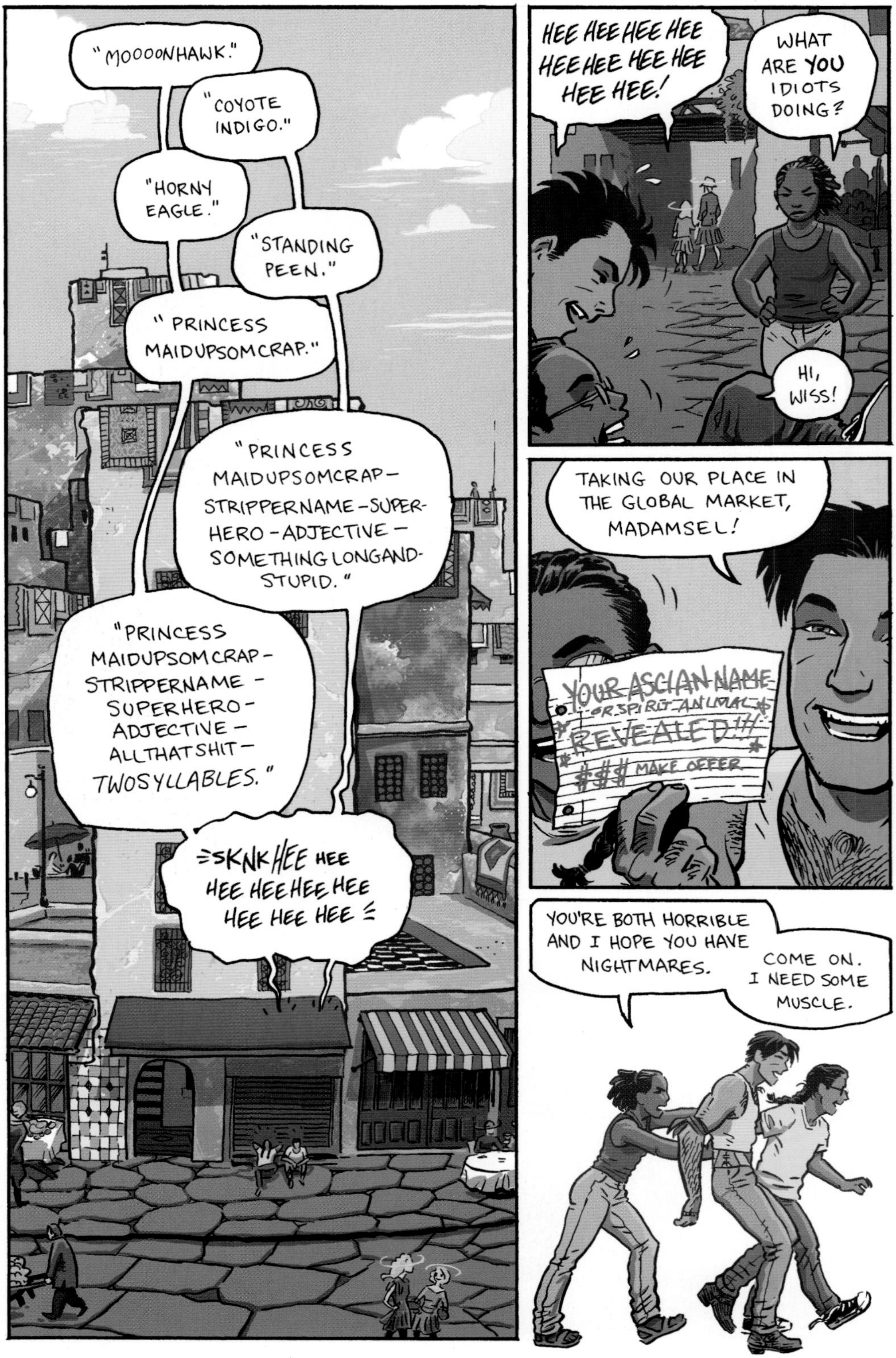
"MOOOONHAWK."
"COYOTE INDIGO."
"HORNY EAGLE."
"STANDING PEEN."
"PRINCESS MAIDUPSOMCRAP."
"PRINCESS MAIDUPSOMCRAP-STRIPPERNAME-SUPER-HERO-ADJECTIVE-SOMETHINGLONGAND-STUPID."
"PRINCESS MAIDUPSOMCRAP-STRIPPERNAME-SUPERHERO-ADJECTIVE-ALLTHATSHIT-TWOSYLLABLES."
SKNK HEE HEE HEE HEE HEE HEE HEE HEE HEE
HEE HEE HEE HEE HEE HEE HEE HEE HEE HEE!
WHAT ARE YOU IDIOTS DOING?
HI, WISS!
TAKING OUR PLACE IN THE GLOBAL MARKET, MADAMSEL!
YOUR ASCIAN NAME
-OR SPIRIT ANIMAL-
REVEALED!!!
$$$ MAKE OFFER
YOU'RE BOTH HORRIBLE AND I HOPE YOU HAVE NIGHTMARES.
COME ON. I NEED SOME MUSCLE.

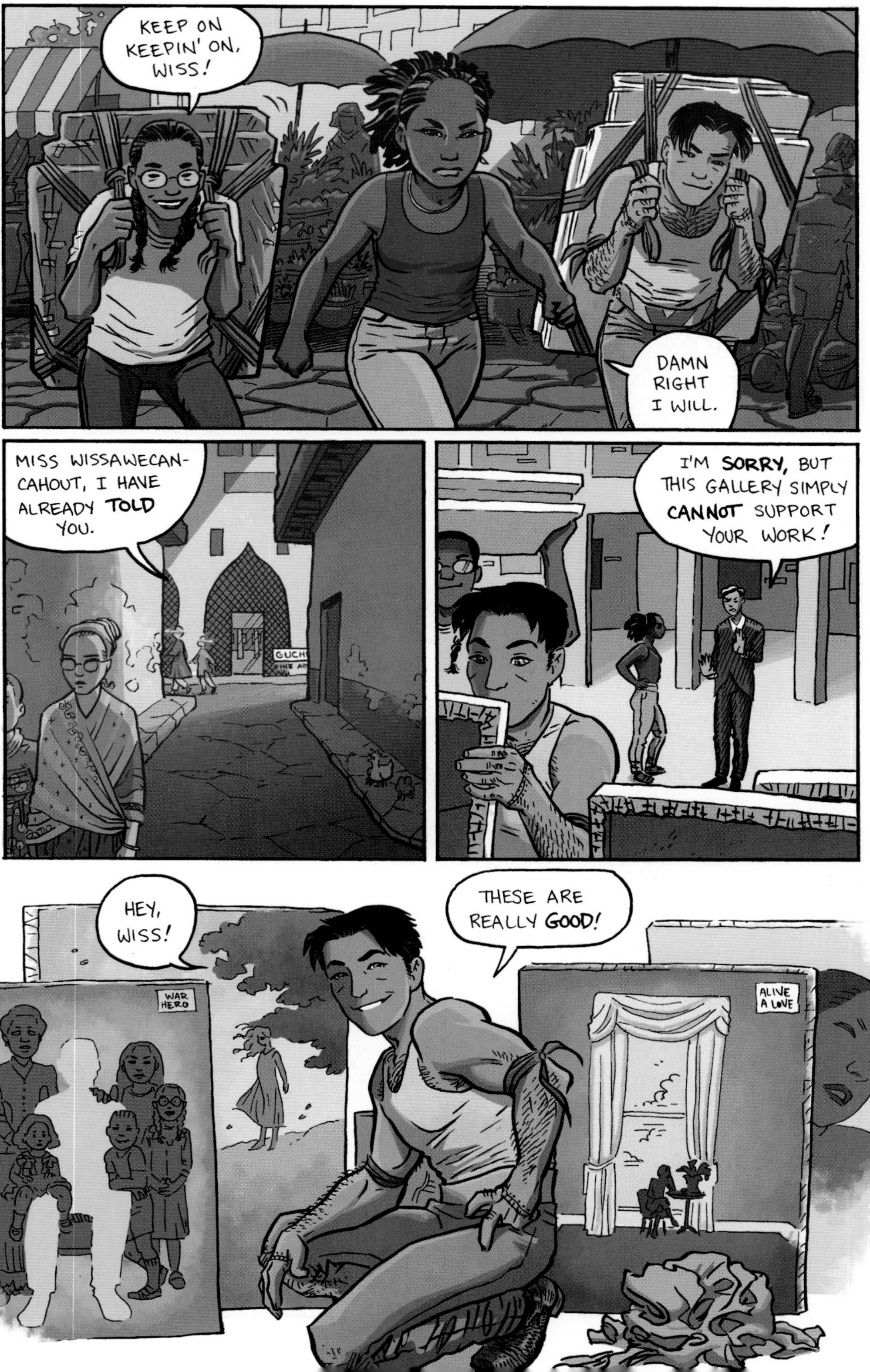
KEEP ON KEEPIN' ON, WISS!
DAMN RIGHT I WILL.
MISS WISSAWECAN-CAHOUT, I HAVE ALREADY **TOLD** YOU.
GUCH
I'M **SORRY,** BUT THIS GALLERY SIMPLY **CANNOT** SUPPORT YOUR WORK!
HEY, WISS!
THESE ARE REALLY **GOOD**!
WAR HERO
ALIVE A LOVE

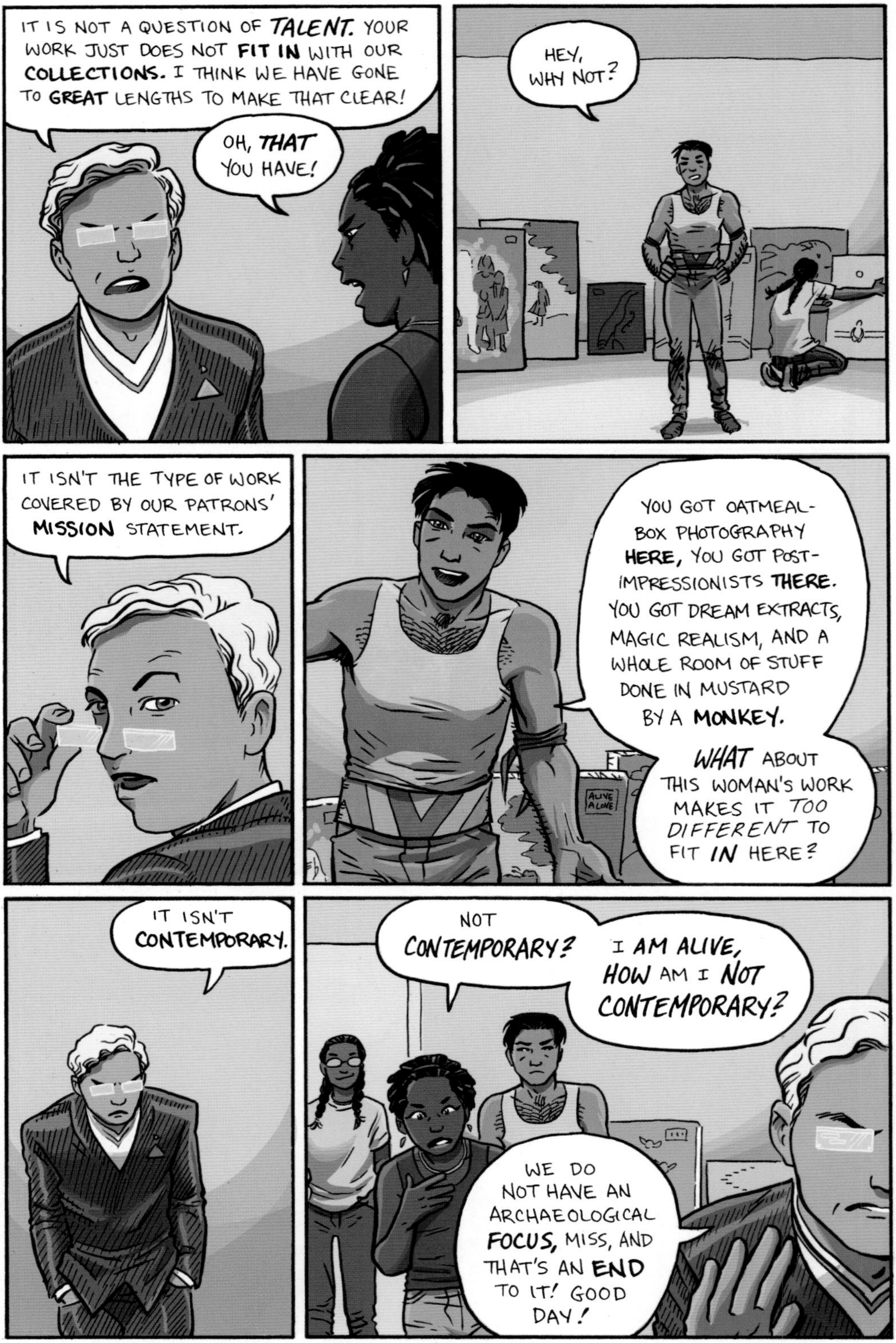
IT IS NOT A QUESTION OF TALENT. YOUR WORK JUST DOES NOT FIT IN WITH OUR COLLECTIONS. I THINK WE HAVE GONE TO GREAT LENGTHS TO MAKE THAT CLEAR!
OH, THAT YOU HAVE!
HEY, WHY NOT?
IT ISN'T THE TYPE OF WORK COVERED BY OUR PATRONS' MISSION STATEMENT.
YOU GOT OATMEAL-BOX PHOTOGRAPHY HERE, YOU GOT POST-IMPRESSIONISTS THERE. YOU GOT DREAM EXTRACTS, MAGIC REALISM, AND A WHOLE ROOM OF STUFF DONE IN MUSTARD BY A MONKEY.
WHAT ABOUT THIS WOMAN'S WORK MAKES IT TOO DIFFERENT TO FIT IN HERE?
ALIVE ALONE
IT ISN'T CONTEMPORARY.
NOT CONTEMPORARY?
I AM ALIVE, HOW AM I NOT CONTEMPORARY?
WE DO NOT HAVE AN ARCHAEOLOGICAL FOCUS, MISS, AND THAT'S AN END TO IT! GOOD DAY!

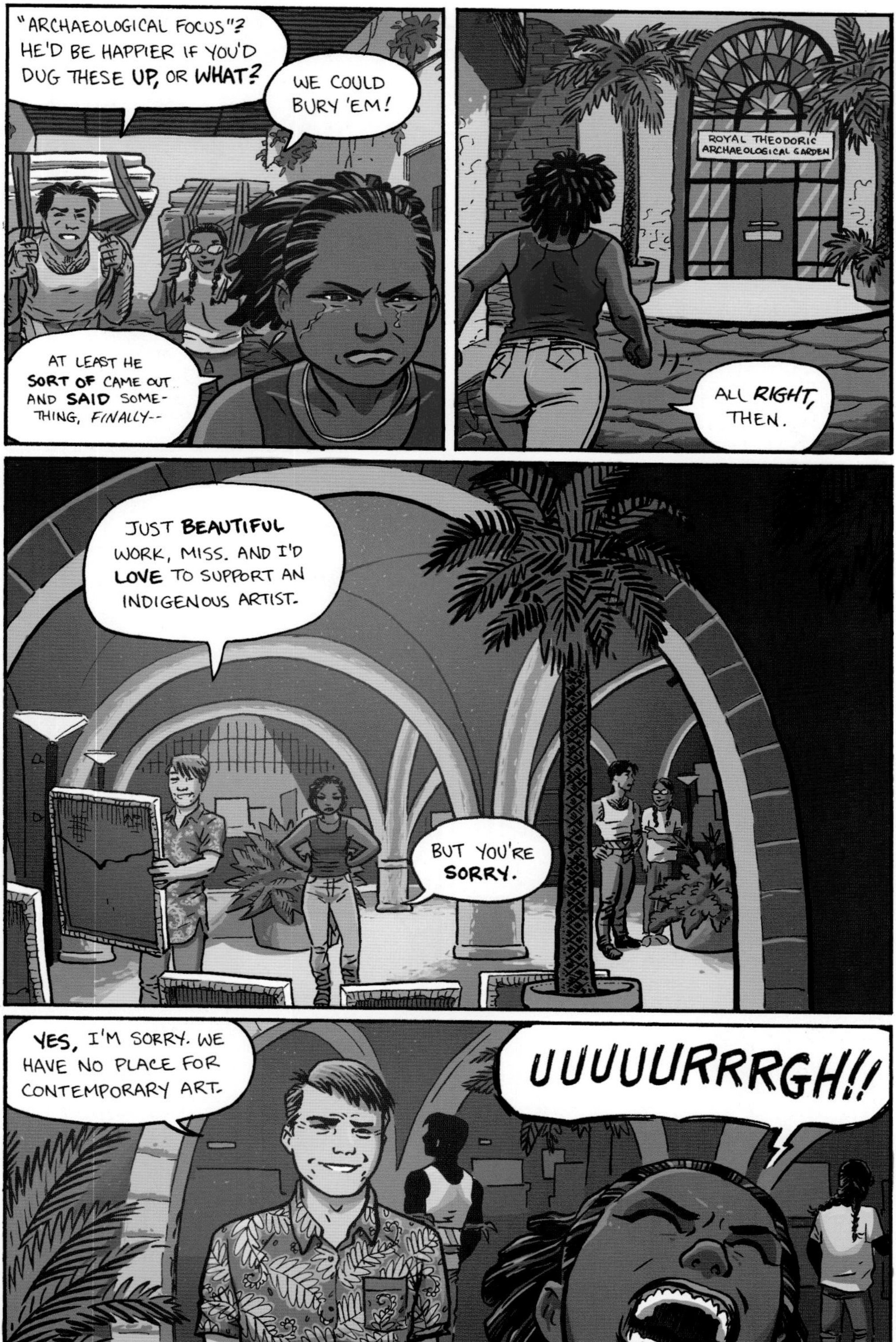
"ARCHAEOLOGICAL FOCUS"? HE'D BE HAPPIER IF YOU'D DUG THESE UP, OR WHAT?
WE COULD BURY 'EM!
AT LEAST HE SORT OF CAME OUT AND SAID SOME-THING, FINALLY--
ROYAL THEODORIC ARCHAEOLOGICAL GARDEN
ALL RIGHT, THEN.
JUST BEAUTIFUL WORK, MISS. AND I'D LOVE TO SUPPORT AN INDIGENOUS ARTIST.
BUT YOU'RE SORRY.
YES, I'M SORRY. WE HAVE NO PLACE FOR CONTEMPORARY ART.
UUUUUURRRGH!!

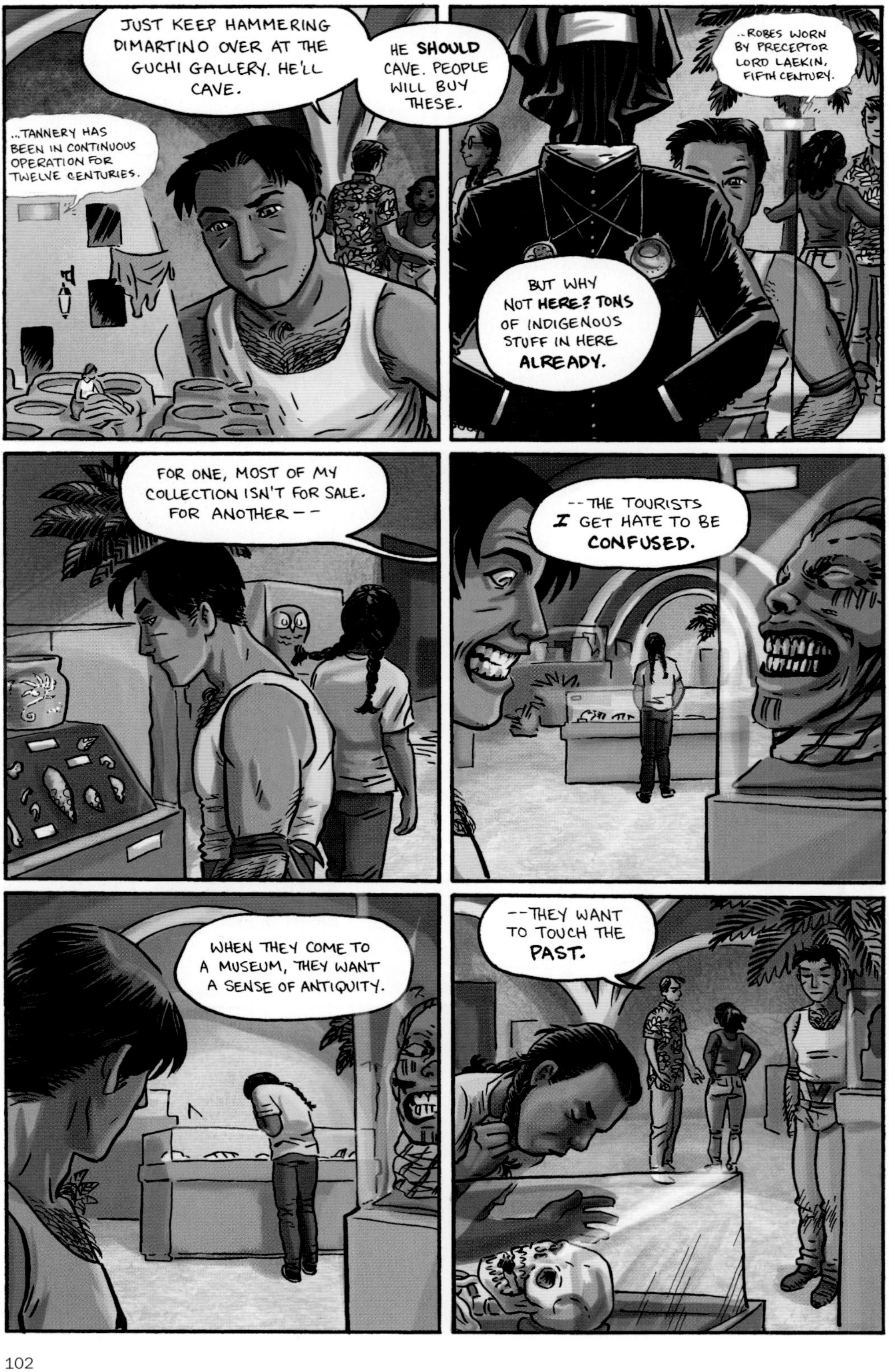
JUST KEEP HAMMERING DIMARTINO OVER AT THE GUCHI GALLERY. HE'LL CAVE.
HE **SHOULD** CAVE. PEOPLE WILL BUY THESE.
...TANNERY HAS BEEN IN CONTINUOUS OPERATION FOR TWELVE CENTURIES.
..ROBES WORN BY PRECEPTOR LORD LAEKIN, FIFTH CENTURY.
BUT WHY NOT **HERE?** TONS OF INDIGENOUS STUFF IN HERE **ALREADY.**
FOR ONE, MOST OF MY COLLECTION ISN'T FOR SALE. FOR ANOTHER--
--THE TOURISTS *I* GET HATE TO BE **CONFUSED.**
WHEN THEY COME TO A MUSEUM, THEY WANT A SENSE OF ANTIQUITY.
--THEY WANT TO TOUCH THE **PAST.**

REE REE REE REE

QUAIYESA, I'VE **ASKED** YOU NOT TO **DO** THAT.

YEAH, QUAIYESA. KISS AIN'T GONNA WAKE **THAT** ONE UP.

NO, BUT SHE KISSED **ME** EVERY NIGHT. LONG AFTER I WAS TOO OLD FOR IT. I'M JUST GIVING 'EM BACK.

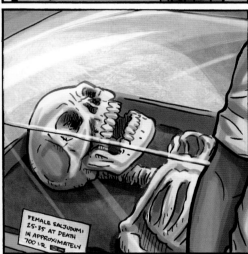

FEMALE SALJUDUM! 25-35 AT DEATH IN APPROXIMATELY 700 I.R.

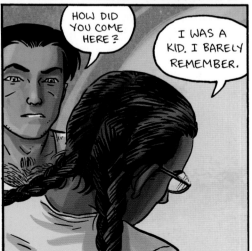

HOW DID YOU COME HERE?

I WAS A KID. I BARELY REMEMBER.

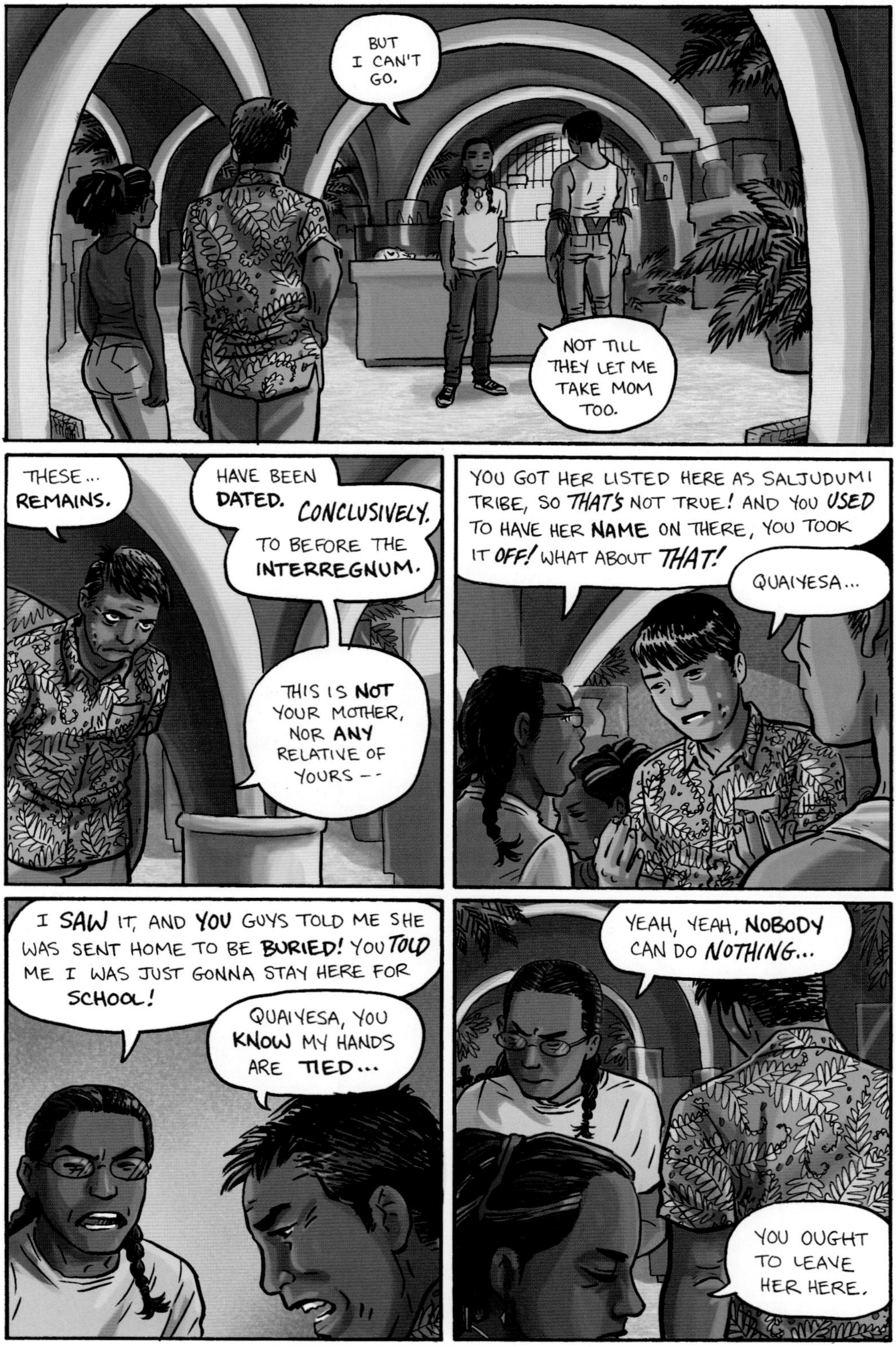
BUT I CAN'T GO.
NOT TILL THEY LET ME TAKE MOM TOO.
THESE... REMAINS.
HAVE BEEN DATED. CONCLUSIVELY.
TO BEFORE THE INTERREGNUM.
THIS IS NOT YOUR MOTHER, NOR ANY RELATIVE OF YOURS --
YOU GOT HER LISTED HERE AS SALJUDUMI TRIBE, SO THAT'S NOT TRUE! AND YOU USED TO HAVE HER NAME ON THERE, YOU TOOK IT OFF! WHAT ABOUT THAT!
QUAIYESA...
I SAW IT, AND YOU GUYS TOLD ME SHE WAS SENT HOME TO BE BURIED! YOU TOLD ME I WAS JUST GONNA STAY HERE FOR SCHOOL!
QUAIYESA, YOU KNOW MY HANDS ARE TIED...
YEAH, YEAH, NOBODY CAN DO NOTHING...
YOU OUGHT TO LEAVE HER HERE.

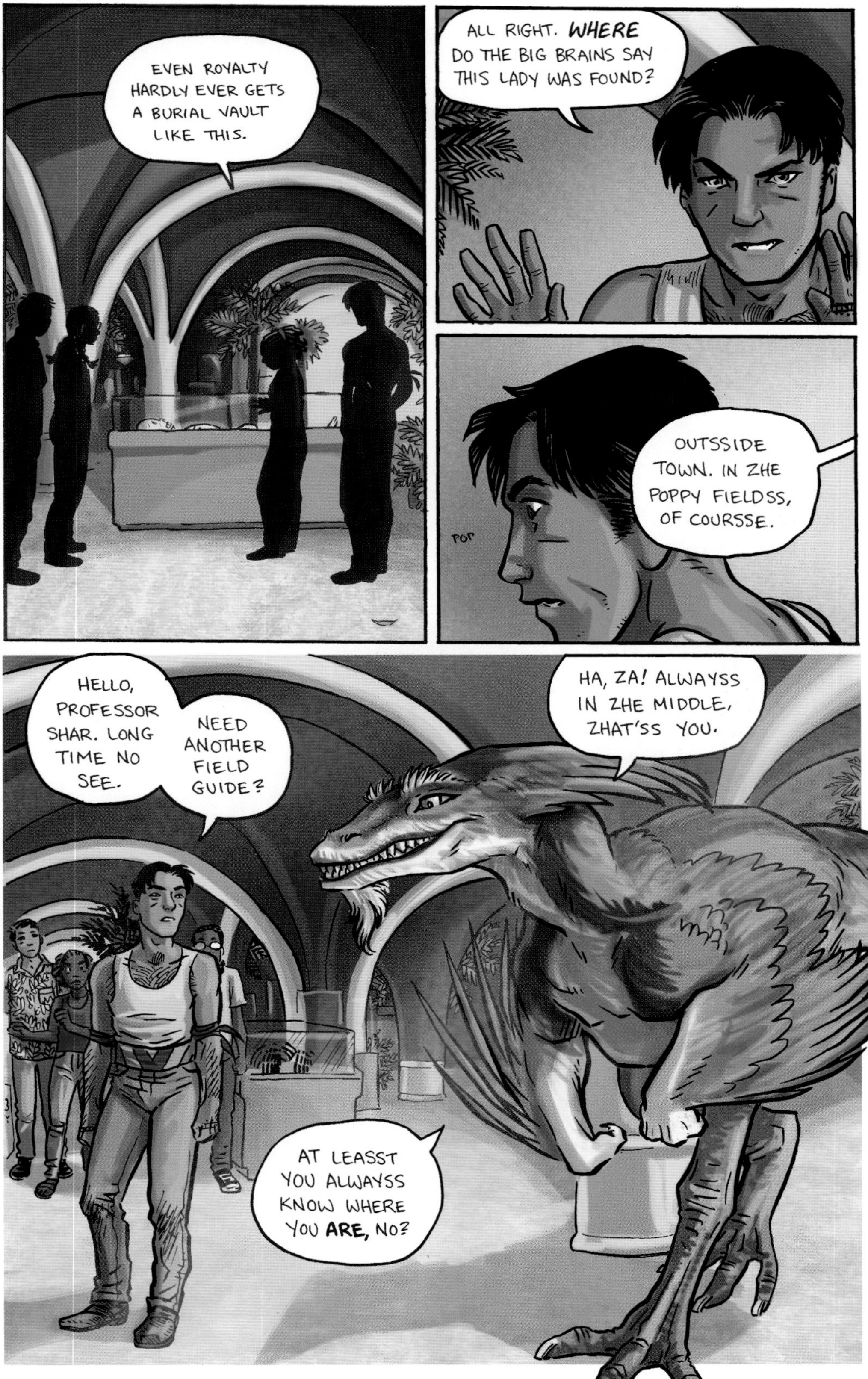
EVEN ROYALTY HARDLY EVER GETS A BURIAL VAULT LIKE THIS.
ALL RIGHT. WHERE DO THE BIG BRAINS SAY THIS LADY WAS FOUND?
OUTSSIDE TOWN. IN ZHE POPPY FIELDSS, OF COURSSE.
POP
HELLO, PROFESSOR SHAR. LONG TIME NO SEE.
NEED ANOTHER FIELD GUIDE?
HA, ZA! ALWAYSS IN ZHE MIDDLE, ZHAT'SS YOU.
AT LEASST YOU ALWAYSS KNOW WHERE YOU ARE, NO?

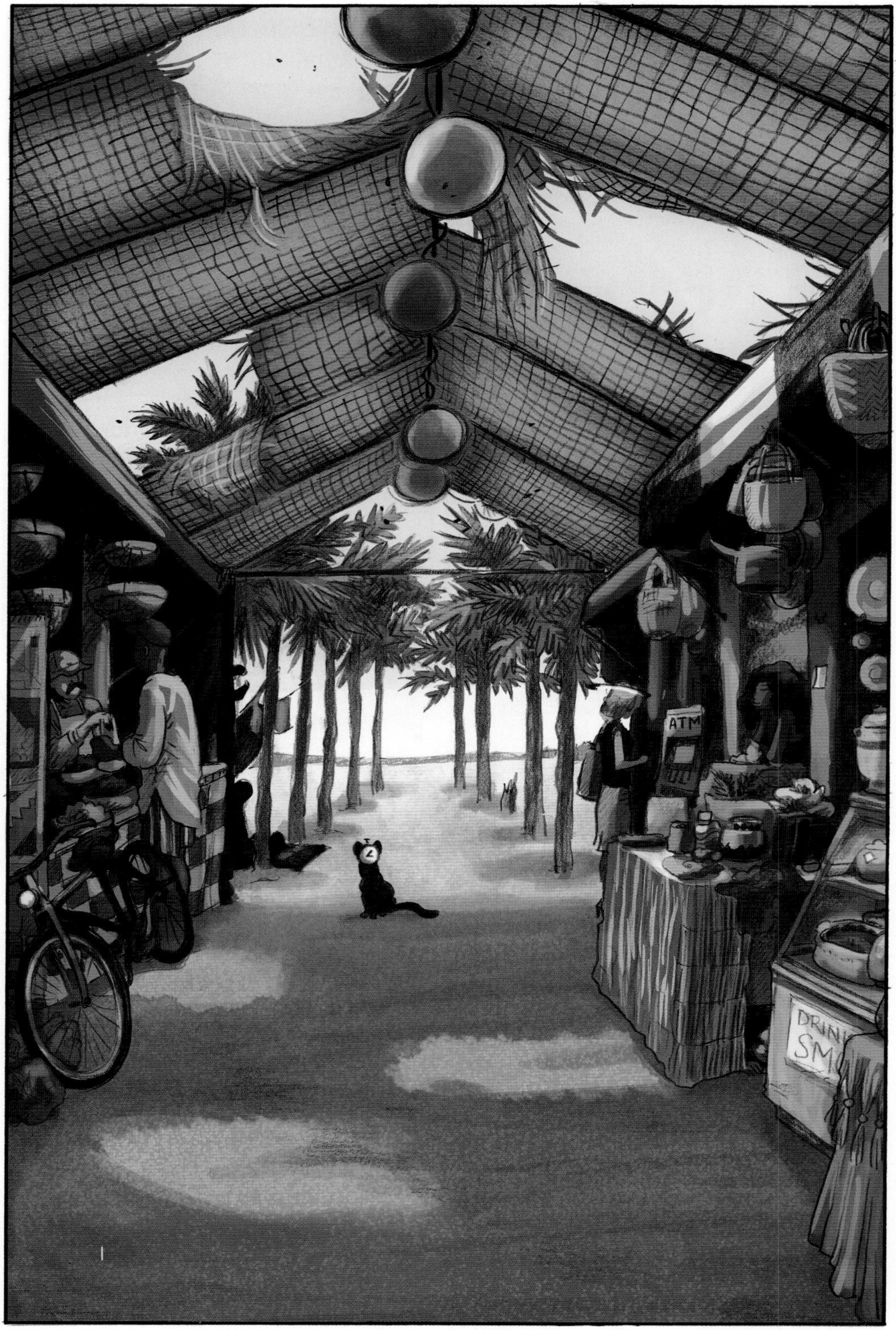
ATM

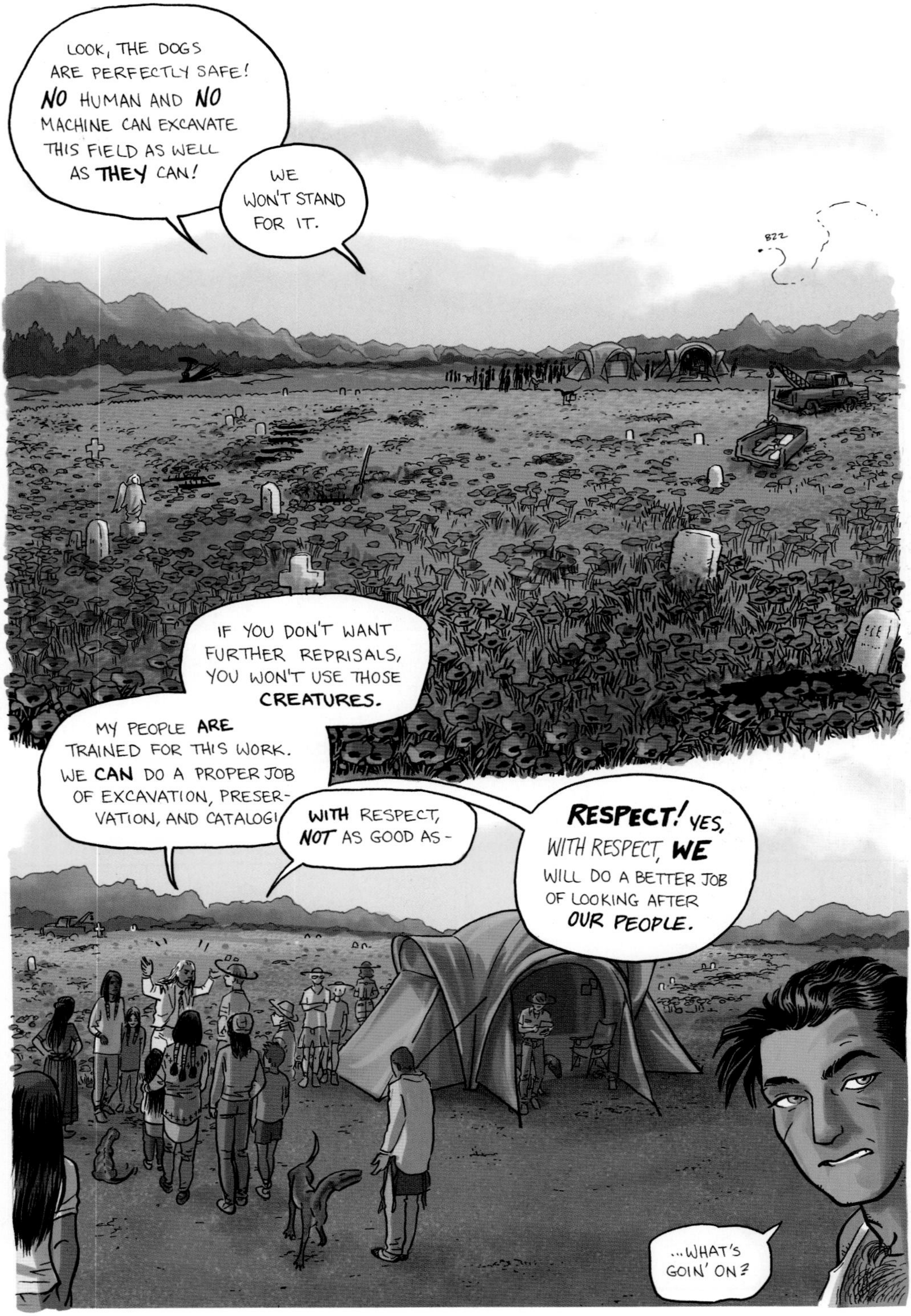
LOOK, THE DOGS ARE PERFECTLY SAFE! NO HUMAN AND NO MACHINE CAN EXCAVATE THIS FIELD AS WELL AS THEY CAN!
WE WON'T STAND FOR IT.
BZZ
IF YOU DON'T WANT FURTHER REPRISALS, YOU WON'T USE THOSE CREATURES.
MY PEOPLE ARE TRAINED FOR THIS WORK. WE CAN DO A PROPER JOB OF EXCAVATION, PRESER-VATION, AND CATALOGI
WITH RESPECT, NOT AS GOOD AS -
RESPECT! YES, WITH RESPECT, WE WILL DO A BETTER JOB OF LOOKING AFTER OUR PEOPLE.
...WHAT'S GOIN' ON?

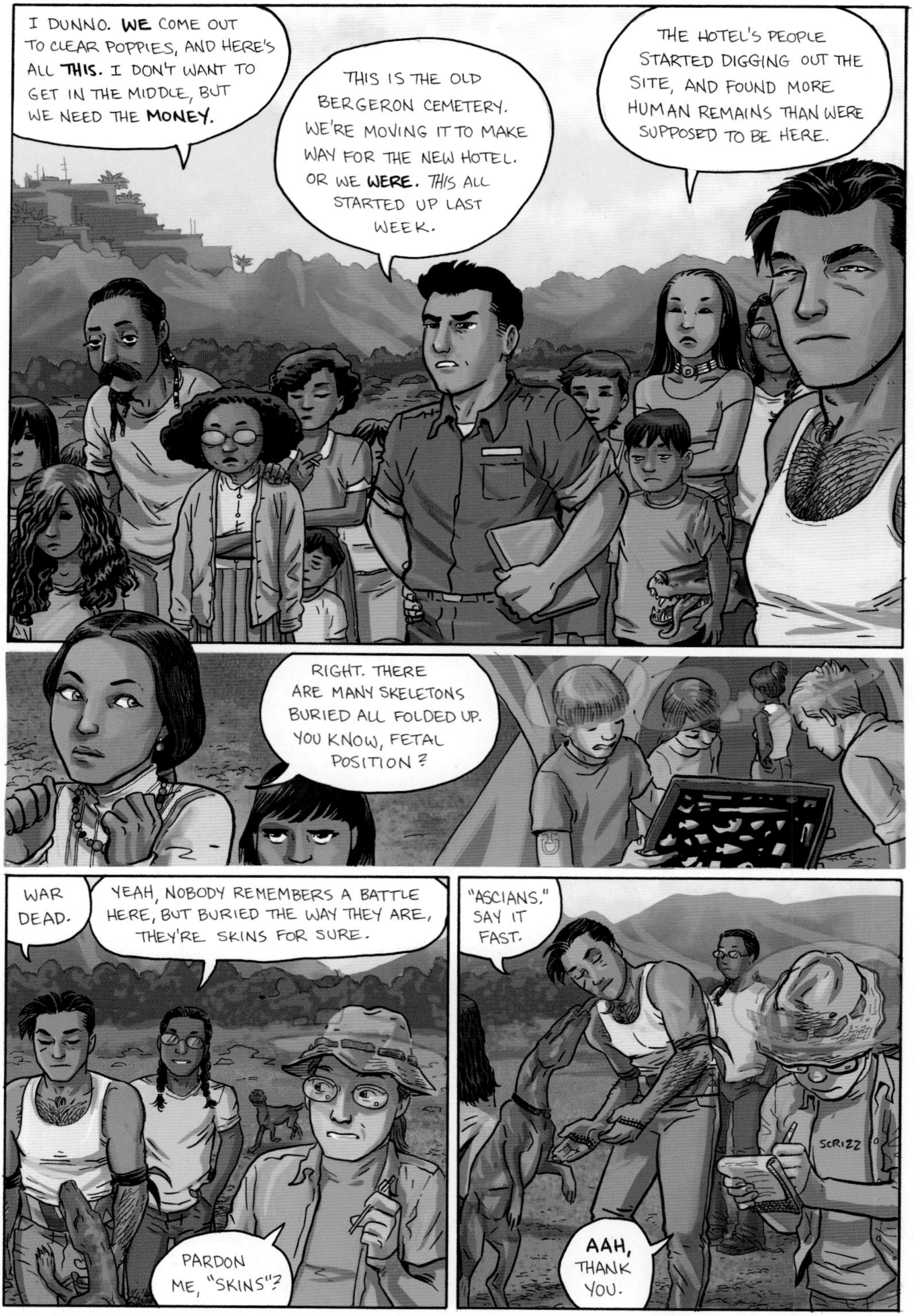
I DUNNO. **WE** COME OUT TO CLEAR POPPIES, AND HERE'S ALL **THIS.** I DON'T WANT TO GET IN THE MIDDLE, BUT WE NEED THE **MONEY.**
THIS IS THE OLD BERGERON CEMETERY. WE'RE MOVING IT TO MAKE WAY FOR THE NEW HOTEL. OR WE **WERE.** THIS ALL STARTED UP LAST WEEK.
THE HOTEL'S PEOPLE STARTED DIGGING OUT THE SITE, AND FOUND MORE HUMAN REMAINS THAN WERE SUPPOSED TO BE HERE.
RIGHT. THERE ARE MANY SKELETONS BURIED ALL FOLDED UP. YOU KNOW, FETAL POSITION?
WAR DEAD.
YEAH, NOBODY REMEMBERS A BATTLE HERE, BUT BURIED THE WAY THEY ARE, THEY'RE SKINS FOR SURE.
PARDON ME, "SKINS"?
"ASCIANS." SAY IT FAST.
AAH, THANK YOU.
SCRIZZ

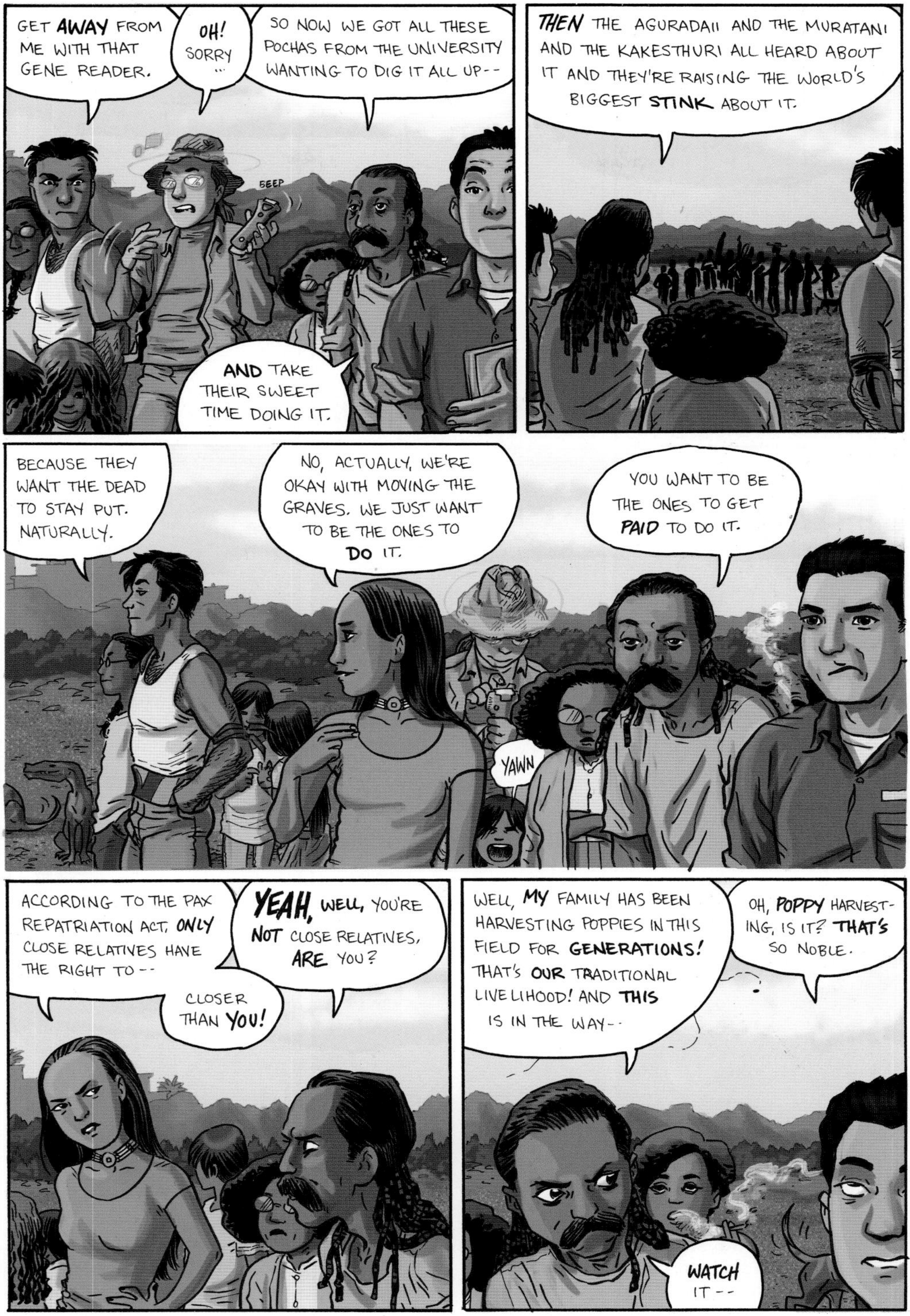
GET AWAY FROM ME WITH THAT GENE READER.
OH! SORRY ...
BEEP
SO NOW WE GOT ALL THESE POCHAS FROM THE UNIVERSITY WANTING TO DIG IT ALL UP--
AND TAKE THEIR SWEET TIME DOING IT.
THEN THE AGURADAII AND THE MURATANI AND THE KAKESTHURI ALL HEARD ABOUT IT AND THEY'RE RAISING THE WORLD'S BIGGEST STINK ABOUT IT.
BECAUSE THEY WANT THE DEAD TO STAY PUT. NATURALLY.
NO, ACTUALLY, WE'RE OKAY WITH MOVING THE GRAVES. WE JUST WANT TO BE THE ONES TO DO IT.
YOU WANT TO BE THE ONES TO GET PAID TO DO IT.
YAWN
ACCORDING TO THE PAX REPATRIATION ACT, ONLY CLOSE RELATIVES HAVE THE RIGHT TO--
YEAH, WELL, YOU'RE NOT CLOSE RELATIVES, ARE YOU?
CLOSER THAN YOU!
WELL, MY FAMILY HAS BEEN HARVESTING POPPIES IN THIS FIELD FOR GENERATIONS! THAT'S OUR TRADITIONAL LIVELIHOOD! AND THIS IS IN THE WAY--
OH, POPPY HARVESTING, IS IT? THAT'S SO NOBLE.
WATCH IT--

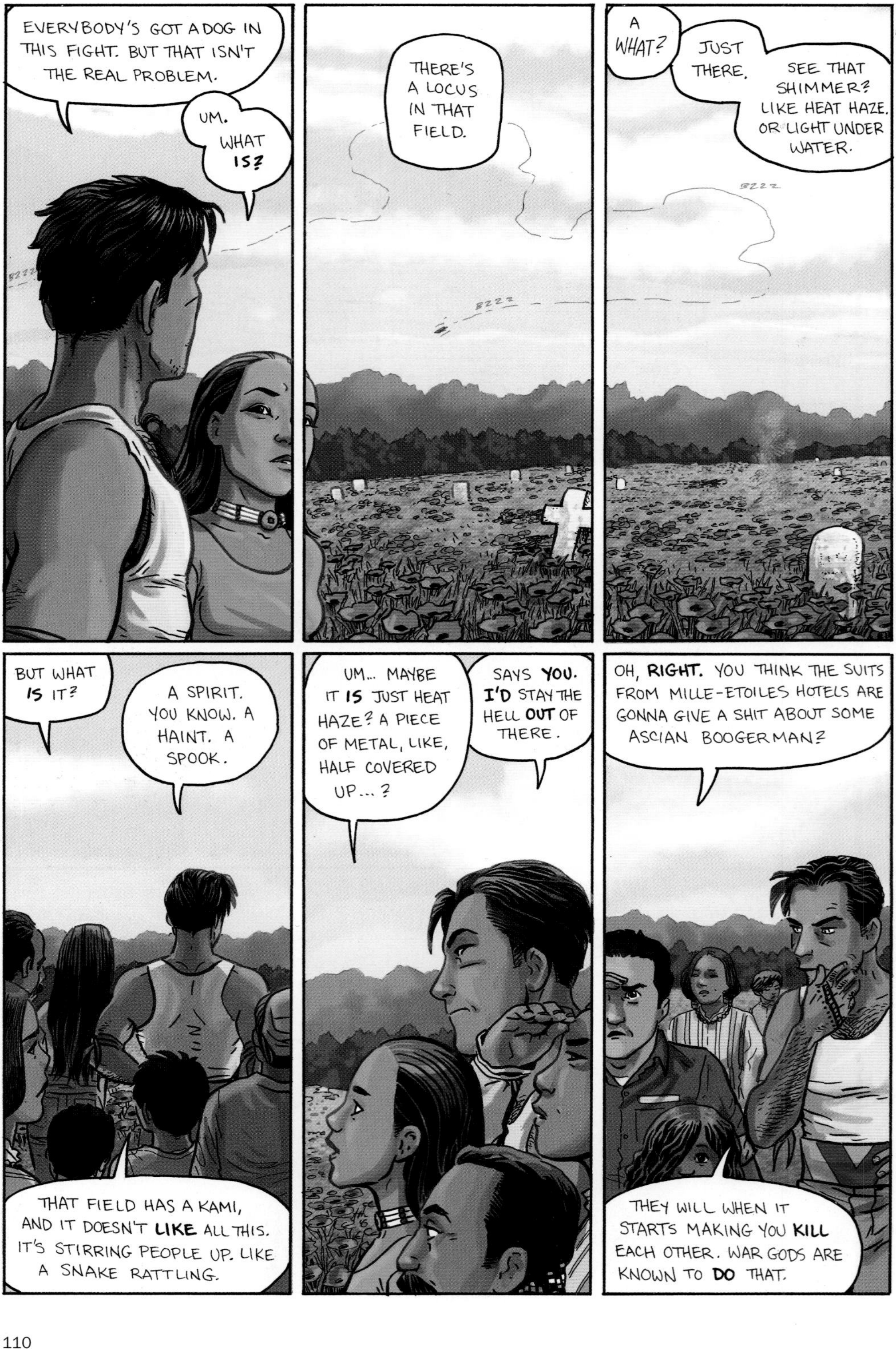
EVERYBODY'S GOT A DOG IN THIS FIGHT. BUT THAT ISN'T THE REAL PROBLEM.
UM. WHAT IS?
BZZZ
THERE'S A LOCUS IN THAT FIELD.
BZZZ
A WHAT?
JUST THERE.
SEE THAT SHIMMER? LIKE HEAT HAZE. OR LIGHT UNDER WATER.
BZZZ
BUT WHAT IS IT?
A SPIRIT. YOU KNOW. A HAINT. A SPOOK.
THAT FIELD HAS A KAMI, AND IT DOESN'T LIKE ALL THIS. IT'S STIRRING PEOPLE UP. LIKE A SNAKE RATTLING.
UM... MAYBE IT IS JUST HEAT HAZE? A PIECE OF METAL, LIKE, HALF COVERED UP...?
SAYS YOU. I'D STAY THE HELL OUT OF THERE.
OH, RIGHT. YOU THINK THE SUITS FROM MILLE-ETOILES HOTELS ARE GONNA GIVE A SHIT ABOUT SOME ASCIAN BOOGERMAN?
THEY WILL WHEN IT STARTS MAKING YOU KILL EACH OTHER. WAR GODS ARE KNOWN TO DO THAT.

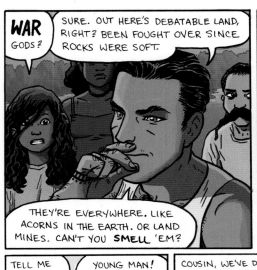

WAR GODS?

SURE. OUT HERE'S DEBATABLE LAND, RIGHT? BEEN FOUGHT OVER SINCE ROCKS WERE SOFT.

THEY'RE EVERYWHERE. LIKE ACORNS IN THE EARTH. OR LAND MINES. CAN'T YOU **SMELL** 'EM?

WE DIG UP LAND MINES EVERY DAY. ACORNS TOO. NOTHING CAN STOP THIS HOTEL FROM GOING IN. HOW CAN WE LEAVE THIS ALONE?

HEY, IT'S NOTHING TO DO WITH ME. I HATE SPOOKS.

TELL ME HOW IT ALL COMES OUT ...

YOUNG MAN! YOUNG MAN! PLEASE WAIT!

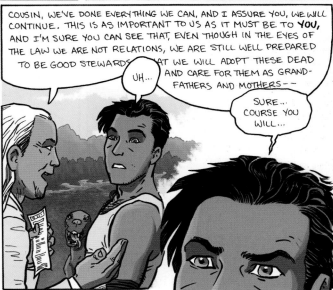

COUSIN, WE'VE DONE EVERYTHING WE CAN, AND I ASSURE YOU, WE WILL CONTINUE. THIS IS AS IMPORTANT TO US AS IT MUST BE TO **YOU**, AND I'M SURE YOU CAN SEE THAT, EVEN THOUGH IN THE EYES OF THE LAW WE ARE NOT RELATIONS, WE ARE STILL WELL PREPARED TO BE GOOD STEWARDS. THAT WE WILL ADOPT THESE DEAD AND CARE FOR THEM AS GRAND-FATHERS AND MOTHERS––

UH...

SURE... COURSE YOU WILL...

BUT NOW **YOU'RE** HERE. IF THERE ARE ANY SPECIFIC BURIAL DETAILS THAT MUST BE CARRIED OUT, YOU NEED ONLY GUIDE US!

AAAAH... SORRY.

I... MISSED... SOMETHING HERE.

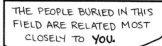

THE PEOPLE BURIED IN THIS FIELD ARE RELATED MOST CLOSELY TO **YOU.**

... GENETIC TESTS ON SOME OF THOSE ALREADY EXHUMED CONFIRM THIS.

HOW...

IT WASN'T ME!

I SWEAR!

IT WAS THE DOGS!

WHAAAT?

THE DIG DOGS!

THEY'RE PROFESSOR SHAR'S INNOVATION! SPECIALLY BRED TO DETECT AND COLLECT GENETIC INFORMATION!

THEY HAVE SKULL COMPUTERS, SO THEY CAN TRANSMIT OVER WIRELESS ANY-THING THEY TASTE OR SMELL!

IT'S AN INGENIOUS COLLECTION SYSTEM! PEOPLE HARDLY NOTICE IT, AND SO USUALLY DON'T OBJECT!

SWELL.

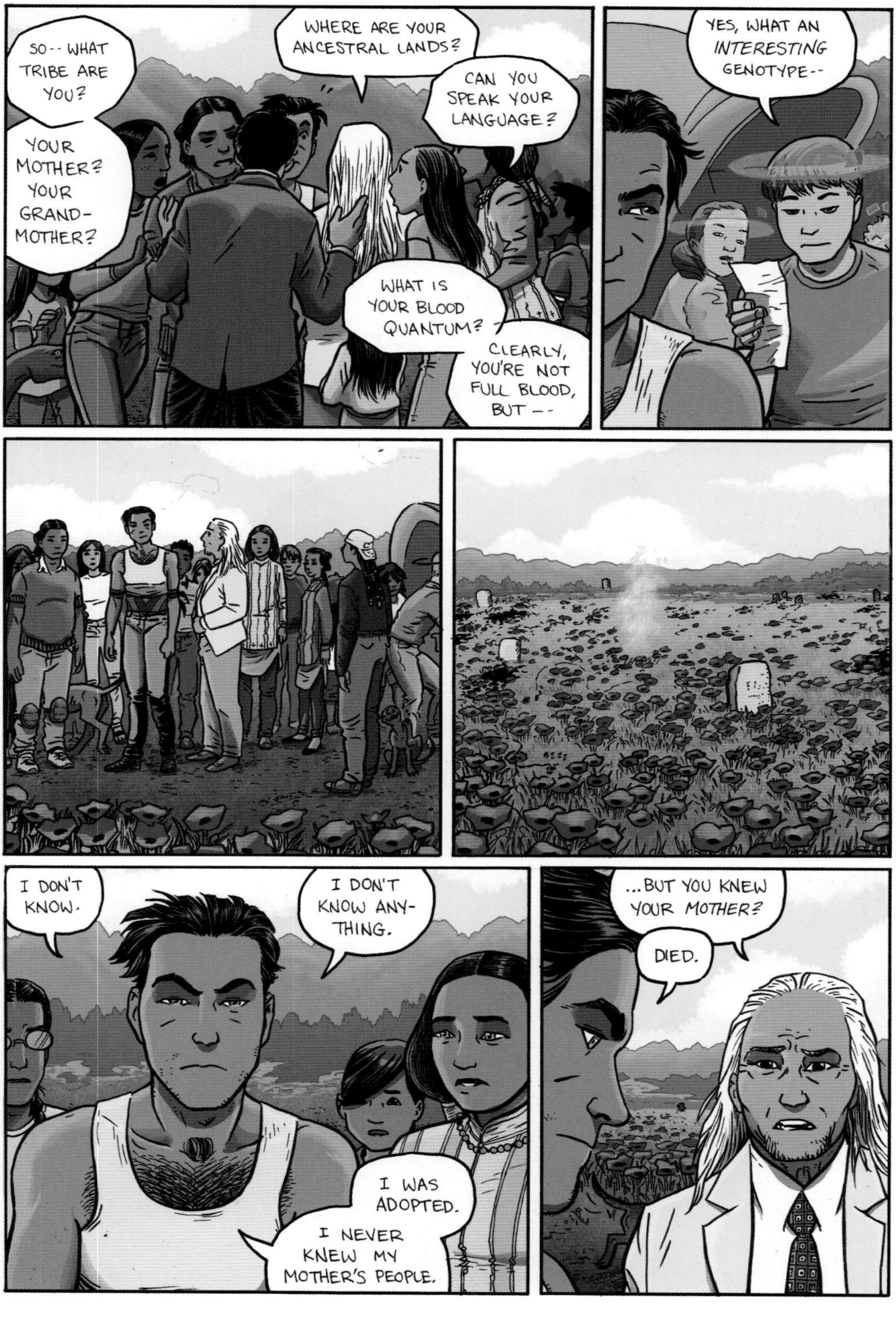
SO-- WHAT TRIBE ARE YOU?
YOUR MOTHER? YOUR GRANDMOTHER?
WHERE ARE YOUR ANCESTRAL LANDS?
CAN YOU SPEAK YOUR LANGUAGE?
WHAT IS YOUR BLOOD QUANTUM?
CLEARLY, YOU'RE NOT FULL BLOOD, BUT --
YES, WHAT AN *INTERESTING* GENOTYPE--
I DON'T KNOW.
I DON'T KNOW ANYTHING.
I WAS ADOPTED.
I NEVER KNEW MY MOTHER'S PEOPLE.
...BUT YOU KNEW YOUR *MOTHER*?
DIED.

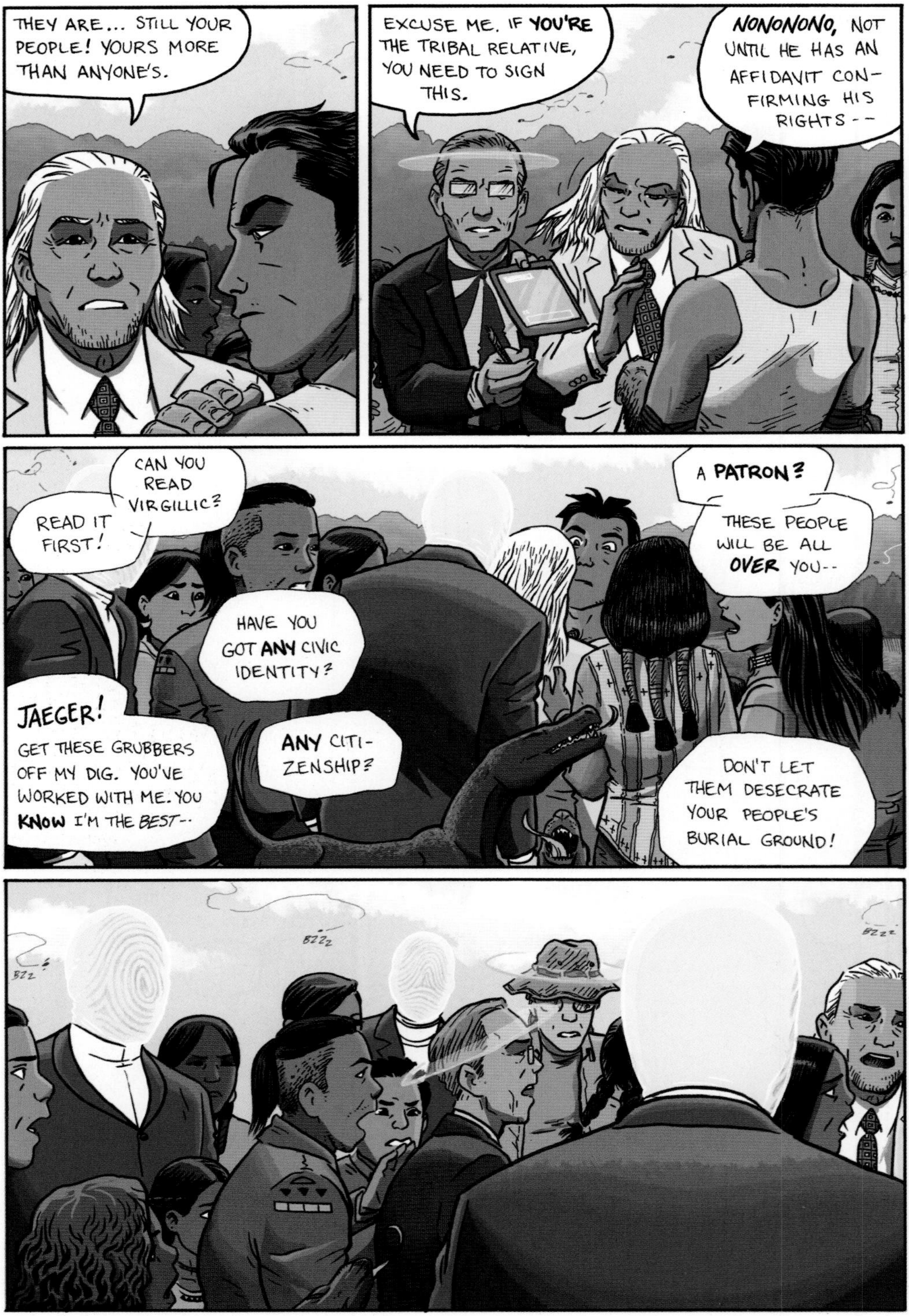
THEY ARE... STILL YOUR PEOPLE! YOURS MORE THAN ANYONE'S.
EXCUSE ME. IF **YOU'RE** THE TRIBAL RELATIVE, YOU NEED TO SIGN THIS.
NONONONO, NOT UNTIL HE HAS AN AFFIDAVIT CONFIRMING HIS RIGHTS--
READ IT FIRST!
CAN YOU READ VIRGILLIC?
A **PATRON**?
THESE PEOPLE WILL BE ALL **OVER** YOU--
HAVE YOU GOT **ANY** CIVIC IDENTITY?
JAEGER! GET THESE GRUBBERS OFF MY DIG. YOU'VE WORKED WITH ME. YOU **KNOW** I'M THE *BEST*--.
ANY CITIZENSHIP?
DON'T LET THEM DESECRATE YOUR PEOPLE'S BURIAL GROUND!

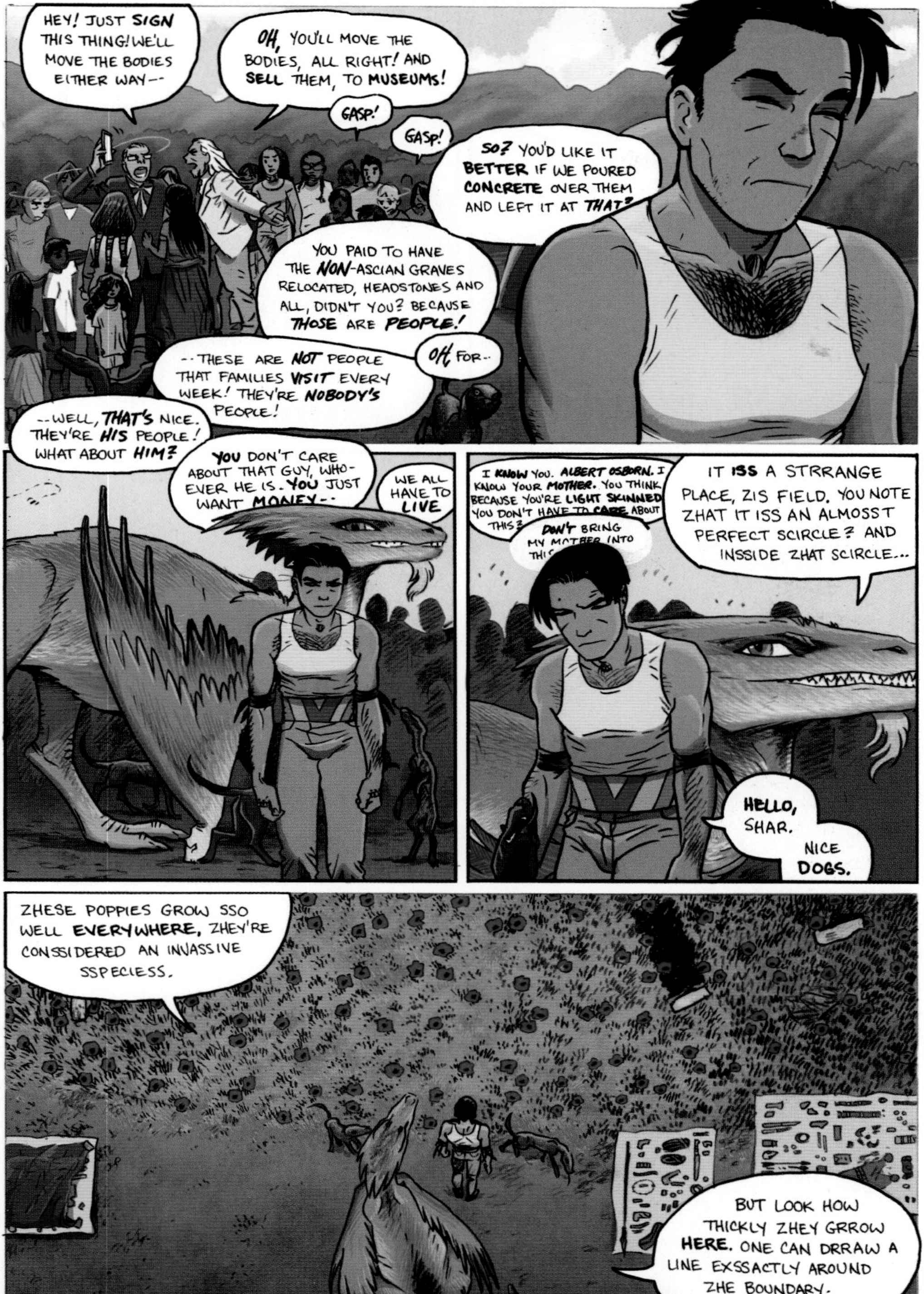

HEY! JUST SIGN THIS THING! WE'LL MOVE THE BODIES EITHER WAY--
OH, YOU'LL MOVE THE BODIES, ALL RIGHT! AND SELL THEM, TO MUSEUMS!
GASP!
GASP!
SO? YOU'D LIKE IT BETTER IF WE POURED CONCRETE OVER THEM AND LEFT IT AT THAT?
YOU PAID TO HAVE THE NON-ASCIAN GRAVES RELOCATED, HEADSTONES AND ALL, DIDN'T YOU? BECAUSE THOSE ARE PEOPLE!
OH, FOR..
--THESE ARE NOT PEOPLE THAT FAMILIES VISIT EVERY WEEK! THEY'RE NOBODY'S PEOPLE!
--WELL, THAT'S NICE. THEY'RE HIS PEOPLE! WHAT ABOUT HIM?
YOU DON'T CARE ABOUT THAT GUY, WHOEVER HE IS. YOU JUST WANT MONEY--
WE ALL HAVE TO LIVE
I KNOW YOU. ALBERT OSBORN. I KNOW YOUR MOTHER. YOU THINK BECAUSE YOU'RE LIGHT SKINNED YOU DON'T HAVE TO CARE ABOUT THIS?
DON'T BRING MY MOTHER INTO THI
IT ISS A STRRANGE PLACE, ZIS FIELD. YOU NOTE ZHAT IT ISS AN ALMOSST PERFECT SCIRCLE? AND INSSIDE ZHAT SCIRCLE...
HELLO, SHAR.
NICE DOGS.
ZHESE POPPIES GROW SSO WELL EVERYWHERE, ZHEY'RE CONSSIDERED AN INVASSIVE SSPECIESS.
BUT LOOK HOW THICKLY ZHEY GRROW HERE. ONE CAN DRRAW A LINE EXSSACTLY AROUND ZHE BOUNDARY.

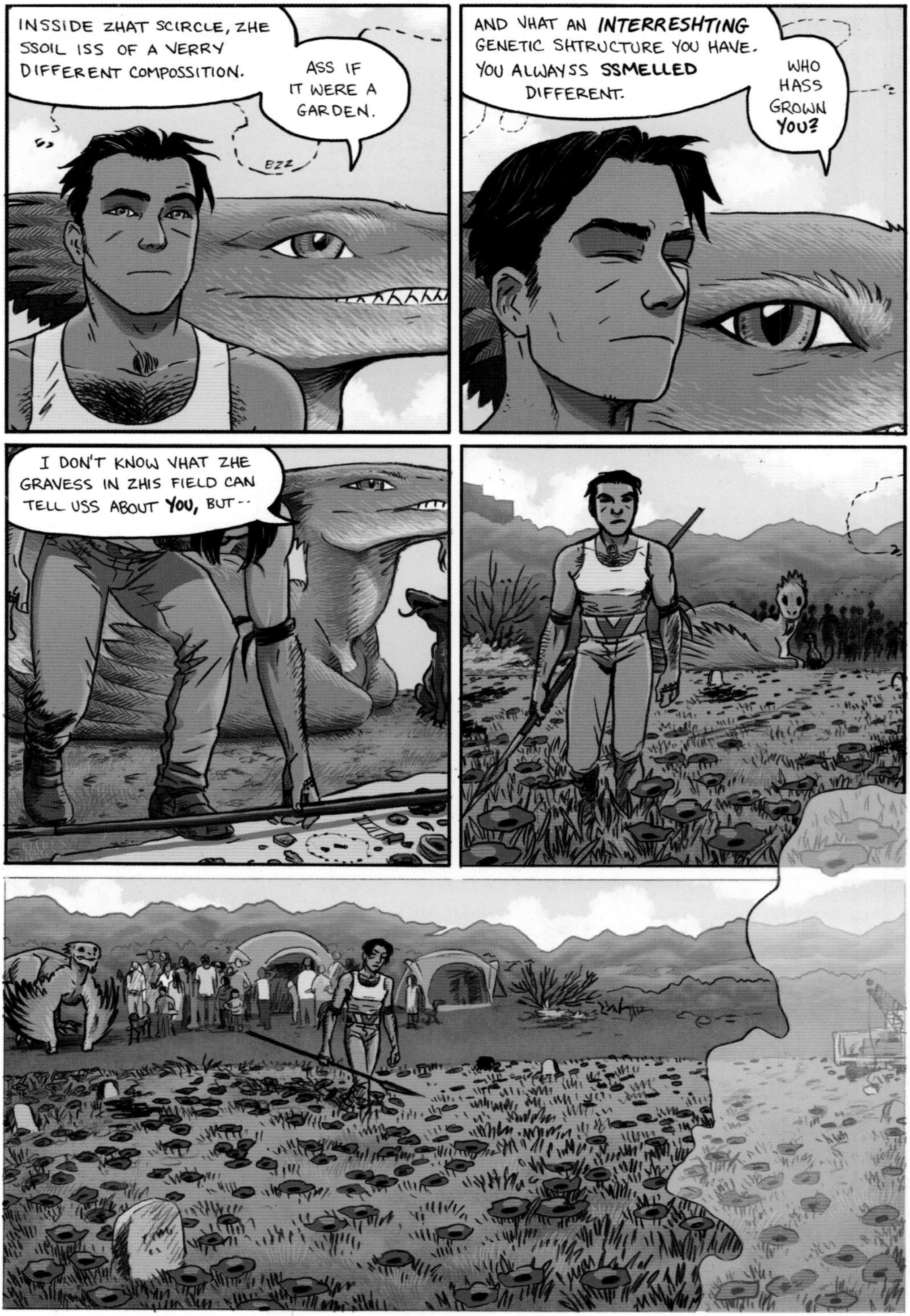

INSSIDE ZHAT SCIRCLE, ZHE SSOIL ISS OF A VERRY DIFFERENT COMPOSSITION.
ASS IF IT WERE A GARDEN.
BZZ
AND VHAT AN **INTERRESHTING** GENETIC SHTRUCTURE YOU HAVE. YOU ALWAYSS **SSMELLED** DIFFERENT.
WHO HASS GROWN **YOU?**
I DON'T KNOW VHAT ZHE GRAVESS IN ZHIS FIELD CAN TELL USS ABOUT **YOU,** BUT--

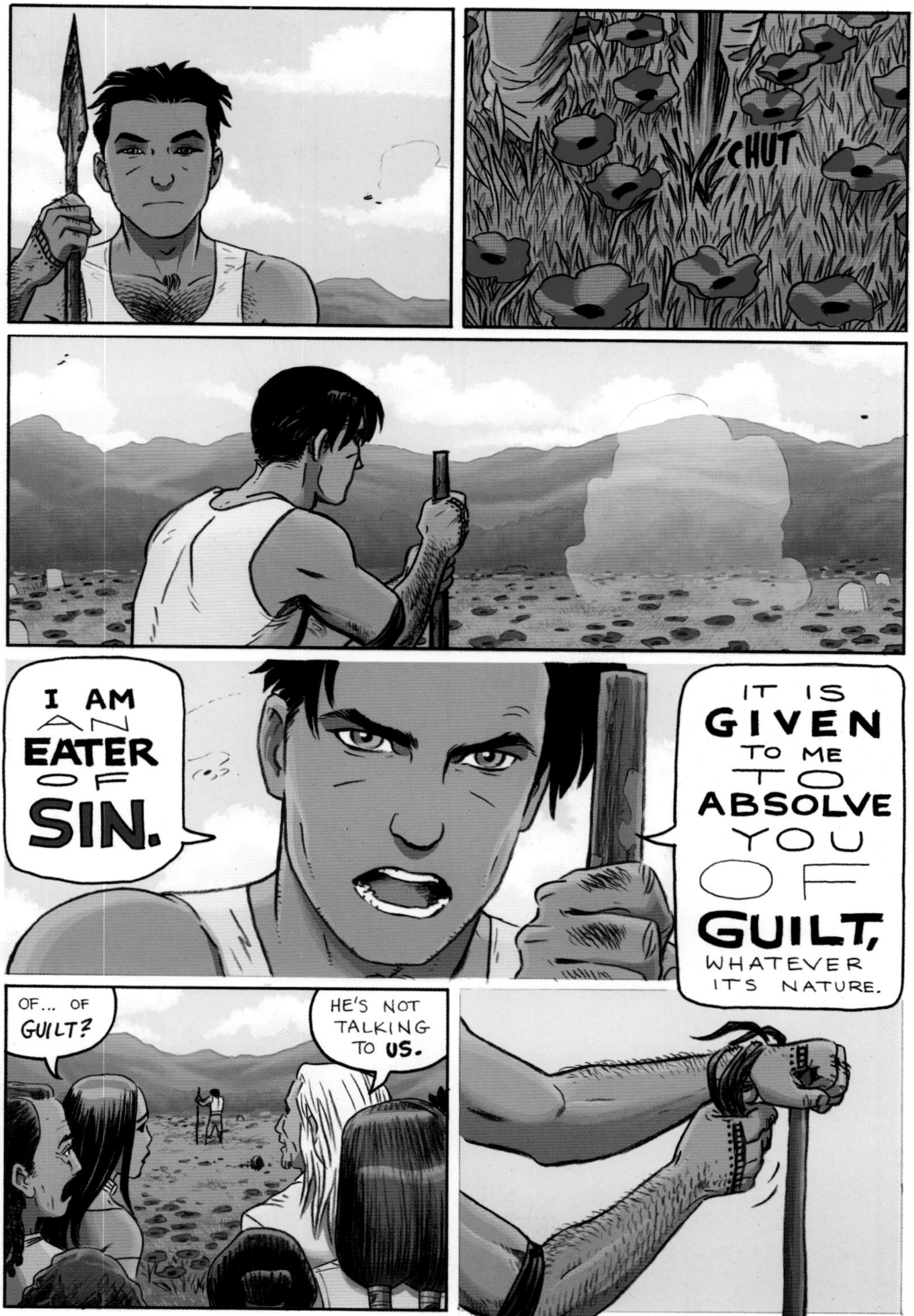
CHUT
I AM AN EATER OF SIN.
IT IS GIVEN TO ME TO ABSOLVE YOU OF GUILT, WHATEVER ITS NATURE.
OF... OF GUILT?
HE'S NOT TALKING TO US.

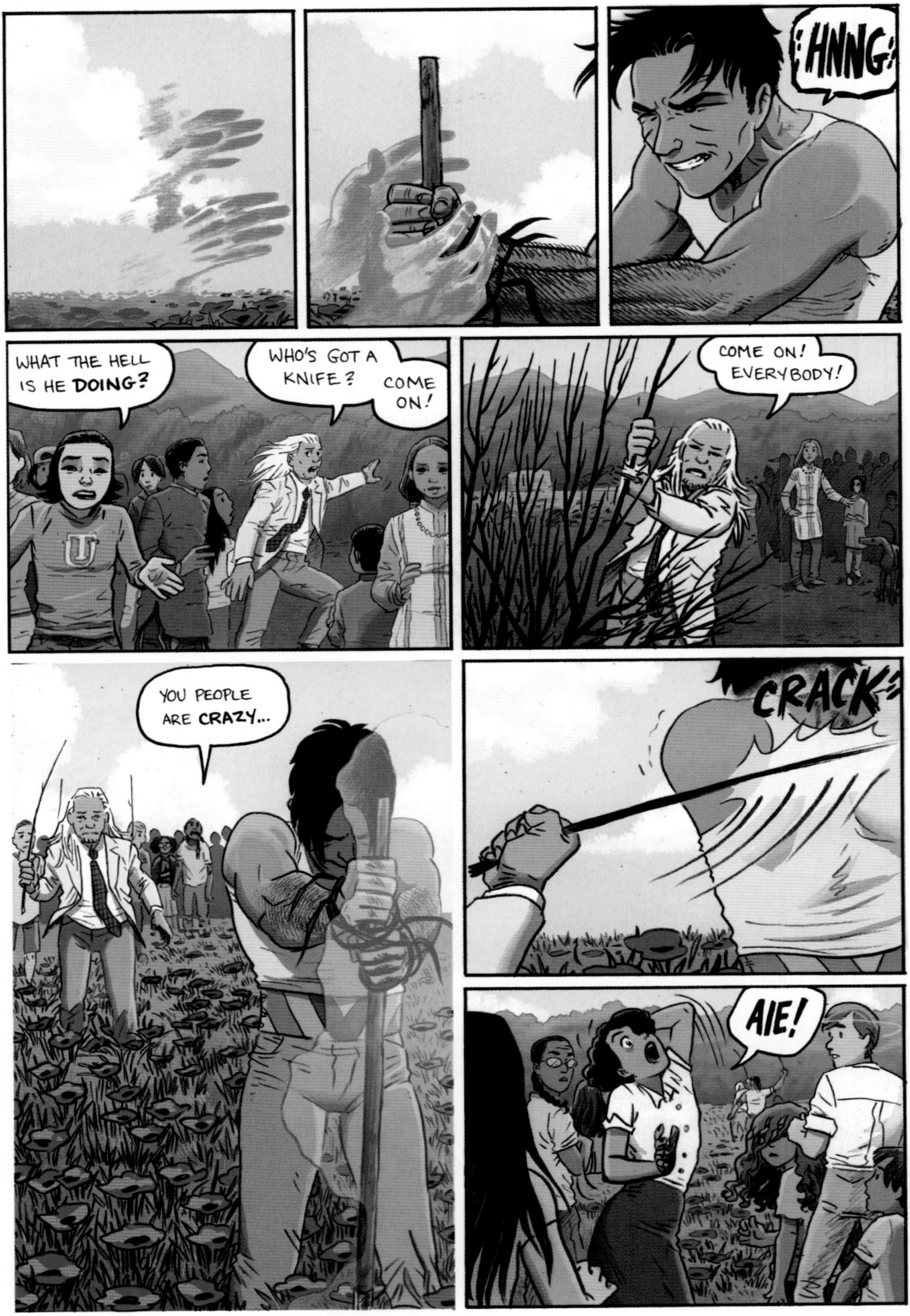
HNNG!
WHAT THE HELL IS HE DOING?
WHO'S GOT A KNIFE?
COME ON!
COME ON! EVERYBODY!
YOU PEOPLE ARE CRAZY...
CRACK
AIE!

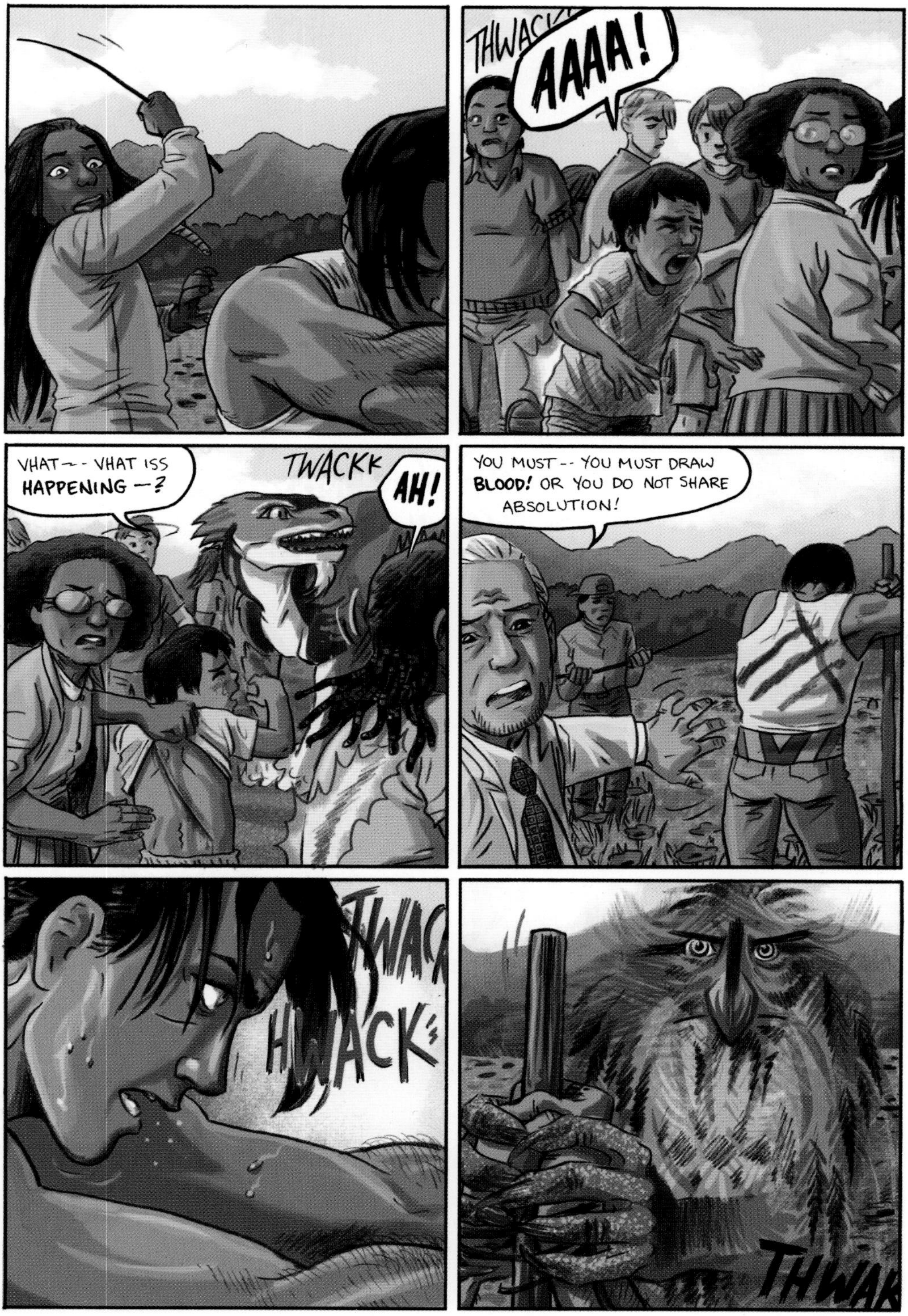
THWACK
AAAA!
VHAT-- VHAT ISS HAPPENING --?
TWACKK
AH!
YOU MUST -- YOU MUST DRAW BLOOD! OR YOU DO NOT SHARE ABSOLUTION!
THWAC
HWACK
THWAK

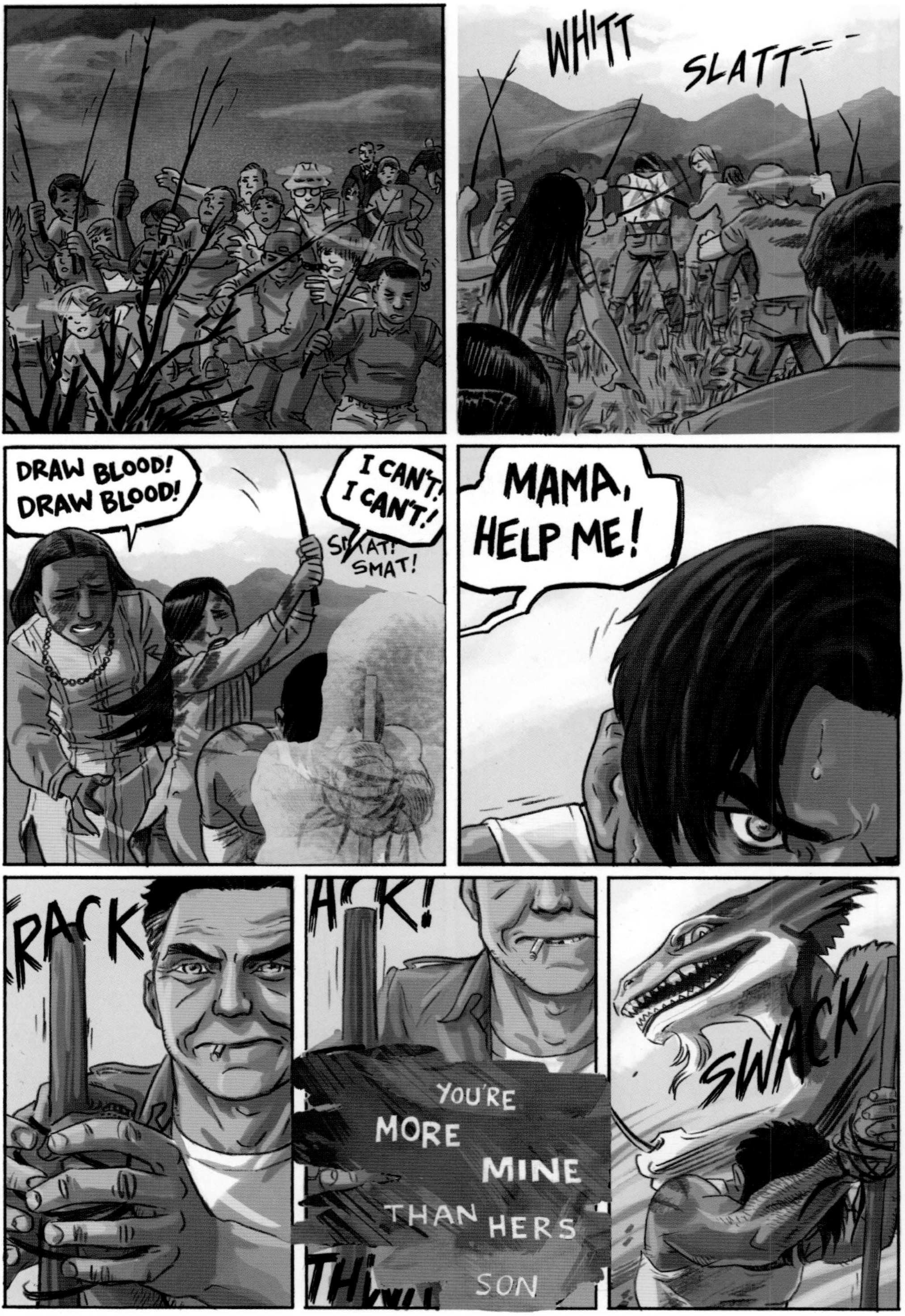
WHITT
SLATT
DRAW BLOOD! DRAW BLOOD!
I CAN'T! I CAN'T!
SMAT! SMAT!
MAMA, HELP ME!
RACK
ACK!
YOU'RE MORE MINE THAN HERS SON
SWACK

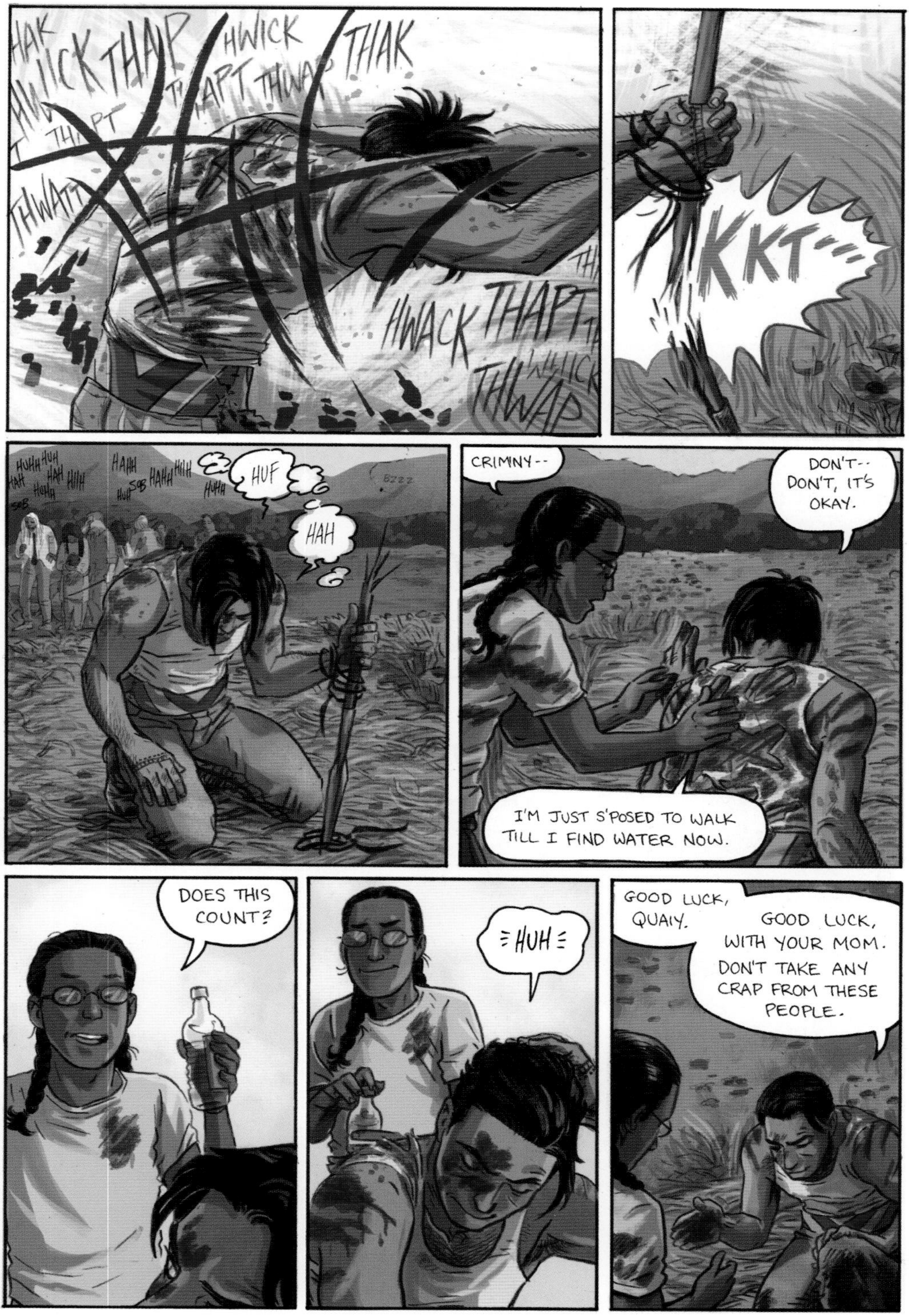
THAK
HWICK
THAP
THAPT
THWAP
THAK
THWAP
HWACK THAPT
THWAP
KKT--
HUF
HAH
CRIMINY--
DON'T-- DON'T, IT'S OKAY.
I'M JUST S'POSED TO WALK TILL I FIND WATER NOW.
DOES THIS COUNT?
HUH
GOOD LUCK, QUAIY.
GOOD LUCK, WITH YOUR MOM. DON'T TAKE ANY CRAP FROM THESE PEOPLE.

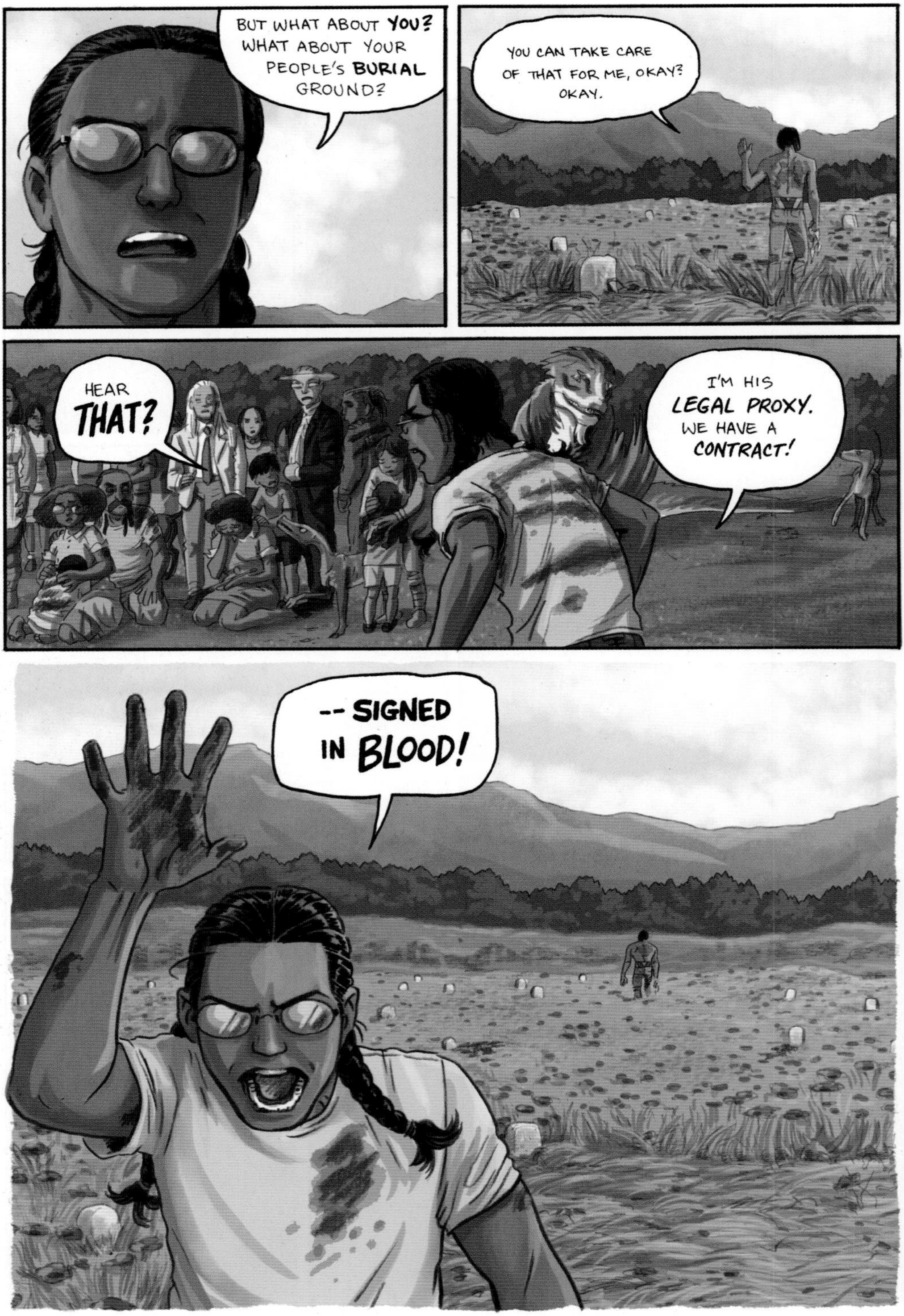
BUT WHAT ABOUT YOU? WHAT ABOUT YOUR PEOPLE'S BURIAL GROUND?
YOU CAN TAKE CARE OF THAT FOR ME, OKAY? OKAY.
HEAR THAT?
I'M HIS LEGAL PROXY. WE HAVE A CONTRACT!
-- SIGNED IN BLOOD!

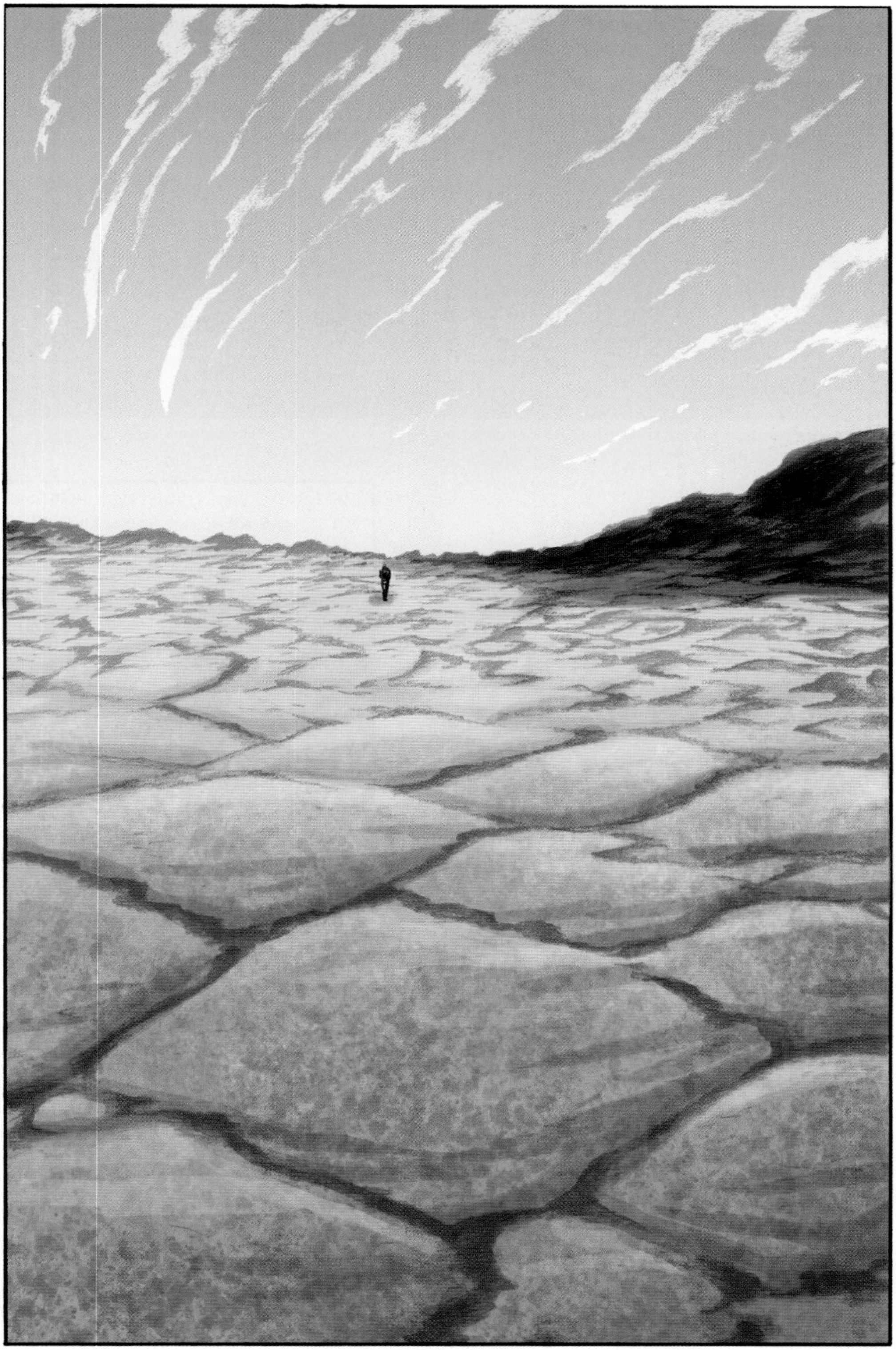

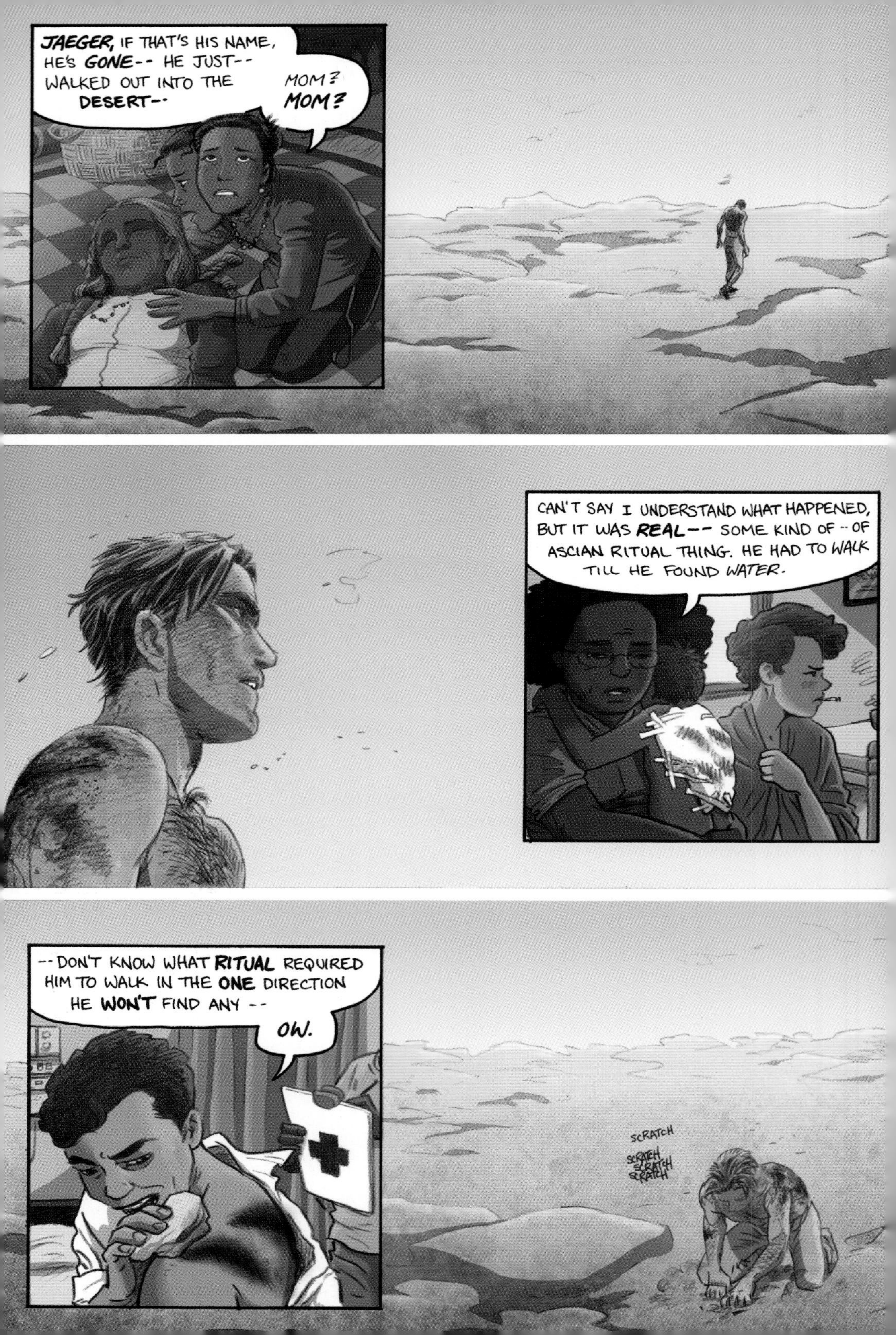
JAEGER, IF THAT'S HIS NAME, HE'S GONE-- HE JUST-- WALKED OUT INTO THE DESERT--
MOM? MOM?
CAN'T SAY I UNDERSTAND WHAT HAPPENED, BUT IT WAS REAL-- SOME KIND OF -- OF ASCIAN RITUAL THING. HE HAD TO WALK TILL HE FOUND WATER.
--DON'T KNOW WHAT RITUAL REQUIRED HIM TO WALK IN THE ONE DIRECTION HE WON'T FIND ANY --
OW.
SCRATCH
SCRATCH SCRATCH SCRATCH

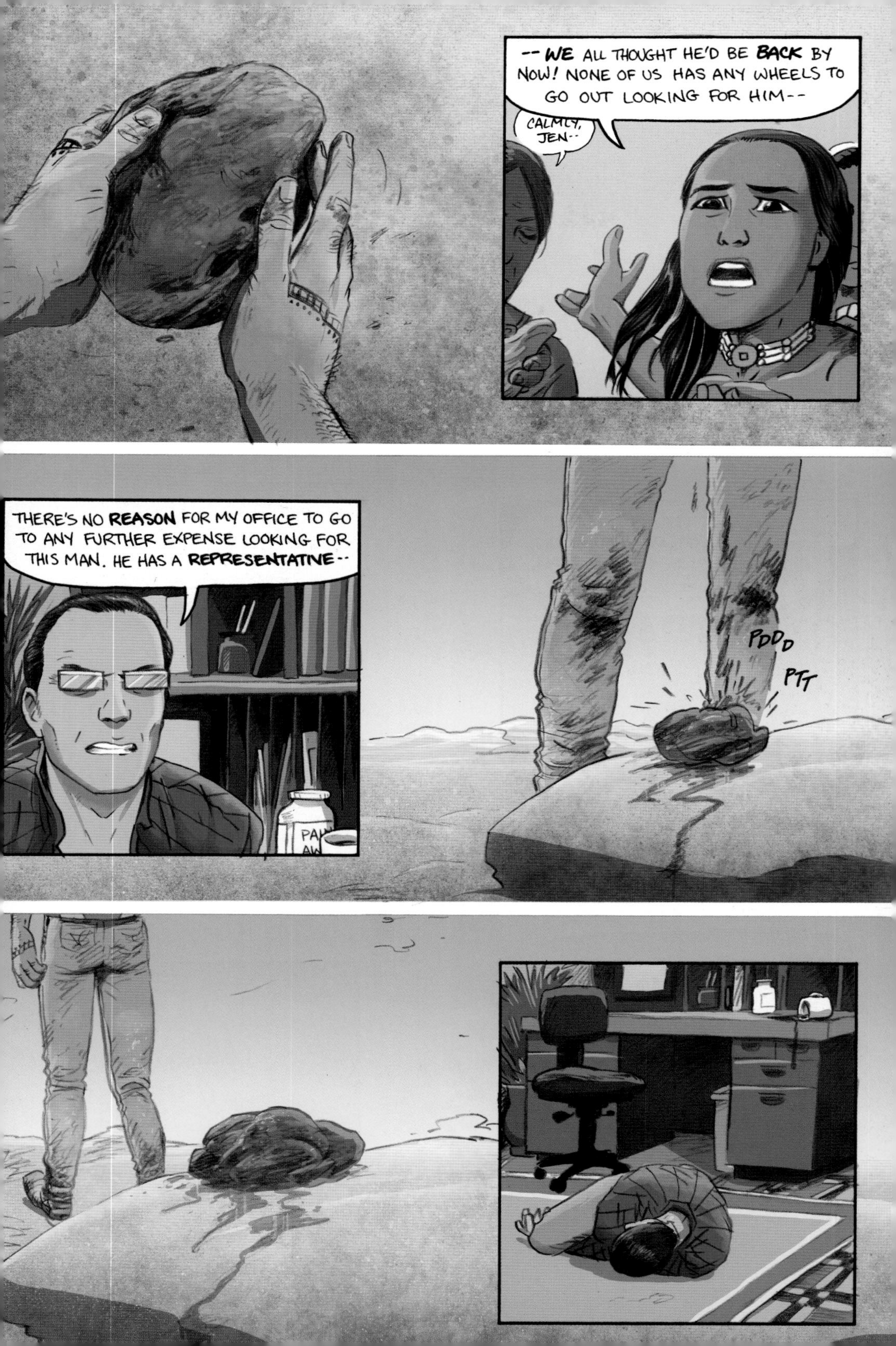
-- WE ALL THOUGHT HE'D BE BACK BY NOW! NONE OF US HAS ANY WHEELS TO GO OUT LOOKING FOR HIM--
CALMLY, JEN--
THERE'S NO REASON FOR MY OFFICE TO GO TO ANY FURTHER EXPENSE LOOKING FOR THIS MAN. HE HAS A REPRESENTATIVE--
PDDD
PTT

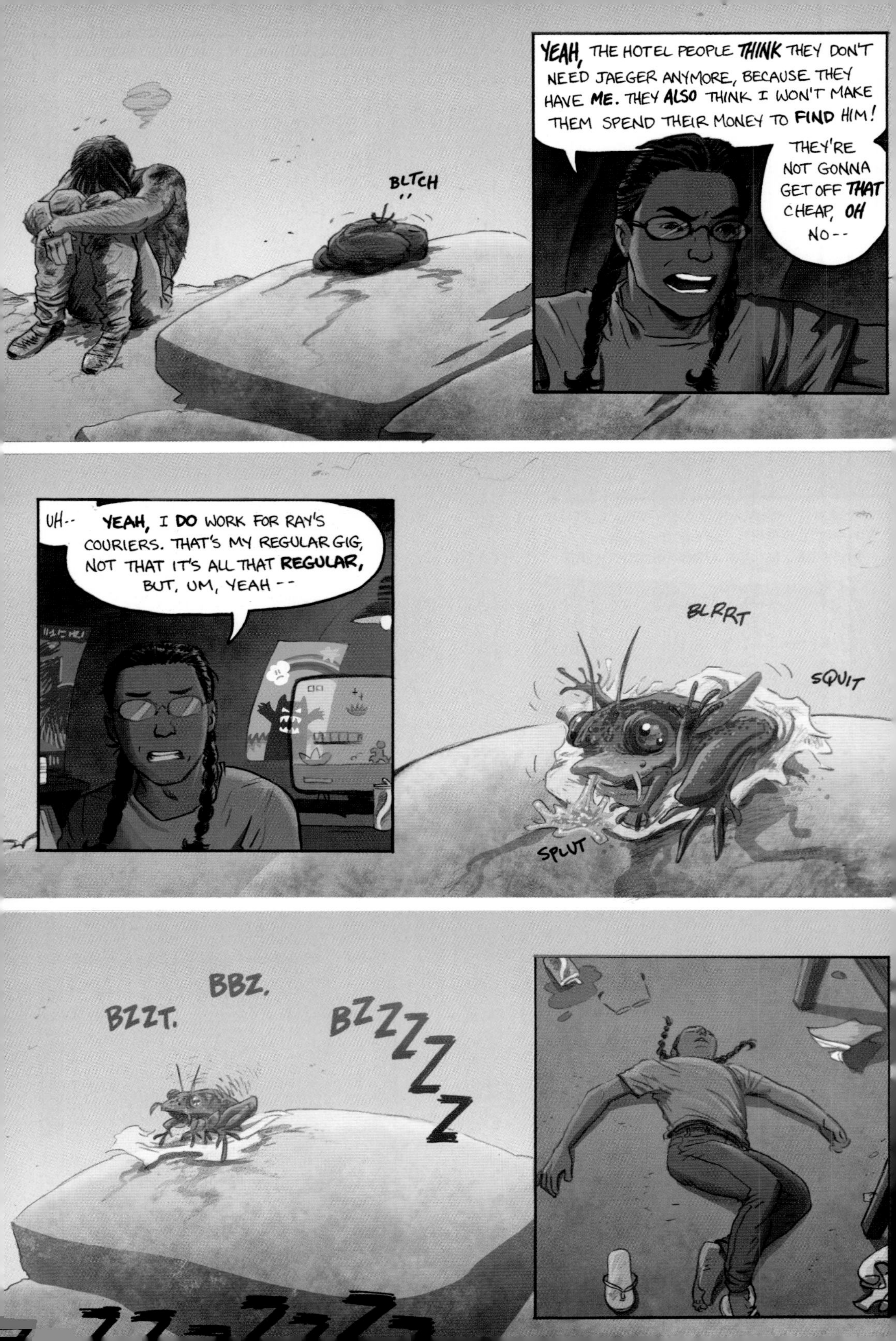

BLTCH
YEAH, THE HOTEL PEOPLE THINK THEY DON'T NEED JAEGER ANYMORE, BECAUSE THEY HAVE ME. THEY ALSO THINK I WON'T MAKE THEM SPEND THEIR MONEY TO FIND HIM!
THEY'RE NOT GONNA GET OFF THAT CHEAP, OH NO--
UH--
YEAH, I DO WORK FOR RAY'S COURIERS. THAT'S MY REGULAR GIG, NOT THAT IT'S ALL THAT REGULAR, BUT, UM, YEAH --
BLRRT
SQUIT
SPLUT
BZZT.
BBZ.
BZZZZZ

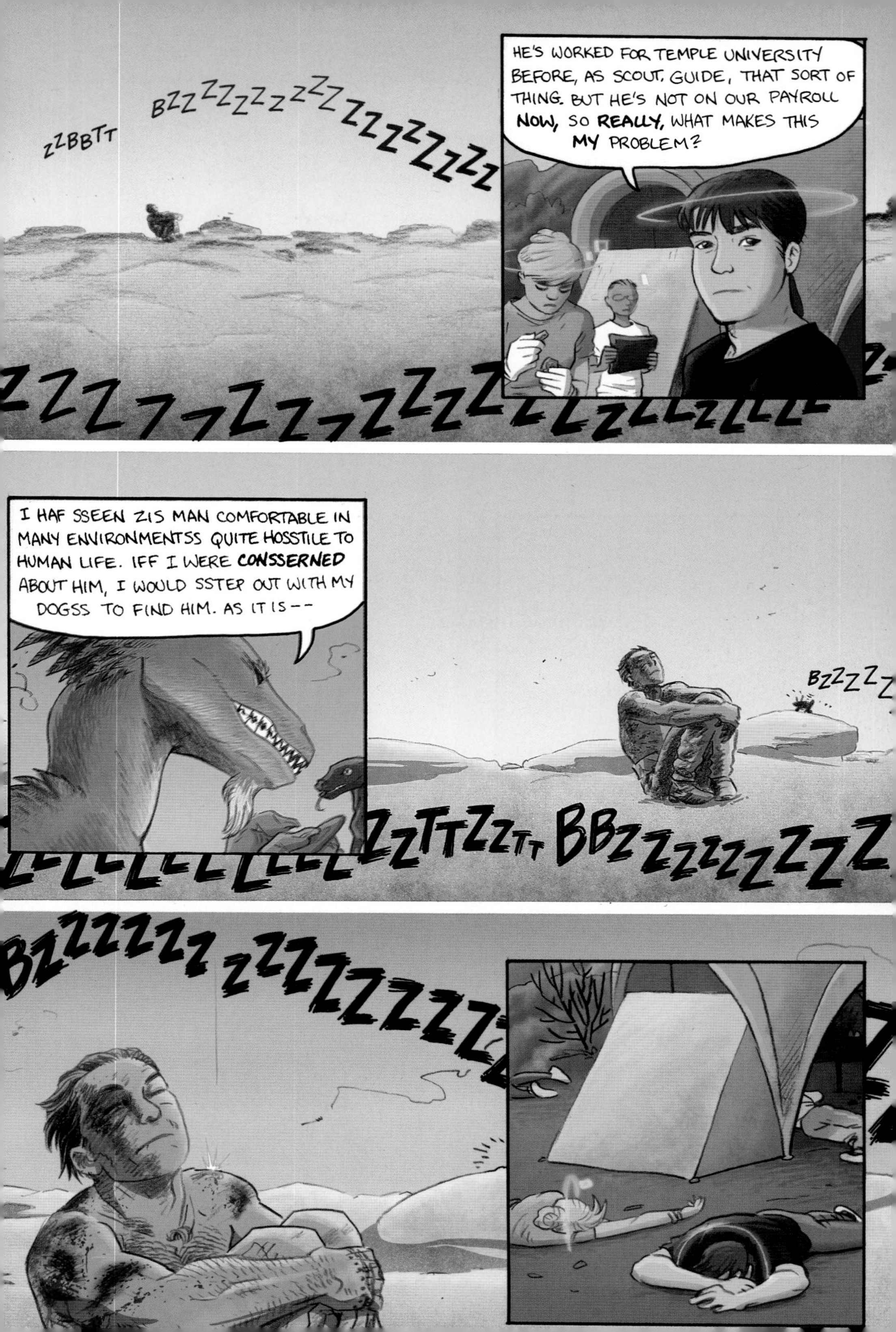
zZBBTT
HE'S WORKED FOR TEMPLE UNIVERSITY BEFORE, AS SCOUT, GUIDE, THAT SORT OF THING. BUT HE'S NOT ON OUR PAYROLL NOW, SO REALLY, WHAT MAKES THIS MY PROBLEM?
I HAF SSEEN ZIS MAN COMFORTABLE IN MANY ENVIRONMENTSS QUITE HOSSTILE TO HUMAN LIFE. IFF I WERE CONSSERNED ABOUT HIM, I WOULD SSTEP OUT WITH MY DOGSS TO FIND HIM. AS IT IS--

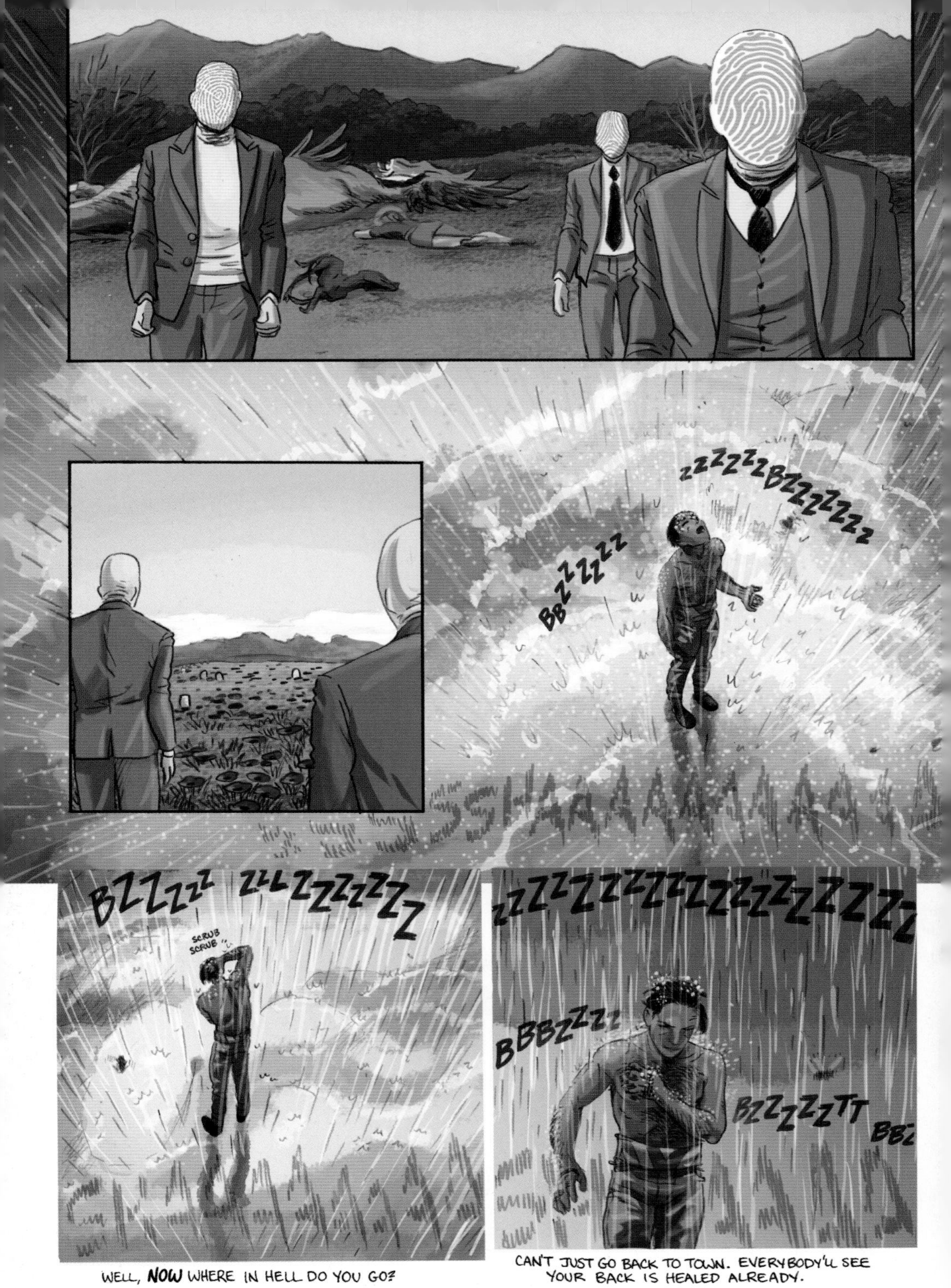
zzzzzzBzzzzzzzzz
BBzzzzzz
BZZzzz zzzzzzzzzZ
SCRUB SCRUB
zzzzzzzzzzzzzzzzzzzz
BBBzzzz
BZZzzzzTT
BBz

WELL, **NOW** WHERE IN HELL DO YOU GO?

CAN'T JUST GO BACK TO TOWN. EVERYBODY'LL SEE YOUR BACK IS HEALED ALREADY.

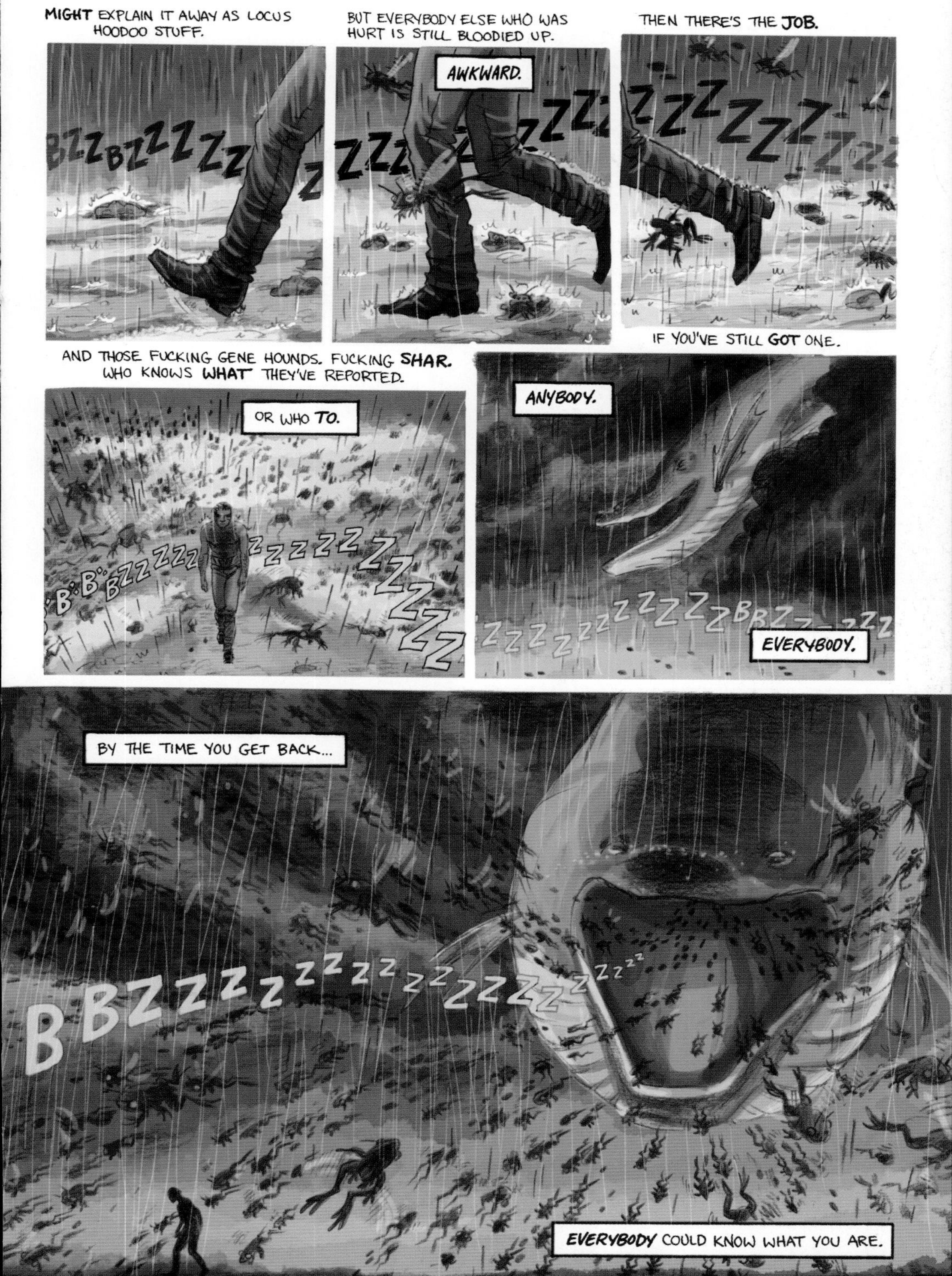
MIGHT EXPLAIN IT AWAY AS LOCUS HOODOO STUFF.
BZZBZZZZZZZ
BUT EVERYBODY ELSE WHO WAS HURT IS STILL BLOODIED UP.
AWKWARD.
ZZZ ZZZZZ
THEN THERE'S THE JOB.
ZZZZZZZ
IF YOU'VE STILL GOT ONE.
AND THOSE FUCKING GENE HOUNDS. FUCKING SHAR. WHO KNOWS WHAT THEY'VE REPORTED.
OR WHO TO.
B:B:BZZZZZ ZZZZZZZZZ
ANYBODY.
ZZZZZZZZZZZBBZZZZ
EVERYBODY.
BY THE TIME YOU GET BACK...
BBZZZZZZZZZZZZZZZZZZZZZ
EVERYBODY COULD KNOW WHAT YOU ARE.

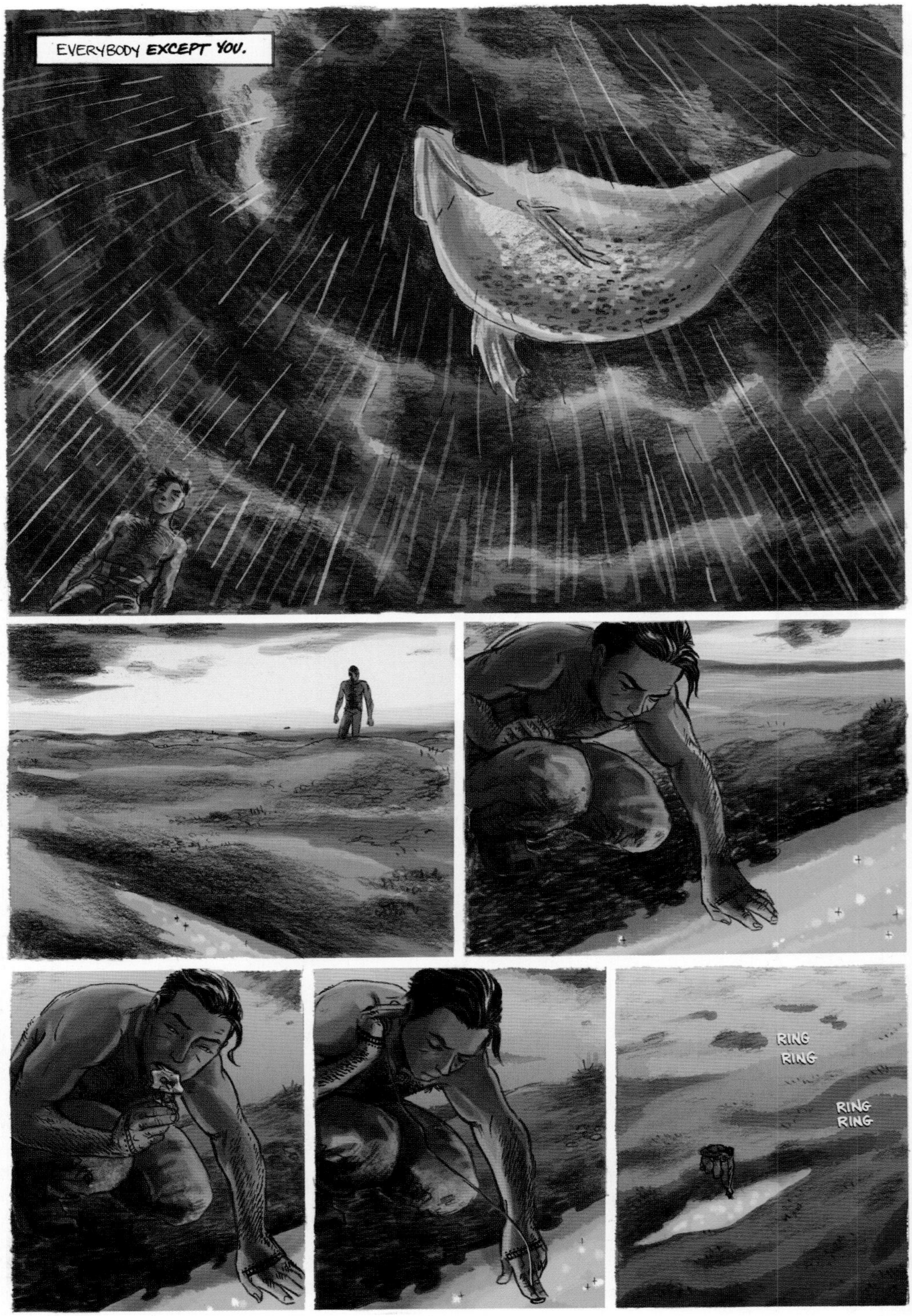
EVERYBODY EXCEPT YOU.
RING
RING
RING
RING

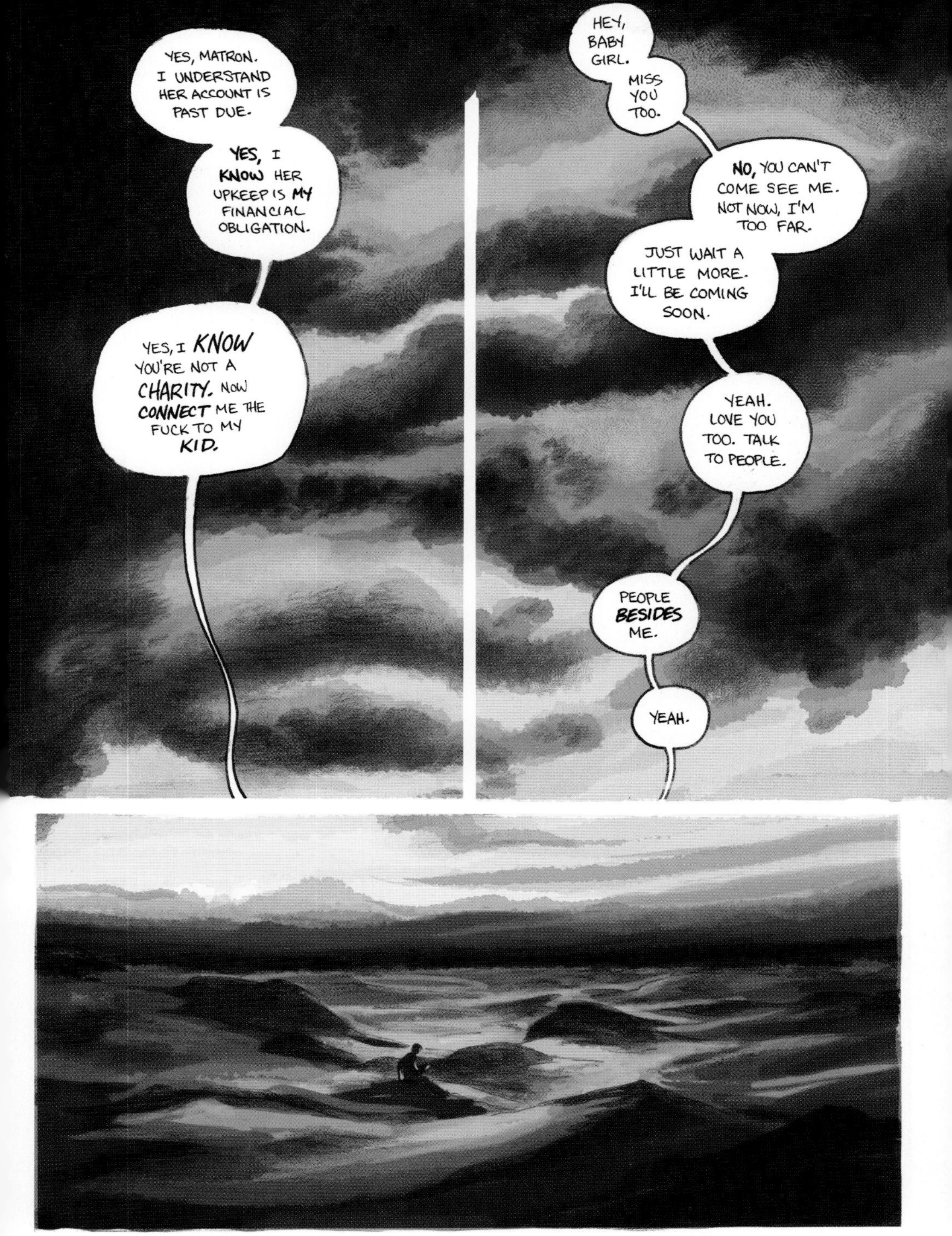
YES, MATRON. I UNDERSTAND HER ACCOUNT IS PAST DUE.
YES, I KNOW HER UPKEEP IS MY FINANCIAL OBLIGATION.
YES, I KNOW YOU'RE NOT A CHARITY. NOW CONNECT ME THE FUCK TO MY KID.
HEY, BABY GIRL.
MISS YOU TOO.
NO, YOU CAN'T COME SEE ME. NOT NOW, I'M TOO FAR.
JUST WAIT A LITTLE MORE. I'LL BE COMING SOON.
YEAH. LOVE YOU TOO. TALK TO PEOPLE.
PEOPLE BESIDES ME.
YEAH.

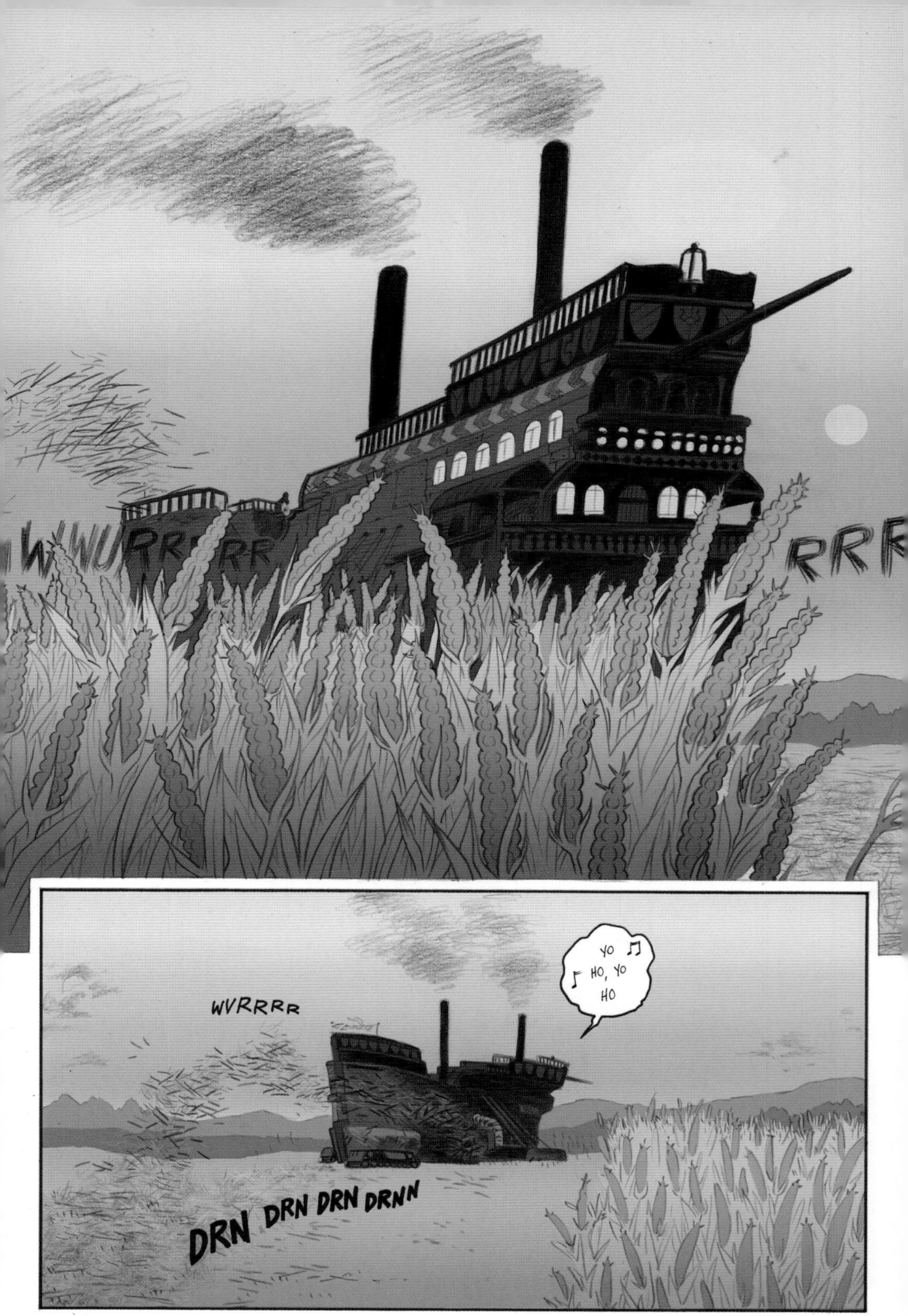
WWURRRRR
RRR
WVRRRR
YO ♪ HO, YO HO
DRN DRN DRN DRNN

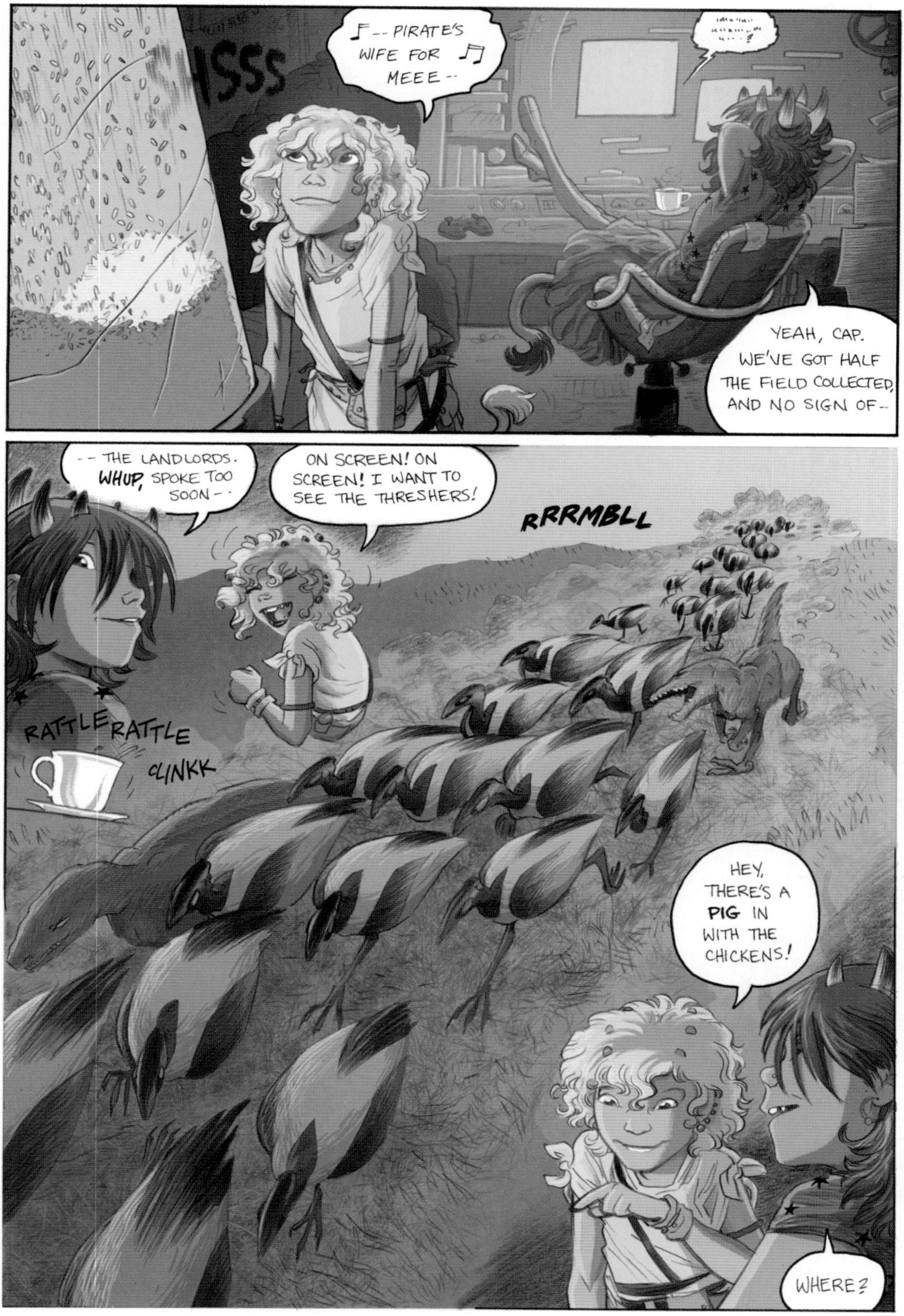
SHSSS
♪ -- PIRATE'S WIFE FOR ♫ MEEE --
YEAH, CAP. WE'VE GOT HALF THE FIELD COLLECTED, AND NO SIGN OF--
-- THE LANDLORDS. WHUP, SPOKE TOO SOON --
ON SCREEN! ON SCREEN! I WANT TO SEE THE THRESHERS!
RRRMBLL
RATTLE RATTLE
CLINKK
HEY, THERE'S A PIG IN WITH THE CHICKENS!
WHERE?

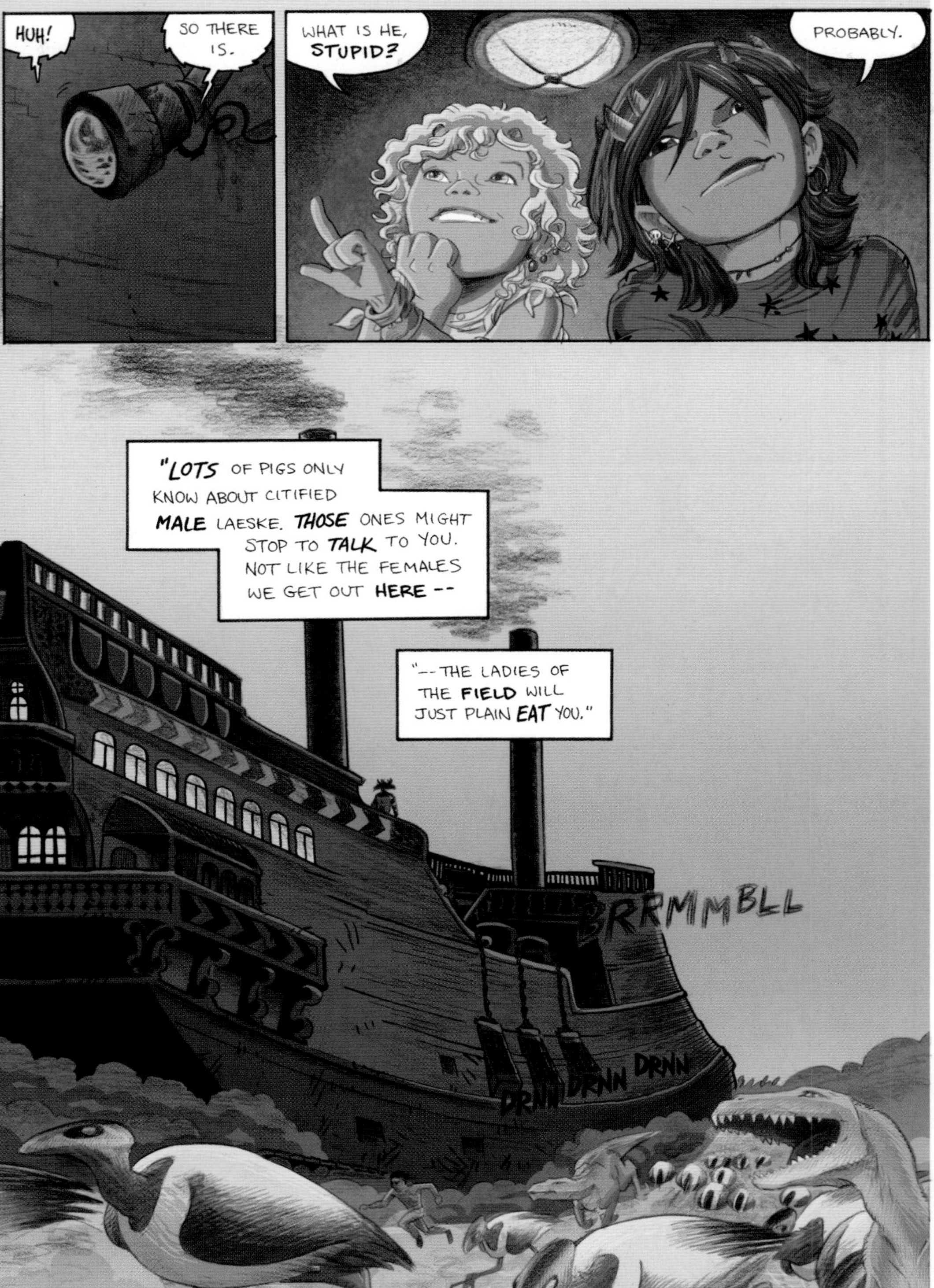
HUH!
SO THERE IS.
WHAT IS HE, STUPID?
PROBABLY.
"LOTS OF PIGS ONLY KNOW ABOUT CITIFIED MALE LAESKE. THOSE ONES MIGHT STOP TO TALK TO YOU. NOT LIKE THE FEMALES WE GET OUT HERE --
"-- THE LADIES OF THE FIELD WILL JUST PLAIN EAT YOU."
BRRMMBLL
DRNN DRNN DRNN

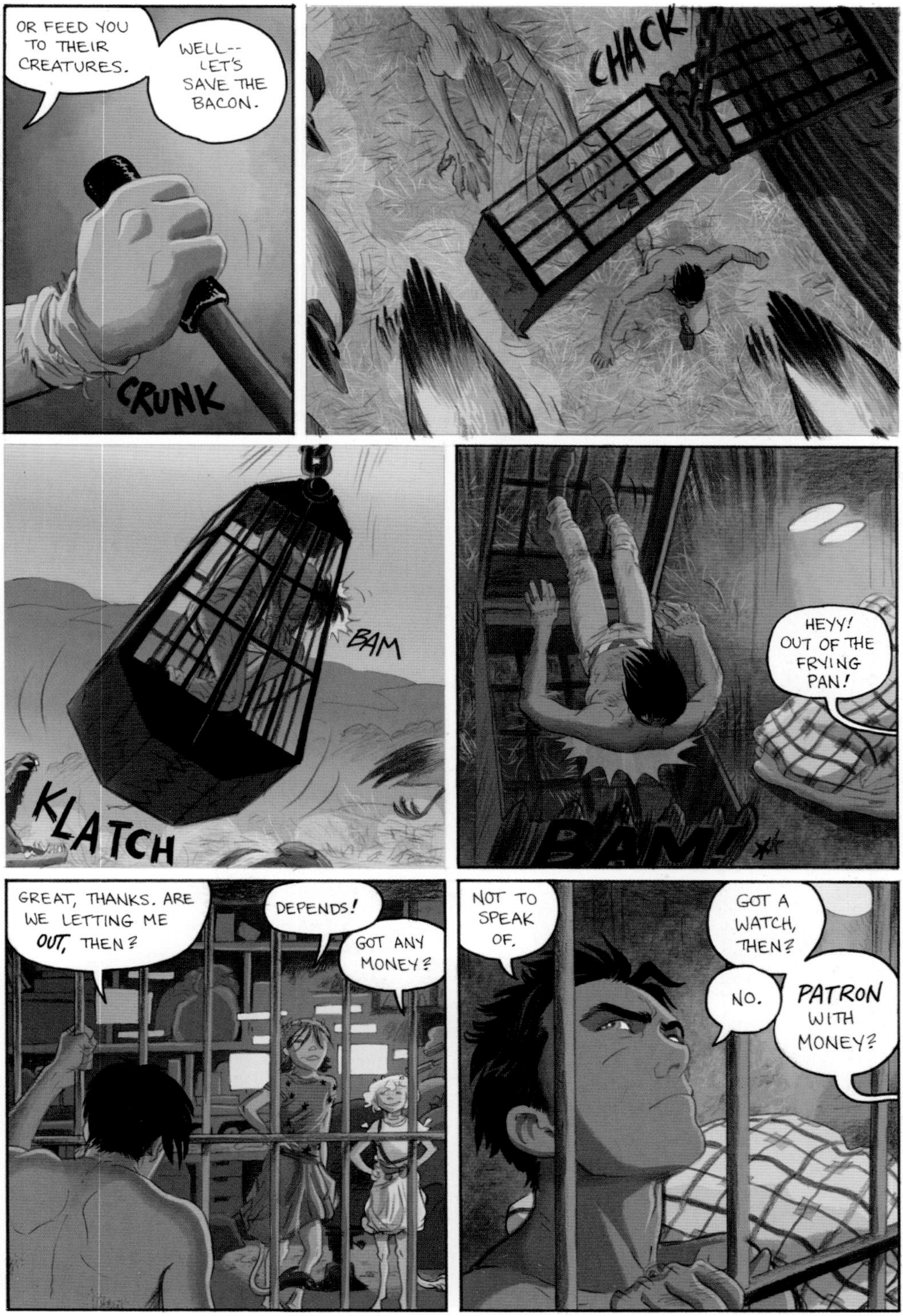
OR FEED YOU TO THEIR CREATURES.
WELL-- LET'S SAVE THE BACON.
CRUNK
CHACK
BAM
KLATCH
HEYY! OUT OF THE FRYING PAN!
BAM!
GREAT, THANKS. ARE WE LETTING ME OUT, THEN?
DEPENDS!
GOT ANY MONEY?
NOT TO SPEAK OF.
GOT A WATCH, THEN?
NO.
PATRON WITH MONEY?

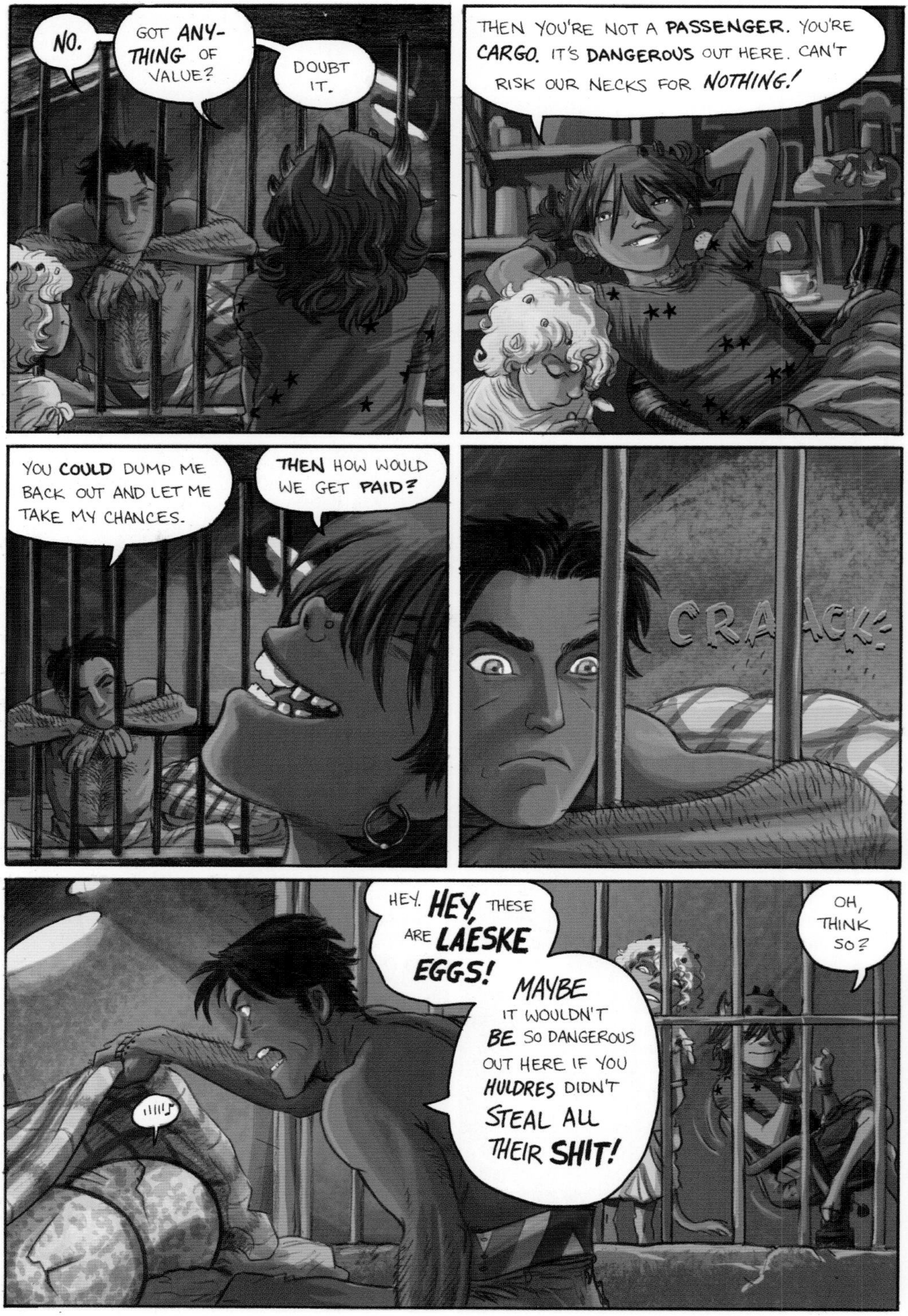
NO.
GOT ANY-THING OF VALUE?
DOUBT IT.
THEN YOU'RE NOT A PASSENGER. YOU'RE CARGO. IT'S DANGEROUS OUT HERE. CAN'T RISK OUR NECKS FOR NOTHING!
YOU COULD DUMP ME BACK OUT AND LET ME TAKE MY CHANCES.
THEN HOW WOULD WE GET PAID?
CRAACK!
HEY. HEY, THESE ARE LAESKE EGGS!
MAYBE IT WOULDN'T BE SO DANGEROUS OUT HERE IF YOU HULDRES DIDN'T STEAL ALL THEIR SHIT!
OH, THINK SO?

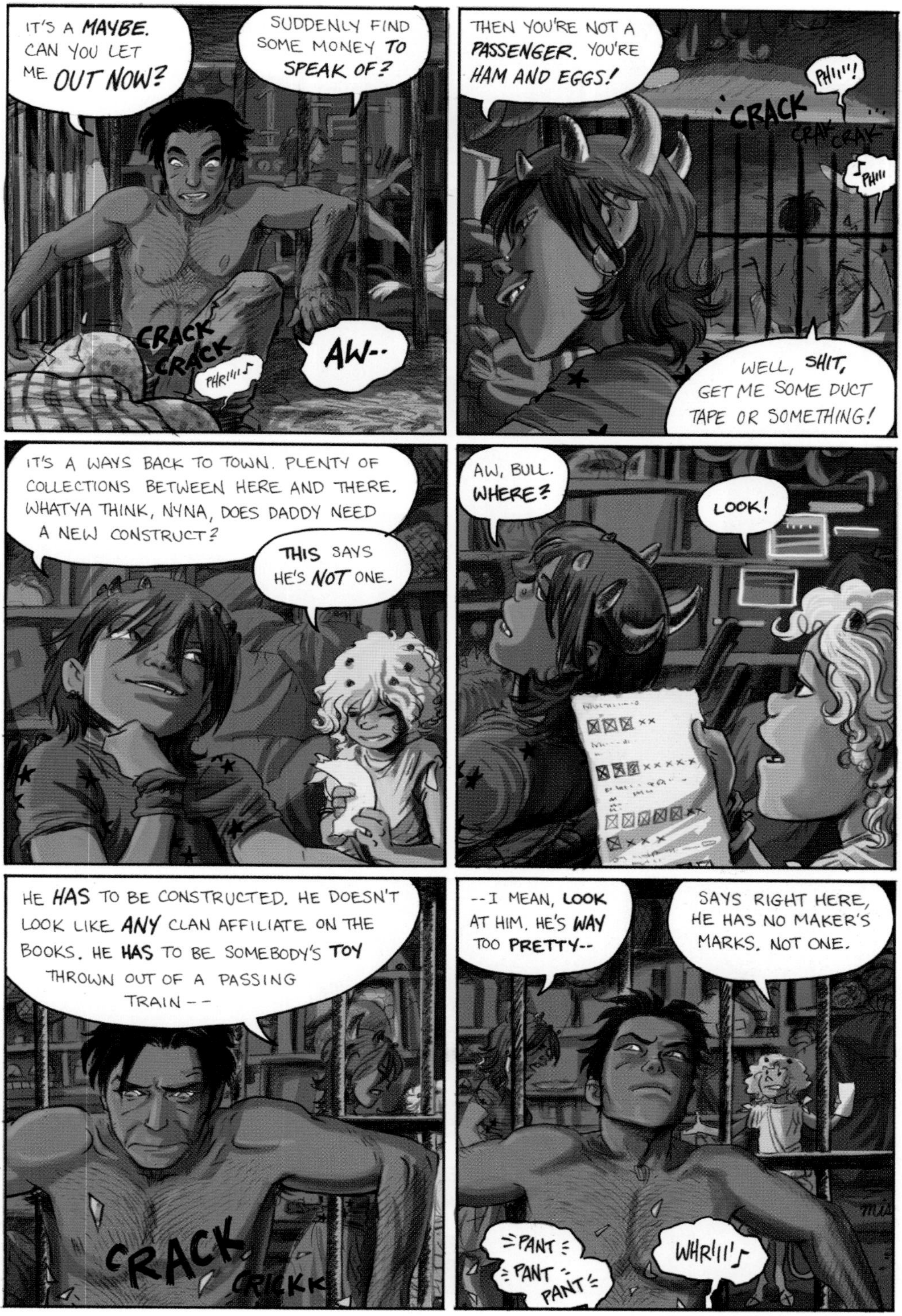
IT'S A MAYBE. CAN YOU LET ME OUT NOW?
SUDDENLY FIND SOME MONEY TO SPEAK OF?
CRACK
CRACK
PHR!!!
AW--
THEN YOU'RE NOT A PASSENGER. YOU'RE HAM AND EGGS!
PHI!!!
CRACK
CRAK
CRAK
PHI!!
WELL, SHIT, GET ME SOME DUCT TAPE OR SOMETHING!
IT'S A WAYS BACK TO TOWN. PLENTY OF COLLECTIONS BETWEEN HERE AND THERE. WHATYA THINK, NYNA, DOES DADDY NEED A NEW CONSTRUCT?
THIS SAYS HE'S NOT ONE.
AW, BULL. WHERE?
LOOK!
HE HAS TO BE CONSTRUCTED. HE DOESN'T LOOK LIKE ANY CLAN AFFILIATE ON THE BOOKS. HE HAS TO BE SOMEBODY'S TOY THROWN OUT OF A PASSING TRAIN--
CRACK
CRICKK
--I MEAN, LOOK AT HIM. HE'S WAY TOO PRETTY--
SAYS RIGHT HERE, HE HAS NO MAKER'S MARKS. NOT ONE.
PANT
PANT
PANT
WHR!!!

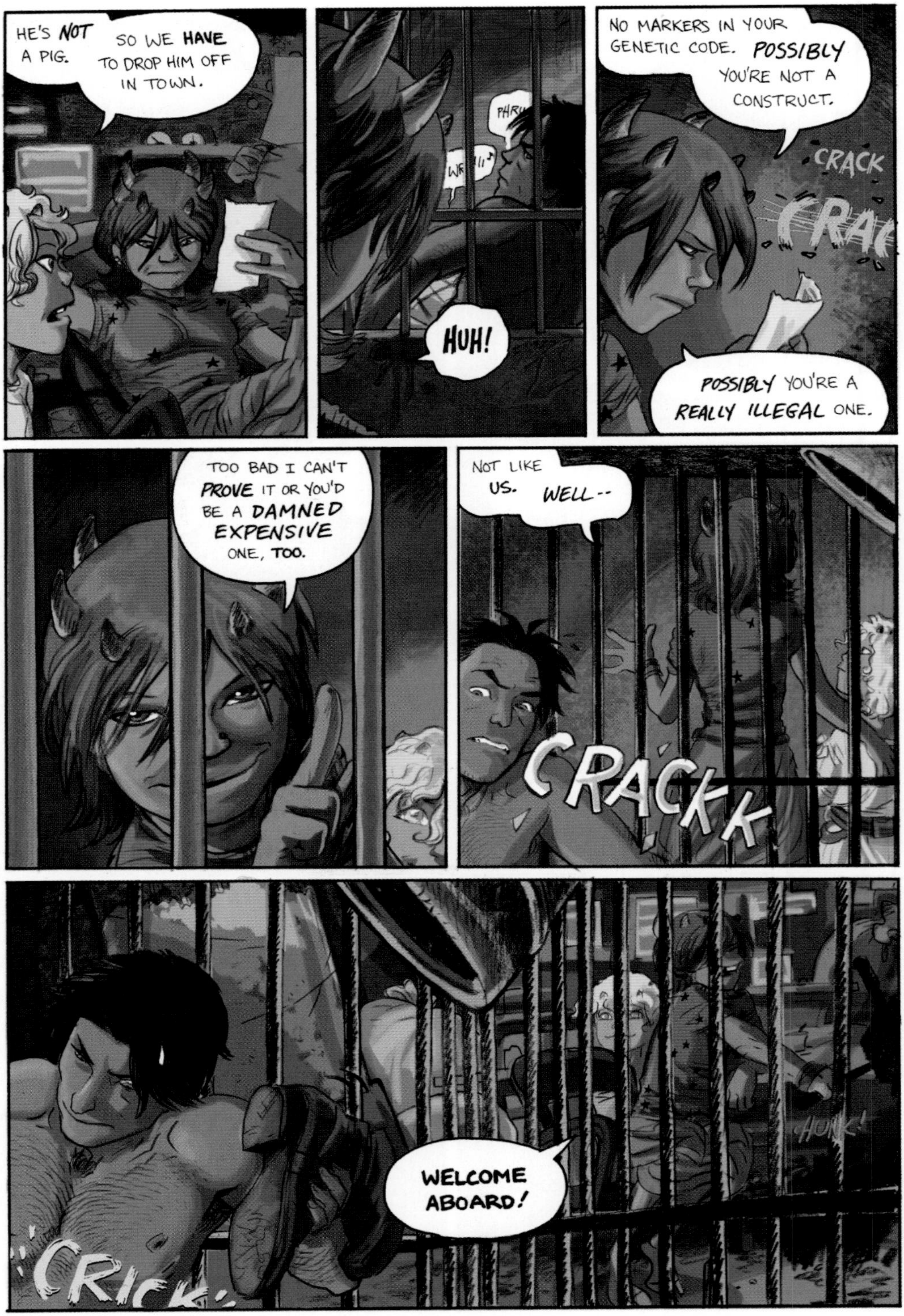
HE'S NOT A PIG.
SO WE HAVE TO DROP HIM OFF IN TOWN.
PHRU
WR!!
HUH!
NO MARKERS IN YOUR GENETIC CODE. POSSIBLY YOU'RE NOT A CONSTRUCT.
CRACK
CRAC
POSSIBLY YOU'RE A REALLY ILLEGAL ONE.
TOO BAD I CAN'T PROVE IT OR YOU'D BE A DAMNED EXPENSIVE ONE, TOO.
NOT LIKE US.
WELL--
CRACKK
CHUNK!
WELCOME ABOARD!
CRICK!

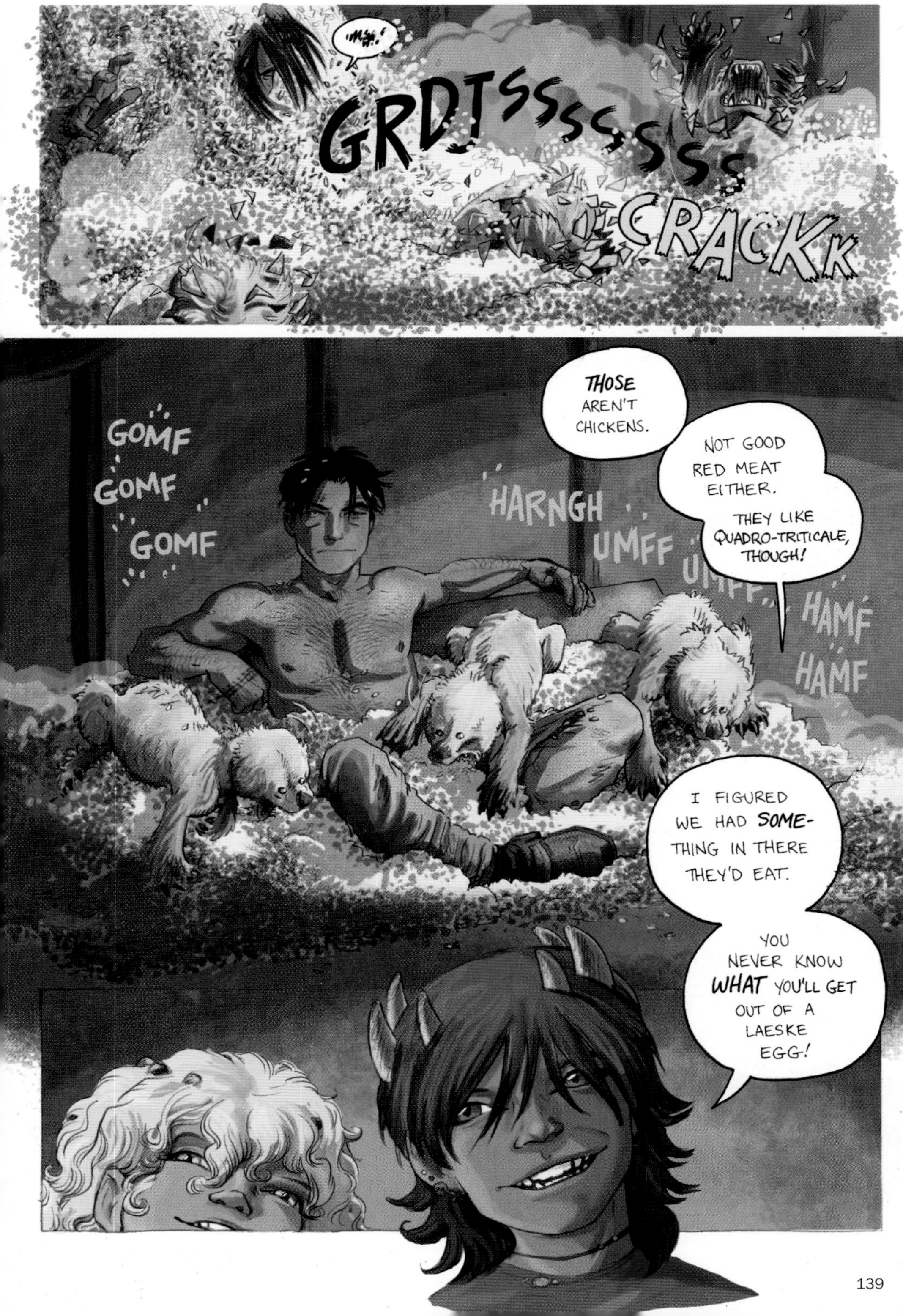
GRDTSSSSSSSS
CRACKK
THOSE AREN'T CHICKENS.
GOMF GOMF GOMF
HARNGH
UMFF
UMFF
HAMF
HAMF
NOT GOOD RED MEAT EITHER.
THEY LIKE QUADRO-TRITICALE, THOUGH!
I FIGURED WE HAD SOME-THING IN THERE THEY'D EAT.
YOU NEVER KNOW WHAT YOU'LL GET OUT OF A LAESKE EGG!

PART THREE

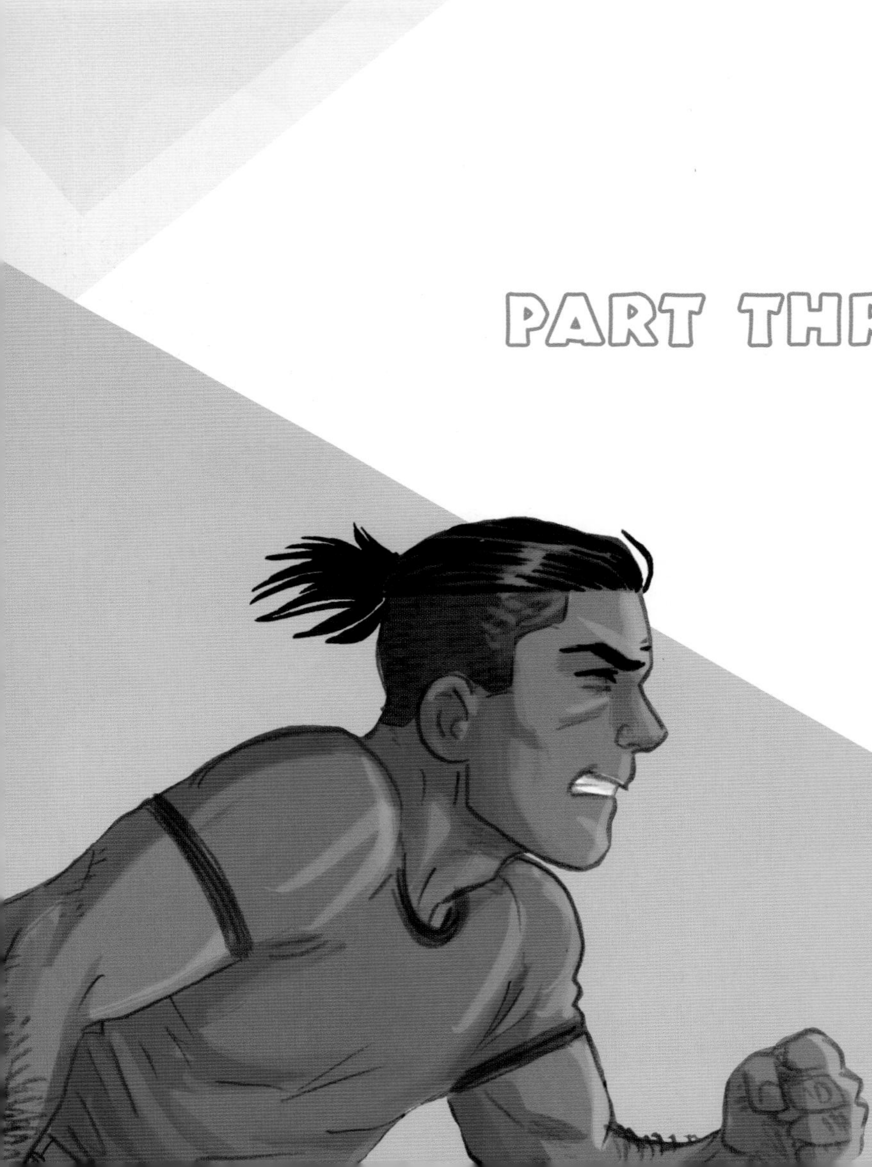

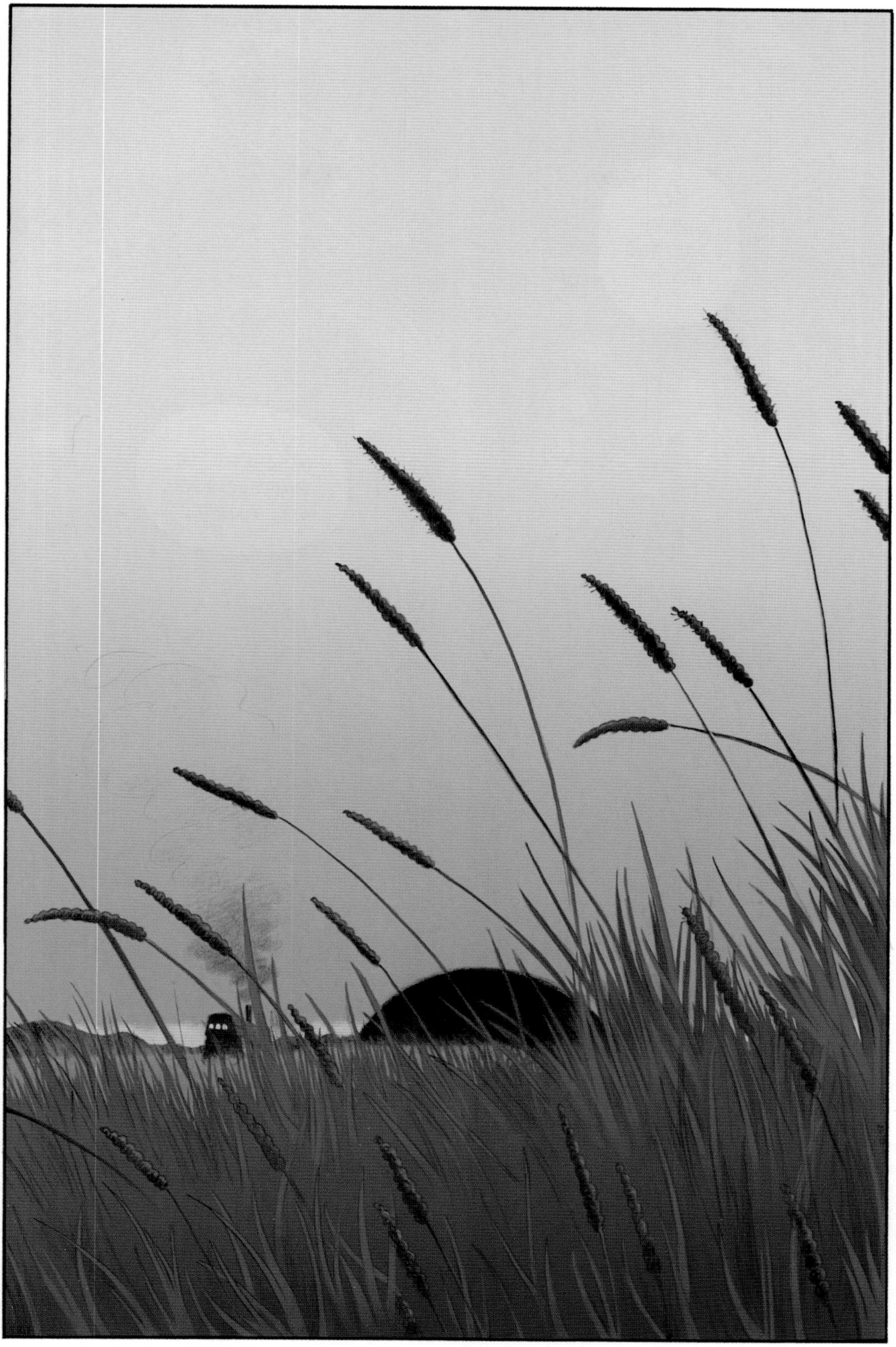

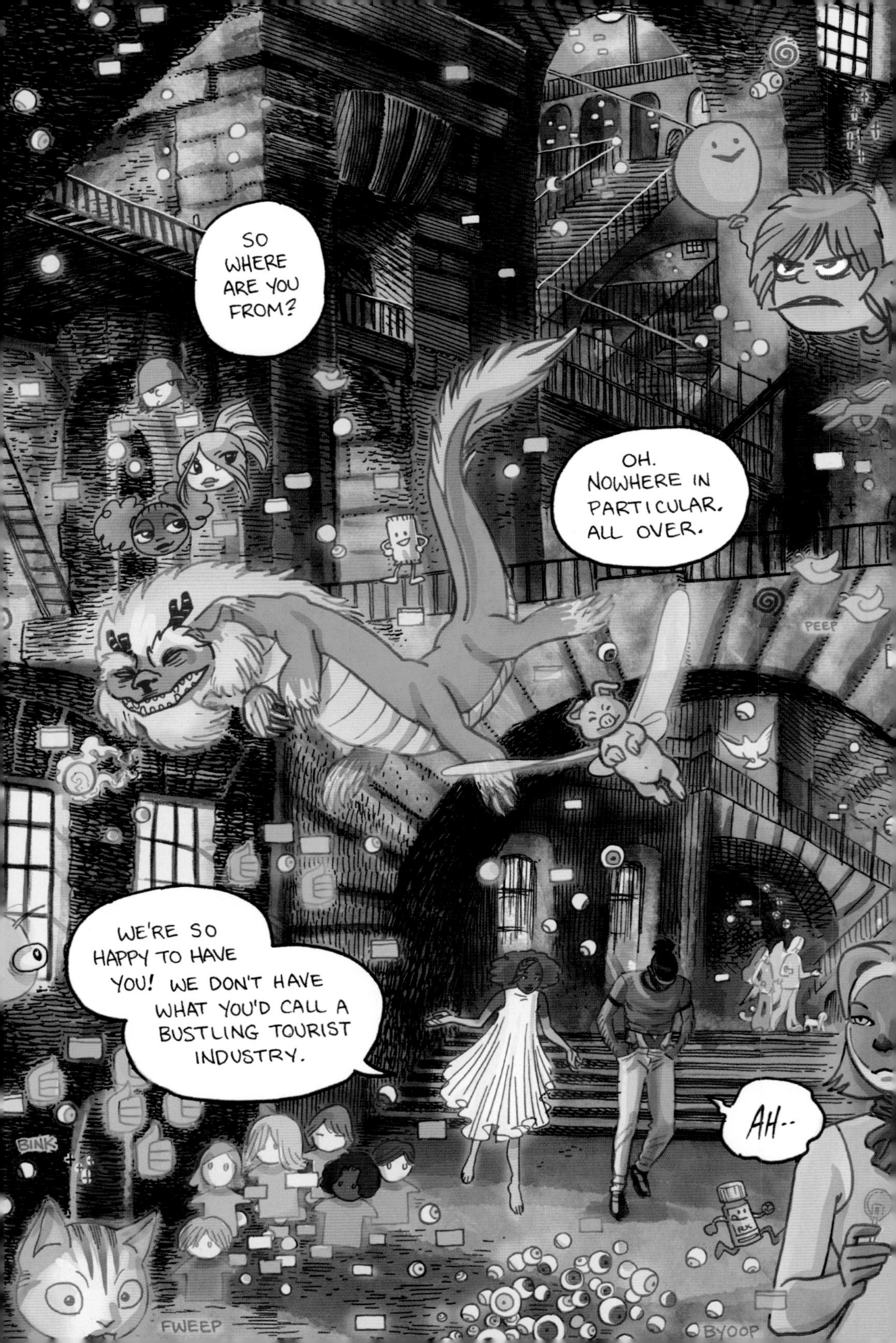
SO WHERE ARE YOU FROM?
OH. NOWHERE IN PARTICULAR. ALL OVER.
PEEP
WE'RE SO HAPPY TO HAVE YOU! WE DON'T HAVE WHAT YOU'D CALL A BUSTLING TOURIST INDUSTRY.
AH--
BINK
FWEEP
BYOOP

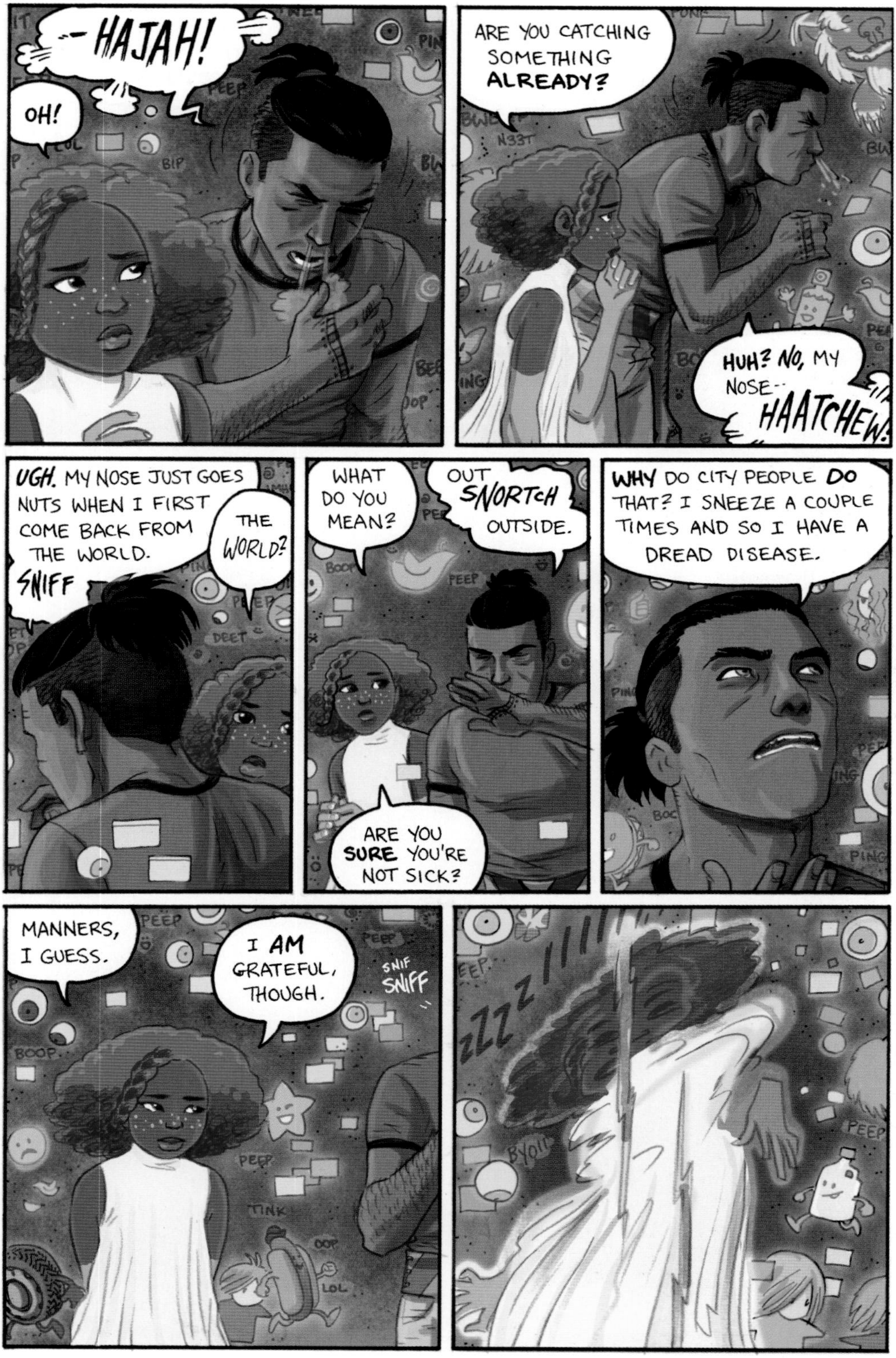
--HAJAH!
OH!
ARE YOU CATCHING SOMETHING ALREADY?
HUH? NO, MY NOSE--
HAATCHEW!
UGH. MY NOSE JUST GOES NUTS WHEN I FIRST COME BACK FROM THE WORLD.
SNIFF
THE WORLD?
WHAT DO YOU MEAN?
OUT
SNORTCH
OUTSIDE.
ARE YOU SURE YOU'RE NOT SICK?
WHY DO CITY PEOPLE DO THAT? I SNEEZE A COUPLE TIMES AND SO I HAVE A DREAD DISEASE.
MANNERS, I GUESS.
I AM GRATEFUL, THOUGH.
SNIF
SNIFF
ZZZZ

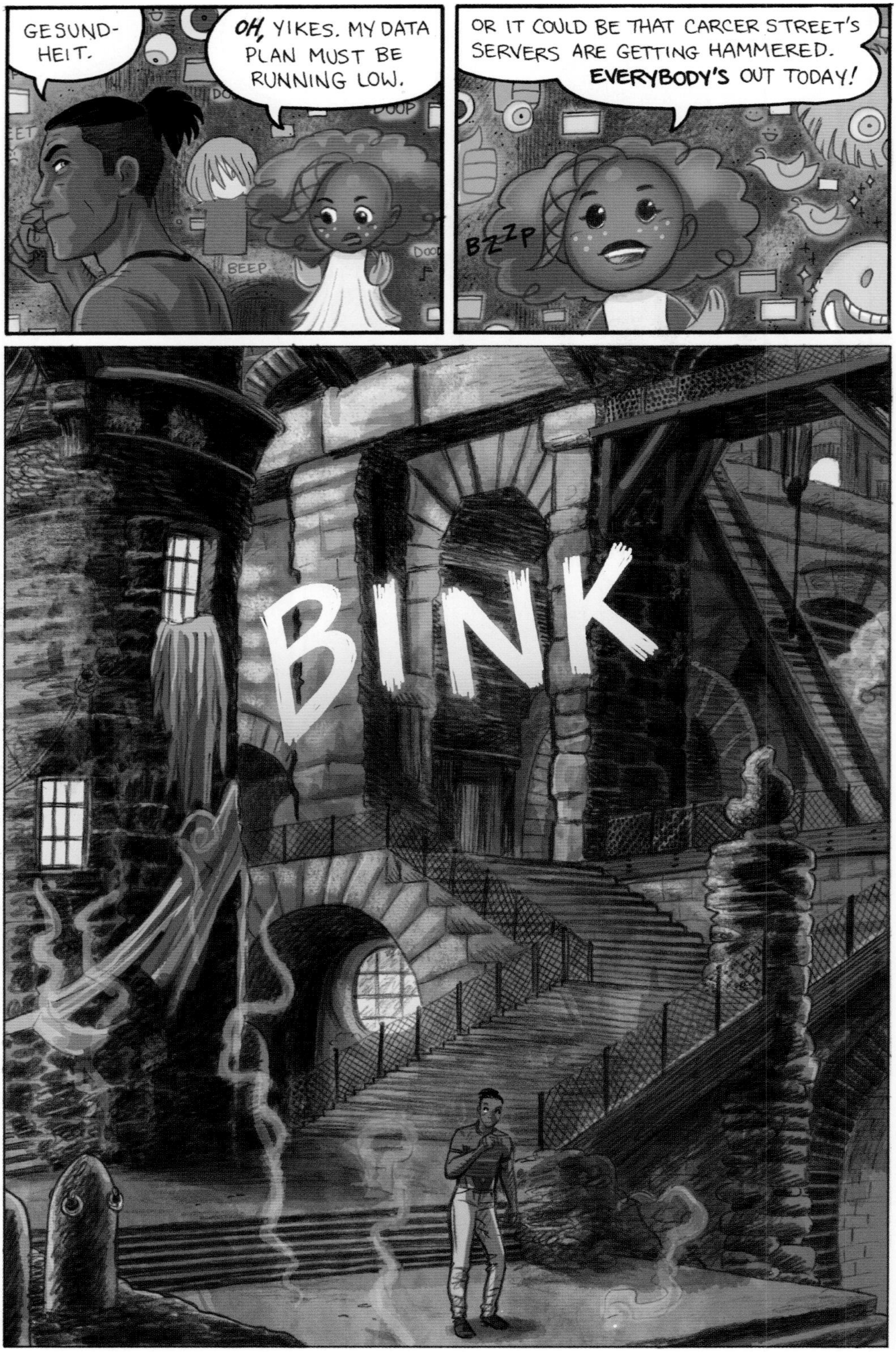
GESUNDHEIT.
OH, YIKES. MY DATA PLAN MUST BE RUNNING LOW.
DOOP
BEEP
OR IT COULD BE THAT CARCER STREET'S SERVERS ARE GETTING HAMMERED. EVERYBODY'S OUT TODAY!
BZZZP
BINK

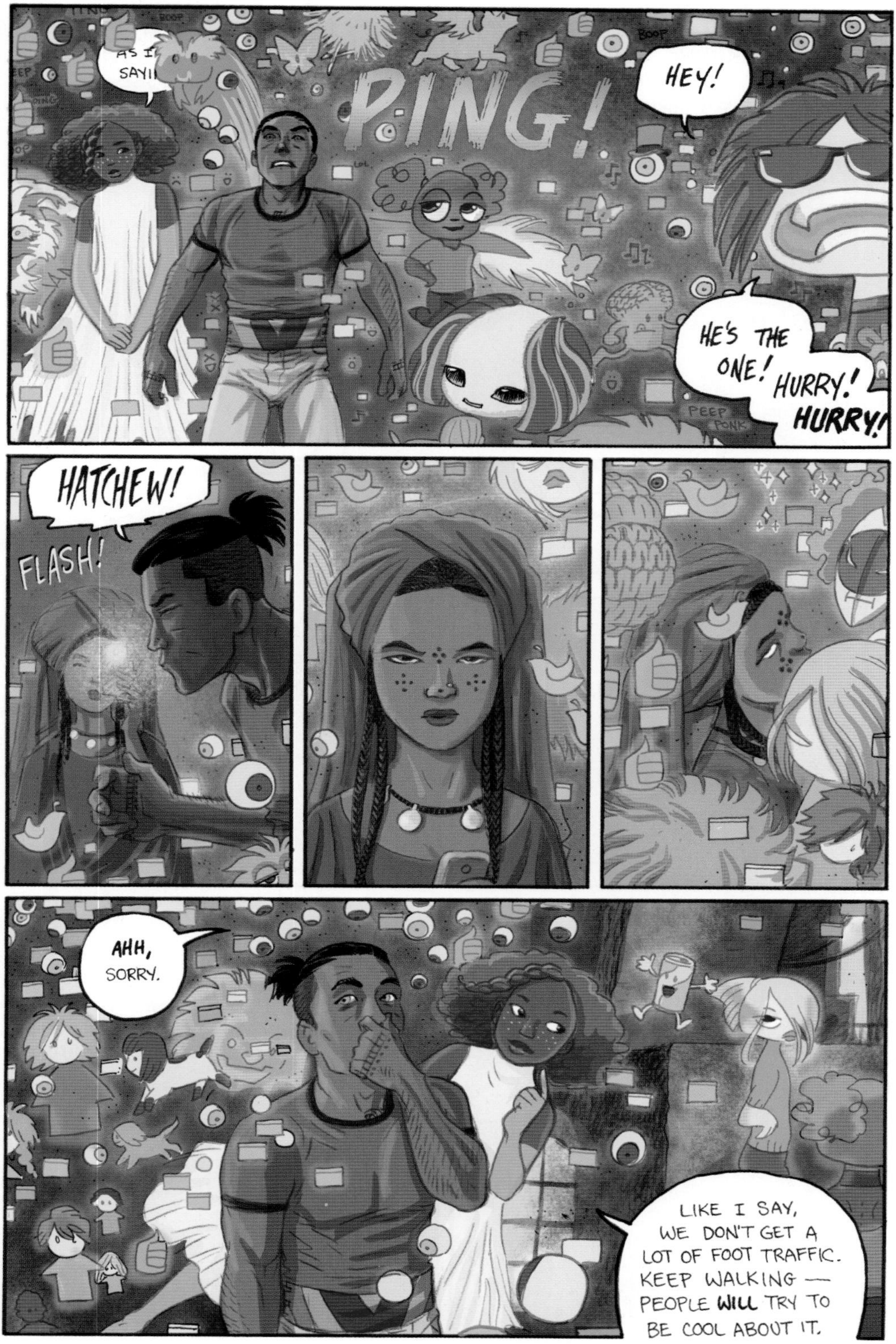

BOOP
PEEP
AS I SAYI
BOOP
PING!
HEY!
HE'S THE ONE!
HURRY!
HURRY!
PEEP
PONK
HATCHEW!
FLASH!
AHH, SORRY.
LIKE I SAY, WE DON'T GET A LOT OF FOOT TRAFFIC. KEEP WALKING — PEOPLE **WILL** TRY TO BE COOL ABOUT IT.

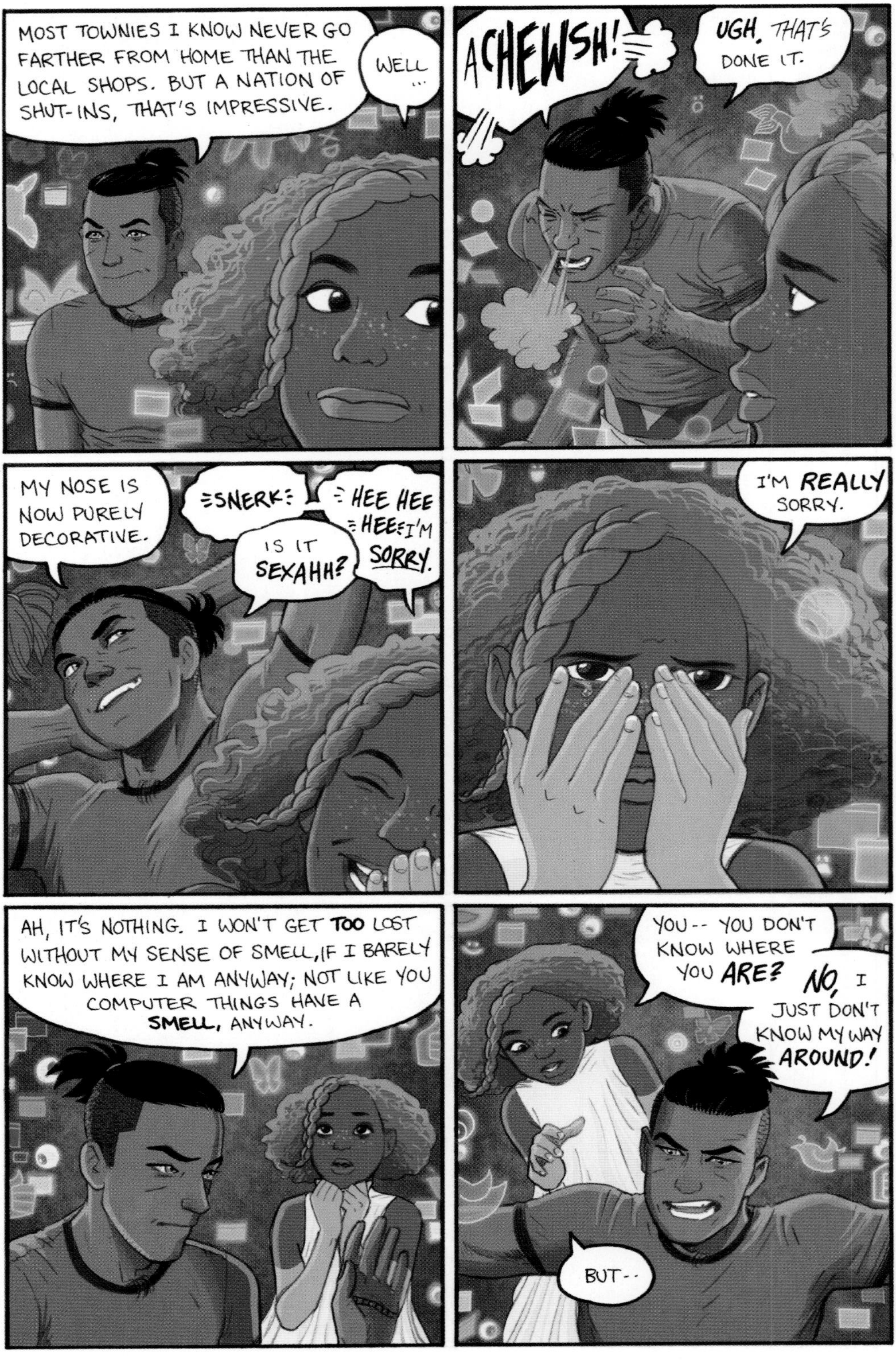

MOST TOWNIES I KNOW NEVER GO FARTHER FROM HOME THAN THE LOCAL SHOPS. BUT A NATION OF SHUT-INS, THAT'S IMPRESSIVE.
WELL...
ACHEWSH!
UGH. THAT'S DONE IT.
MY NOSE IS NOW PURELY DECORATIVE.
SNERK
IS IT SEXAHH?
HEE HEE HEE I'M SORRY.
I'M REALLY SORRY.
AH, IT'S NOTHING. I WON'T GET TOO LOST WITHOUT MY SENSE OF SMELL, IF I BARELY KNOW WHERE I AM ANYWAY; NOT LIKE YOU COMPUTER THINGS HAVE A SMELL, ANYWAY.
YOU-- YOU DON'T KNOW WHERE YOU ARE?
NO, I JUST DON'T KNOW MY WAY AROUND!
BUT--

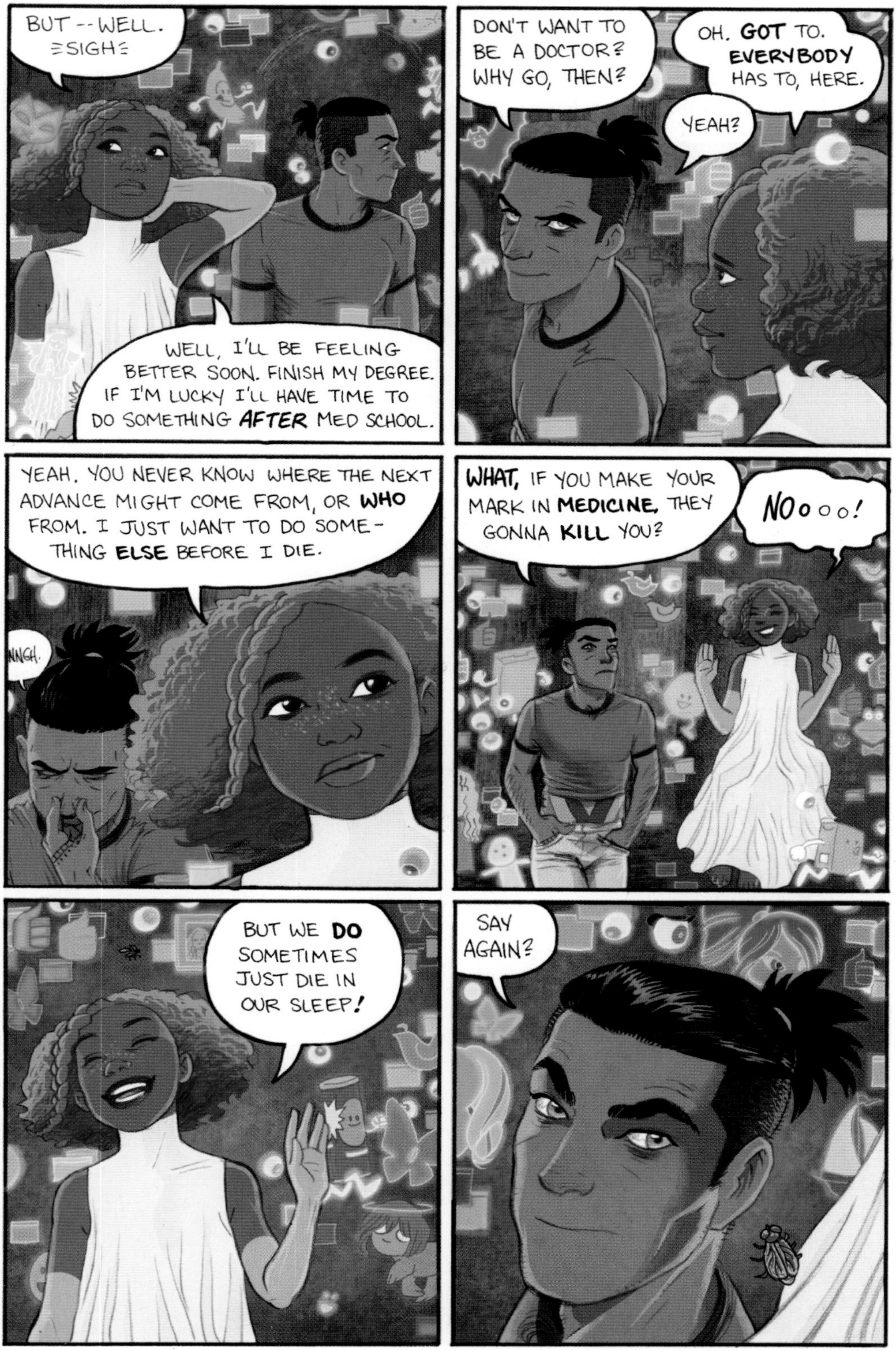

BUT--WELL.
≡SIGH≡
WELL, I'LL BE FEELING BETTER SOON. FINISH MY DEGREE. IF I'M LUCKY I'LL HAVE TIME TO DO SOMETHING AFTER MED SCHOOL.
DON'T WANT TO BE A DOCTOR? WHY GO, THEN?
OH. GOT TO. EVERYBODY HAS TO, HERE.
YEAH?
YEAH. YOU NEVER KNOW WHERE THE NEXT ADVANCE MIGHT COME FROM, OR WHO FROM. I JUST WANT TO DO SOME-THING ELSE BEFORE I DIE.
NNGH.
WHAT, IF YOU MAKE YOUR MARK IN MEDICINE, THEY GONNA KILL YOU?
NOooo!
BUT WE DO SOMETIMES JUST DIE IN OUR SLEEP!
SAY AGAIN?

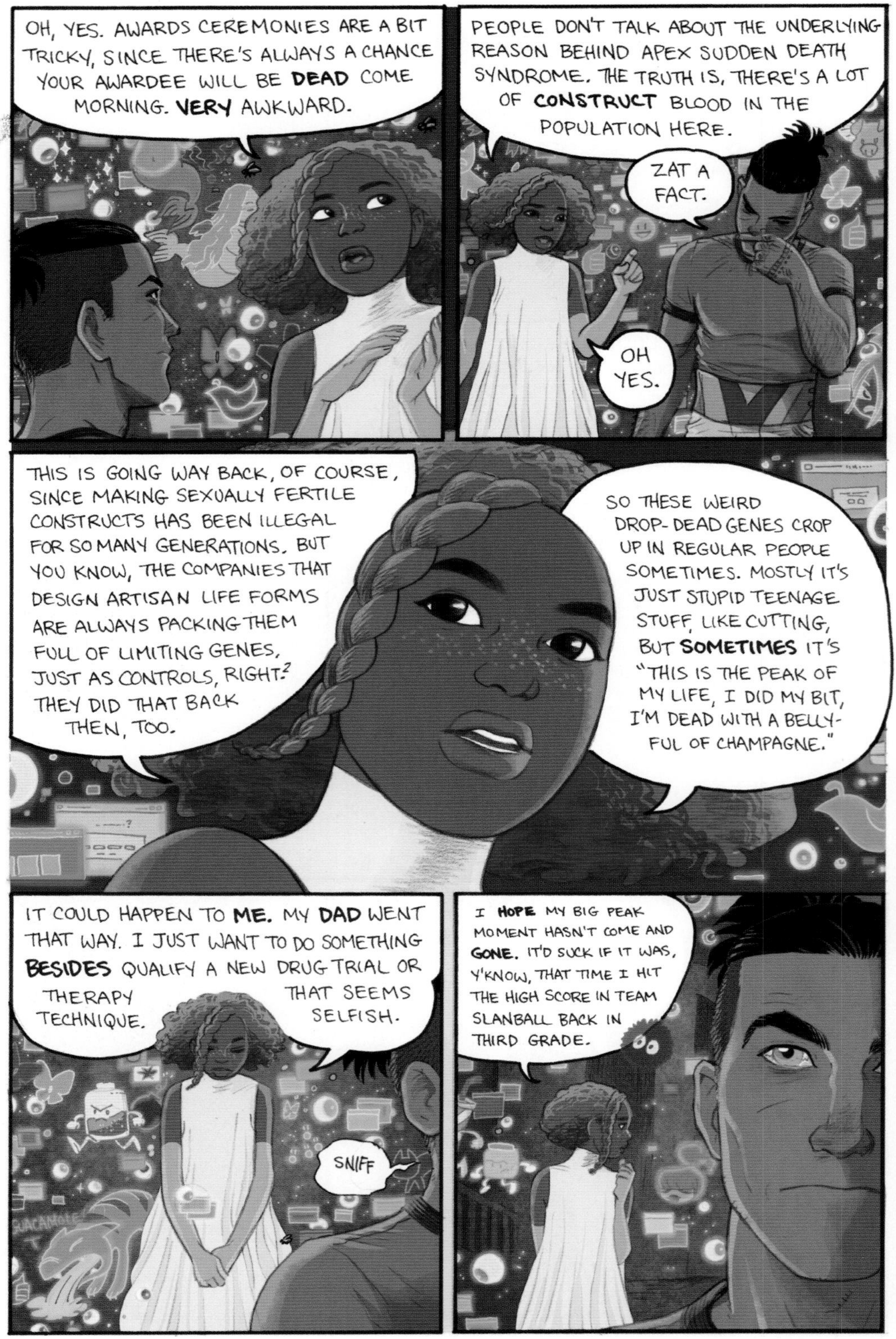

OH, YES. AWARDS CEREMONIES ARE A BIT TRICKY, SINCE THERE'S ALWAYS A CHANCE YOUR AWARDEE WILL BE **DEAD** COME MORNING. **VERY** AWKWARD.
PEOPLE DON'T TALK ABOUT THE UNDERLYING REASON BEHIND APEX SUDDEN DEATH SYNDROME. THE TRUTH IS, THERE'S A LOT OF **CONSTRUCT** BLOOD IN THE POPULATION HERE.
ZAT A FACT.
OH YES.
THIS IS GOING WAY BACK, OF COURSE, SINCE MAKING SEXUALLY FERTILE CONSTRUCTS HAS BEEN ILLEGAL FOR SO MANY GENERATIONS. BUT YOU KNOW, THE COMPANIES THAT DESIGN ARTISAN LIFE FORMS ARE ALWAYS PACKING THEM FULL OF LIMITING GENES, JUST AS CONTROLS, RIGHT? THEY DID THAT BACK THEN, TOO.
SO THESE WEIRD DROP-DEAD GENES CROP UP IN REGULAR PEOPLE SOMETIMES. MOSTLY IT'S JUST STUPID TEENAGE STUFF, LIKE CUTTING, BUT **SOMETIMES** IT'S "THIS IS THE PEAK OF MY LIFE, I DID MY BIT, I'M DEAD WITH A BELLYFUL OF CHAMPAGNE."
IT COULD HAPPEN TO **ME.** MY **DAD** WENT THAT WAY. I JUST WANT TO DO SOMETHING **BESIDES** QUALIFY A NEW DRUG TRIAL OR THERAPY TECHNIQUE.
THAT SEEMS SELFISH.
SNIFF
I **HOPE** MY BIG PEAK MOMENT HASN'T COME AND **GONE.** IT'D SUCK IF IT WAS, Y'KNOW, THAT TIME I HIT THE HIGH SCORE IN TEAM SLANBALL BACK IN THIRD GRADE.

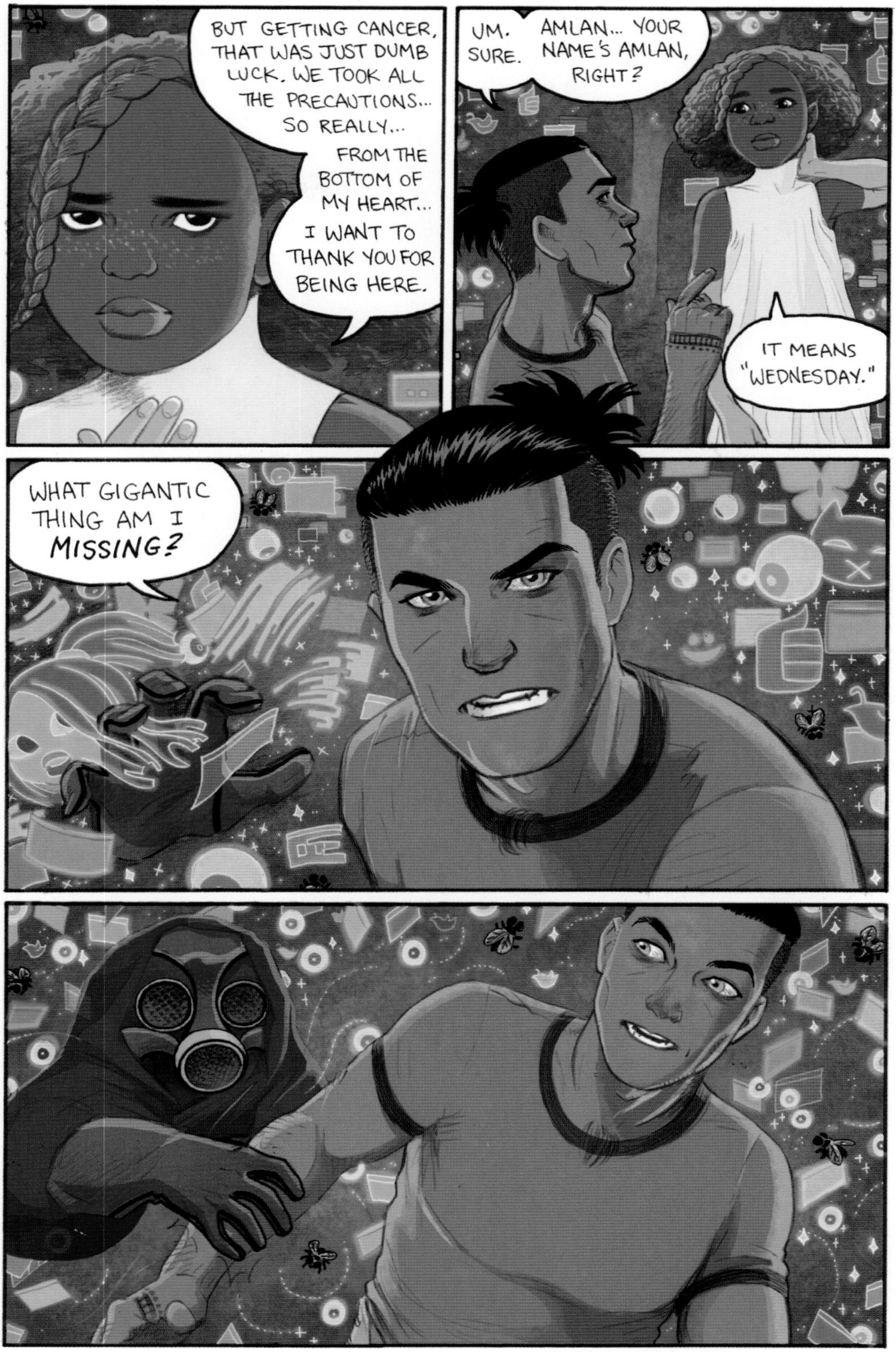
BUT GETTING CANCER, THAT WAS JUST DUMB LUCK. WE TOOK ALL THE PRECAUTIONS... SO REALLY...
FROM THE BOTTOM OF MY HEART...
I WANT TO THANK YOU FOR BEING HERE.
UM. SURE.
AMLAN... YOUR NAME'S AMLAN, RIGHT?
IT MEANS "WEDNESDAY."
WHAT GIGANTIC THING AM I *MISSING?*

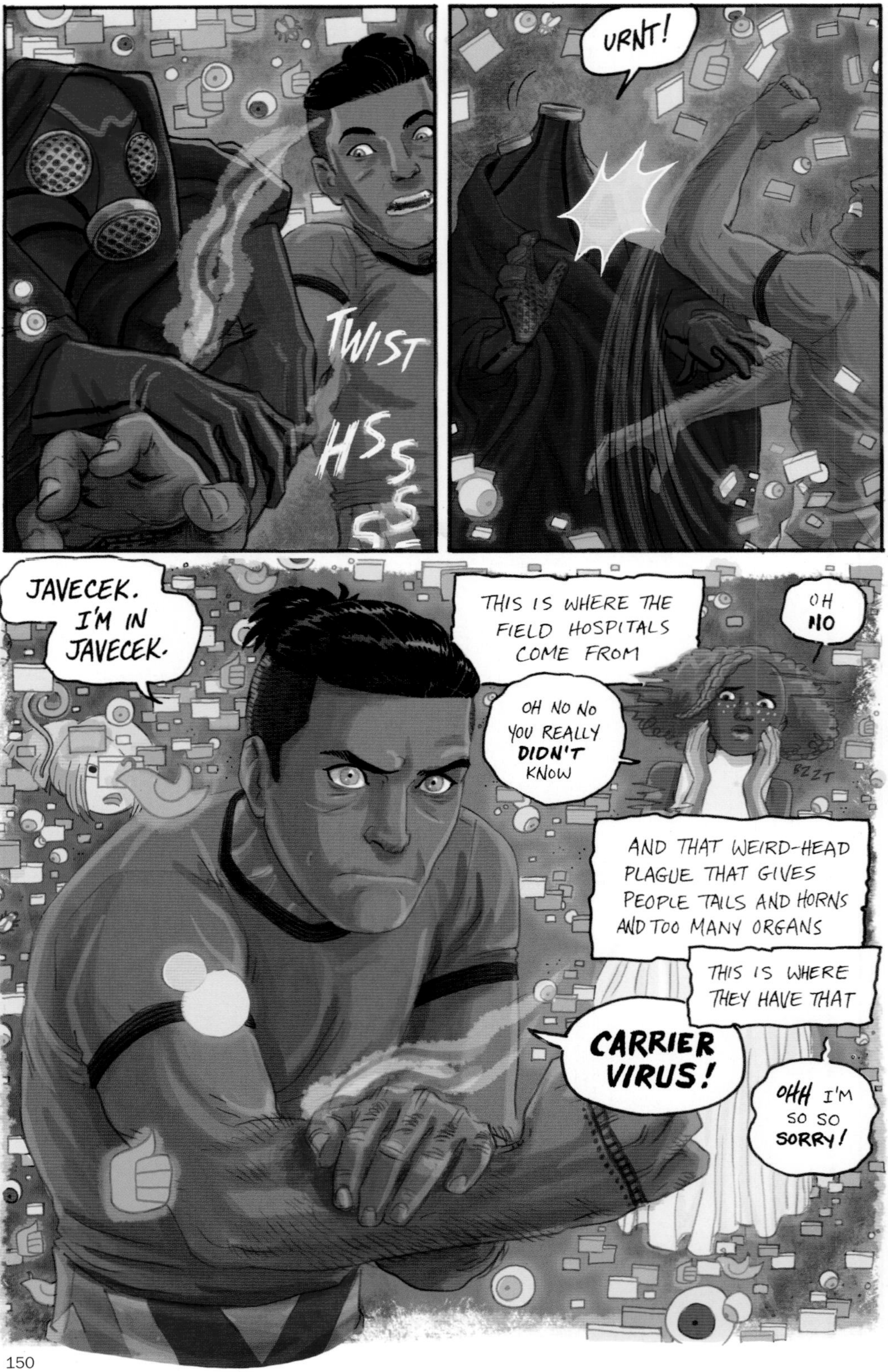
TWIST
HSSSS
URNT!
JAVECEK. I'M IN JAVECEK.
THIS IS WHERE THE FIELD HOSPITALS COME FROM
OH NO
OH NO NO YOU REALLY DIDN'T KNOW
BZZT
AND THAT WEIRD-HEAD PLAGUE THAT GIVES PEOPLE TAILS AND HORNS AND TOO MANY ORGANS
THIS IS WHERE THEY HAVE THAT
CARRIER VIRUS!
OHH I'M SO SO SORRY!

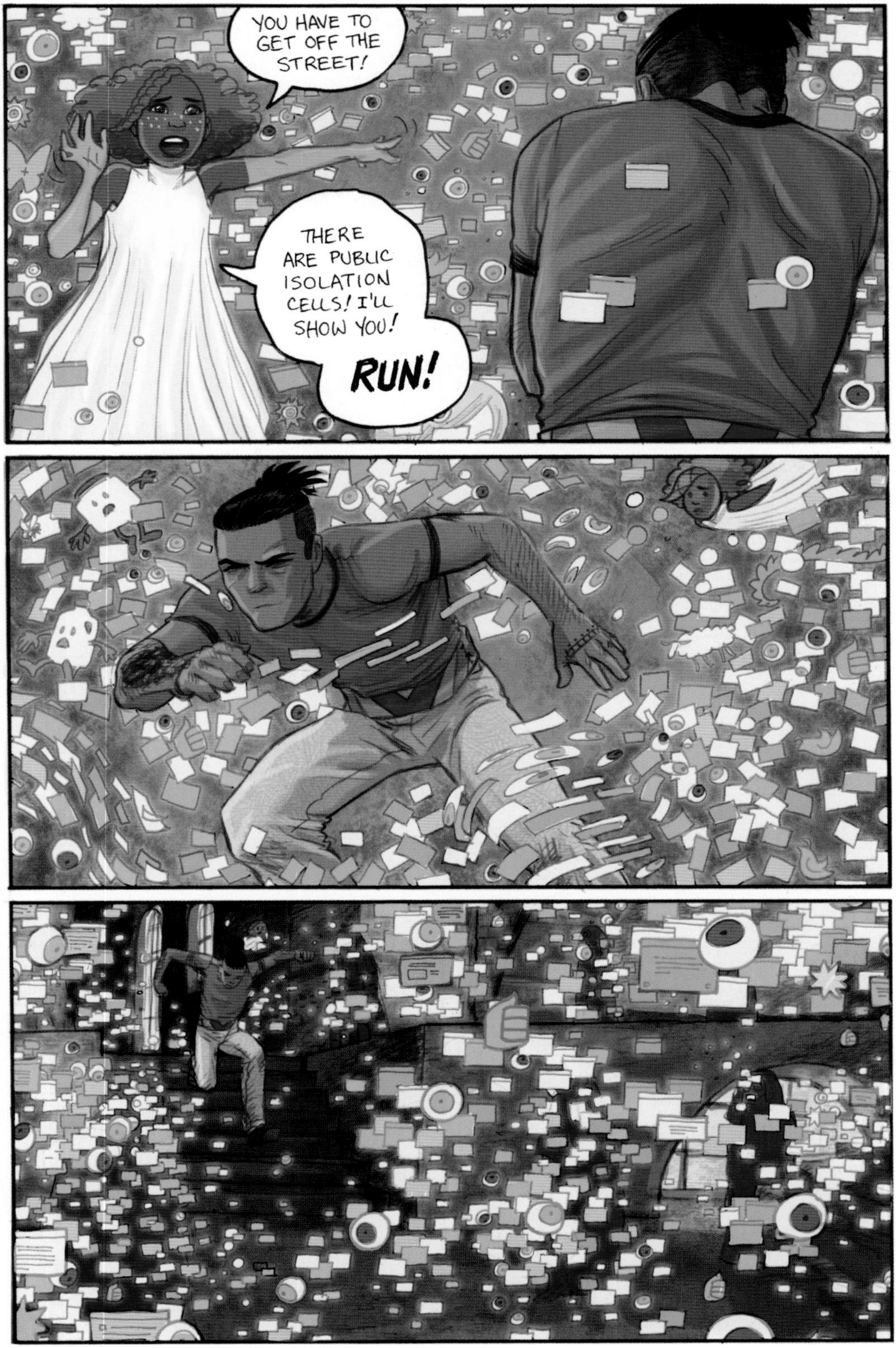
YOU HAVE TO GET OFF THE STREET!
THERE ARE PUBLIC ISOLATION CELLS! I'LL SHOW YOU!
RUN!

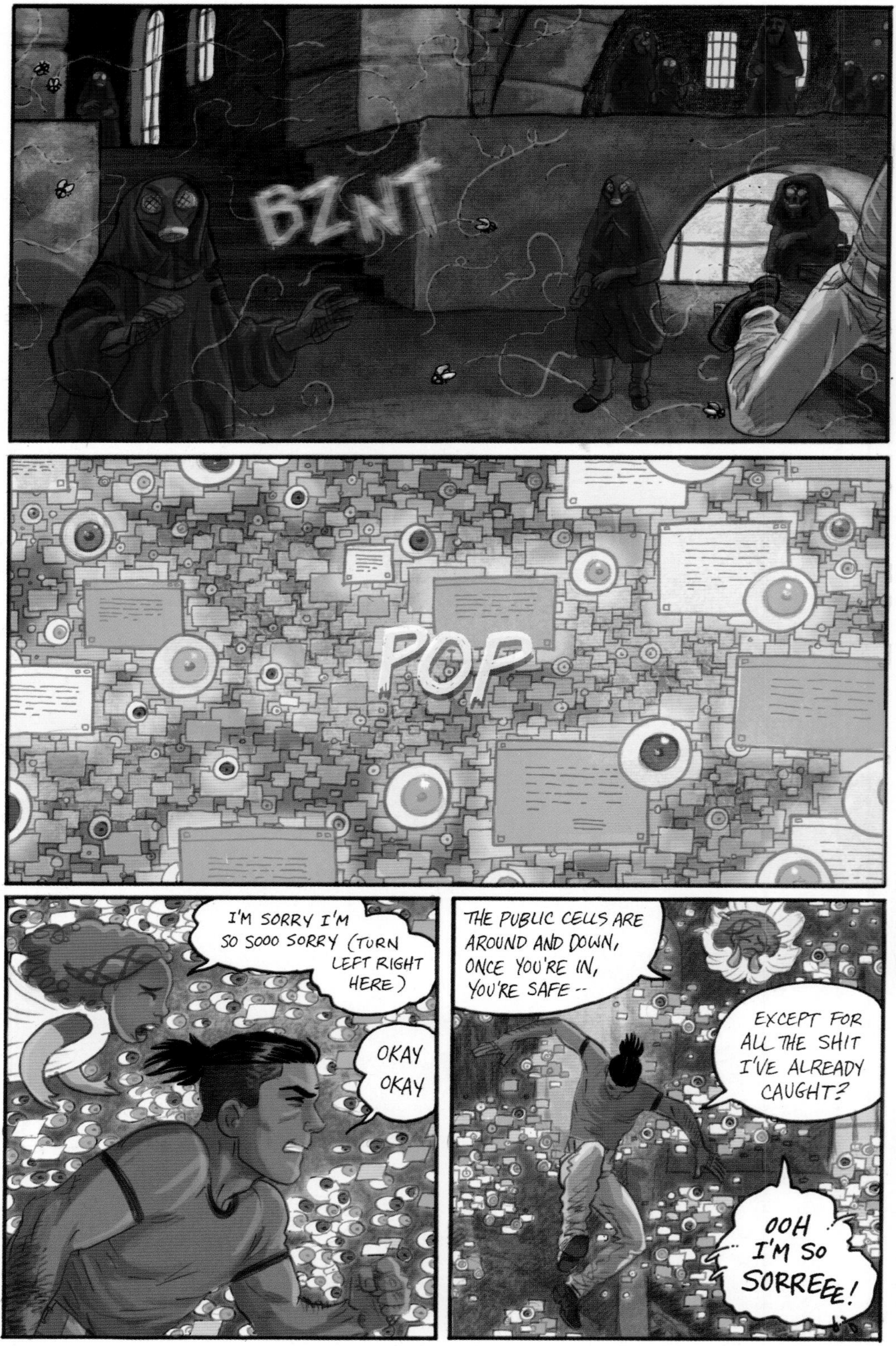
BZNT
POP
I'M SORRY I'M SO SOOO SORRY (TURN LEFT RIGHT HERE)
OKAY OKAY
THE PUBLIC CELLS ARE AROUND AND DOWN, ONCE YOU'RE IN, YOU'RE SAFE --
EXCEPT FOR ALL THE SHIT I'VE ALREADY CAUGHT?
OOH I'M SO SORREEEE!

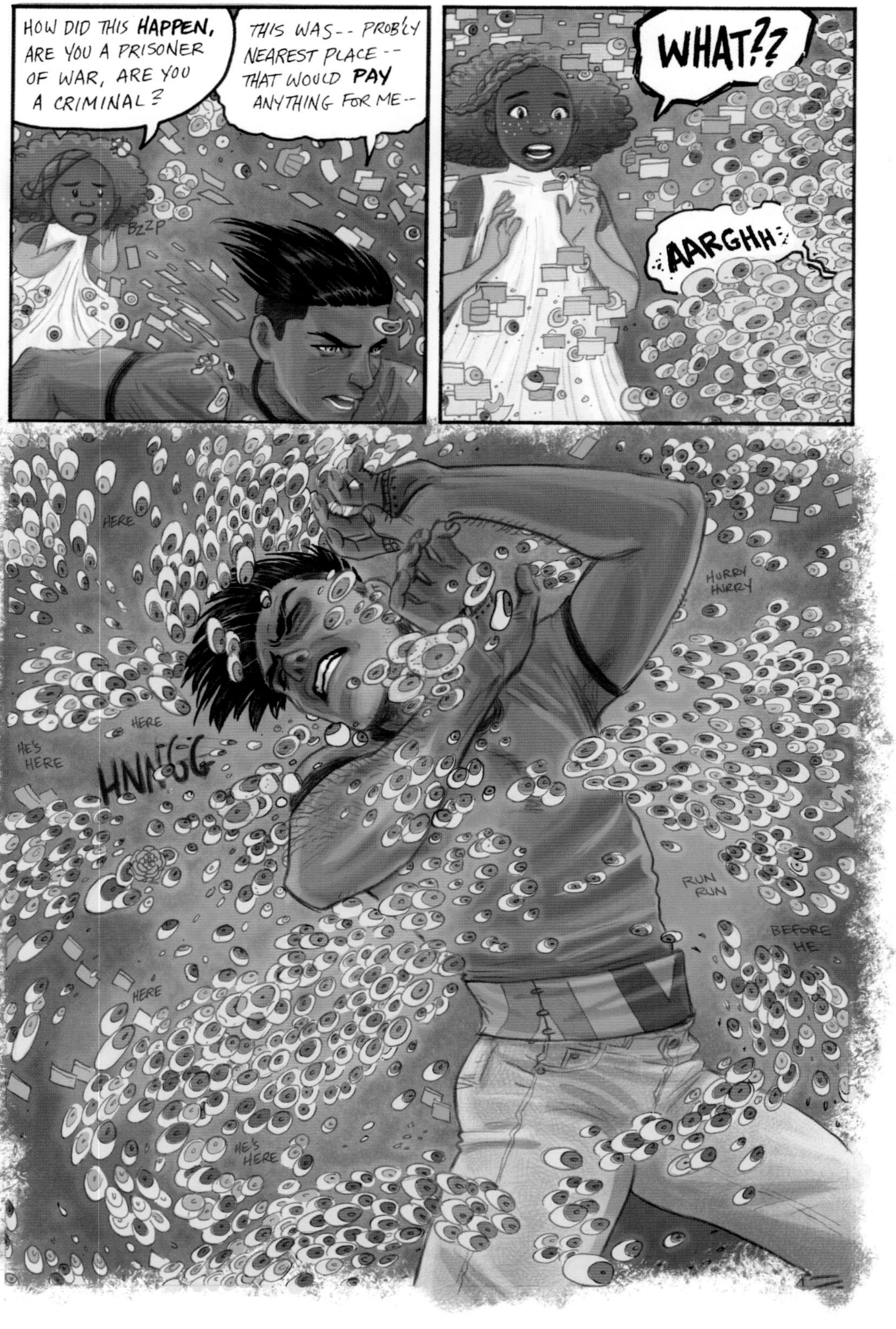
HOW DID THIS HAPPEN, ARE YOU A PRISONER OF WAR, ARE YOU A CRIMINAL?
THIS WAS-- PROB'LY NEAREST PLACE -- THAT WOULD PAY ANYTHING FOR ME--
BZZP
WHAT?!?
AARGHH
HERE
HURRY HURRY
HERE
HE'S HERE
HNNGG
RUN RUN
BEFORE HE
HERE
HE'S HERE

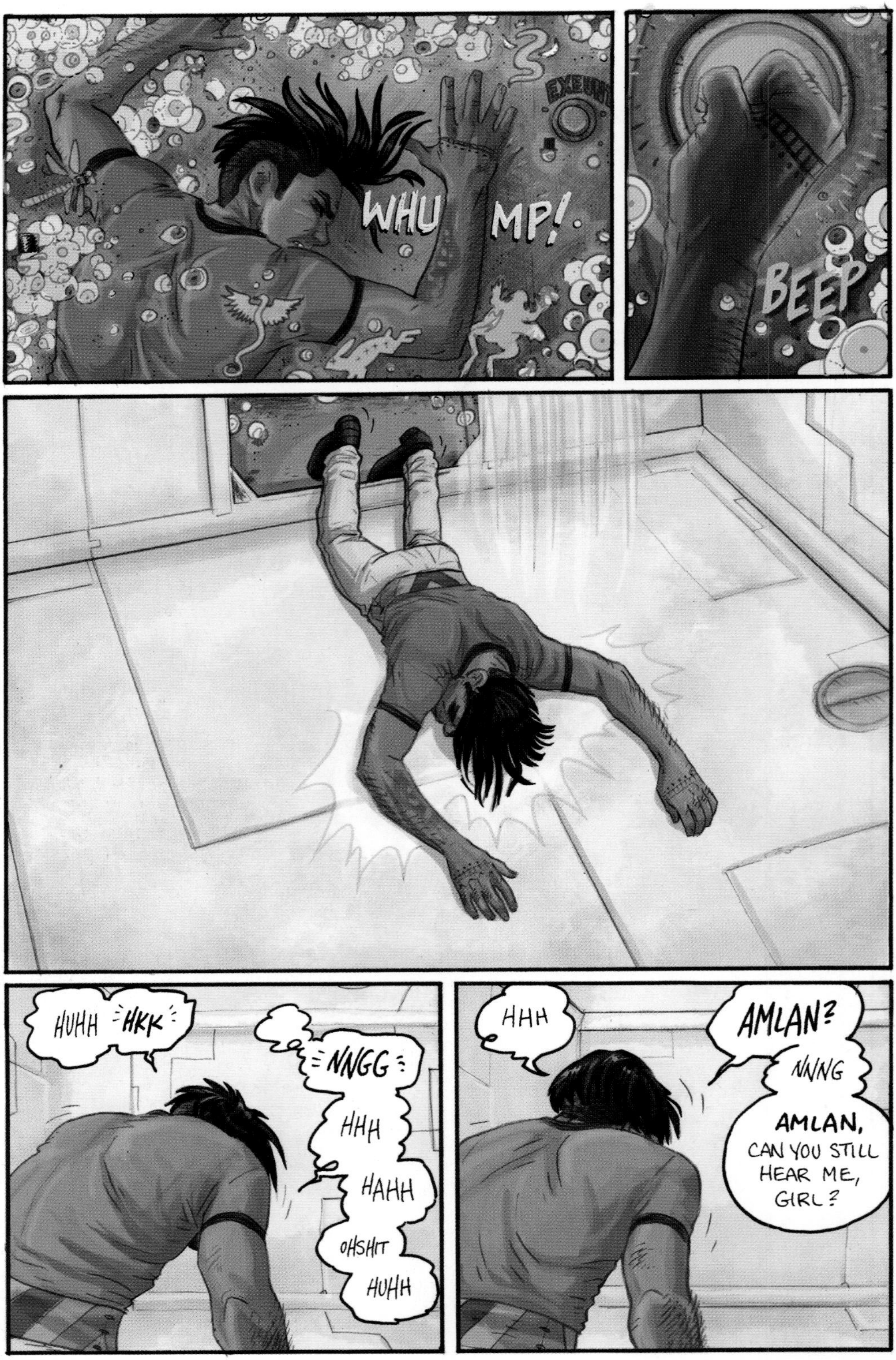
EXEUNT
WHU MP!
BEEP
HUHH HKK
NNGG
HHH
HAHH
OHSHIT
HUHH
HHH
AMLAN?
NNNG
AMLAN, CAN YOU STILL HEAR ME, GIRL?

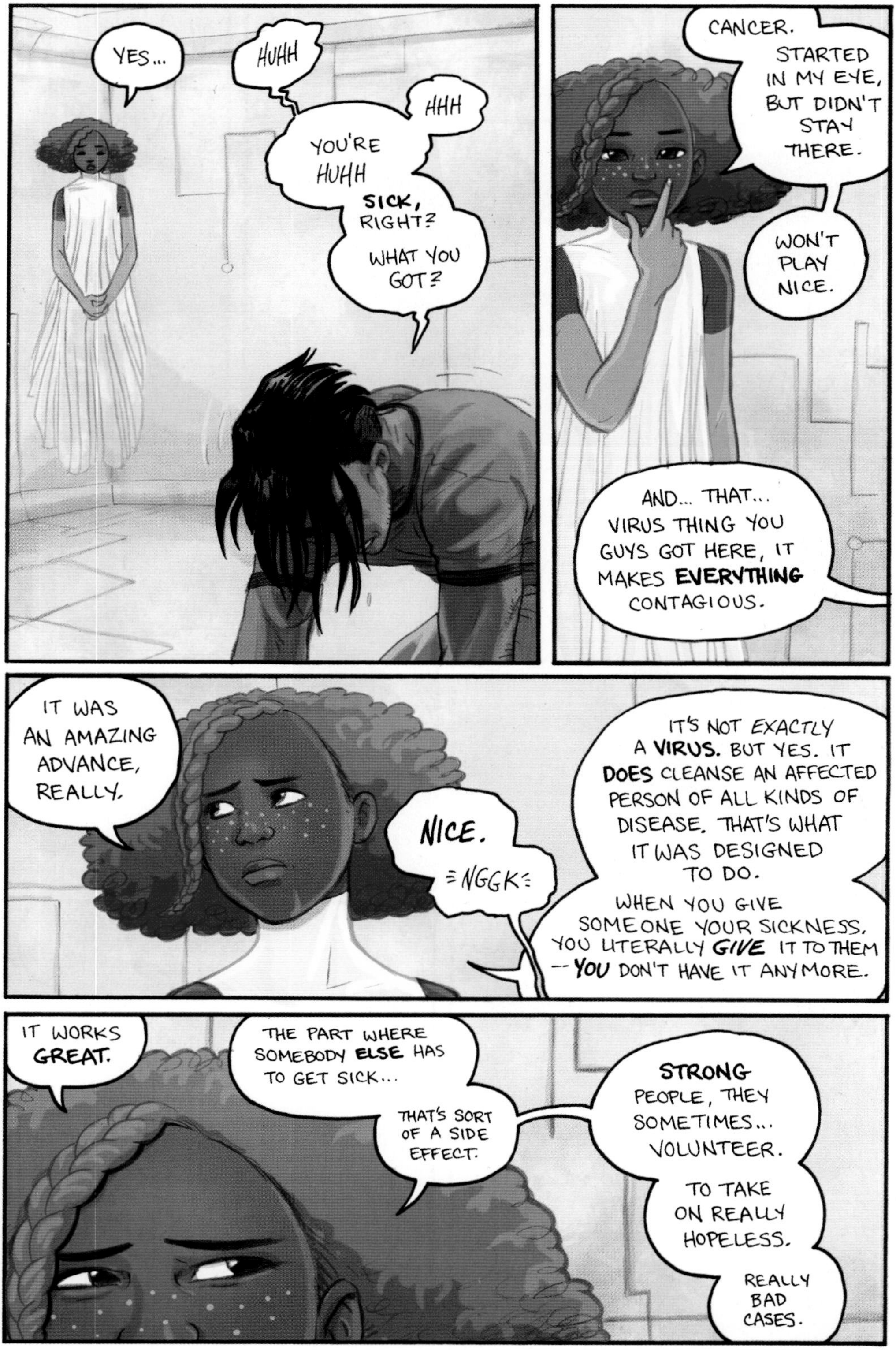
YES...
HUHH
HHH
YOU'RE HUHH **SICK,** RIGHT?
WHAT YOU GOT?
CANCER.
STARTED IN MY EYE, BUT DIDN'T STAY THERE.
WON'T PLAY NICE.
AND... THAT... VIRUS THING YOU GUYS GOT HERE, IT MAKES **EVERYTHING** CONTAGIOUS.
IT WAS AN AMAZING ADVANCE, REALLY.
NICE.
NGGK
IT'S NOT *EXACTLY* A **VIRUS.** BUT YES. IT **DOES** CLEANSE AN AFFECTED PERSON OF ALL KINDS OF DISEASE. THAT'S WHAT IT WAS DESIGNED TO DO.
WHEN YOU GIVE SOMEONE YOUR SICKNESS, YOU LITERALLY ***GIVE*** IT TO THEM --***YOU*** DON'T HAVE IT ANYMORE.
IT WORKS **GREAT.**
THE PART WHERE SOMEBODY **ELSE** HAS TO GET SICK...
THAT'S SORT OF A SIDE EFFECT.
STRONG PEOPLE, THEY SOMETIMES... VOLUNTEER.
TO TAKE ON REALLY HOPELESS.
REALLY BAD CASES.

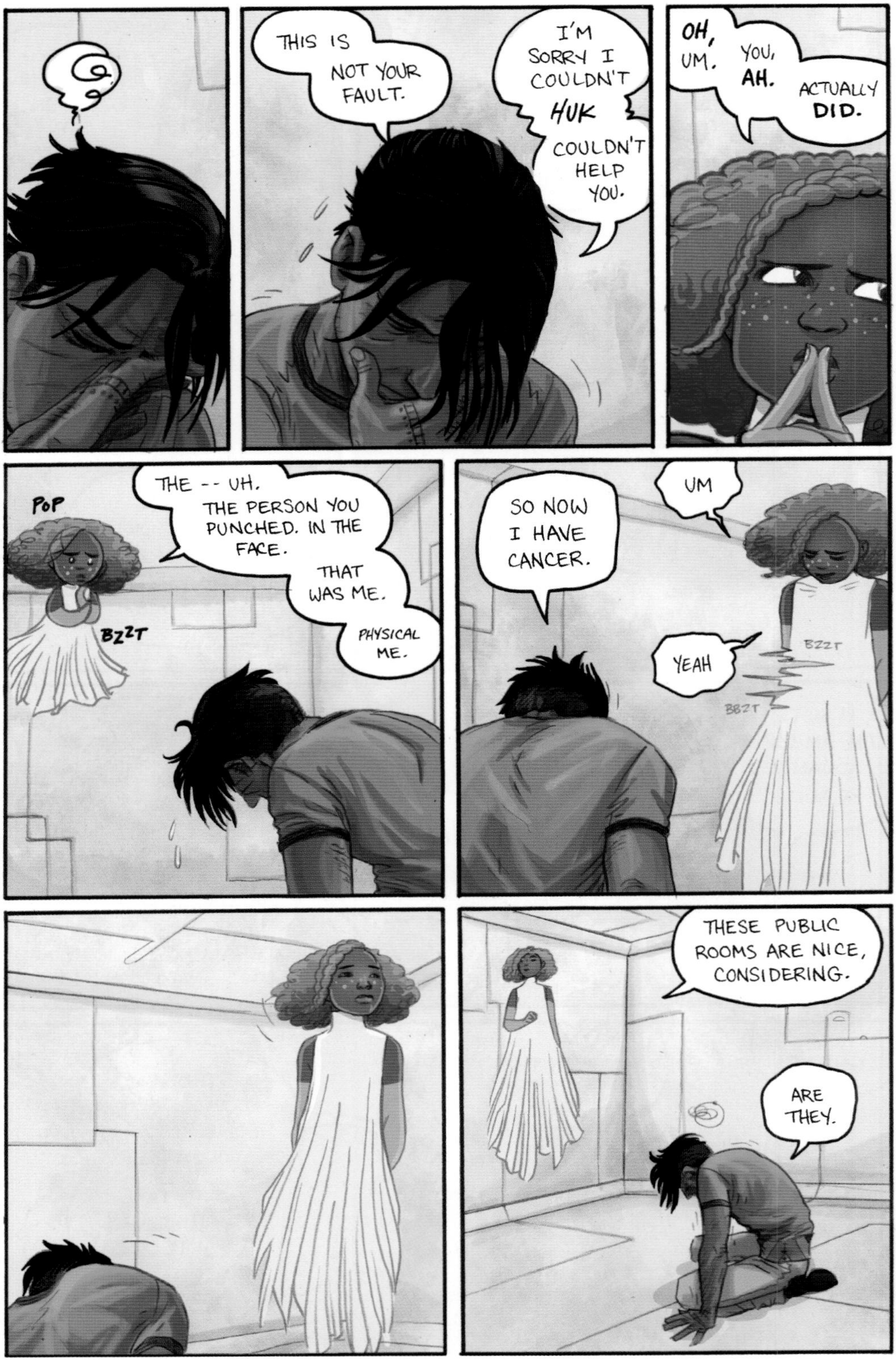
THIS IS NOT YOUR FAULT.
I'M SORRY I COULDN'T HUK COULDN'T HELP YOU.
OH, UM.
YOU, AH.
ACTUALLY DID.
POP
THE -- UH. THE PERSON YOU PUNCHED. IN THE FACE.
THAT WAS ME.
PHYSICAL ME.
BZZT
SO NOW I HAVE CANCER.
UM
YEAH
BZZT
BBZT
THESE PUBLIC ROOMS ARE NICE, CONSIDERING.
ARE THEY.

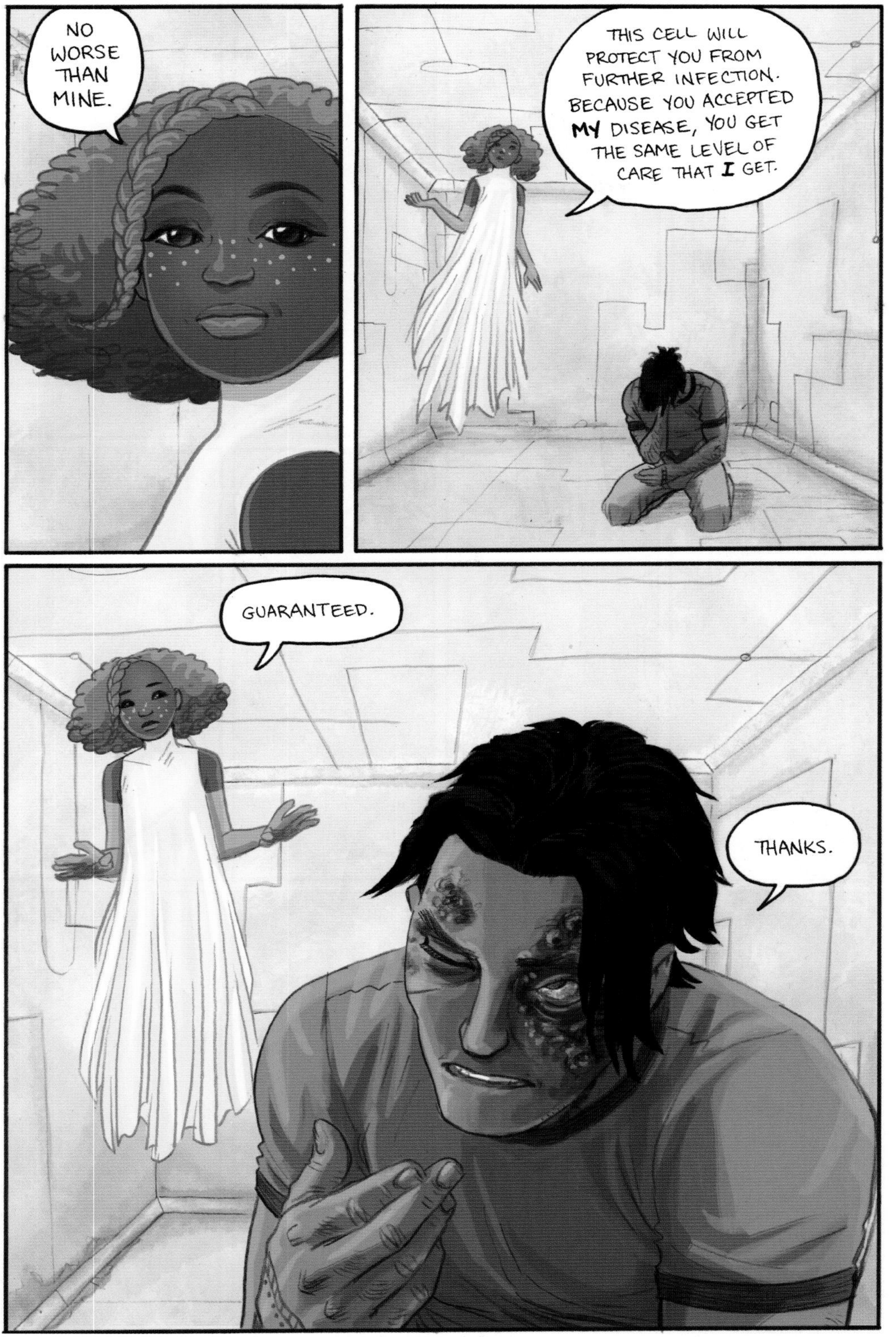
NO WORSE THAN MINE.
THIS CELL WILL PROTECT YOU FROM FURTHER INFECTION. BECAUSE YOU ACCEPTED MY DISEASE, YOU GET THE SAME LEVEL OF CARE THAT I GET.
GUARANTEED.
THANKS.

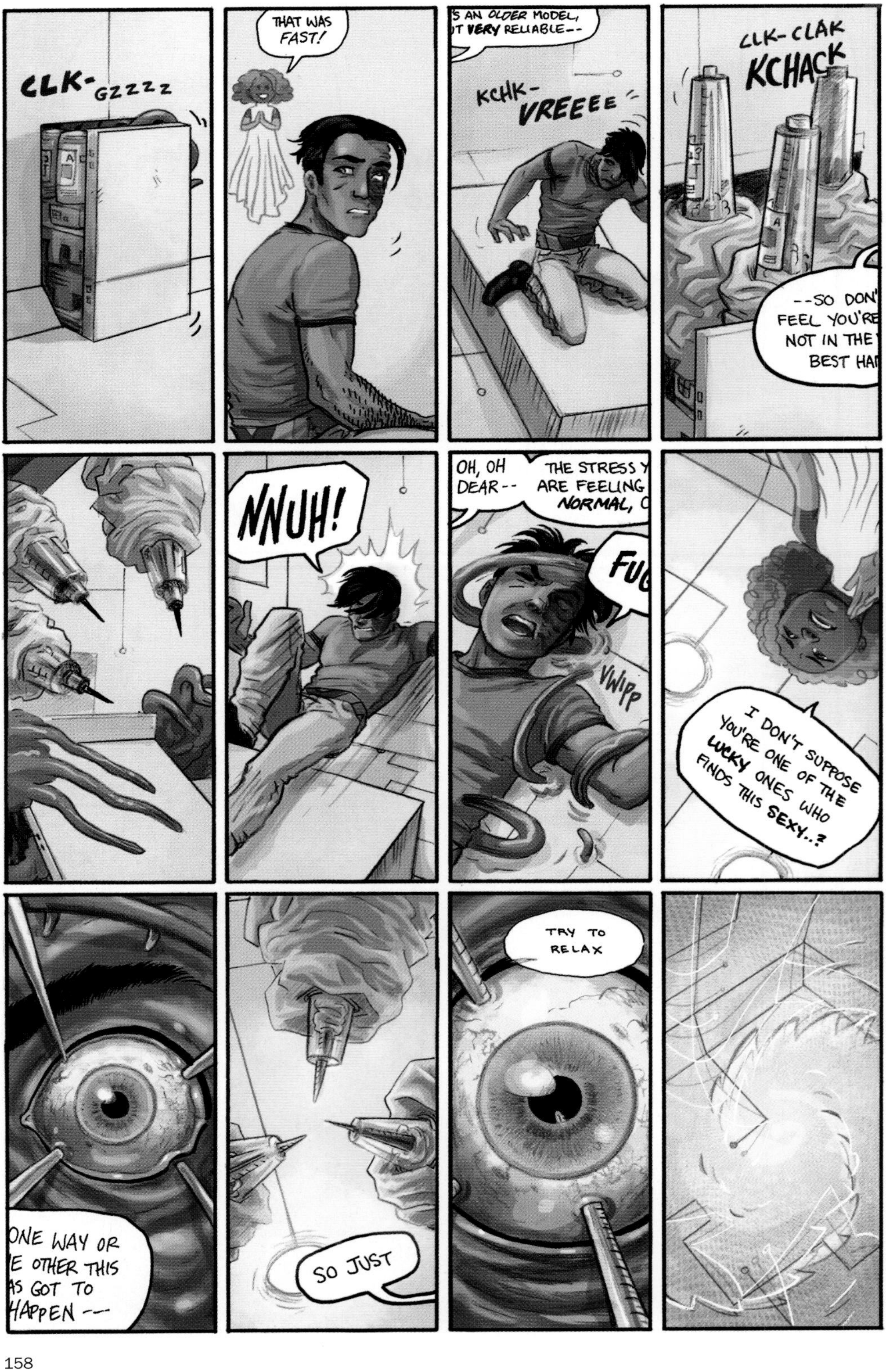
CLK-GZZZZ
THAT WAS FAST!
'S AN OLDER MODEL, T VERY RELIABLE--
KCHK-VREEEE
CLK-CLAK KCHACK
--SO DON' FEEL YOU'RE NOT IN THE BEST HA
NNUH!
OH, OH DEAR--
THE STRESS Y ARE FEELING NORMAL, C
FU
VWIPP
I DON'T SUPPOSE YOU'RE ONE OF THE LUCKY ONES WHO FINDS THIS SEXY..?
ONE WAY OR E OTHER THIS AS GOT TO HAPPEN --
SO JUST
TRY TO RELAX

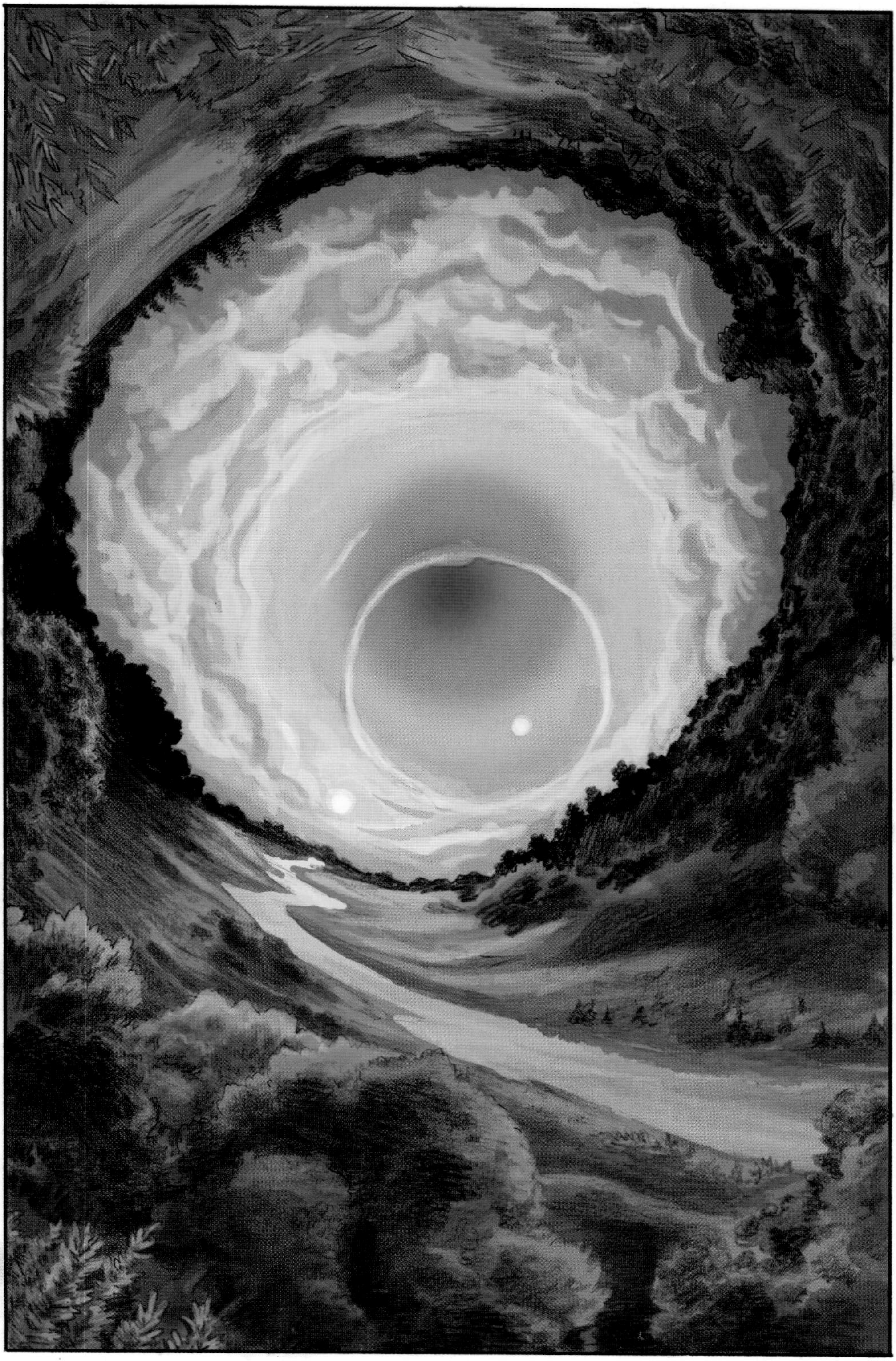

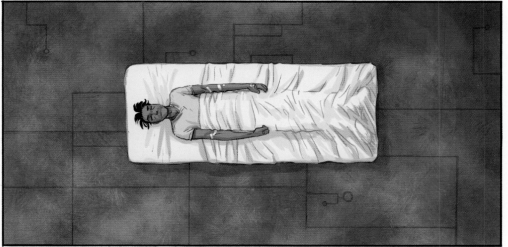

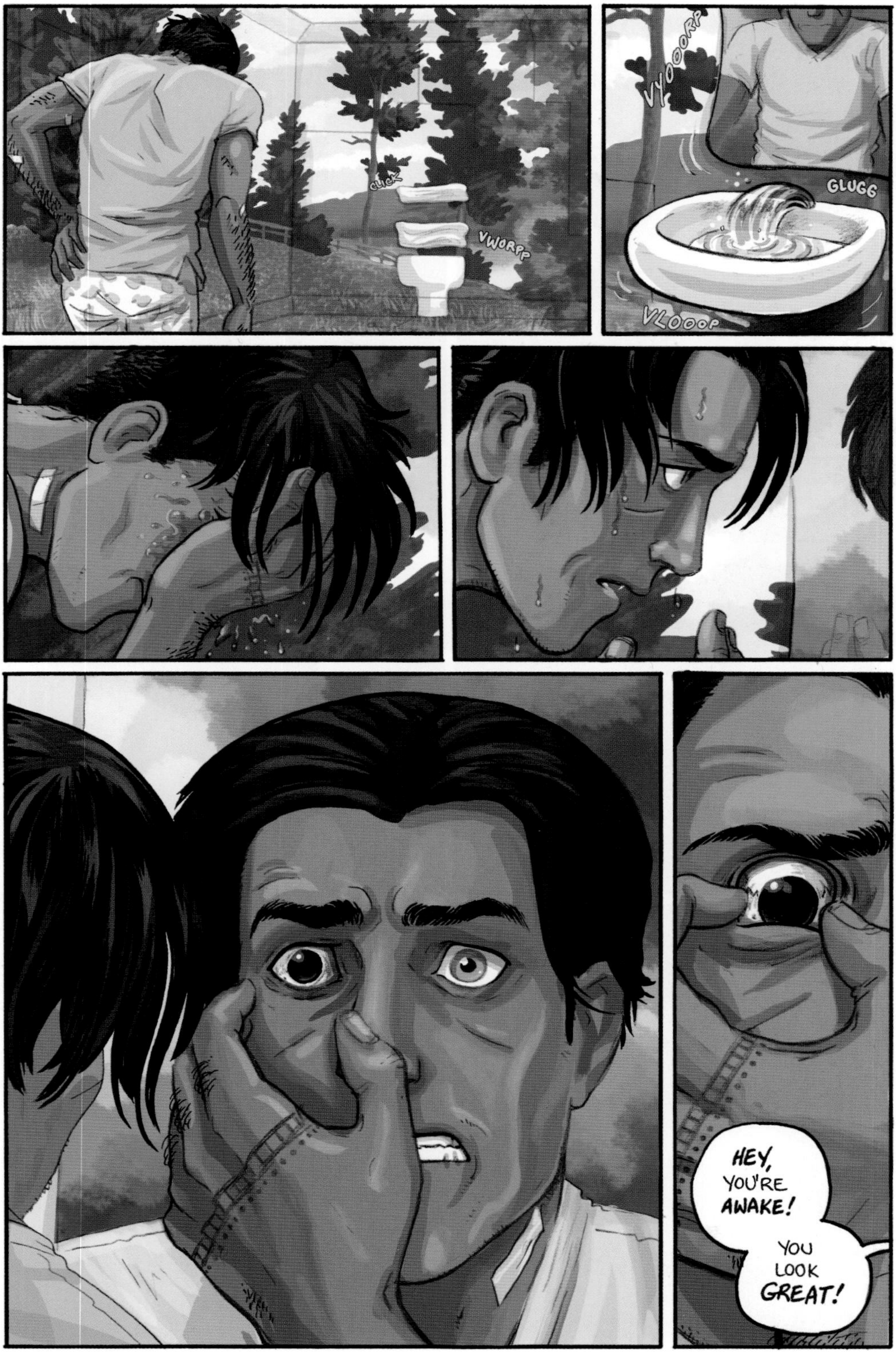
CLICK
VWORPP
VYOOORP
GLUGG
VLOOOP
HEY, YOU'RE AWAKE!
YOU LOOK GREAT!

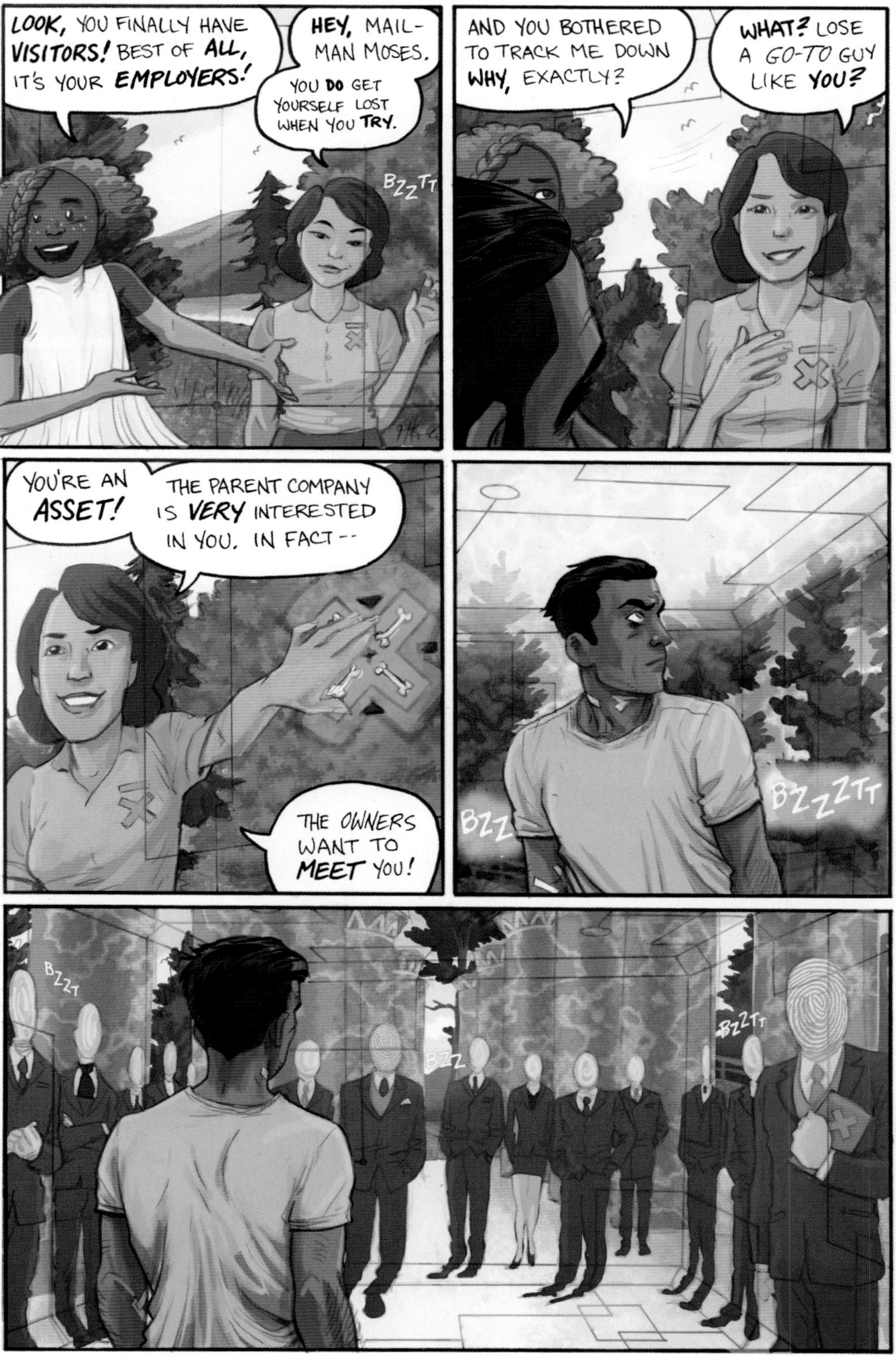
LOOK, YOU FINALLY HAVE VISITORS! BEST OF ALL, IT'S YOUR EMPLOYERS!
HEY, MAIL-MAN MOSES.
YOU DO GET YOURSELF LOST WHEN YOU TRY.
BZZTT
AND YOU BOTHERED TO TRACK ME DOWN WHY, EXACTLY?
WHAT?! LOSE A GO-TO GUY LIKE YOU?
YOU'RE AN ASSET!
THE PARENT COMPANY IS VERY INTERESTED IN YOU. IN FACT--
THE OWNERS WANT TO MEET YOU!
BZZ
BZZZTT
BZZT
BZZ
BZZTT

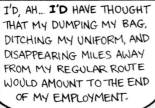

I'D, AH... **I'D** HAVE THOUGHT THAT MY DUMPING MY BAG, DITCHING MY UNIFORM, AND DISAPPEARING MILES AWAY FROM MY REGULAR ROUTE WOULD AMOUNT TO THE END OF MY EMPLOYMENT.

A TALENTED COURIER LIKE **YOU?** WE PURSUE **EXCELLENCE,** MR. AYERS, AND WE TRY VERY HARD NOT TO LET IT GET AWAY!

HAHA!

IN ADDITION TO A **PAY** RAISE, WE'VE AGREED TO FINANCE A **SIGNIFICANT PHYSICAL** UPGRADE FOR YOU!

STEP THROUGH THESE DOORS, AND THE BEST WETWARE SURGEONS IN JAVECEK WILL INSTALL THE LATEST, BEST-MODEL CEREBRAL ACCESS JACK FOR YOU!

BZZT

BZZT

BZZT

.... WHY.

THOSE THINGS ARE. NOT CHEAP.

WELL, **NO,** BUT **YOU'RE WORTH** IT!

THE TRACKING DEVICES EMBEDDED IN X-RAY'S PACKAGING TO REDUCE SHIPPING LOSSES REVEAL INTRIGUING ANOMALIES IN YOU!

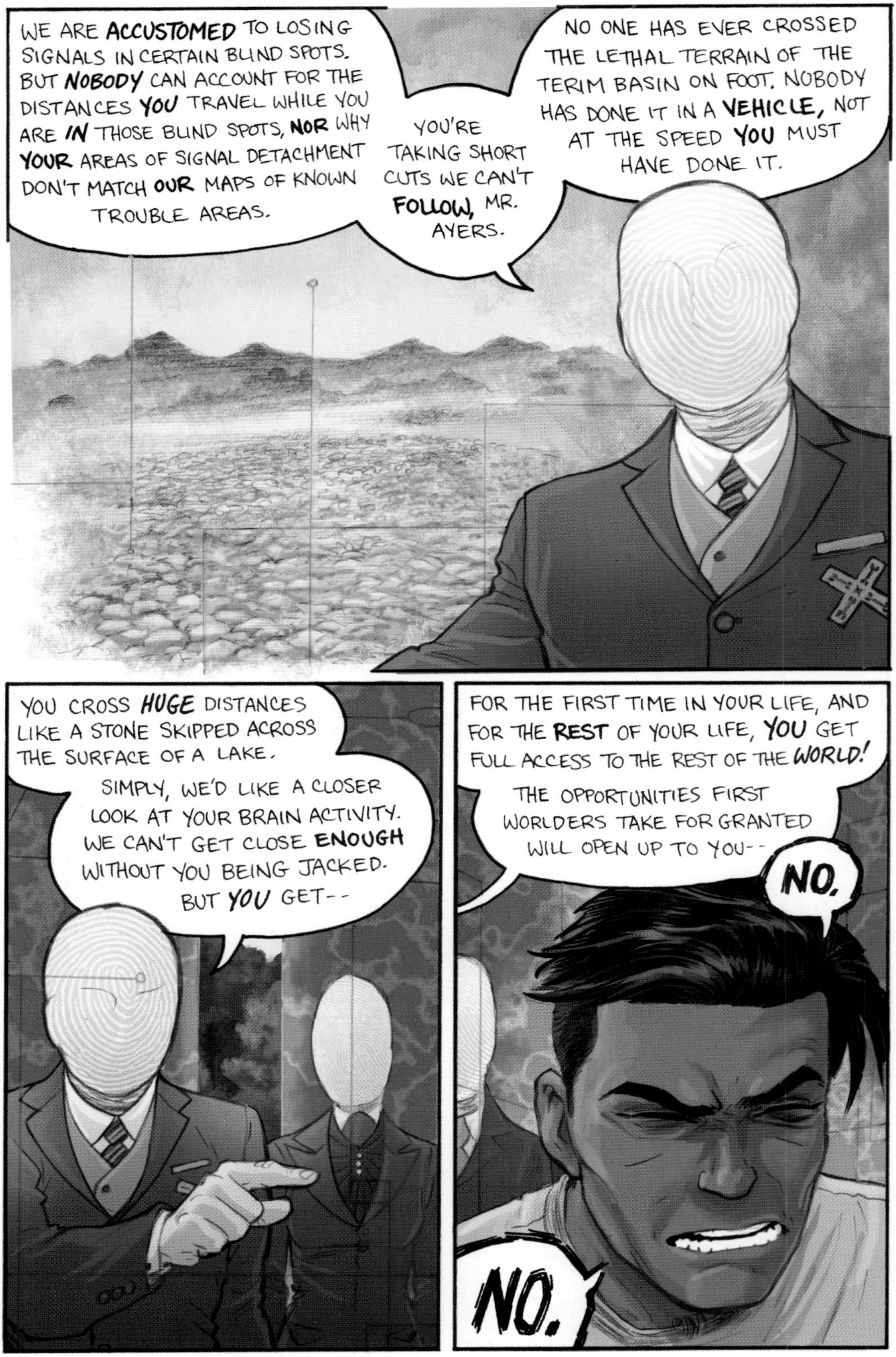

WE ARE ACCUSTOMED TO LOSING SIGNALS IN CERTAIN BLIND SPOTS. BUT NOBODY CAN ACCOUNT FOR THE DISTANCES YOU TRAVEL WHILE YOU ARE IN THOSE BLIND SPOTS, NOR WHY YOUR AREAS OF SIGNAL DETACHMENT DON'T MATCH OUR MAPS OF KNOWN TROUBLE AREAS.
YOU'RE TAKING SHORT CUTS WE CAN'T FOLLOW, MR. AYERS.
NO ONE HAS EVER CROSSED THE LETHAL TERRAIN OF THE TERIM BASIN ON FOOT. NOBODY HAS DONE IT IN A VEHICLE, NOT AT THE SPEED YOU MUST HAVE DONE IT.
YOU CROSS HUGE DISTANCES LIKE A STONE SKIPPED ACROSS THE SURFACE OF A LAKE.
SIMPLY, WE'D LIKE A CLOSER LOOK AT YOUR BRAIN ACTIVITY. WE CAN'T GET CLOSE ENOUGH WITHOUT YOU BEING JACKED. BUT YOU GET--
FOR THE FIRST TIME IN YOUR LIFE, AND FOR THE REST OF YOUR LIFE, YOU GET FULL ACCESS TO THE REST OF THE WORLD!
THE OPPORTUNITIES FIRST WORLDERS TAKE FOR GRANTED WILL OPEN UP TO YOU--
NO.
NO.

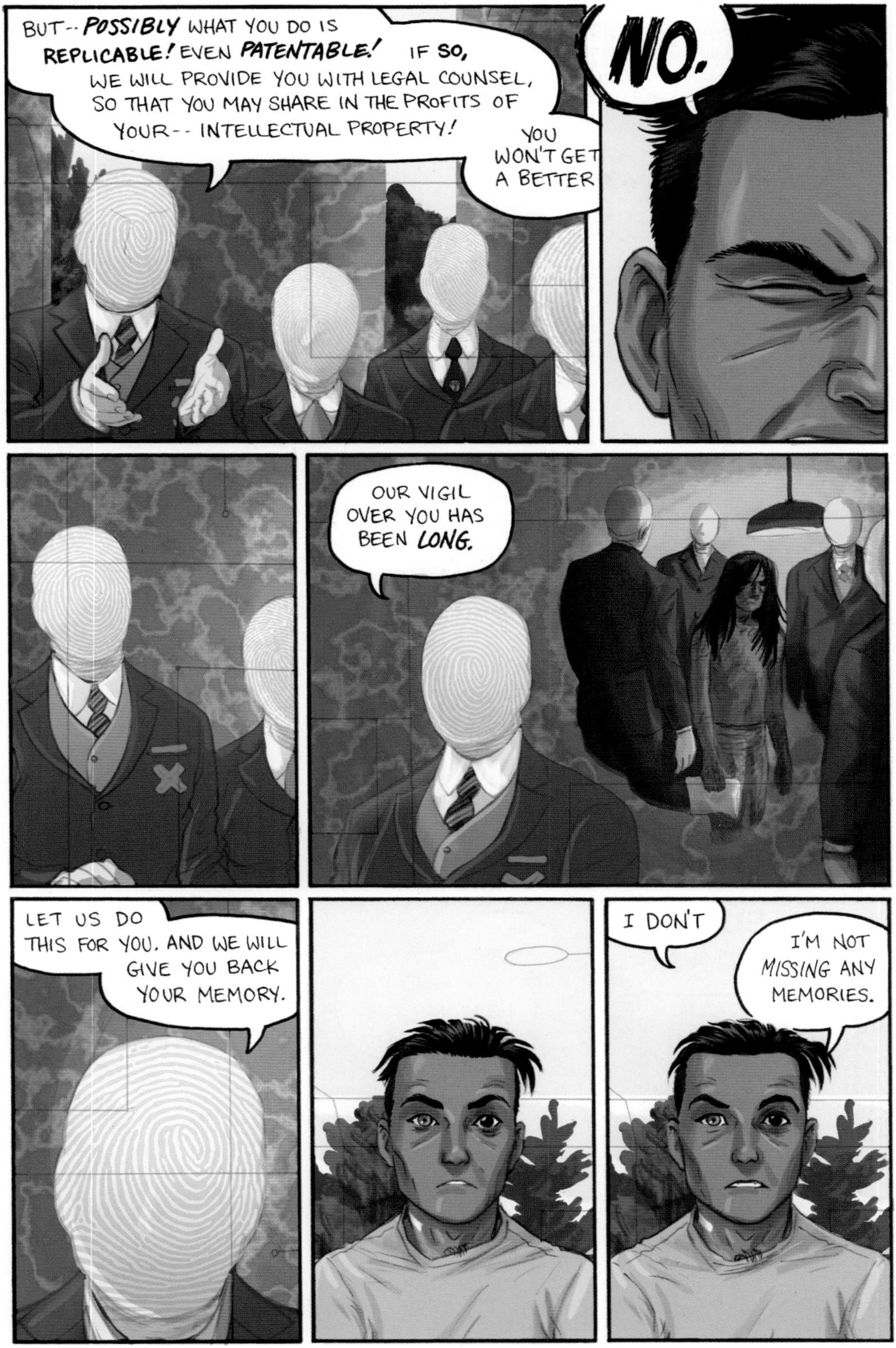
BUT-- POSSIBLY WHAT YOU DO IS REPLICABLE! EVEN PATENTABLE! IF SO, WE WILL PROVIDE YOU WITH LEGAL COUNSEL, SO THAT YOU MAY SHARE IN THE PROFITS OF YOUR-- INTELLECTUAL PROPERTY!
YOU WON'T GET A BETTER
NO.
OUR VIGIL OVER YOU HAS BEEN LONG.
LET US DO THIS FOR YOU. AND WE WILL GIVE YOU BACK YOUR MEMORY.
I DON'T
I'M NOT MISSING ANY MEMORIES.

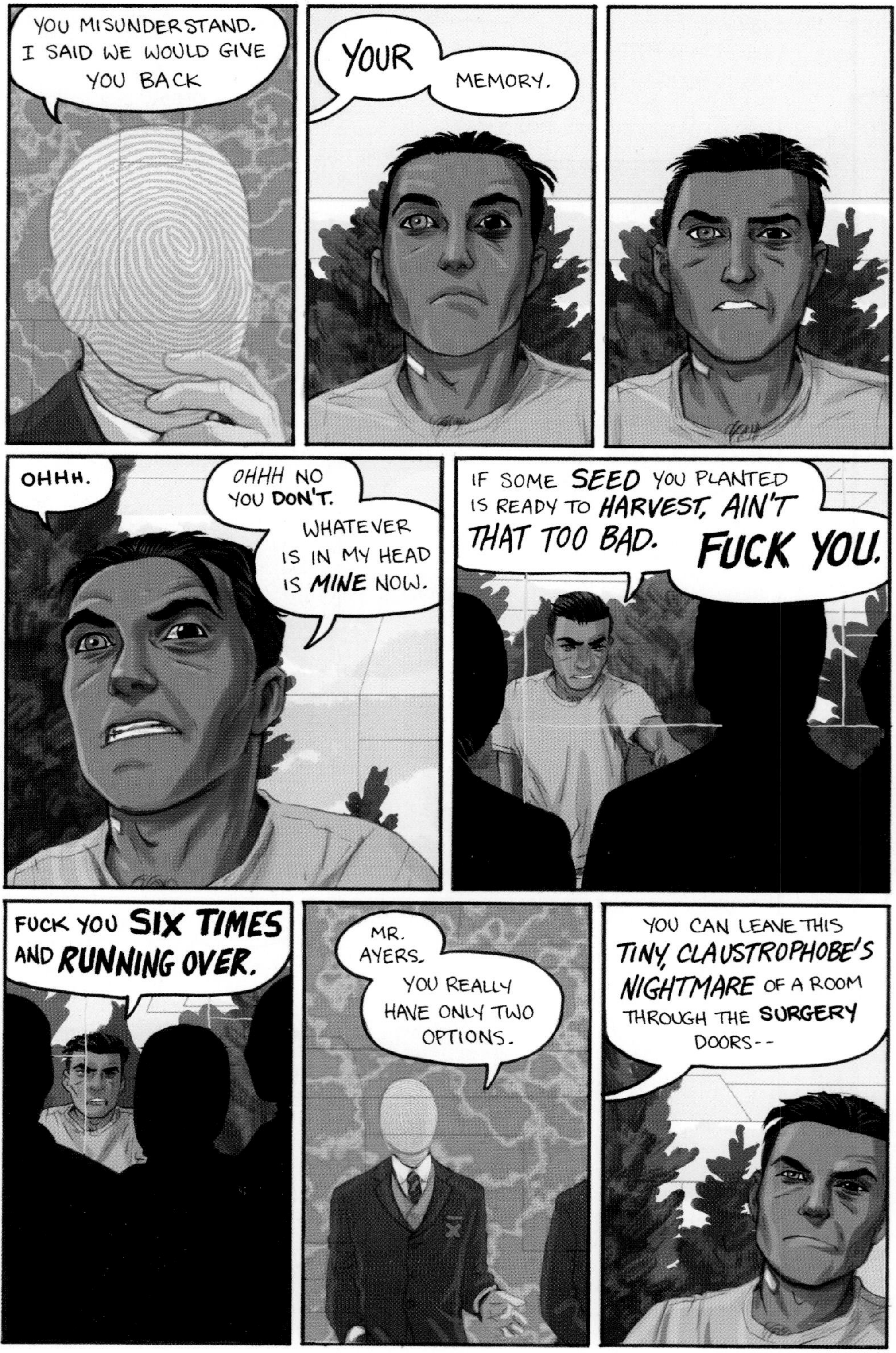
YOU MISUNDERSTAND. I SAID WE WOULD GIVE YOU BACK
YOUR
MEMORY.
OHHH.
OHHH NO YOU DON'T.
WHATEVER IS IN MY HEAD IS MINE NOW.
IF SOME SEED YOU PLANTED IS READY TO HARVEST, AIN'T THAT TOO BAD.
FUCK YOU.
FUCK YOU SIX TIMES AND RUNNING OVER.
MR. AYERS.
YOU REALLY HAVE ONLY TWO OPTIONS.
YOU CAN LEAVE THIS TINY, CLAUSTROPHOBE'S NIGHTMARE OF A ROOM THROUGH THE SURGERY DOORS--

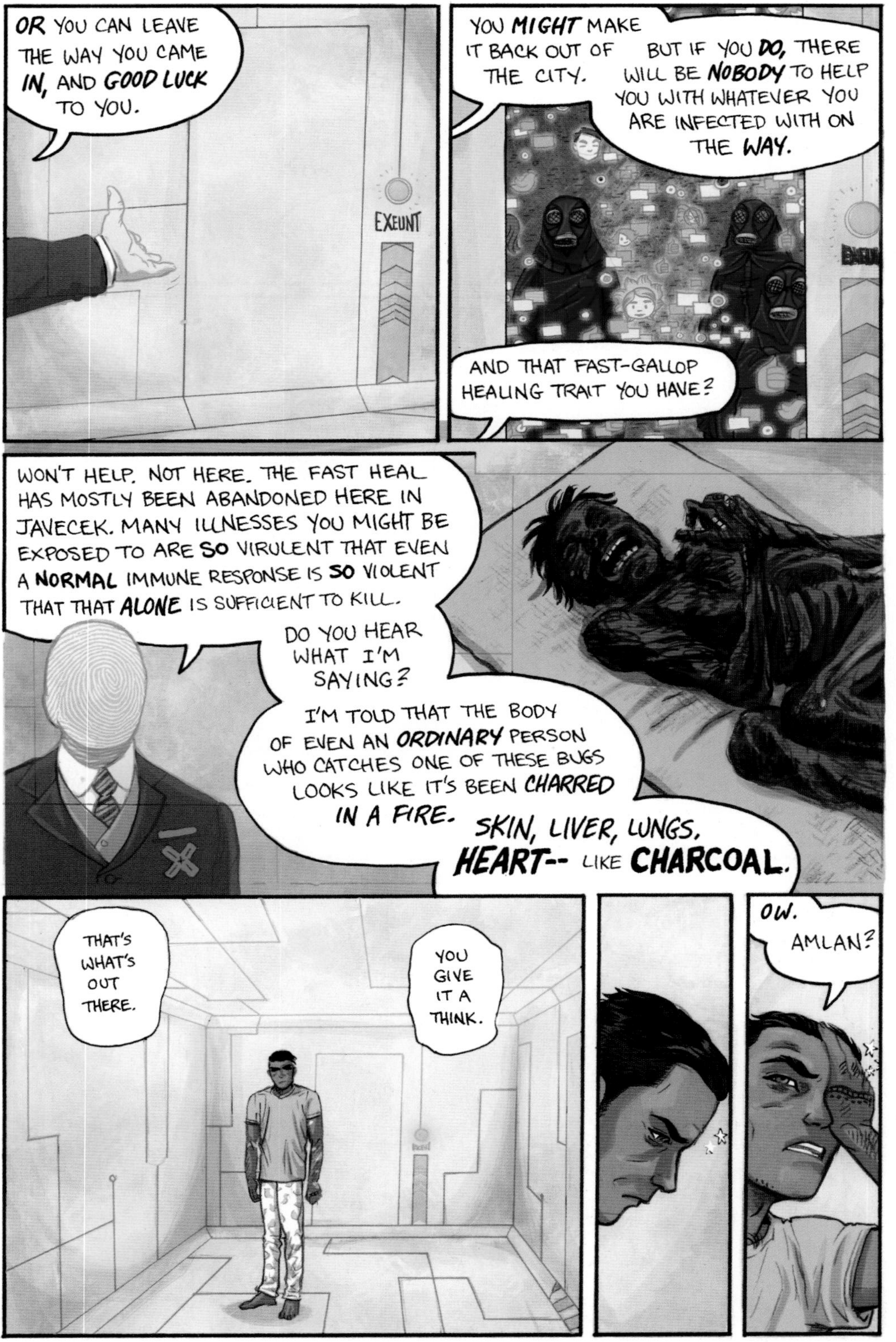
OR YOU CAN LEAVE THE WAY YOU CAME IN, AND GOOD LUCK TO YOU.
EXEUNT
YOU MIGHT MAKE IT BACK OUT OF THE CITY.
BUT IF YOU DO, THERE WILL BE NOBODY TO HELP YOU WITH WHATEVER YOU ARE INFECTED WITH ON THE WAY.
AND THAT FAST-GALLOP HEALING TRAIT YOU HAVE?
WON'T HELP. NOT HERE. THE FAST HEAL HAS MOSTLY BEEN ABANDONED HERE IN JAVECEK. MANY ILLNESSES YOU MIGHT BE EXPOSED TO ARE SO VIRULENT THAT EVEN A NORMAL IMMUNE RESPONSE IS SO VIOLENT THAT THAT ALONE IS SUFFICIENT TO KILL.
DO YOU HEAR WHAT I'M SAYING?
I'M TOLD THAT THE BODY OF EVEN AN ORDINARY PERSON WHO CATCHES ONE OF THESE BUGS LOOKS LIKE IT'S BEEN CHARRED IN A FIRE.
SKIN, LIVER, LUNGS, HEART-- LIKE CHARCOAL.
THAT'S WHAT'S OUT THERE.
YOU GIVE IT A THINK.
OW.
AMLAN?

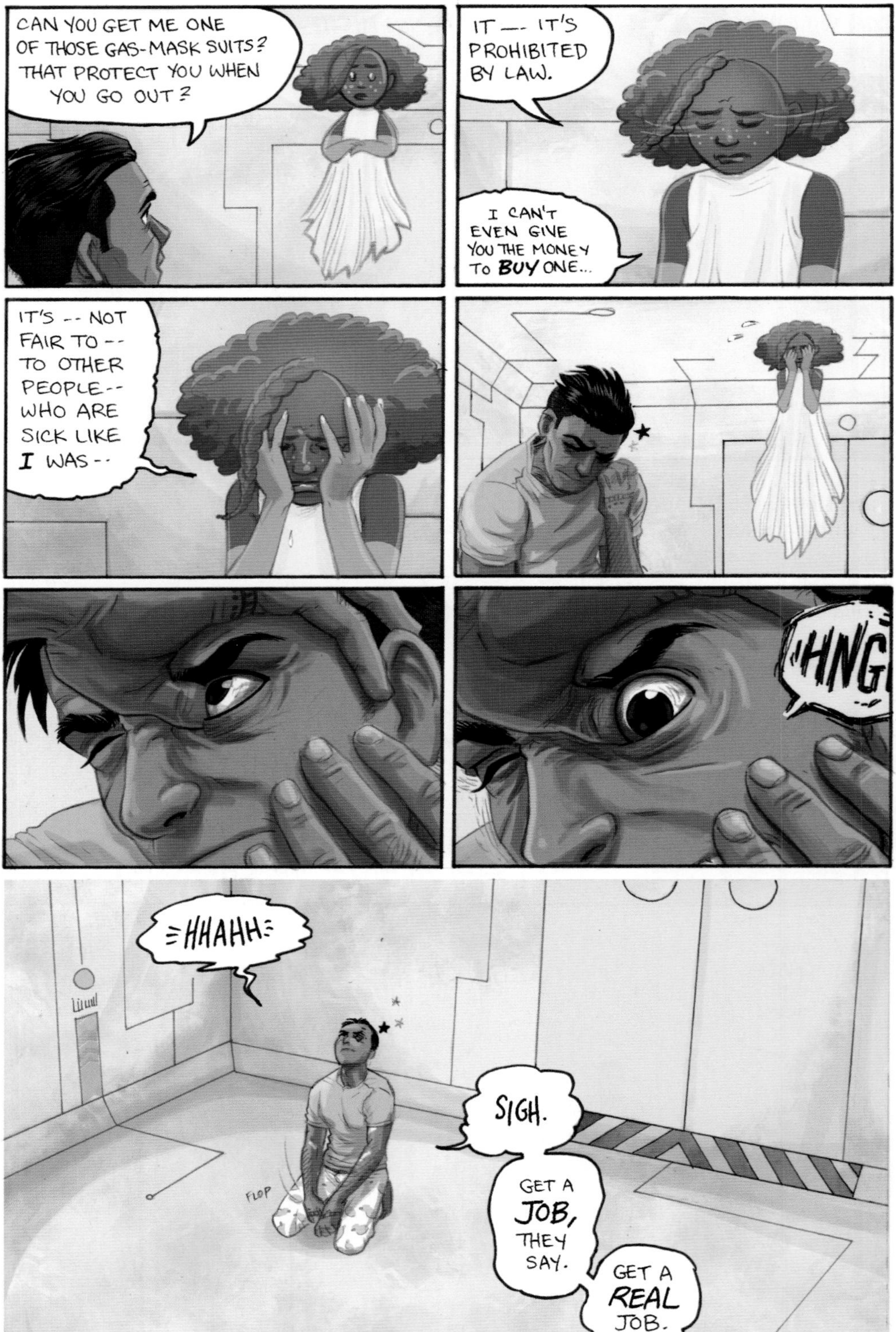
CAN YOU GET ME ONE OF THOSE GAS-MASK SUITS? THAT PROTECT YOU WHEN YOU GO OUT?
IT -- IT'S PROHIBITED BY LAW.
I CAN'T EVEN GIVE YOU THE MONEY TO BUY ONE...
IT'S -- NOT FAIR TO -- TO OTHER PEOPLE-- WHO ARE SICK LIKE I WAS--
HNG
HHAHH
SIGH.
FLOP
GET A JOB, THEY SAY.
GET A REAL JOB.

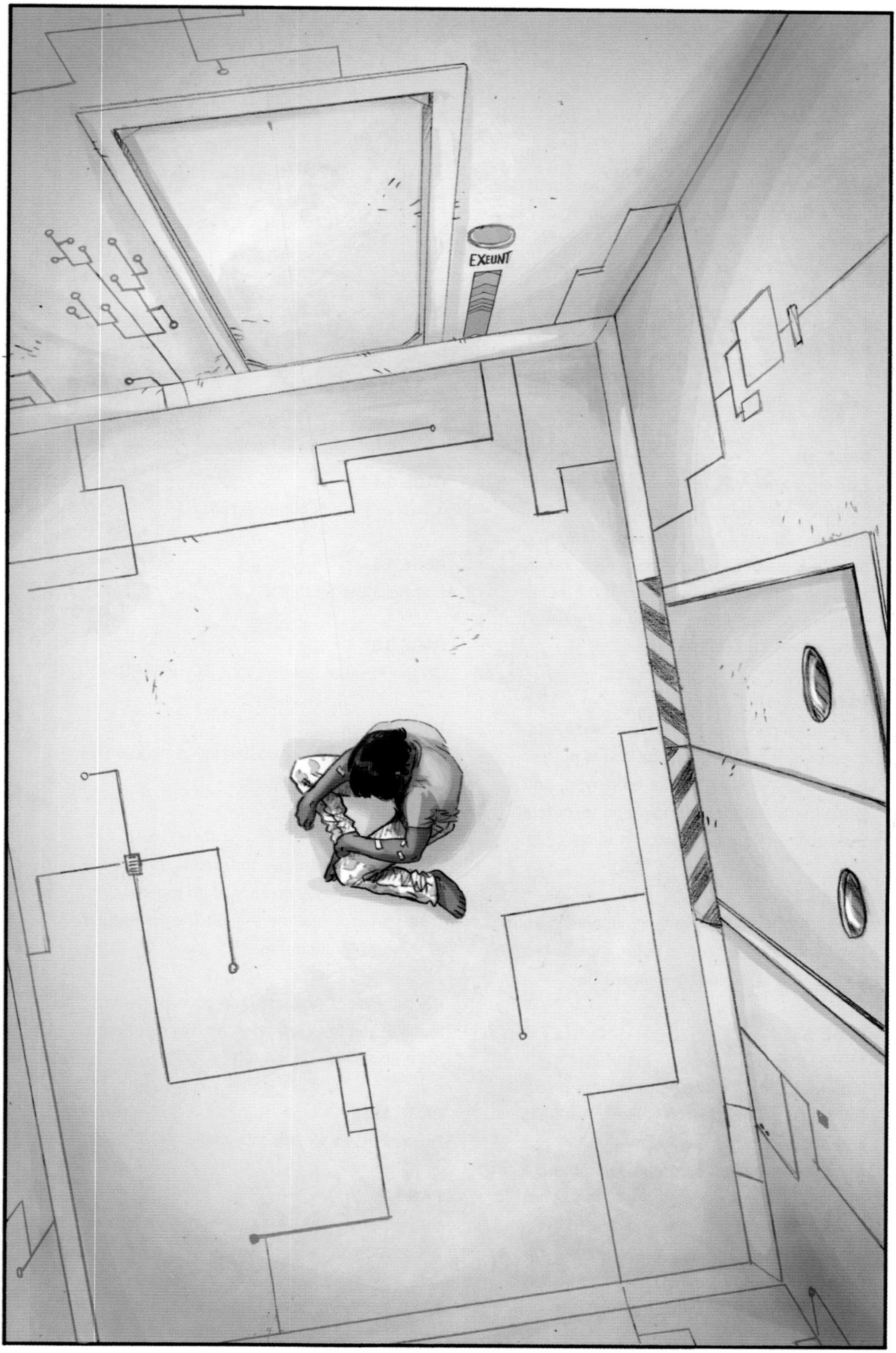
EXEUNT

NOTES

PAGE 8
Part 1. This image is based on drawings of the now-defunct walled city of Kowloon. A lot of Anvard, the city in which most of *Finder* is set, is like this. The nicer parts of the city are less like an anthill.

PAGE 9
This is Jaeger. Hi, Jaeger. He hates filling out forms.

PAGE 10
This employment agent has vitiligo, which causes permanent breakdown of melanin in the skin. Many people in Anvard come from close groups of associated extended families, and she is no exception. Most of the people in her clan have vitiligo, and it is regarded as normal, even a sign of maturity.

PAGE 11
She's nobody's fool. She knows what kind of work he's really done. But she is in the business of keeping people employed, and she's hardheaded, practical, and resourceful. Businesses like Ray's pay for referrals.

PAGE 12
Jaeger has worked in varying capacities for a few families. Muscle and gofer, mostly. Here's a chance for him to move up a little!

PAGE 13
The city of Anvard is like a giant termite mound. It's a city built on many, many levels. Buildings or neighborhoods may have a simple internal layout, but outside is a mess of skywalks—sections of streets laid out on a grid that are at a thirty-degree angle to the next chunk of streets on a grid, holes and byways galore. The "sky" of one street is the underside of the next street. Richer people can afford to live in areas where those undersides are prettied up.

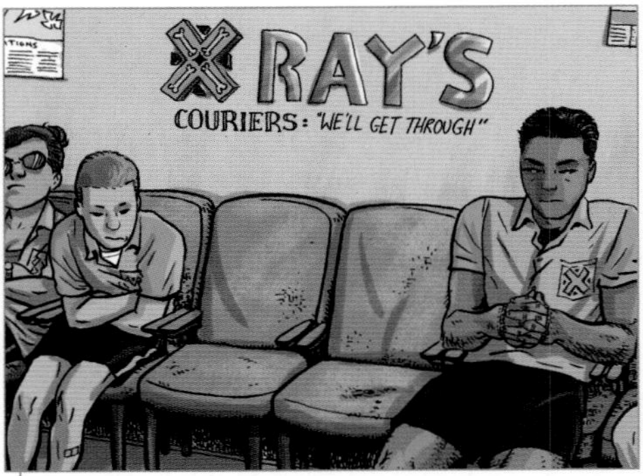
RAY'S
COURIERS: "WE'LL GET THROUGH"

PAGE 14
A courier's life is complicated.

PAGE 15
Cue hero theme music.

PAGE 16
Do the job that defines you! DO IT HARD.

PAGE 17
Grimy streets below, casino lights above. This is what I like about cities.

PAGE 18
Mermaid casino! I love mermaids, and I hate casinos—but they do kind of go together. These are not real mermaids. They're regular land trout. In costumes.

Because all of Anvard is effectively "inside," loads of markets are open air. Fancier shops have doors and decor.

PAGE 19
He was made for this job, really.

PAGE 20
But the pay's not as good, certainly, and one loses one's friends.

There are elevators of enormous girth, like vertical buses, in various locations.

PAGE 21

Mully is cosplaying as Katara from *Avatar: The Last Airbender*, just Katara as a lowlife smuggler. Cosplay should be interpretive.

PAGE 22

The cop's line is "We found no one!" which is me being too clever. *Nemo* means "no one," but it kills the joke.

All the cops look alike because nearly all the cops belong to a clan called Medawar. The twelve major clans are the ruling class, and those twelve are, individually, quite weird. Major clans are powerfully uniform within themselves and have a distinctive look. Medawars all look like this, and they make up most of the police and military. Minor clans are united in other ways.

PAGE 23

This scene is informally titled "Pigeonleg." All the smuggling methods seen here are straight from the Internet, and so they must be real.

For my fellow Americans: an aubergine is a regular purple eggplant. Apparently, though I've never seen nor eaten one, there is also a species of eggplant that is small and white and looks—ta da!—like an egg. Evidently Medawars are more familiar with that kind.

Pidj, you dick. Who needs the moral high ground anyway? It *is* true that Jaeger is an Ascian nomad, and the cops would give him a much harder time even than the regular smugglers.

PAGE 24

The pigeon smuggler I read about had short chunks of PVC pipe duct taped to his shins. The pigeons were stuffed down into the pipes. Birds have no diaphragms, and so it's easy to squeeze them to death. That's why the rigid pipes, I guess. The guy just had skinny legs, I guess. But pigeons do make distinctive noises, and an air steward on his flight got suspicious.

PAGE 25

Jaeger has never walked casually out the front door of a police precinct in his life. Death glares from his former friends mean nothing to him now.

PAGES 26–33

This eight-page chunk was informally titled "Anyroad." It derives partly from an unfinished Shirley Jackson short story about an older woman who takes a sleeping pill while riding on an all-night bus trip, and gets put off the bus in the middle of nowhere by mistake. Hijinks ensue.

PAGE 27

So the old lady gives him an impromptu dance lesson. Nobody can learn it this fast, but everyone's gotta start somewhere.

Center panel is an homage to Jacek Yerka, whose dreamscapes are stunning.

PAGES 28–29

The coffered drum vault overhead comes from the DC-area metro. Coffering is deeper on the ceiling, then progressively shallower as it approaches the floor. Makes the arch stronger but lighter.

PAGE 30

Now we're getting into nicer neighborhoods. Some even have a proper day-to-night cycle. Others are always lit; still others always dark. House hunting can be problematic, but everybody sells blackout curtains and color-correcting sunlamps.

PAGE 31
She's never missed a funeral or a birth. I'm imagining the baby's name being Lio.

PAGE 32
In the forests of the north, in the olden days, every section of woods had its jaegers, or wardens. Jaeger's dad was one. His mother wasn't. His milk name isn't really Jaeger, that's just what he goes by.

PAGE 33
The builders of Anvard have made some attempts at systematic design. For instance, they did try to separate supply traffic from privately owned vehicles and cars from foot traffic. It sort of worked.

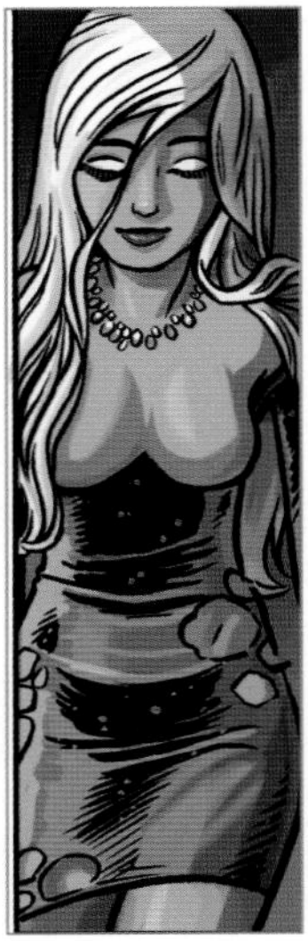

PAGE 35
"Lost Girls." This party girl's dress is supposed to look like that, rips and all. So is she, basically; she's spent her inheritance on plastic surgery. She has no nipples. So she looks like a Malibu Barbie.

"Helen, Please Come Home" is another Shirley Jackson story. Read some Jackson. She's still the best.

PAGE 36
The runaway daughter gig is a staple of detective fiction.

PAGE 37
Ronia has Ideas about life.

PAGES 38–39
There is an abundant and vigorous virtual life in Anvard, and in the other big cities. Kids from clan families get skull computers built into their heads at an early age, partly for school, partly for health—hack your kid when he's sick. Of course it's heavily regulated, and of course those bounds are overstepped.

Many people who live in the city don't have skull computers. They don't have access to the larger community's resources of all kinds—libraries, news, current events, social media. And pictures of cats. But they also don't have to worry about being infested by completely legal area-defense software, such as Jaeger is describing. She needs an escort back to her own home, because she can't remember how to get there. Her parents have cut her off.

PAGE 40
Pretty neighborhood. Not on the ground level. Leaks from pools and parks are a big problem for the multileveled city of tomorrow.

Her name is, or was, Ronia, as in "Ronia, the Robber's Daughter," by Astrid Lindgren, also author of *Pippi Longstocking*.

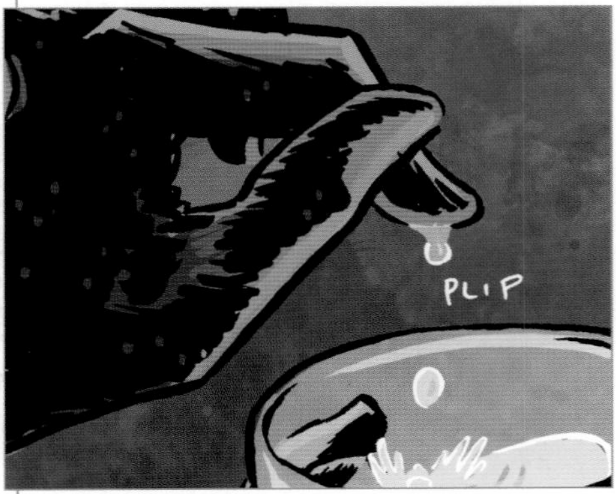
PLIP

PAGES 41–42
Soul jar. In some funerary traditions, family bones are exhumed after burial and cleaned, and the water poured into a well. It is assumed then that the soul of the dead family member has joined a larger spirit world. The water, in whole or in part, may also be kept for a while, for various reasons—not all of them benevolent. Ronia's parents assume that their other daughter is dead, but Ronia implies that she's just . . . like Ronia.

PAGE 43

I meant Lucy to look a little like an adult Lucy Van Pelt. Dunno how successful I was.

The Laeske are a nonhuman race responsible for much of the biologically based technology in this world. They look like big, feathery theropod dinosaurs.

PAGE 44

A lot of the things Jaeger eats would gross out the city folks. They're not really used to food coming out of "weeds."

PAGE 45

Duuuuu. Uuuude.

PAGE 46

I think lots of academics have dreamed of doing something similar (and been glad they couldn't).

PAGE 47

This record collector's story didn't make it into this book. I guess I'll save it for something else. The gramophone figures into it also.

PAGES 49–50

The belt Jaeger wears is indicative of his own tribal clan affiliation, which is not the same thing as clan membership in the city. Every year Anvard has a huge street party, like Carnival or Mardi Gras, and the drum chiefs are among the costumed throng. These paraders are not ethnically the same as Jaeger's mother's people, though the Ascian chiefs he's used to are also called drum chiefs. The bird design on the big beaded patch the girl is holding up in panel 5 on page 49 is Jaeger's own clan symbol. He's adopted, so he's a little startled.

The drum chiefs are at a level of organization still lower, socioeconomically, than the minor clans. Twelve major clans run the city, numerous minor ones struggle to maintain their rights, and then there are various societies that try to help and protect their members. The drum chiefs belong to that last group. Jaeger belongs to the mass of people who aren't part of any group. It really isn't very romantic.

PAGE 51

A street parade, like a second-line march in New Orleans. Not as raucous as true Carnival time.

PAGES 52–53

Everybody knows what a process server is, right? Certain legal paperwork, such as summonses, have to be placed in the hands of the person named in the paperwork, so they can't say they never got it and so that's why they never showed up in court. Under certain circumstances, people who are geared up for protracted and bloodthirsty legal battles go to great lengths to avoid receiving that kind of paperwork. Process servers sometimes have to be sneaky about it.

PAGE 54

Sad little birthday party, with no other kids invited. Dad's doing his best.

PAGES 55–56

She really wants custody.

PAGES 57–59

Jaeger hates ghosts. Prejudice is an ugly thing.

PAGE 60

It will come up through a decorative wishing well twelve streets above, then pop when it hits a hot streetlight.

PAGE 61

Parkour, Anvard style!

PAGE 63

Putt, putt, putt. The car is based on a model I own that now I cannot find. I suspect children may be involved.

PAGE 64

The lines on the road are purely decorative.

PAGES 65–66

This is a three-dimensional fractal made by my friend Dave Dodge. Jaeger calls it Space Spider City, or he *will* once he gets his eyes back in his head.

PAGE 67

See? This neighborhood can afford a pretty backlit "sky" with moving images of the sun, stars, and clouds.

PAGE 68

Jaeger feels all "less special."

PAGE 70

Part 2. These water holes are called *goblin pots*. They exist in red-rock deserts and aren't always there, so they usually harbor very little life.

PAGES 71–73

This is Jaeger's memory of a conversation he had with Lynne, who doesn't appear in this book, when Lynne was very young.

Jaeger doesn't know it, but he has a small iron deposit in the bridge of his nose, which, with the right nerves, makes him sensitive to magnetic north.

PAGE 74

I think Jaeger should look like this all the time.

PAGE 75

Shadow Man has a thumbprint where he should have a face. Isn't it odd that faces are often so similar, and yet we're attuned to a person's identity as being based on their face? Fingerprints are all unique, but to the casual eye they're just a bewildering collection of meaningless lines.

PAGES 76–77

Maryana is never really surprised to see him, either.

PAGE 78

Train's here, Mar.

Maryana is wearing a "halo," which does several things for her. It's part of a personal force shield which protects her from the "dangerous radiation" outside the city— well, it does protect her from heat stroke and UV radiation, so she doesn't need much sunscreen. It also serves as a hotspot for her skull computer, providing better connectivity, and it serves as a desktop. She can call up air-screen windows and place them, still open, up above her head so they won't bother her when she doesn't want to look at them.

As force fields go, it can't save her from being stabbed or shot, but it does summon the local constabulary, assuming there is one.

PAGE 79
Dirigibles are great for areas with no roads. The designers tried to make this one look less like a flying link sausage, with some success.

PAGE 80
The interiors of these dirigibles are structural. They carry a lot of freight, but don't afford much of a view—except of the ground. They do have lots of cameras, which passengers can access through their browsers, and that improves the view.

PAGE 81
Flies are pretty weird.

These little fliers actually do work, but they tend to flip over. Personal safety is not really at the forefront of people's concerns in this world. Speculative fiction is fun that way.

PAGE 82
But the job came back, the very next day. The job came back; he thought it was a goner . . .

PAGE 85
Next town over.

Anvard has a protective dome and a latticed support structure. There aren't a lot of these domed cities, but they're very densely populated. Cities outside the domes are less populated even when they sprawl, and much of the land is unpopulated.

PAGE 86
People who live in Third World worry less about radiation.

PAGE 87
I made this image chiefly to compare it to Anvard. The old and the new sitting alongside is still there, but in Third World, there's less new.

PAGES 88–89
Based on the great Moroccan tanneries, the oldest factories in the world. The white ones are lime pits, the colored ones, obviously, are dyes. What with all the megafauna, collecting animal effluvia for tanning is pretty easy. Tanneries do not freshen the air.

What's in a name? It's all in who you ask.

PAGE 90
The preceptor. He'll be around.

PAGE 91
There is a political concept that calls nomads the "fifth estate." The fourth estate was the powerful journalists, and the third the better-known aristocracy, clergy, and commoners. I have seen other definitions, and it seems very contentious. I liked the resonance between that system, and the Jewish kabbalah series of related emanatory worlds of varying character, and the belief of the Navajo people that the world has been destroyed three times, and that they (and by extension we) now live in the Fourth World, the Glittering World. Like the physical streets of Anvard, you don't know where you are until you get there, and you consider where you are as shaped by how you got there. If you went up three flights of stairs to get to the street you live on, do you live on a different floor than your neighbor, who came up five flights with an elevator ride for good measure?

Nomads often think of settled people as living in their own filth. They may have a point, but there comes a time when there is no more "away" to go.

PAGE 92
People do everything in public fountains.

PAGE 93
Dumping the job means ditching the obligations *first*, but he never thinks of this.

PAGE 94
Here's the local guy who was supposed to go out to meet the train. Very much an Ascian slacker. There are urban Ascians, and Quaiyesa is one. He's lived in town all his life, unlike Jaeger.

PAGE 95
Poor Jaeger, he still doesn't quite know where he is.

PAGES 96–97
Race to the bank machine. Whoever deposits it first gets the money. Jaeger is not entirely *not* playing.

PAGE 98
Street peddlers.

Wiss is short for "Wissawecancahout," which means "laundry basket." Wiss is not from the same tribe as Quaiy. *Quaiyesa* means "last one." He was the youngest.

PAGES 99–102
Wiss's predicament is one that Native American artists have struggled with. In some areas, their art is well known and accepted. In others, the prevailing attitude is that Native art is somehow only antique and should never be presented as contemporary, leaving artists caught in a very stupid quandary. Wiss isn't going to quit till she wears someone down. Enlisting the local layabouts to help her lug her paintings around is her prerogative.

PAGE 103
Quaiyesa, what are you doing?

FEMALE SALJUDUMI
25-35 AT DEATH
IN APPROXIMATELY
700 I.R.

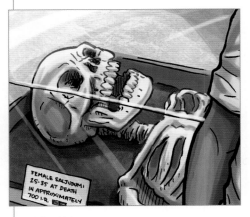

PAGE 104
Quaiyesa's story is based on the story of Minik, a very young Inuit boy brought to New York from Greenland in 1897 with his father and four others of their tribe. It is unlikely that they were aware they were traveling not for adventure but to be studied by the American Museum of Natural History. They had been told they would be returned to their home, but the adults and another child caught tuberculosis and died soon after arriving. Minik and a young man survived. The man went back

home, but the museum curator adopted Minik and kept him. A fake funeral was staged to satisfy the boy, but his father's body was defleshed and put on display in the museum. Minik had to find this out from his schoolmates.

He did return to Greenland as a young man. It isn't completely clear to what extent the curator, William Wallace, is to be excoriated in this history. After having been fired from the museum, he fought bitterly with the museum's other authorities for the remains to be restored to Minik for return to Greenland, and for the museum to support Minik

financially, to fund his return home. Minik had been so long away from his own people that he didn't even speak his birth language anymore. He came back to America and found work as a lumberman, later dying in the Spanish flu epidemic in 1918. The remains of his father and the other three adult Inuit weren't returned to Greenland until 1993.

PAGE 105

That is an adult Laeske named Hexoholoi Shar, an archaeologist for whom Jaeger has worked as a field guide. Laeske do their best with human languages; they invented skull computers, but there's only so much they can do about their accent.

PAGE 106

Many souks are covered like this. They aren't really roofed; it's just something to cut the glare.

PAGE 107

"In Flanders fields the poppies blow / Between the crosses, row on row / That mark our place; and in the sky / The larks, still bravely singing, fly / Scarce heard amid the guns below." (Poetry from *In Flanders Fields and Other Poems* by John McCrae.) The poppies

grow there, where hardly anything else does, because poppies can tolerate the lime in the soil that the war dead are buried in. Quicklime, incidentally, doesn't make a body decompose faster. It just cuts down on the smell. It is actually a pretty good preservative.

PAGE 108

In one corner, we have a hotel construction company that wants to build someplace pretty with air conditioning. In another, we have local Ascians who want to move the people buried in this field according to Ascian rites and rebury them somewhere else. The people buried are not related to the Ascians protesting, and there are non-Ascians buried there as well. In a third corner, we have local non-Ascians who want to gather poppies to sell. And then we have an archaeological team who want to excavate the field and learn whatever they can about what happened there.

Then there's Jaeger.

PAGE 110

Ascians, in general, don't like ghosts. They have elaborate burial rites designed to send the dead along on their way.

PAGE 112
Jaeger, *This Is Your Life*. You just don't know it.

Laeske technology is based on genetic manipulation. Shar wanted a way to gather genetic data from people, living and dead, and from animals and other sources, without alarming them. So, after many iterations, he created these lizard-like creatures with terrific noses and tongues for gathering chemical information and skull computers to transmit information directly to him. Shar didn't have these creatures the last time Jaeger worked for him.

PAGE 113
Jaeger spends a lot of time avoiding questions about himself, because there's a lot of stuff he just doesn't know. He feels separate from his adopted people because of this.

PAGE 115
Circular sections of earth, such as this meadow, are so common people accept them as natural.

PAGE 116
Jaeger could find out the details of his past and settle things, but he has a large number of reasons not to do so.

PAGE 117
As an adopted young adult without a family affiliation and without a sponsor having chosen him as a kind of apprentice, Jaeger was made a sin-eater, which is both a priest and a scapegoat all at once. It made him very important and even more separate. He hasn't lived with the Northern Anemoi tribe that adopted him for many, many years, and he always feels guilty when he meets Ascians and doesn't immediately tell them he is a sin-eater.

PAGES 118–120
Ghosts do bad things sometimes.

PAGE 122
Quaiy is good at standing firm, but not so much at moving forward.

PAGE 123
Water is holy to Ascians. Every form of water has a different significance. Having performed this exorcism, Jaeger's just supposed to keep going till he finds water.

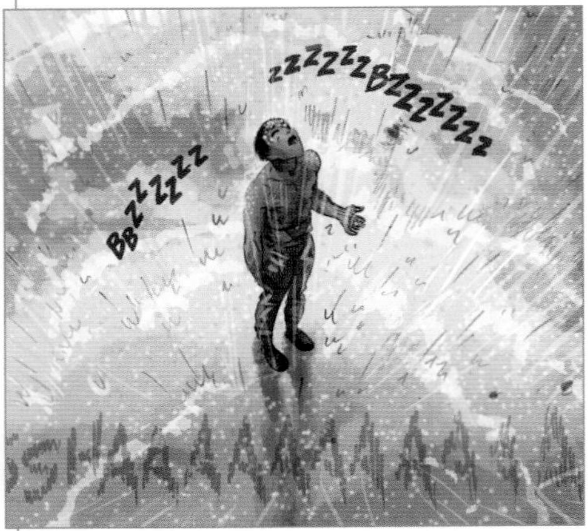

zzzzzzBzzzzzzz
BBzzzzzz

PAGE 124
However long that takes.

PAGE 126
Splurt. Snow White and Sleeping Beauty get a kiss. Not so the hibernating rainmaker.

PAGE 127
I pictured this noise as being a stridulation, like the sound cicada make.

PAGES 128–129
These people are wearing blur camouflage. They don't like to lose track of Jaeger, as they often do.

Jaeger heals really, really quickly. He hides this fact from people because he is in utter denial about its significance.

Airwhal! A simple arrangement: The rainmakers conjure rain, swarm, and get inhaled by airwhals. Other plants and animals do their best with what rain they get.

PAGE 130
The support lattice that provides structure for the multileveled interior of the dome cities

runs a long, long way out from them. It also transmits all kinds of communications, some of which originate with the human inhabitants.

So Jaeger is making a call.

PAGE 131
Jaeger's kid's name is Leah.

PAGES 132–133
Land pirates! Meet the huldres. They are not strictly human. The word *huldre* comes from Scandinavian mythology. The Scandinavian huldre or huldra is a forest-nymph kind of creature—a beautiful girl who may have a hollow behind or a cow's tail or something similar. These huldres are a construct race, meaning they were created by Laeske and have since gotten away from their creators. The Laeske grow enormous crops, which these huldres are busy stealing.

The local Laeske have grown a bunch of big flightless birds to trample the grain and separate it from its stalks, which they are herding at a gallop across the field in an effort to save the crop from the pirate combine. It's a lot harder to winnow the grain from the straw if it's run down like this, and the combine can't get it at all.

PAGE 134
Most Laeske are female, and are euphemistically called the Ladies of the Field.

PAGE 135
Fishing for bystanders.

PAGE 136
The older girl is Ada; the younger, Nyna. Not very imaginative, but it gets the job done.

PAGE 137
Laeske eggs may hatch carnivorous things.

The girls assume Jaeger is a construct, also made by a Laeske, which is pretty much his worst fear and the source of his tight-lipped attitude. He just does not want to know.

PAGE 138
The huldres only have three fingers in addition to their opposable thumbs, which was an agreed-upon convention to mark humanoid constructs. It's a convention, though, not a necessity.

PAGE 139
Quadro-triticale is the grain the tribbles devour in "The Trouble with Tribbles"—*Star Trek* (original series) episode #44.

PAGE 141
Part 3. Lovely, scenic Javecek. Another domed city. Everything's pretty . . . till you get up close.

PAGE 142
Streets of Javecek, packed tight with all kinds of foot traffic, pretty as a day at Disneyland.

PAGE 143

Sneeze noises are always fun to write.

Jaeger's friend's name is Amlan Addams. What you see is her digital avatar, a pretty fancy one, free to roam the streets as if it was a real person. The whole city is wired for holos and simulations of varying degrees and types.

PAGE 144

The sets for the city of Javecek were inspired by Giovanni Battista Piranesi's *Carceri* series. Piranesi is a true original. His infernal prison-scapes have sunk into the skulls of Coleridge and Poe and Terry Gilliam alike. When Javecek suffers a brownout, Jaeger can see (his nose is on the blink) that the throngs of Javecek are entirely made up of sims and holos.

PAGE 145

Way better signal strength now.

The sophistication of an avatar is no indication that it necessarily represents a living person. It's a matter of money and personal preference, and the type of street browsing you want to do. Amlan manifested her fancy sim to be friendly.

PAGE 146

Amlan is making assumptions.

PAGE 147

Flies on the wall.

PAGE 148

More about constructs, but Jaeger isn't listening.

Slanball is a game invented by the amazing Joan Slonczewski in her book *The Highest Frontier*.

PAGE 149

That's what you're missing, Jaeger, but it's too late now.

PAGE 150

The Javeceki civilization is a dangerous one. They continually tinker with biological technology. They stay insulated in their homes. When people marry, they often shift housing around any way they can so that their homes can be adjacent to existing extended family, making complicated prairie-dog burrows of linked apartments—so nobody has to go out on the streets if they can help it. Every adult has a medical degree, and new superbugs escape from Javecek frequently. Its neighboring cities do not have peaceful relations with Javecek.

Then there are the field hospitals. The Javeceki do not precisely think of the field hospitals as aggressive army units, but everyone else does.

Travelers are at risk of being subjected to unwanted treatment by the field hospitals. Many Javeceki do not support the field hospitals, but they are not numerous enough to put a stop to them.

PAGES 151–152

You can't walk the streets without one of those biohazard suits without catching a whole witch's brew of different ailments, but some things require more direct contact.

PAGE 153

Amlan assumed that Jaeger was willing and prepared to accept major infection. People do occasionally decide to do what he appeared to be doing. That he might have been a prisoner of war did give her a twinge, but the idea that he might have been sent blindly into her city is a shock.

PAGE 154

Javeceki ethics are complicated. They do maintain these public isolation cells free of charge for people to use in case of emergencies. The cells have the same access to medical treatment as anywhere in the city, assuming the inmate can afford it.

PAGES 155–156

Amlan had cancer. Now Jaeger has it. The carrier virus is capable of making all kinds of things contagious that normally aren't. It was an attempt to make a viral therapy that would compare a sick body to a healthy body and destroy the ailment, but it had the unintended effect of re-creating the ailment in the healthy body. When you give someone your disease, you literally *give* it to them so you are free of it. The person in the biohazard suit that grabbed Jaeger by the arm was Amlan, who had to stagger out of her bed and meet Jaeger in the flesh to activate the carrier virus and heal herself. She truly thought that's why he was out on the streets practically naked.

PAGE 157

The Javeceki government will sponsor Jaeger's treatment, because, knowingly or not, he took on a citizen's disease. So he doesn't have to pay rent or buy food or pay for his treatment. And he has Amlan's huge guilt complex to watch over him.

PAGES 158–160

I have a problem with hospitals. This isn't really therapeutic.

Many of the lines on the walls are in motion. They indicate various things—where a room divider can be raised or various pieces of furniture or storage spaces can appear. Doors can open along those lines, or lighting, or medical machinery can run at you from out of the darkness. Or the room can make you a bed to sleep on. Or a pleasing vista to try to help you forget you're inside a battered tin can of a smart room.

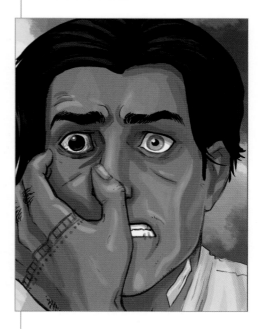

PAGE 161

This is one of those scenes I've been waiting years to draw. Amlan's sponsorship is enough to keep most unwanted treatments off of him. But not the eye.

PAGES 162–163
They have interests in a lot of companies, actually.

Jaeger's horror is informed by the fact that they are trying to do something to him which, if he actually wanted it, would cost a bomb load to do. The fact that they're willing to spend a lot of money on him—and are trying to make it sound like the best thing that could happen to him—is deeply terrifying.

PAGE 164
He's always insisted that there's nothing strange about him—that anyone could do what he does if they just set themselves to do it. "Anything's easy if it's all you do" has been his motto. Being forced to see that he really *is* an anomaly is one of the worst things that's ever happened to him.

PAGE 165
The blurs have been keeping tabs on him since childhood. They tried to put the screws into him once before, when he was a teenager.

PAGES 166–167
Lady or tiger. Of course, this "lady" is carrying several scalpels, and that "tiger" is composed of a bunch of nasty superbugs in conjunction with a hypercompetent immune response.

Sufferers of certain hemorrhagic fevers can, at death, look as though they have been burned to this extent.

PAGES 168–169
Amlan can't count on anything she says or does being private. She can't operate out of the bounds of the law without facing severe penalties. The blurs have done their best to make sure Jaeger has no way out but their way. This is where this little director's narration ends; I'm looking forward to drawing Jaeger's attempts to escape while wearing ducky jammies.

FINDER

CARLA SPEED McNEIL

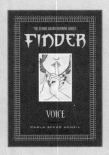

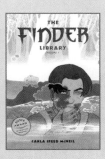

FINDER: VOICE	THE FINDER LIBRARY VOLUME 1	THE FINDER LIBRARY VOLUME 2	FINDER: TALISMAN Special edition hardcover
ISBN 978-1-59582-651-0	ISBN 978-1-59582-652-7	ISBN 978-1-59582-653-4	ISBN 978-1-61655-027-1
$19.99	$24.99	$24.99	$19.99

LOSE YOURSELF IN A WORLD BEYOND YOUR WILDEST DREAMS...

Since 1996, *Finder* has set the bar for science-fiction storytelling, with a lush, intricate world and compelling characters. Now, Dark Horse is proud to present Carla Speed McNeil's groundbreaking series in newly revised, expanded, afford-ablypriced volumes!

Follow enigmatic hero Jaeger through a "glorious, catholic pileup of high-tech SF, fannish fantasy, and street-level culture clash" (*Village Voice*), and discover the lush world and compelling characters that have carved *Finder* a permanent place in the pantheon of independent comics.

To find a comics shop in your area, call 1-888-266-4226
For more information or to order direct: On the web:
DarkHorse.com
E-mail: mailorder@darkhorse.com
Phone: 1-800-862-0052
Mon–Fri 9 AM to 5 PM Pacific Time

DARK HORSE COMICS®
DarkHorse.com

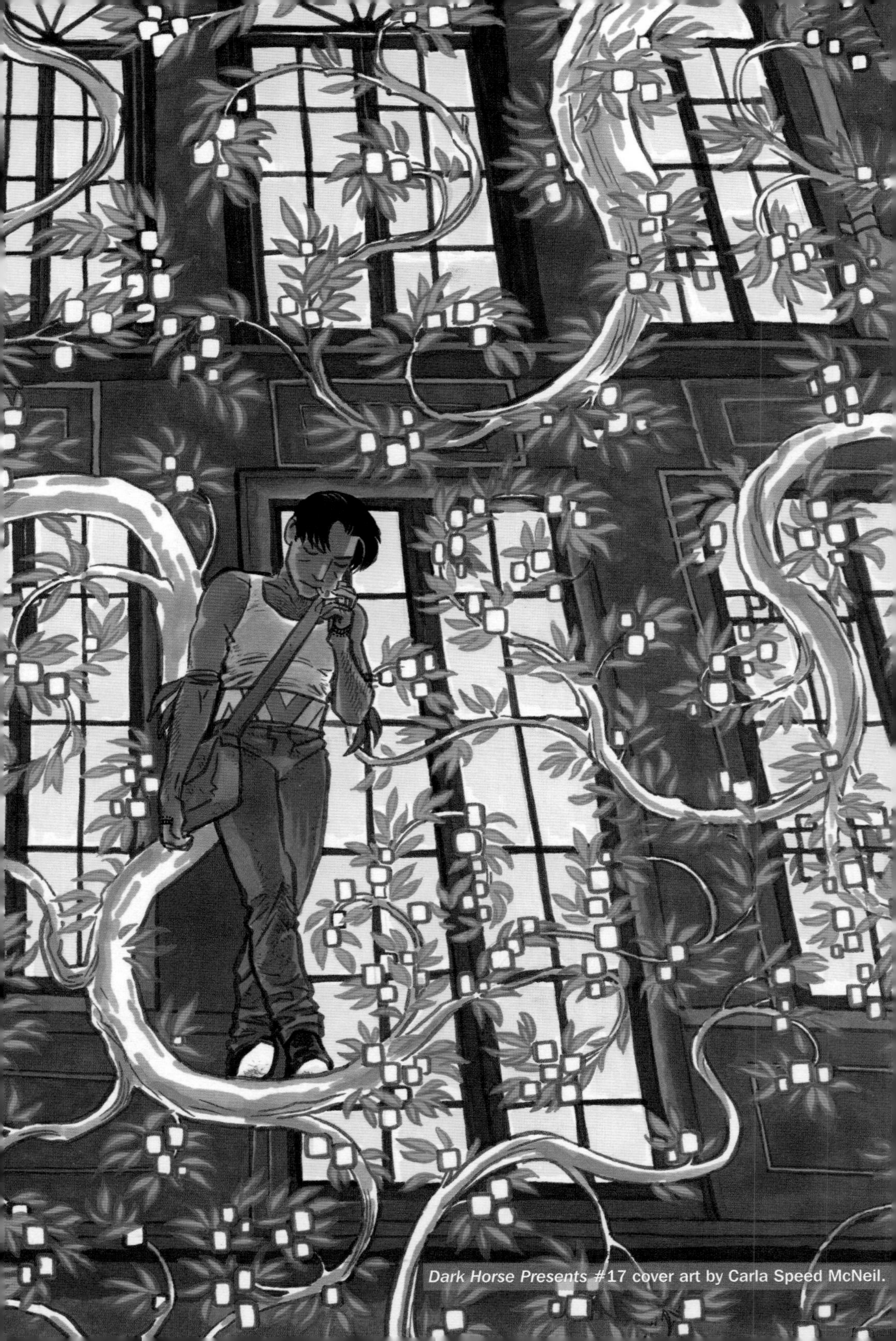

Dark Horse Presents #17 cover art by Carla Speed McNeil.